CompTIA®
Server+®
Study Guide

Exam SK0-005
Second Edition

CompTIA®
Server+®
Study Guide
Exam SK0-005
Second Edition

Troy McMillan

SYBEX®
A Wiley Brand

For my wife, Heike, who makes the hard work all worth it

Acknowledgments

Special thanks go to Kristi Bennett for keeping me on schedule and ensuring all the deadlines are met. Also I'd like to thank David Clinton for the excellent technical edit that saved me from myself at times. Finally, as always, I'd like to acknowledge Kenyon Brown for his continued support of all my writing efforts.

About the Author

Troy McMillan writes practice tests, study guides, and online course materials for CyberVista, while also running his own consulting and training business. He holds over 30 industry certifications. Troy can be reached at mcmillantroy@hotmail.com.

About the Technical Editor

David Clinton is the author of books and video courses on Linux and AWS administration, data analytics, container virtualization, and IT security.

Contents at a Glance

Contents

Table of Exercises

Introduction

The Server+ certification program was developed by CompTIA to provide an industry-wide means of certifying the competency of computer server technicians. The Server+ certification, which is granted to those who have attained the level of knowledge and troubleshooting skills that are needed to provide capable support to the most commonly used server and storage systems, is similar to other certifications in the computer industry. The theory behind these certifications is that if you needed to have service performed on any of their products, you would sooner call a technician who has been certified in one of the appropriate programs than you would just call the first so-called "expert" listed online.

CompTIA's Server+ exam objectives are periodically updated to keep the certification applicable to the most recent hardware and software. This is necessary because a technician must be able to work on the latest equipment. The most recent revisions to the objectives—and to the whole program—were introduced in 2021 and are reflected in this book.

This book is a tool to help you prepare for this certification—and for the new areas of focus of a modern server technician's job.

What Is Server+ Certification?

The Server+ certification program was created to offer a wide-ranging certification in the sense that it's intended to certify competence with servers from many different makers and vendors. Everyone must take and pass one exam: SK0-005.

The Server+ certification isn't awarded until you've passed the test. For the latest pricing on the exams and updates to the registration procedures, call Pearson VUE at (877) 551-7587. You can also go to the website, www.vue.com, for additional information or to register online. If you have further questions about the scope of the exams or related CompTIA programs, refer to the CompTIA website at www.comptia.org.

Who Should Buy This Book?

If you want to acquire a solid foundation in servers and the storage systems they use, and your goal is to prepare for the exams by filling in any gaps in your knowledge, this book is for you. You'll find clear explanations of the concepts you need to grasp and plenty of help to achieve the high level of professional competency you need in order to succeed in your chosen field.

If you want to become certified as a Server+ holder, this book is definitely what you need. However, if you just want to attempt to pass the exam without really understanding the basics of personal computers, this guide isn't for you. It's written for people who want to acquire skills and knowledge of servers and storage systems.

What Does This Book Cover?

This book covers everything you need to know to pass the CompTIA Server+ exam.

What's Included in the Book

We've included several learning tools throughout the book:

Objective Map and Opening List of Objectives   We have included a detailed exam objective map showing you where each of the exam objectives is covered. In addition, each chapter opens with a list of the exam objectives it covers. Use these resources to see exactly where each of the exam topics is covered.

Assessment Test   We have provided an assessment test that you can use to check your readiness for the exam at the end of this Introduction. Take this test before you start reading the book; it will help you determine the areas on which you might need to brush up. The answers to the assessment test questions appear on a separate page after the last question of the test. Each answer includes an explanation and a note telling you the chapter in which the material appears.

Exam Essentials   Each chapter, just before the summary, includes a number of exam essentials. These are the key topics that you should take from the chapter in terms of areas on which you should focus when preparing for the exam.

Chapter Review Questions   To test your knowledge as you progress through the book, there are review questions at the end of each chapter. As you finish each chapter, answer the review questions and then check your answers—the correct answers appear in the Appendix. You can go back to reread the section that deals with each question you got wrong to ensure that you answer correctly the next time you're tested on the material.

Interactive Online Learning Environment and Test Bank

The interactive online learning environment that accompanies CompTIA Server+ Exam SK0-005 provides a test bank with study tools to help you prepare for the certification exams and increase your chances of passing them the first time. The test bank includes the following elements:

Sample Tests   All of the questions in this book, including the assessment test, which you'll find at the end of this Introduction, and the chapter tests that include the review questions at the end of each chapter are provided with answers and explanations. In addition, there are two practice exams. Use these questions to test your knowledge of the study guide material. The online test bank runs on multiple devices.

Flashcards   One set of questions is provided in digital flashcard format (a question followed by a single correct answer). You can use the flashcards to reinforce your learning and provide last-minute test prep before the exam.

Glossary The key terms from this book and their definitions are available as a fully searchable PDF.

Go to www.wiley.com/go/sybextestprep to register and gain access to this interactive online learning environment and test bank with study tools.

> **NOTE** Like all exams, the Server+ certification from CompTIA is updated periodically and may eventually be retired or replaced. At some point after CompTIA is no longer offering this exam, the old editions of our books and online tools will be retired. If you have purchased this book after the exam was retired, or are attempting to register in the Sybex online learning environment after the exam was retired, please know that we make no guarantees that this exam's online Sybex tools will be available once the exam is no longer available.

How to Use This Book

If you want a solid foundation for preparing for the Server+ exam, this is the book for you. We've spent countless hours putting together this book with the sole intention of helping you prepare for the exams.

This book is loaded with valuable information, and you will get the most out of your study time if you understand how we put the book together. Here's a list that describes how to approach studying:

1. Take the assessment test immediately following this Introduction. It's okay if you don't know any of the answers—that's what this book is for. Carefully read over the explanations for any question you get wrong, and make note of the chapters where that material is covered.

2. Study each chapter carefully, making sure you fully understand the information and the exam objectives listed at the beginning of each one. Again, pay extra-close attention to any chapter that includes material covered in questions you missed on the assessment test.

3. Read over the summary and exam essentials. These will highlight the sections from the chapter with which you need to be familiar before sitting for the exam.

4. Answer all of the review questions at the end of each chapter. Specifically note any questions that confuse you, and study the corresponding sections of the book again. Don't just skim these questions! Make sure that you understand each answer completely.

5. Go over the electronic flashcards. These help you prepare for the latest Server+ exam, and they're really great study tools.

6. Take the practice exam.

Performance-Based Questions

CompTIA includes performance-based questions on the Server+ exams. These are not the traditional multiple-choice questions with which you're probably familiar. These questions require the candidate to know how to perform a specific task or series of tasks. The candidate will be presented with a scenario and will be asked to complete a task. They will be taken to a simulated environment where they will have to perform a series of steps and will be graded on how well they complete the task.

Tips for Taking the Server+ Exam

Here are some general tips for taking your exams successfully:

- Bring two forms of ID with you. One must be a photo ID, such as a driver's license. The other can be a major credit card or a passport. Both forms must include a signature.

- Arrive early at the exam center so you can relax and review your study materials, particularly tables and lists of exam-related information.

- Read the questions carefully. Don't be tempted to jump to an early conclusion. Make sure you know exactly what the question is asking.

- Don't leave any unanswered questions. Unanswered questions are scored against you.

- There will be questions with multiple correct responses. When there is more than one correct answer, a message at the bottom of the screen will prompt you to either "Choose two" or "Choose all that apply." Be sure to read the messages displayed to know how many correct answers you must choose.

- When answering multiple-choice questions you're not sure about, use a process of elimination to get rid of the obviously incorrect answers first. Doing so will improve your odds if you need to make an educated guess.

- On form-based tests (nonadaptive), because the hard questions will eat up the most time, save them for last. You can move forward and backward through the exam.

- For the latest pricing on the exams and updates to the registration procedures, visit CompTIA's website at www.comptia.org.

The CompTIA Server+ Exam Objectives

CompTIA goes to great lengths to ensure that its certification programs accurately reflect the IT industry's best practices. The company does this by establishing Cornerstone Committees for each of its exam programs. Each committee consists of a small group of IT professionals, training providers, and publishers who are responsible for establishing the exam's baseline competency level and who determine the appropriate target audience level.

Once these factors are determined, CompTIA shares this information with a group of hand-selected subject matter experts (SMEs). These folks are the true brainpower behind the certification program. They review the committee's findings, refine them, and shape them into the objectives you see before you. CompTIA calls this process a job task analysis (JTA).

Finally, CompTIA conducts a survey to ensure that the objectives and weightings truly reflect the job requirements. Only then can the SMEs go to work writing the hundreds of questions needed for the exam. And, in many cases, they have to go back to the drawing board for further refinements before the exam is ready to go live in its final state. So, rest assured, the content you're about to learn will serve you long after you take the exam.

Exam objectives are subject to change at any time without prior notice and at CompTIA's sole discretion. Please visit the certification page of CompTIA's website at `www.comptia.org` for the most current listing of exam objectives.

CompTIA also publishes relative weightings for each of the exam's objectives. The following tables list the objective domains and the extent to which they're represented on each exam.

SK0-005 Exam Domains	% of Exam
1.0 Server Hardware Installation and Management	18%
2.0 Server Administration	30%
3.0 Security and Disaster Recovery	24%
4.0 Troubleshooting	28%
Total	100%

The following sections look at the objectives beneath each of these domains in more detail.

CompTIA SK0-005 Exam

1.1 Given a scenario, install physical hardware.

- Enclosure sizes
- Unit sizes
  - 1U, 2U, 3U, etc.
- Rack layout
  - Cooling management
  - Safety
    - Proper lifting techniques
    - Rack balancing
    - Floor load limitations

- Power distribution unit (PDU)
- Keyboard-video mouse (KVM) placement
- Rail kits
- Power cabling
  - Redundant power
    - Uninterruptible power supply (UPS)
    - Separate circuits
    - Separate providers
  - Power connector types
  - Cable management
- Network cabling
  - Redundant networking
  - Twisted pair
  - Fiber
    - SC
    - LC
    - Single mode
    - Multimode
  - Gigabit
  - 10 GigE
  - Small form factor pluggable (SFP)
  - SFP+
  - Quad small form factor pluggable (QSFP)
  - Cable management
- Server chassis types
  - Tower
  - Rack mount
  - Blade enclosure
- Server components
  - Hardware compatibility list (HCL)
  - Central processing unit (CPU)
  - Graphics processing unit (GPU)
  - Memory

- Bus types
- Interface types
- Expansion cards

1.2 Given a scenario, deploy and manage storage.

- RAID levels and types
  - 0
  - 1
  - 5
  - 6
  - 10
  - Just a bunch of disks (JBOD)
  - Hardware vs. software
- Capacity planning
- Hard drive media types
  - Solid state drive (SSD)
    - Wear factors
      - Read intensive
      - Write intensive
  - Hard disk drive (HDD)
    - Rotations per minute (RPM)
      - 15,000
      - 10,000
      - 7,200
  - Hybrid
- Interface types
  - Serial attached SCSI (SAS)
  - Serial ATA (SATA)
  - Peripheral component interconnect (PCI)
  - External serial advanced technology attachment (eSATA)
  - Universal serial bus (USB)
  - Secure digital (SD)
- Shared storage
  - Network attached storage (NAS)

- Network file system (NFS)
- Common Internet file system (CIFS)
- Storage area network (SAN)
  - Internet small computer systems interface (iSCSI)
  - Fibre Channel
  - Fibre Channel over Ethernet (FCoE)

1.3 Given a scenario, perform server hardware maintenance.

- Out-of-band management
  - Remote drive access
  - Remote console access
  - Remote power on/off
  - Internet protocol keyboard video-mouse (IP KVM)
- Local hardware administration
  - Keyboard-video-mouse (KVM)
  - Crash cart
  - Virtual administration console
  - Serial connectivity
  - Console connections
- Components
  - Firmware upgrades
- Drives
- Hot-swappable hardware
  - Drives
  - Cages
  - Cards
  - Power supplies
  - Fans
- Basic input/output system (BIOS)/Unified Extensible Firmware Interface (UEFI)

2.1 Given a scenario, install server operating systems.

- Minimum operating system (OS) requirements
- Hardware compatibility list (HCL)

- Installations
  - Graphical user interface (GUI)
  - Core
  - Bare metal
  - Virtualized
  - Remote
  - Slip streamed/unattended
    - Scripted installations
    - Additional drivers
    - Additional applications and utilities
    - Patches
- Media installation type
  - Network
  - Optical
  - Universal serial bus (USB)
  - Embedded
- Imaging
  - Cloning
    - Virtual machine (VM) cloning
    - Physical clones
    - Template deployment
    - Physical to virtual (P2V)
- Partition and volume types
  - Global partition table (GPT) vs. master boot record (MBR)
  - Dynamic disk
  - Logical volume management (LVM)
- File system types
  - ext4
  - New technology file system (NTFS)
  - VMware file system (VMFS)
  - Resilient file system (ReFS)
  - Z file system (ZFS)

2.2 Given a scenario, configure servers to use network infrastructure services.

- IP configuration
- Virtual local area network (VLAN)
- Default gateways
- Name resolution
  - Domain name service (DNS)
  - Fully qualified domain name (FQDN)
  - Hosts file
- Addressing protocols
  - IPv4
    - Request for comments (RFC) 1918 address spaces
  - IPv6
- Firewall
  - Ports
- Static vs. dynamic
  - Dynamic host configuration protocol (DHCP)
  - Automatic private IP address (APIPA)
- MAC addresses

2.3 Given a scenario, configure and maintain server functions and features

- Server roles requirements
  - Print
  - Database
  - File
  - Web
  - Application
  - Messaging
  - Baselining
    - Documentation
    - Performance metrics

- Directory connectivity
- Storage management
  - Formatting
  - Connectivity
  - Provisioning
  - Partitioning
  - Page/swap/scratch location and size
  - Disk quotas
  - Compression
  - Deduplication
- Monitoring
  - Uptime
  - Thresholds
  - Performance
    - Memory
    - Disk
      - Input output operations per second (IOPS)
      - Capacity vs. utilization
    - Network
    - Central processing unit (CPU)
  - Event logs
    - Configuration
    - Shipping
    - Alerting
    - Reporting
    - Retention
    - Rotation
- Data migration and transfer
  - Infiltration
  - Exfiltration
  - Disparate OS data transfer
    - Robocopy
    - File transfer

- Fast copy
- Secure copy protocol (SCP)

- Administrative interfaces
  - Console
  - Remote desktop
  - Secure shell (SSH)
  - Web interface

2.4 Explain the key concepts of high availability for servers.

- Clustering
  - Active-active
  - Active-passive
  - Failover
  - Failback
  - Proper patching procedures
  - Heartbeat
- Fault tolerance
  - Server-level redundancy vs. component redundancy
- Redundant server network infrastructure
  - Load balancing
    - Software vs. hardware
    - Round robin
    - Most recently used (MRU)
  - Network interface card (NIC) teaming and redundancy
    - Failover
    - Link aggregation

2.5 Summarize the purpose and operation of virtualization.

- Host vs. guest
- Virtual networking
  - Direct access (bridged)

- Network address translation (NAT)
- vNICs
- Virtual switches
- Resource allocation and provisioning
  - CPU
  - Memory
  - Disk
  - NIC
  - Overprovisioning
  - Scalability
- Management interfaces for virtual machines
- Cloud models

  - Public
  - Private
  - Hybrid

2.6 Summarize scripting basics for server administration.

- Script types
  - Bash
  - Batch
  - PowerShell
  - Virtual basic script (VBS)
- Environment variables
- Comment syntax
- Basic script constructs
  - Loops
  - Variables
  - Conditionals
  - Comparators
- Basic data types
  - Integers
  - Strings
  - Arrays

- Common server administration scripting tasks
  - Startup
  - Shut down
  - Service
  - Login
  - Account creation
  - Bootstrap

2.7 Explain the importance of asset management and documentation.

- Asset management
  - Labeling
  - Warranty
  - Leased vs. owned devices
  - Life-cycle management
    - Procurement
    - Usage
    - End of life
    - Disposal/recycling

- Inventory
  - Make
  - Model
  - Serial number
  - Asset tag
- Documentation management
  - Updates
  - Service manuals
  - Architecture diagrams
  - Infrastructure diagrams
  - Workflow diagrams
  - Recovery processes
  - Baselines
  - Change management

- Server configurations
- Company policies and procedures
  - Business impact analysis (BIA)
  - Mean time between failure (MTBF)
  - Mean time to recover (MTTR)
  - Recovery point objective (RPO)
  - Recovery time objective (RTO)
  - Service level agreement (SLA)
  - Uptime requirements
- Document availability
- Secure storage of sensitive documentation

2.8 Explain licensing concepts.

- Models
  - Per-instance
  - Per-concurrent user
  - Per-server
  - Per-socket
  - Per-core
  - Site-based
  - Physical vs. virtual
  - Node-locked
  - Signatures
- Open source
- Subscription
- License vs. maintenance and support
- Volume licensing
- License count validation
  - True up
- Version compatibility
  - Backward compatible
  - Forward compatible

3.1 Summarize data security concepts.

- Encryption paradigms
  - Data at rest
  - Data in transit
- Retention policies
- Data storage
  - Physical location storage
  - Off-site vs. on-site
- UEFI/BIOS passwords
- Bootloader passwords
- Business impact
  - Data value prioritization
  - Life-cycle management
  - Cost of security vs. risk and/or replacement

3.2 Summarize physical security concepts.

- Physical access controls
- Bollards
- Architectural reinforcements
  - Signal blocking
  - Reflective glass
  - Datacenter camouflage
- Fencing
- Security guards
- Security cameras
- Locks
  - Biometric
  - Radio frequency identification (RFID)
  - Card readers
  - Mantraps
  - Safes
- Environmental controls
  - Fire suppression
  - Heating, ventilation, and cooling (HVAC)
  - Sensors

3.3 Explain important concepts pertaining to identity and access management for server administration.

- User accounts
- User groups
- Password policies
  - Length
  - Lockout
  - Enforcement
- Permissions and access controls
  - Role-based
  - Rule-based
  - Scope based
  - Segregation of duties
  - Delegation
- Auditing
  - User activity
  - Logins
  - Group memberships
  - Deletions
- Multifactor authentication (MFA)
  - Something you know
  - Something you have
  - Something you are
- Single sign-on (SSO)

3.4 Explain data security risks and mitigation strategies.

- Security risks
  - Hardware failure
  - Malware
  - Data corruption
  - Insider threats
  - Theft
    - Data loss prevention (DLP)
    - Unwanted duplication
    - Unwanted publication

3.5 Given a scenario, apply server hardening methods.

- Host security
  - Antivirus
  - Anti-malware
  - Host intrusion detection system (HIDS)/Host intrusion prevention system (HIPS)
- Hardware hardening
  - Disable unneeded hardware
  - Disable unneeded physical ports, devices, or functions
  - Set BIOS password
  - Set boot order
- Patching
  - Testing
  - Deployment
  - Change management

3.6 Summarize proper server decommissioning concepts.

- Proper removal procedures
  - Company policies
  - Verify non-utilization
  - Documentation
    - Asset management
    - Change management
- Media destruction
  - Disk wiping
  - Physical
    - Degaussing
    - Shredding
    - Crushing
    - Incineration
  - Purposes for media destruction
- Media retention requirements
- Cable remediation
  - Power
  - Networking

- Electronics recycling
  - Internal vs. external
  - Repurposing

3.7 Explain the importance of backups and restores.

- Backup methods
  - Full
  - Synthetic full
  - Incremental
  - Differential
  - Archive
  - Open file
  - Snapshot
- Backup frequency
- Media rotation
- Backup media types
  - Tape
  - Cloud
  - Disk
  - Print
- File-level vs. system-state backup
- Restore methods
  - Overwrite
  - Side by side
  - Alternate location path
- Backup validation
  - Media integrity
  - Equipment
  - Regular testing intervals
- Media inventory before restoration

3.8 Explain the importance of disaster recovery.

- Site types
  - Hot site
  - Cold site
  - Warm site
  - Cloud
  - Separate geographic locations
- Replication
  - Constant
  - Background
  - Synchronous vs. asynchronous
  - Application consistent
  - File locking
  - Mirroring
  - Bidirectional
- Testing
  - Tabletops
  - Live failover
  - Simulated failover
  - Production vs. non-production

4.1 Explain the troubleshooting theory and methodology.

- Identify the problem and determine the scope.
  - Question users/stakeholders and identify changes to the server/environment.
  - Collect additional documentation/logs.
  - If possible, replicate the problem as appropriate.
  - If possible, perform backup before making changes.
  - Escalate, if necessary.
- Establish a theory of probable cause (question the obvious).
  - Determine whether there is a common element or symptom causing multiple problems.

- Test the theory to determine the cause.
  - Once the theory is confirmed, determine the next steps to resolve the problem.
  - If the theory is not confirmed, establish a new theory.
- Establish a plan of action to resolve the problem.
  - Notify impacted users.
- Implement the solution or escalate.
  - Make one change at a time and test/confirm the change has resolved the problem.
  - If the problem is not resolved, reverse the change, if appropriate, and implement a new change.
- Verify full system functionality and, if applicable, implement preventive measures.
- Perform a root cause analysis.
- Document findings, actions, and outcomes throughout the process.

4.2 Given a scenario, troubleshoot common hardware failures.

- Common problems
  - Predictive failures
  - Memory errors and failures
    - System crash
      - Blue screen
      - Purple screen
      - Memory dump
    - Utilization
    - Power-on self-test (POST) errors
    - Random lockups
    - Kernel panic
  - Complementary metal-oxide-semiconductor (CMOS) battery failure
  - System lockups
  - Random crashes
  - Fault and device indication
    - Visual indicators
    - Light-emitting diode (LED)
    - Liquid crystal display (LCD) panel readouts
      - Auditory or olfactory cues
      - POST codes

- Misallocated virtual resources
- Causes of common problems
  - Technical
    - Power supply fault
    - Malfunctioning fans
    - Improperly seated heat sink
    - Improperly seated cards
    - Incompatibility of components
    - Cooling failures
    - Backplane failure
    - Firmware incompatibility
    - CPU or GPU overheating
  - Environmental
    - Dust
    - Humidity
    - Temperature
- Tools and techniques
  - Event logs
  - Firmware upgrades or downgrades
  - Hardware diagnostics
  - Compressed air
  - Electrostatic discharge (ESD) equipment
  - Reseating or replacing components and/or cables

4.3 Given a scenario, troubleshoot storage problems.

- Common problems
  - Boot errors
  - Sector block errors
  - Cache battery failure
  - Read/write errors
  - Failed drives
  - Page/swap/scratch file or partition

- Partition errors
- Slow file access
- OS not found
- Unsuccessful backup
- Unable to mount the device
- Drive not available
- Cannot access logical drive
- Data corruption
- Slow I/O performance
- Restore failure
- Cache failure
- Multiple drive failure
- Causes of common problems
  - Disk space utilization
    - Insufficient disk space
  - Misconfigured RAID
  - Media failure
  - Drive failure
  - Controller failure
  - Hot bus adapter (HBA) failure
  - Loose connectors
  - Cable problems
  - Misconfiguration
  - Corrupt boot sector
  - Corrupt file system table
  - Array rebuild
  - Improper disk partition
  - Bad sectors
  - Cache battery failure
  - Cache turned off
  - Insufficient space
  - Improper RAID configuration
  - Mismatched drives
  - Backplane failure

- Tools and techniques
  - Partitioning tools
  - Disk management
  - RAID and array management
  - System logs
  - Disk mounting commands
    - net use
    - mount
  - Monitoring tools
  - Visual inspections
  - Auditory inspections

4.4 Given a scenario, troubleshoot common OS and software problems.

- Common problems
  - Unable to log on
  - Unable to access resources
  - Unable to access files
  - System file corruption
  - End of life/end of support
  - Slow performance
  - Cannot write to system logs
  - Service failures
  - System or application hanging
  - Freezing
  - Patch update failure
- Causes of common problems
  - Incompatible drivers/modules
  - Improperly applied patches
  - Unstable drivers or software
  - Server not joined to domain
  - Clock skew
  - Memory leaks

- Buffer overrun
- Incompatibility
  - Insecure dependencies
  - Version management
  - Architecture
- Update failures
- Missing updates
- Missing dependencies
- Downstream failures due to updates
- Inappropriate application level permissions
- Improper CPU affinity and priority
- OS and software tools and techniques
  - Patching
    - Upgrades
    - Downgrades
  - Package management
  - Recovery
    - Boot options
      - Safe mode
      - Single user mode
    - Reload OS
    - Snapshots
  - Proper privilege escalations
    - runas/Run As
    - sudo
    - su
  - Scheduled reboots
  - Software firewalls
    - Adding or removing ports
    - Zones
  - Clocks
    - Network time protocol (NTP)
    - System time

- Services and processes
  - Starting
  - Stopping
  - Status identification
  - Dependencies
- Configuration management
  - System center configuration manager (SCCM)
  - Puppet/Chef/Ansible
  - Group Policy Object (GPO)
- Hardware compatibility list (HCL)

4.5 Given a scenario, troubleshoot network connectivity issues.

- Common problems
  - Lack of Internet connectivity
  - Resource unavailable
  - Receiving incorrect DHCP information
  - Non-functional or unreachable
  - Destination host unreachable
  - Unknown host
  - Unable to reach remote subnets
  - Failure of service provider
  - Cannot reach server by host-name/fully qualified domain name (FQDN)
- Causes of common problems
  - Improper IP configuration
  - IPv4 vs. IPv6 misconfigurations
  - Improper VLAN configuration
  - Network port security
  - Component failure
  - Incorrect OS route tables
  - Bad cables
  - Firewall (misconfiguration, hardware failure, software failure)

- Misconfigured NIC
- DNS and/or DHCP failure
- DHCP server misconfigured
- Misconfigured hosts file
- Tools and techniques
  - Check link lights
  - Confirm power supply
  - Verify cable integrity
  - Check appropriate cable selection
  - Commands
    - ipconfig
    - ip addr
    - ping
    - tracert
    - traceroute
    - nslookup
    - netstat
    - dig
    - telnet
    - nc
    - nbtstat
    - route

4.6 Given a scenario, troubleshoot security problems.

- Common problems
  - File integrity
  - Improper privilege escalation
    - Excessive access
  - Applications will not load
  - Cannot access network file shares
  - Unable to open files

- Causes of common problems
  - Open ports
  - Services
    - Active
    - Inactive
    - Orphan/zombie

  - Intrusion detection configurations
  - Anti-malware configurations
  - Improperly configured local/group policies
  - Improperly configured firewall rules
  - Misconfigured permissions
  - Virus infection
  - Malware
  - Rogue processes/services
  - Data loss prevention (DLP)
  - Security tools
  - Port scanners
  - Sniffers
  - Telnet clients
  - Anti-malware
  - Antivirus
  - File integrity
    - Checksums
    - Monitoring
    - Detection
    - Enforcement

  - User access controls
    - SELinux
    - User account control (UAC)

Objective Map

The following objective map shows you where the exam objectives are covered in the chapters. Use it as a reference to find the information you're looking for.

SK0-004 Exam Objectives

Objective	Chapter
1.0 Server Hardware Installation and Management	
1.1 Given a scenario, install physical hardware.	1
1.2 Given a scenario, deploy and manage storage.	4
1.3 Given a scenario, perform server hardware maintenance.	3
2.0 Server Administration	
2.1 Given a scenario, install server operating systems.	2
2.2 Given a scenario, configure servers to use network infrastructure services.	8
2.3 Given a scenario, configure and maintain server functions and features.	2
2.4. Explain the key concepts of high availability for servers.	5
2.5 Summarize the purpose and operation of virtualization.	2
2.6 Summarize scripting basics for server administration.	8
2.7 Explain the importance of asset management and documentation.	4
2.8 Explain licensing concepts.	3
3.0 Security and Disaster Recovery	
3.1 Summarize data security concepts.	7
3.2 Summarize physical security concepts.	6
3.3 Explain important concepts pertaining to identity and access management for server administration.	7
3.4 Explain data security risks and mitigation strategies.	6
3.5 Given a scenario, apply server hardening methods.	6
3.6 Summarize proper server decommissioning concepts.	7
3.7 Explain the importance of backups and restores.	9

Exam specifications and content are subject to change at any time without prior notice and at CompTIA's sole discretion. Please visit CompTIA's website (`www.comptia.org`) for the most current information on the exam content.

How to Contact the Publisher

If you believe you have found a mistake in this book, please bring it to our attention. At John Wiley & Sons, we understand how important it is to provide our customers with accurate content, but even with our best efforts an error may occur.

In order to submit your possible errata, please email it to our Customer Service Team at `wileysupport@wiley.com` with the subject line "Possible Book Errata Submission."

Assessment Test

1. Which of the following is *not* part of the form factor of a server?
   A. Size
   B. Appearance
   C. Dimensions
   D. Security

2. Which function is made easier when a server has a rail kit?
   A. Installation
   B. Maintenance
   C. Configuration
   D. Network access

3. Which of the following is the unit of measurement when discussing rack components?
   A. M
   B. I
   C. U
   D. C

4. Which of the following is another term for RAID 1?
   A. Duplicating
   B. Doubling
   C. Duplexing
   D. Mirroring

5. What is the primary function of PXE?
   A. Remote booting
   B. Secure routing
   C. Remote administration
   D. Redundant connections

6. Shares are used to allocate which of the following to VMs?
   A. ROM
   B. CPU
   C. NVRAM
   D. L2 cache

7. What is the most common protocol a SAN uses?

   A. IPX

   B. IP

   C. Ethernet

   D. Fibre Channel

8. Which of the following is true of a NAS?

   A. A NAS has lower latency and higher reliability than a SAN.

   B. A NAS typically supports only RAID 5.

   C. A NAS does not support high throughput.

   D. Implementing a NAS is inexpensive.

9. Which of the following is a standard firmware interface for servers and PCs designed to replace BIOS?

   A. SCSI

   B. ISCSI

   C. UEFI

   D. FDDI

10. What is the role of a DHCP server in a network?

    A. Issues IP configurations

    B. Translates private to public addresses

    C. Authenticates users

    D. Resolves IP addresses to hostnames

11. The metric IOPS is used to describe the performance of which resource?

    A. Memory

    B. Disk

    C. CPU

    D. Network

12. As the number of users assigned to a printer increases, which resource should be increased?

    A. Disk

    B. Network

    C. CPU

    D. Memory

13. What is the function of the command-line utility wevtutil?

    A. Manages log files

    B. Manages network connections

    C. Manages memory issues

    D. Manages CPU affinity

14. Which of the following are simply whole numbers?

   A. Strings

   B. Arrays

   C. Integers

   D. Conditionals

15. Which RAID version requires at least three drives?

   A. RAID 0

   B. RAID 1

   C. RAID 5

   D. RAID 10

16. Which of the following statements is true with respect to safes?

   A. No safes are fireproof.

   B. Consumer Reports assigns ratings to safes that you can use to assess the suitability of the safe.

   C. Those that are fire-resistant will protect a backup tape from being damaged.

   D. When considering a safe, you should focus on two items: the cost and the size.

17. Which of the following is true of an HIDS?

   A. A high number of false negatives can cause a lax attitude on the part of the security team.

   B. An HIDS cannot address authentication issues.

   C. Encrypted packets can be analyzed.

   D. An HIDS monitors only traffic destined for the machine on which it is installed.

18. Which of the following is a compact, hot-pluggable transceiver not standardized by any governing body like the IEEE?

   A. SELinux

   B. PXE

   C. SPF

   D. QoS

19. Which of the following would Joe use to digitally sign a document so that Sally can verify his signature?

   A. Joe's private key

   B. Sally's private key

   C. Joe's public key

   D. Sally's public key

20. Which authentication mechanism is an example of something you are?

 A. Password

 B. Username

 C. Smartcard

 D. Retina scan

21. What is a common host-based firewall on Linux-based systems?

 A. iptables

 B. nessus

 C. tripwire

 D. scannow

22. Which of the following can be accomplished using port security?

 A. Set the minimum number of MAC addresses that can be seen on a port.

 B. Set the maximum number of IP addresses that can be seen on a port.

 C. Define which MAC addresses are not allowed on the port.

 D. Set the maximum number of MAC addresses that can be seen on a port.

23. Which of the following is one that is a process, completes its work, but is mistakenly marked as a dead process, preventing it from ending?

 A. Orphan

 B. Active

 C. Zombie

 D. Inactive

24. Which is the minimum category of cable required for 100 Mbps transmissions?

 A. CAT3

 B. CAT5

 C. CAT5e

 D. CAT6

25. Which of the following services uses port number 443?

 A. SFTP

 B. NTP

 C. HTTP

 D. HTTPS

26. Backdoors are also sometimes called which of the following?

 A. Teardrops

 B. Remote access trojans

 C. Trapdoors

 D. Rootkits

27. Which of the following parts of a MAC address is unique for each interface made by a vendor?

    A. UAA

    B. BAA

    C. OUI

    D. EUI-64

28. How many sets of backup tapes are used in the GFS system?

    A. 2

    B. 3

    C. 4

    D. 5

29. When creating a backup, what function can be used to verify the integrity of the results?

    A. Checksums

    B. Encryption

    C. Digital signatures

    D. Transaction logs

30. If you perform a full backup once a week and use a differential backup scheme the rest of the week, how many tapes are required for a restore four days after the full backup is taken?

    A. 1

    B. 2

    C. 3

    D. 4

31. Which of the following components is a system responsible for preventing attacks?

    A. HIDS

    B. NIDS

    C. IPS

    D. DC

32. Which of the following is a suite of protocols that establishes a secure channel between two devices?

    A. IPsec

    B. SPI

    C. iSCSI

    D. VLAN

33. Which of the following is not true about server backplanes?

    A. They can be a single point of failure.

    B. They provide data and control signal connectors for CPU.

    C. Backplane failures are uncommon.

    D. You should implement redundant backplanes.

34. Which of the following steps in the CompTIA troubleshooting method comes first?

    A. Verify full system functionality and, if applicable, implement preventive measures.

    B. Document findings, actions, and outcomes throughout the process.

    C. Identify the problem and determine the scope.

    D. Perform a root cause analysis.

35. Which command is used on a Windows computer to identify the path taken to a destination network?

    A. `traceroute`

    B. `tracert`

    C. `ipconfig/trace`

    D. `trace`

36. On which type of device is port security used?

    A. Hub

    B. Switch

    C. Router

    D. Multiplexer

37. You receive a destination unreachable message with a source IP address. Where is it coming from?

    A. A remote router

    B. A remote DNS server

    C. A local DNS server

    D. The local router

38. The `sudo fdisk -l` command lists the partitions on what type of system?

    A. Windows

    B. Mac

    C. Novell

    D. Linux

39. In Linux, what is `fstab` used for?

  A. To mount partitions on boot

  B. To create partitions

  C. To format a partition

  D. To defragment a drive

40. What component locates the operating system in Linux?

  A. NTLDR

  B. GRUB

  C. Bootmgr

  D. `boot.ini`

Answers to Assessment Test

1. D. Form factor refers to the physical appearance and dimensions of the server.

2. B. Rail kits, when implemented, allow for the server to be slid out of the rack for maintenance.

3. C. Each U is 1.75 inches (4.445 cm) high.

4. D. RAID 1 is also known as disk mirroring. This is a method of producing fault tolerance by writing all data simultaneously to two separate drives.

5. A. The Preboot Execution Environment (PXE) is an industry standard client/server interface that allows networked computers that are not yet loaded with an operating system to be configured and booted remotely by an administrator.

6. B. There are three ways the allocation of the use of the physical CPU(s) can be controlled. These methods are as follows:

- Shares: Using values such as Low, Normal, High, and Custom (in VMWare, for example), these values are compared to the sum of all shares of all virtual machines on the server. Therefore, they define the relative percentage each VM can use.

- Reservation: Guaranteed CPU allocation for a VM.

- Limit: Upper limit for a VM's CPU allocation.

7. D. In a classic SAN, devices communicate using the Fibre Channel protocol over a fiber network of storage devices typically connected to a Fibre Channel switch.

8. D. Implementing a NAS is inexpensive when compared to implementing a SAN.

9. C. Some advantages of UEFI firmware are:

- Better security; protects the preboot process

- Faster startup times and resuming from hibernation

- Support for drives larger than 2.2 terabytes (TB)

- Support for 64-bit firmware device drivers

- Capability to use BIOS with UEFI hardware

10. A. DHCP servers are used to automate the process of providing an IP configuration to devices in the network. These servers respond to broadcast-based requests for a configuration by offering an IP address, subnet mask, and default gateway to the DHCP client.

11. B. IOPS (input/output operations per second) is a common disk metric that describes how fast the disk subsystem is able to read and write to the drive. The higher this value, the better.

12. D. Print servers need lots of memory to hold the print jobs waiting in the print queue. The exact amount will depend on the number of users assigned to the printers being managed by this print server.

13. A. Managing log files can be done at the command line using the following command, inserting the name of the log file and the maximum size in bytes:

```
wevtutil sl <LogName> /ms:<MaxSizeInBytes>
```

14. C. Integers are simply whole numbers. This data type can be used to:

- Assign a value to a variable
- Set the parameters of a loop
- Define a condition to be met

15. C. A minimum of three drives is required for RAID 5.

16. C. With respect to fire, no safe is fireproof. Many are fire-resistant and will protect a document from being destroyed, which occurs at a much higher temperature than many of the other items (such as backup tapes and CDs) can tolerate without damage. For these reasons, items such as backup tapes should be stored off-site.

17. D. A host-based system is installed on the device (for purposes of our discussion, a server) and the system focuses solely on identifying attacks on that device only.

18. C. The small form-factor pluggable (SFP) is a compact, hot-pluggable transceiver that, though not standardized by any governing body like the IEEE, was created through a multisource agreement (MSA) between competing manufacturers. For this reason, you may find that there is not full compatibility among these from various sources.

19. A. Since Sally will use Joe's public key to verify the signature, he must sign it with his private key.

20. D. While passwords and usernames are examples of something you know and a smartcard is an example of something you possess, a retina scan provides something you are.

21. A. On Linux-based systems a common host-based firewall is `iptables`, which replaces a previous package called `ipchains`. It has the ability to accept or drop packets.

22. D. It is possible to specify a maximum number of MAC addresses allowed on a port.

23. C. A zombie process (work performed on behalf of services is done using processes) is one that is a child of another process. It becomes a zombie when it completes its work but is mistakenly marked as a dead process, preventing it from ending.

24. B. CAT5 transmits data at speed up to 100 Mbps and specifies cable lengths up to 100 meters.

25. D. HTTPS is a secure form of HTTP that uses port 443.

26. B. A Trojan horse can create a backdoor. These backdoors are also sometimes called remote access Trojans (RATs) because they allow the hacker to connect to the machine without going through any sort of authentication process.

27. C. Each part of this address communicates information. The left half of the address is called the organizationally unique identifier (OUI). It identifies the vendor who made the interface. The right half is called the universally administered address (UAA). It will be unique for each interface made by the vendor. Together they make a globally unique MAC address.

28. B. In the Grandfather-Father-Son (GFS) backup scheme, three sets of backups are defined. Most often these three definitions are daily, weekly, and monthly.

29. A. If you create the backup using checksums (which is an option with many utilities), it will allow you to check that the data has not changed since it was made or that it has been corrupted or damaged.

30. B. You will need the last full backup tape and the last differential tape. Each differential tape contains all changes that occurred since the last full backup.

31. C. An IPS is a system responsible for preventing attacks. When an attack begins, an IPS takes actions to contain the attack.

32. A. Internet Protocol Security (IPsec) is a suite of protocols that establishes a secure channel between two devices. IPsec is commonly implemented over VPNs, but that is not its only use.

33. B. Backplanes are advantageous in that they provide data and control signal connectors for the hard drives. They also provide the interconnection for the front I/O board, power and locator buttons, and system/component status LEDs. Unfortunately, this creates a serious single point of failure because if the backplane fails, we lose communication with the servers to which it is connected.

34. C. The steps in order are:

1. Identify the problem and determine the scope.

2. Establish a theory of probable cause.

3. Test the theory to determine the cause.

4. Establish a plan of action to resolve the problem and notify impacted users.

5. Implement the solution or escalate as appropriate.

6. Verify full system functionality and, if applicable, implement preventive measures.

7. Perform a root cause analysis.

8. Document findings, actions, and outcomes throughout the process.

35. B. The `tracert` command (`traceroute` in Linux and Unix) is used to trace the path of a packet through the network on routers.

36. B. Switches can be used to implement port security. Some of the things you can specify using port security are the only MAC address or addresses allowed to send traffic in the port, the total number of MAC addresses that can transmit on the port, and an action to be taken when a violation occurs (either shut the port down or prevent transmissions by the guilty MAC address).

37. A. If the message comes with no source IP address, that means the message is coming from the local router (the default gateway of the sender). If it has a source IP address of the sender, then it is another router in the path.

38. D. The `sudo fdisk -l` command lists the partitions on a Linux system.

39. A. `fstab` (File System Table) is a file used by Linux operating systems to mount partitions on boot.

40. B. In Linux this is handled by GRUB.

Chapter

1

Server Hardware

COMPTIA SERVER+ EXAM OBJECTIVES
COVERED IN THIS CHAPTER:

✓ **1.1   Given a scenario, install physical hardware.**

- Enclosure sizes
- Unit sizes
    - 1U, 2U, 3U, etc.
- Rack layout
    - Cooling management
    - Safety
    - Proper lifting techniques
    - Rack balancing
    - Floor load limitations
    - Power distribution unit (PDU)
    - Keyboard-video-mouse (KVM) placement
    - Rail kits
- Power cabling
    - Redundant power
        - Uninterruptible power supply (UPS)
        - Separate circuits
        - Separate providers
    - Power connector types
    - Cable management
- Network cabling
    - Redundant networking
    - Twisted pair
    - Fiber
        - SC

While servers and workstations have many of the same hardware components and in many cases use the same or similar operating systems, their roles in the network and therefore the requirements placed upon them are quite different. For this reason, CompTIA has developed the Server+ certification to validate the skills and knowledge required to design, install, and maintain server systems in the enterprise. Although many of the skills required to maintain workstations are transferable to maintaining servers, there are certainly enough differences both in the devices themselves and in the environment in which they operate to warrant such a certification. This book is designed to prepare you for the SK0-005 exam, otherwise known as the CompTIA Server+ exam.

Racking

Racking is the process of installing rack systems and then populating the rack systems with rack-mounted devices such as routers, switches, servers, intrusion detection system (IDS) devices, and many other types of network gear. In the opening section of this chapter, you'll learn about issues related to racking.

Enclosure Sizes

Racks come in different sizes, and we refer to the space the rack provides as the enclosure size. For example, the Dell PowerEdge rack enclosures are offered in three height options: 24U (2420), 42U (4220), and 48U (4820). Each U is 1.75 inches (44.45 mm) high.

Unit Sizes

Rack systems can accommodate a variety of device sizes. Each device is a unit, and in this section you'll learn about standard unit sizes.

1U, 2U, 3U, etc.

Rack mount servers are those that are designed to be bolted into a framework called a rack and thus are designed to fit one of several standard size rack slots, or *bays*. They also require *rail kits*, which when implemented allow you to slide the server out of the rack for maintenance. One of the benefits of using racks to hold servers, routers, switches, and other hardware appliances is that a rack gets the equipment off the floor, while also making more efficient use of the space in the server room and maintaining good air circulation. A rack with a server and other devices installed is shown in Figure 1.1.

FIGURE 1.1   Server in a rack

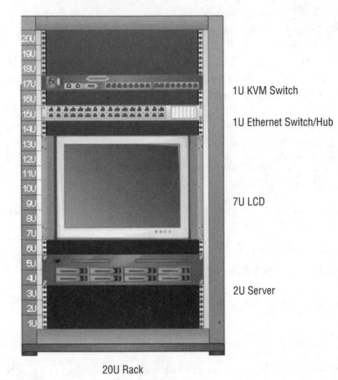

1U KVM Switch

1U Ethernet Switch/Hub

7U LCD

2U Server

20U Rack

Dimensions

As you may have noticed in Figure 1.1, there are several items in the rack and they take up various amounts of space in the rack. While both 19- and 23-inch-wide racks are used, this is a 19-inch-wide rack. Each module has a front panel that is 19 inches (482.6 mm) wide. The dimension where the devices or modules differ is in their height. This dimension is measured in *rack units*, or U for short. Each U is 1.75 inches (44.45 mm) high. While in Figure 1.1 the liquid crystal display (LCD) takes up 7U, there are four standard sizes for servers:

1U   These are for very small appliances or servers that are only 1.75 inches high. In Figure 1.1, there is a KVM switch (which provides a common keyboard, mouse, and monitor to use for all devices in the rack) and an Ethernet switch or hub that uses a 1U bay.

2U This is the middle of the most common sizes. In Figure 1.1 there is a server in the bottom of the rack that is using a 2U bay.

3U While not as common, 3U servers are also available.

4U Although there are no devices in the rack shown in Figure 1.1 that use 4U, this is a common bay size for servers. A 4U server is shown in Figure 1.2. For comparison, this server has twice the height of the 2U server in Figure 1.1.

FIGURE 1.2 A 4U server

It is also worth knowing that there are enclosures for blade servers that can be 10U in size. The typical rack provides 42U of space.

Rack Layout

Rack systems have many options to accommodate various power and cooling requirements. Moreover, there are additional components that you need to know about to successfully install and manage rack systems.

Cooling Management

When all power considerations have been satisfied, your attention should turn to ensuring that the servers do not overheat. The CPUs in a server produce a lot of heat, and this heat needs to be dealt with. In this section, we'll look at the sources of heat in a server room or datacenter and approaches used to control this heat so that it doesn't cause issues such as reboots (or worse).

Airflow

Airflow, both within the server and in the server room or datacenter in general, must be maintained and any obstructions to this flow must be eliminated if possible. Inside the server case, if you add any fans, avoid making the following common mistakes:

- Placing intake and exhaust in close proximity on the same side of the chassis, which causes exhausted warm air to flow back into the chassis, lowering overall cooling performance
- Installing panels and components, such as the graphics card, motherboard, and hard drives, in the way of airflow

You must also consider the airflow around the rack of servers and, in some cases, around the rows of racks in a large datacenter. We'll look at some approaches to that in the "Baffles/Shrouds" section later in this chapter.

Thermal Dissipation

Heat is generated by electronic devices and must be dissipated. There are a number of techniques to accomplish this. Heatsinks are one approach with which you are probably already familiar. Although heatsinks may pull the heat out of the CPU or the motherboard, we still have to get the heat out of the case, and we do that with fans. Finally, we need to get the collected heat from all of the servers out of the server room, or at least create a flow in the room that keeps the hot air from reentering the devices.

One of the ways to do that is through the use of hot and cold aisle arrangements. The goal of a hot aisle/cold aisle configuration is to conserve energy and lower cooling costs by managing airflow. It involves lining up server racks in alternating rows with cold air intakes facing one way and hot air exhausts facing the other. The cold aisles face air conditioner output ducts. The hot aisles face air conditioner return ducts. This arrangement is shown in Figure 1.3.

FIGURE 1.3   Hot aisle/cold aisle configuration

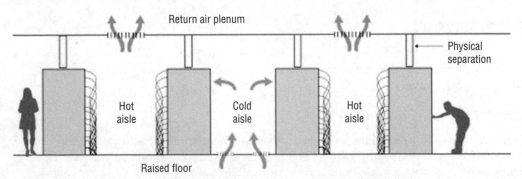

Baffles/Shrouds

Another technique used both inside the case and in the server room is deploying baffles or shrouds to direct and alter the flow of air. Inside the case they are used to channel the air in the desired direction. For example, in Figure 1.4 they are used to direct the air over components that might block the desired airflow.

FIGURE 1.4 Baffles

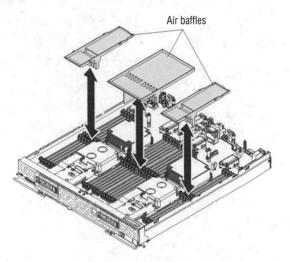

In the server room or datacenter, baffles may be deployed to channel the air in a desirable fashion as well. Here they are usually used to cover open rack slots, and in some cases, they are used under the raised floor to close holes there as well. Closing off these holes improves the airflow. You may have learned that open slots on the back of a tower computer should be closed with spacers. That recommendation is made for the same reason: improved airflow.

Fans

Fans are used in several places inside the server case. There may be one on top of the heatsink used to assist the heatsink in removing the heat from the CPU. However, there will also be at least one, if not two, case fans used to move the hot air out of the case.

In server rooms and datacenters, the racks in which servers reside will probably also have multiple fans to pull the air out of the rack. An example of the fans in the back of a rack system is shown in Figure 1.5. In this instance the fans are located in an external unit that can be bought and placed on the back of a rack that either has no fans or has insufficient fans.

FIGURE 1.5   Rack fans

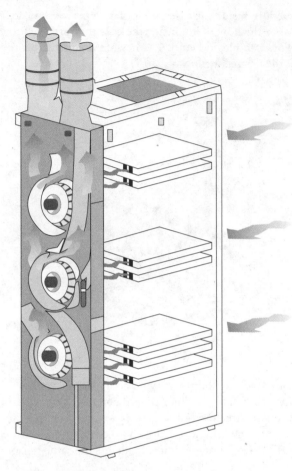

Liquid Cooling

In cases where passive heat removal is insufficient, liquid cooling may be deployed inside the case. In large datacenters this may be delivered from outside the case to the chips that need cooling. When done in this fashion, each server receives cool water from a main source, the heated water from all the servers is returned to a central location, and then the process repeats itself. Figure 1.6 shows a server receiving liquid cooling in this way.

Safety

Equipment can be replaced but not humans. When working with electric equipment, much of it heavy and difficult to move, proper safety practices should be followed. In this section you'll learn about safety issues.

FIGURE 1.6   Liquid cooling

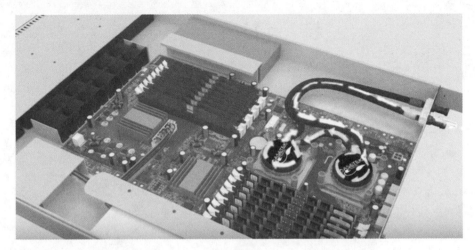

Proper Lifting Techniques

An easy way to get hurt is by moving equipment in an unsafe or improper way. Here are some safe lifting techniques to always keep in mind:

- Lift with your legs, not your back. When you have to pick something up, bend at the knees, not at the waist. You want to maintain the natural curve of the back and spine when lifting.

- Be careful to not twist when lifting. Keep the weight on your centerline.

- Keep objects as close to your body as possible and at waist level.

- Where possible, push instead of pull.

Rack Balancing

The racks in your server room will probably hold significant amounts of weight. The devices that reside there can be fragile, so for both your and the equipment's safety the racks must be stable. Racks that are solidly connected to both the floor and the ceiling will be the least of your worries if they are properly secure at all posts.

Considering that some racks may be on wheels, you may want to consider using rack stabilizers to prevent them from falling over. Then go underneath the rack and secure the rack to the floor, as shown in Figure 1.7.

The goal in lifting should be to reduce the strain on lower back muscles as much as possible since muscles in the lower back aren't nearly as strong as those in the legs or other parts of the body. Some people use a back belt or brace to help maintain the proper position while lifting.

FIGURE 1.7   Rack stabilizer

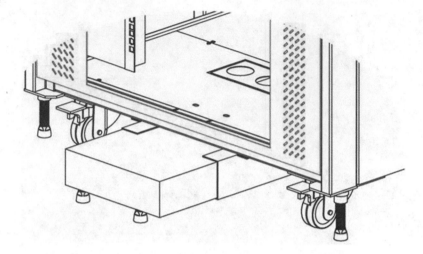

Floor Load Limitations

Whether your server room or datacenter has a raised floor (which is highly advisable) or not, you must ensure that the floor has the ability to support the weight of the equipment. You should determine the total weight of all the equipment and the racks in the room. This includes everything that will be in the room. Then when the raised floor is constructed, you must ensure it has the load capacity. If you are in an area where earthquakes are possible, you need go beyond that and consult load experts who can tell you how much additional load capacity may be required for the intensity of any of these events that occur.

Most server room or datacenter floors have tile panels that can be removed to access things such as cabling that might be under the floor. Your floor load calculations should be done with the tiles installed because they will increase the load capacity when they are all in place.

SHARP EDGES AND PINCH POINTS

In the process of working with the servers and the racks in which they may be installed, there will be several inescapable hazards you may encounter, but a dose of patience and awareness can help you avoid them. Although manufacturers try to minimize this fact, you may encounter sharp edges that can cut you if you aren't careful. These include metal corners of cases, edges of cards, and subassemblies. If you go slow and exercise care, you can avoid cutting yourself.

There also will be occasions when certain procedures may expose you to a "pinch point," which is simply an opportunity to pinch your fingers between two objects when performing the procedure. In some cases the documentation describing the procedure will call out this hazard, another good reason to "read the directions." For example, Figure 1.8 shows a callout that precedes instructions on removing the power distribution board on a Sun Netra 440 server. Always heed these warnings.

FIGURE 1.8   Pinch point warning

 Caution - There are several pinch points on the power supplies, so use caution when removing or installing a power supply in the system. Refer to the caution label on the power supplies for more information.

Power Distribution Unit (PDU)

A power distribution unit (PDU) is a device that looks much like a simple power strip with multiple outlets, but depending on the model it can be much more than that. Some are large, freestanding devices. Some of the features these devices can provide besides multiple outlets are:

- Power conditioning (evening out sags and surges)
- Surge protection
- Environmental monitoring
- Case alarms

Figure 1.9 shows an example of a rack mount PDU that is installed in a rack cabinet.

FIGURE 1.9   Rack PDU

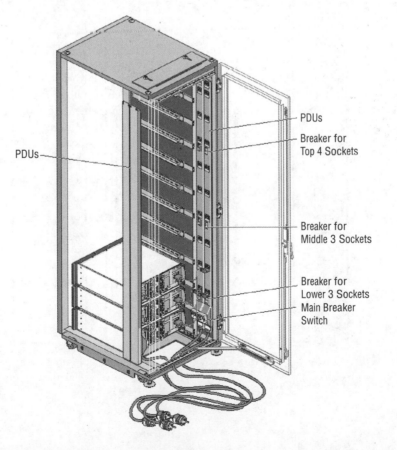

PDU Ratings

PDUs are rated according to the power load they can handle. You should ensure that no single PDU is connected to more devices than it can handle. So a PDU that is rated at 24 amps cannot provide more power at a time to the servers to which it is connected than that. It is also useful to know that PDUs will have two ratings in that regard. The National Electric Code, which is published by the National Fire Protection Association, requires that the continuous current drawn from a branch circuit not exceed 80 percent of the circuit's maximum rating. Therefore, PDUs have a maximum input value and a de-rated value. The de-rated value will be 80 percent of the maximum input value. So a PDU with a maximum value of 30 amps will have a de-rated value of 24 amps.

In cases where every possible effort must be made to keep the servers running, you may decide to deploy multiple rack PDUs in a rack or cabinet, as shown in Figure 1.10, where there are two PDUs.

FIGURE 1.10   Redundant PDUs

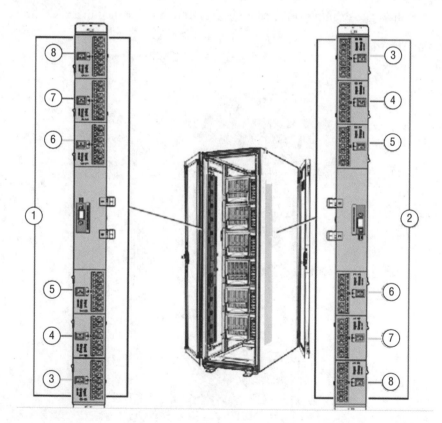

   If you do this it for redundancy, you may want to connect each to different circuits so that if one entire circuit goes dead, the rack can still be powered by the second power source.

Keyboard-Video-Mouse (KVM) Placement

When working with servers locally—that is, standing in the same room with the server—one of the most common ways technicians connect to the server is through a KVM. A keyboard, video, and mouse (KVM) device allows you to plug multiple PCs (usually servers) into the device and to switch easily back and forth from system to system using the same mouse, monitor, and keyboard. The KVM is actually a switch that all of the systems plug into. There is usually no software to install. Just turn off all the systems, plug them all into the switch, and turn them back on; then you can switch from one to another using the same keyboard, monitor, and mouse device connected to the KVM switch. The way in which this switch connects to the devices is shown in Figure 1.11.

FIGURE 1.11   Standard KVM switch

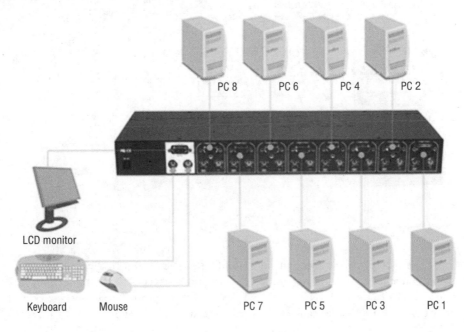

Serial

Although serial connections have been largely replaced by the use of KVM switches, it is still possible to connect to a server using a serial connection. The issue that arises is that even if a technician's laptop had a serial port (which is unlikely today), there would be at most one. This conundrum led to the development of the serial device server. It provides a number of serial ports, which are then connected to the serial ports of other equipment, such as servers, routers, or switches. The consoles of the connected devices can then be accessed by connecting to the console server over a serial link such as a modem, or over a network with terminal emulator software such as Telnet or SSH, maintaining survivable connectivity that allows remote users to log in the various consoles without being physically nearby. This arrangement is shown in Figure 1.12. One of the advantages of this is the ability to get to the servers "out of band." This means even if the network is down, servers can be reached through the serial ports either locally or through the modem.

FIGURE 1.12   Serial device server

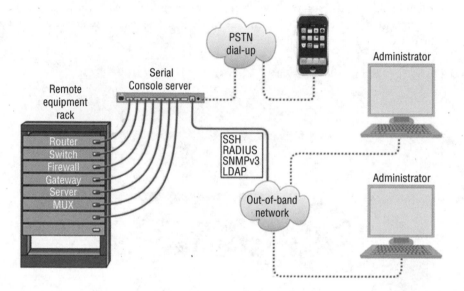

Rail Kits

Rail kits are used to provide a mechanism for sliding the server out of the rack. The rail kits have an inner rack and an outer rack. The inner rack attaches to the server, whereas the outer one attaches to the rack. The inner rack is designed to fit inside the outer rack and then it "rides" or slides on the outer rack. The installation steps are shown in Figure 1.13.

Power Cabling

Computing equipment of any kind, including servers, require a certain level of power and an environment that is cool enough to keep the devices from overheating. When discussing power it is helpful to define some terms that relate to power. In this section we'll do that, and we'll also look at power consumption and power redundancy. Finally, we'll explore power plug types you may encounter when dealing with servers in the enterprise.

FIGURE 1.13   Rail kit installation

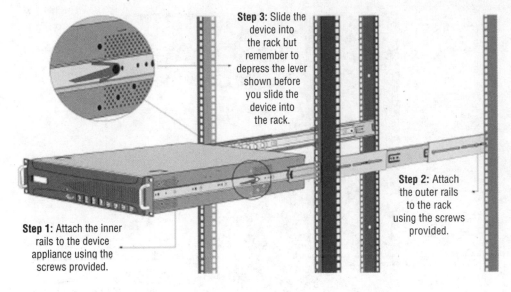

Step 3: Slide the device into the rack but remember to depress the lever shown before you slide the device into the rack.

Step 2: Attach the outer rails to the rack using the screws provided.

Step 1: Attach the inner rails to the device appliance using the screws provided.

Voltage

Two terms that are thrown about and often confused when discussing power are voltage and amperage. *Voltage* is the pressure or force of the electricity, whereas *amperage* is the amount of electricity. They together describe the *wattage* supplied. The watts required by a device are the amps multiplied by the voltage.

Amps multiplied by the volts give you the wattage (watts), a measure of the work that electricity does per second.

Power supplies that come in servers (and in all computers for that matter) must be set to accept the voltage that is being supplied by the power outlet to which it is connected. This voltage is standardized but the standard is different in different countries. Almost all IT power supplies are now autosensing and universal voltage–capable (100-250 V) to allow the same product to operate worldwide. Those that do not will provide a switch on the outside of the case that allows you to change the type of power the supply is expecting, as shown in Figure 1.14.

Single-Phase vs. Three-Phase Power

There are two types of power delivery systems: single-phase and three-phase. Single-phase power refers to a two-wire alternating current (AC) power circuit. Typically there is one power wire and one neutral wire. In the United States, 120V is the standard single-phase voltage, with one 120V power wire and one neutral wire. In some countries, 230V is the standard single-phase voltage, with one 230V power wire and one neutral wire. Power flows between the power wire (through the load) and the neutral wire.

FIGURE 1.14   Voltage switch

Three-phase power refers to three-wire AC power circuits. Typically there are three (phase A, phase B, phase C) power wires (120 degrees out of phase with one another) and one neutral wire. For example, a three-phase, four-wire 208V/120V power circuit provides three 120V single-phase power circuits and one 208V three-phase power circuit. Installing three-phase systems in datacenters helps to consolidate the power distribution in one place, reducing the costs associated with installing multiple distribution units.

Single-phase is what most homes have whereas three-phase is more typically found in industrial settings.

110V vs. 220V vs. 48V

Although 110V is used in some parts of the world and 220V in others, the two systems have advantages and disadvantages. While 220V is more efficient in that it suffers less transmission loss (and it can use wiring rated for less current), 110V is safer if someone is electrocuted. Some datacenters deliver power to a rack at 220V and then use a transformer to step it down to 110V to the equipment if required.

Some equipment also is made for – 48V DC power rather than 110/220 AC power. 48V is the common power scheme used in central offices and many datacenters. Many telcos can deliver 48V DC power to the facility and many are currently doing so. The advantage of using it is heat output. You no longer have the AC/DC conversion inside each device—just a DC/DC conversion. Less heat output means less (smaller) HVAC equipment. You will, however, need a rectifier, which is a small device that receives the 48V power and makes it –48V.

120/208V vs. 277/480V

Earlier you learned that systems can be one-phase or three-phase. Most commercial systems use one of two versions of three-phase. The first we mentioned earlier: 120/208V. To review, that power circuit provides three 120V single-phase power circuits and one 208V three-phase power circuit.

The 277/480V circuit provides two 277V single-phase power circuits and one 480V three-phase power circuit. Server power supplies that operate directly from 480/277V power distribution circuits can reduce the total cost of ownership (TCO) for a high-performance cluster by reducing both infrastructure and operating cost. The trade-off is that 277/480V systems are inherently more dangerous.

Wattage

Earlier you learned that voltage is the pressure or force of the electricity, whereas amperage is the amount of electricity. They together describe the wattage supplied. Amps multiplied by the volts give you the wattage (watts), a measure of the work that electricity does per second. The power supply must be able to provide the wattage requirements of the server and any devices that are also attached and dependent on the supply for power.

Consumption

Servers vary in their total consumption of power. However, there have been studies over the years that can give you an idea of what a server and some of its components draw in power. The following can be used as a rough guideline for planning:

- **1U rack mount x86:** 300 W–350 W
- **2U rack mount, 2-socket x86:** 350 W–400 W
- **4U rack mount, 4-socket x86:** average 600 W, heavy configurations, 1000 W
- **Blades:** average chassis uses 4500 W; divide by number of blades per chassis (example: 14 per chassis, so about 320 per blade server)

Keep in mind that these are values for the server only. In a datacenter, much additional power is spent on cooling and other requirements. A value called power usage effectiveness (PUE) is used to measure the efficiency of the datacenter. It is a number that describes the relationship between the amount of power used by the entire datacenter and the power used by the server only. For example, a value of 3 means that the datacenter needs three times the power required by the servers. A lower value is better. Although this is changing, the general rule of thumb is that PUE is usually 2.0, which means a datacenter needs twice the power required by the servers.

Redundant Power

Datacenters usually deploy redundant power sources to maintain constant power. Redundancy can be provided in several ways:

- Parallel redundancy, or the N+1 option, describes an architecture where there is always a single extra UPS available (that's the +1) and the N simply indicates the total number of UPSs required for the datacenter. Because the system runs in two feeds and there is only one redundant UPS, this system can still suffer failures.

- 2N redundancy means the datacenter provides double the power it requires. This ensures that the system is fully redundant.

Redundancy also refers to using redundant power supplies on the devices. Many servers come with two supplies, and you can buy additional power supplies as well. Always ensure that the power supply you buy can accommodate all the needs of the server. As you saw earlier in the section "Consumption," many 4U rack and blade servers use a lot of power.

Total Potential Power Draw

The power consumption of any individual server will vary. It's unlikely but there may be a point in time when all of your devices require what's called *critical power* at the same time. You need to calculate that value and ensure that if this occurs, you have sufficient power. If the circuit is overloaded, it can cause a complete outage. This means every link in the chain, including the PDU, UPS, and the circuit to these devices, must be capable of the load. When determining that load, use the following guidelines:

- Add up the wattages listed on each device. If the wattage is not listed on the device, multiply the current (amps) by the voltage of the device to get the volt-amperes (VA).

- Multiply the VA by 0.67 to estimate the actual power, in watts, that the critical load will represent.

- Divide the number by 1,000 to establish the kilowatt (kW) load level of the anticipated critical load.

- Don't forget that your needs will not be static, so build in some additional capacity to allow for growth.

Remember, power is the lifeline of the datacenter. One of your goals is to ensure that all systems have a constant, clean source of power. In this section, we'll look at the proper use of uninterruptable power supplies (UPSs) and discuss what power distribution units (PDUs) are. We'll also talk about how to plan to ensure you have sufficient capacity to serve your devices. Finally, we'll explore the use of redundant power supplies and the use of multiple circuits to enhance availability.

Uninterruptible Power Supply (UPS)

All systems of any importance to the continued functioning of the enterprise should be connected to a UPS. These devices have a battery attached that can provide power to the systems in the case of a power outage. You may also be aware that these systems are designed to provide only short-term power to the systems; that is a length of time sufficient to allow someone to gracefully shut down the devices. In this section, we'll dig a bit deeper and identify some of the features of these devices. We'll also go over best practices with regard to ensuring your UPS solution provides the protection you intended.

Runtime vs. Capacity

Two important metrics that are related but *not* the same when assessing a UPS are its runtime and its capacity. The *runtime* is the amount of time that the UPS can provide power at a given power level. This means you can't evaluate this metric without knowing the amount of load you will be placing on the UPS. Documentation that comes with the UPS should reveal to you the number of minutes expected at various power levels. So if you doubled the number of like devices attached to the UPS, you should expect the time to be cut in half (actually, it will be cut more than in half in reality because the batteries discharge quicker at higher loads).

Capacity is the maximum amount of power the UPS can supply at any moment in time. So if it has a capacity of 650 VA and you attempt to pull 800 VA from the UPS, it will shut itself down. So both of the values must be considered. You need to know the total amount of power the devices may require (capacity) and, based on that figure, select a UPS that can provide that for the amount of time you will need to shut down all the devices.

One good thing to know is that some UPS vendors can supply expansion packs for existing units that increase their capacity and runtime. That would be a favorable feature to insist on to allow your system to grow.

Automated Graceful Shutdown of Attached Devices

Today's enterprise-level UPS system tends to offer the ability to shut down a server to which it is attached when the power is lost. If all devices were thus equipped, it could reduce the amount of runtime required and eliminate the race to shut servers down.

There are several approaches that vendors have taken to this. In some cases if you purchase a special network card for the UPS, a single UPS can provide the automatic shutdown to multiple servers. The agent on each server communicates with the network card in the UPS.

Another option is to use a dedicated UPS for each server and attach the server to the UPS using a serial or USB cable. The disadvantage of this approach is that it requires a UPS for each device and you will be faced with the cable length limitations of serial and USB cables.

In either case, using the software that comes with the UPS, you can also have scripts run prior to the shutdown, and you can configure the amount of time to wait for the shutdown so that the script has time to execute, as shown in Figure 1.15. You can set a notification of this event.

FIGURE 1.15   Automatic shutdown

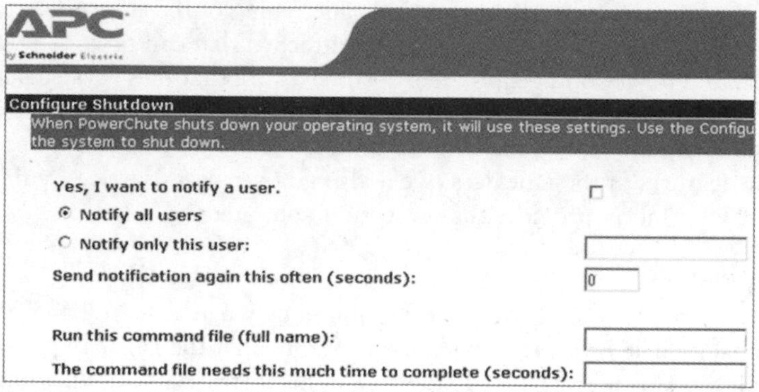

Periodic Testing of Batteries

Just as you would never wait until there is a loss of data to find out if the backup system is working, you should never wait until the power goes out to see whether the UPS does its job. Periodically you should test the batteries to ensure they stand ready to provide the expected runtime.

While the simplest test would be to remove power and see what happens, if you have production servers connected when you do this it could cause a resume generating event (RGE). In most cases, the software that came with the UPS will have the ability to report the current expected runtime based on the current state of the battery, as shown in Figure 1.16.

Even with this information, it is probably advisable to test the units from time to time with devices connected that you don't care about just to make sure the process of switching over to the battery succeeds and the correct runtime is provided.

Maximum Load

Although the capacity of a UPS is rated in VA, that is not the same as maximum load. The capacity value assumes that all of the attached devices are pulling the maximum amount of power, which they rarely do. As a rule of thumb, if you multiply the VA times 0.8, you will get a rough estimate of the maximum load your UPC may undergo at any particular time. So a UPS that is rated for 650 VA cannot provide more than 520 watts. If either of these values is exceeded during operation, the UPS will fail to provide the power you need.

Bypass Procedures

Putting a UPS in bypass mode removes the UPS from between the device and the wall output conceptually, without disconnecting it. A *static bypass* is one in which the UPS, either by the administrator invoking the bypass manually or by an inverter failure in the UPS, switches the power path back to the main line and removes itself from the line.

FIGURE 1.16   Checking the battery level

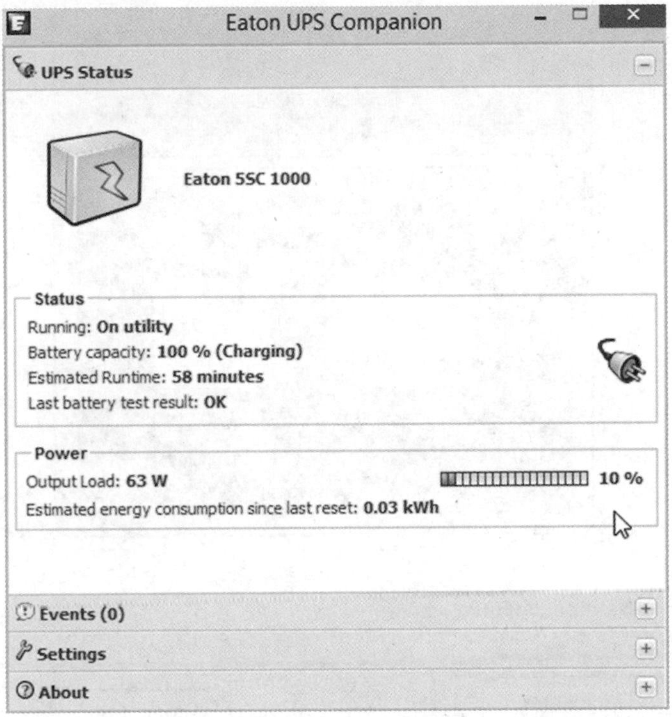

A *maintenance bypass* is possible when the UPS is augmented with an external appliance called the bypass cabinet. This allows for enabling the bypass and then working with the UPS without concerns about the power being on (although it can be enabled while leaving the power to the UPS on). This concept is shown in Figure 1.17. Notice the two switches on the bypass cabinet that can be opened and shut to accomplish this power segregation.

Separate Circuits

If you have a single power circuit and it fails, you will only be up as long as your batteries last or as long as the generator can run. Many datacenters commission multiple power circuits to prevent this. A comparison of a center with a single circuit to one with two circuits is shown in Figure 1.18. In this case the engineers have gone beyond circuit redundancy and implemented a main power panel, auto transfer switch, power panel, maintenance bypass (MBP), and UPS redundancy as well. An MBP is used to bypass the UPS when either changing the UPS or performing maintenance on it.

FIGURE 1.17   Maintenance bypass

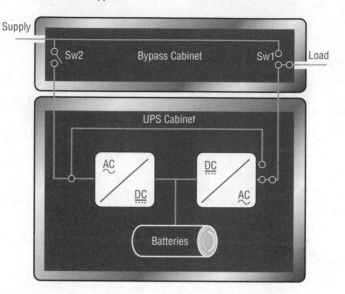

FIGURE 1.18   Multiple circuits

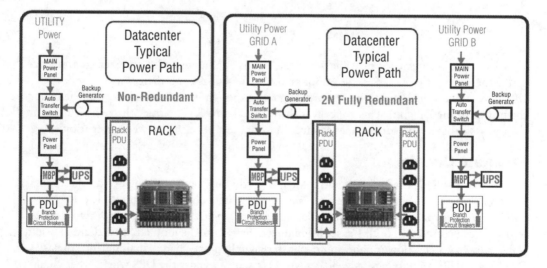

Connect Redundant Power Supplies to Separate PDUs

If you deploy multiple PDUs for redundancy, you may want to connect each to different circuits so that if one entire circuit goes dead, the rack can still be powered by the second power source. Another approach is to attach two UPSs to the PDU, with one going to the main power and the other to secondary power or to a generator, as shown in Figure 1.19.

FIGURE 1.19   Redundant UPS with single PDU

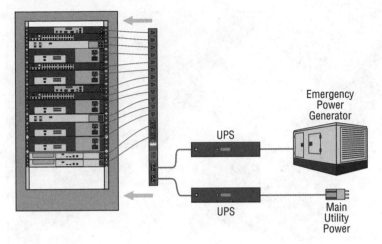

Separate Providers

All this redundancy sounds great, but what if your ISP goes down? Yes, it does happen. Many organizations engage multiple ISPs and maintain connections to all of them; that way, if one of the providers suffers an issue, a quick switchover can solve the issue.

Power Connector Types

You'll encounter several types of power plugs with servers. Let's examine each.

NEMA

Power plugs that conform to the U.S. National Electrical Manufacturers Association (NEMA) standards are called NEMA plugs. There are many types of these plugs, and they differ in the orientation of the plugs and their shape. The two basic classifications of a NEMA device are straight-blade and locking.

Edison

The term *Edison plug* refers to the standard three-prong grounded or two-prong ungrounded plugs with which we are all familiar. Both are shown in Figure 1.20. Keep in mind the shape of the plug may differ somewhat.

Twist Lock

Twist-locking connectors refer to NEMA locking connectors manufactured by any company, although "Twist-Lock" remains a registered trademark of Hubbell Inc. The term is applied generically to locking connectors that use curved blades. The plug is pushed into the receptacle and turned, causing the now-rotated blades to latch.

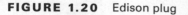

FIGURE 1.20 Edison plug

A sample of this connector for a 6000 W power supply is shown in Figure 1.21.

FIGURE 1.21 Locking plug

Power Supply Sockets

The midplane or backplane also supplies power connections to various components. When a midplane is in use, connections are provided on the back side for power modules. The power connectors on an IBM midplane are shown in Figure 1.22. The blade power connector is where the blade servers get their power, and the power module connector is for the cable that plugs into the power sockets.

FIGURE 1.22   Midplane power

Power module connector →

← Power module connector

Blade power connector →

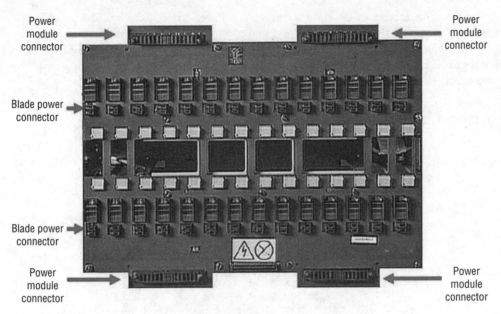

Blade power connector →

Power module connector →

← Power module connector

Cable Management

One of the challenges in the server room is to keep control of all the cables. When you consider the fact that servers use rail kits to allow you to slide the servers out for maintenance, there must be enough slack in both the power cable and the data cable(s) to permit this. On the other hand, you don't want a bunch of slack hanging down on the back of the rack for each device. To provide the slack required and to keep the cables from blanketing the back of the rack and causing overheating, you can use *cable management arms* (see Figure 1.23). These arms contain the slack and are designed to follow the server when you slide it out of the bay.

FIGURE 1.23   Cable management arm

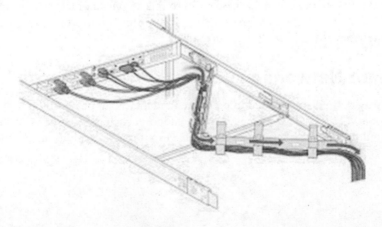

Cable Ties

Throughout the datacenter or server room, you will need to organize bundles of cable and in some cases attach these bundles to trays and channels. For this operation, you will use cable ties, which come in various sizes and strengths. You should have plenty of these ties in all sizes at all times. In Figure 1.24 a variety of cable ties are shown along with a bundle of cable neatly organized using the cable ties.

FIGURE 1.24   Cable ties

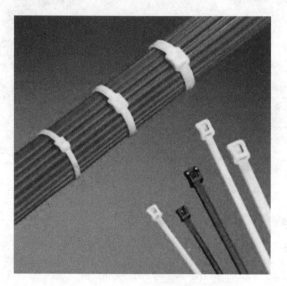

Network Cabling

In order for all of these devices in all these racks to talk to one another we have to have network cabling, and in the datacenter there will be lots of this cabling. In this section you'll learn about network cabling and how to manage it.

Redundant Networking

In the same way that you must build in power redundancy, you must also build in network redundancy. This could be achieved on an endpoint such as a server by installing and connecting multiple network interface cards (NICs) so if one fails additional connections are available.

Multiple connections between switches and routers in the datacenter should also be configured. Study the network diagrams and eliminate any network single points of failure.

Network Modules/Switches

Blade enclosures can accept several types of modules in addition to blade servers. At least one and probably two switch modules will be present to provide networking for the servers. This switch module is typically Ethernet but not always.

Twisted Pair

Copper cabling uses electrical signals to represent the ones and zeroes in a transmission. The most common type of copper cabling in use is twisted pair cabling. There are two primary types of twisted pair cabling: shielded twisted pair (STP) and unshielded twisted pair (UTP). In both cases, the cabling consists of pairs of wires twisted around each other, as shown in Figure 1.25.

FIGURE 1.25 Twisted pair cable

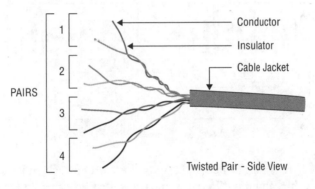

UTP offers no shielding (hence the name) and is the network cabling type most prone to outside interference. The interference can be from fluorescent light ballast, an electrical motor, or other such source (known as electromagnetic interference [EMI]) or from wires being too close together and signals jumping across them (known as crosstalk). STP adds a foil shield around the twisted wires to protect against EMI.

Patch Cables

While any twisted pair cable can be called a patch cable, there are actually three types of patch cables (different in the way in which they are wired and in the situation in which they are required), and these cables come in specifications called categories used to describe their capabilities. Let's first look at the three ways in which these cables can be wired.

Crossover and Straight Through

Two wiring standards are commonly used with twisted pair cabling: T568A and T568B (sometimes referred to simply as 568A and 568B). These are telecommunications standards from TIA and EIA that specify the pin arrangements for the RJ-45 connectors on UTP or STP cables. The number 568 refers to the order in which the wires within the Category 5 cable are terminated and attached to the connector. The signal is identical for both.

T568A was the first standard, released in 1991. Ten years later, in 2001, T568B was released. Figure 1.26 shows the pin number assignments for the 568A and 568B standards. Pin numbers are read left to right, with the connector tab facing down. Notice that the pin-outs stay the same, and the only difference is in the color coding of the wiring.

FIGURE 1.26   Pin assignments for T568A and T568B

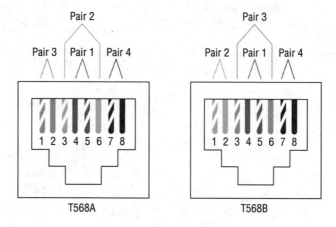

The bottom line here is that if the same standard is used on each end, the cable will be a straight-through cable, and if a different standard is used on either end, it will be a crossover cable.

Crossover cables are used to connect like devices, whereas straight-through cables are used to connect dissimilar devices. For example, to connect a router to another router or a switch to another switch, use a crossover cable. To connect a router to a switch or a computer to a switch, use a straight-through cable. There is one exception: to connect a host to a router, use crossover. Having said all that, most NICs today have the ability to sense the required pin-out pattern for the connection and use that. This function is called Auto-MDI-X.

Rollover

A rollover cable is a cable using a completely reversed wiring pattern. It is used to connect to a router, switch, or access point console port to manage the device using a HyperTerminal application. The pin-out is shown in Figure 1.27.

FIGURE 1.27   Rollover pin-out

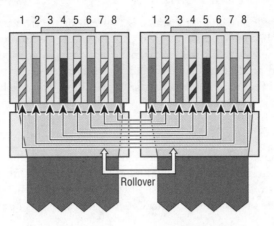

CAT5

Category 5 cabling transmits data at speeds up to 100 Mbps and is used with Fast Ethernet (operating at 100 Mbps) with a transmission range of 100 meters. It contains four twisted pairs of copper wire to give the most protection. Although it had its share of popularity (it's used primarily for 10/100 Ethernet networking), it is now an outdated standard. Newer implementations use the 5e standard.

RJ-45 and RJ-11

Twisted pair cabling uses a connector type called an RJ (registered jack) connector. You are probably familiar with RJ connectors. Most landline phones connect with an RJ-11 connector. The connector used with UTP cable is called RJ-45. The RJ-11 has room for two pairs (four wires), and the RJ-45 has room for four pairs (eight wires). In almost every case, UTP uses RJ connectors; a crimper is used to attach an RJ connector to a cable. Figure 1.28 shows an RJ-11 and an RJ-45 connector.

FIGURE 1.28   RJ-45 and an RJ-11 connector

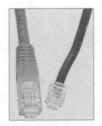

Fiber

Because fiber-based media use light transmissions instead of electronic pulses, such problems as EMI and crosstalk become nonissues. Fiber gets around the limitations on almost everything else except cost and is well suited for transferring data, video, and voice transmissions. Since anyone trying to access data signals on a fiber-optic cable must physically tap into the medium, it is the most secure of all cable media. It does have distance limitations based on the mode in use and the cable type.

SC

The subscriber connector (SC), also sometimes known as a square connector, is shown in Figure 1.29. SCs are latched connectors, making it virtually impossible for you to pull out the connector without releasing its latch, usually by pressing a button or release. SCs work with either single-mode or multimode optical fibers. They aren't as popular as ST connectors for LAN connections.

ST

The straight tip (ST) fiber-optic connector, developed by AT&T, is probably the most widely used fiber-optic connector. It uses a BNC attachment mechanism that makes connections and disconnections fairly easy. The ease of use of the ST is one of the attributes that makes this connector so popular. Figure 1.29 shows an ST connector along with an SC and a local connector.

LC

The local connector (LC), which was developed by Lucent Technologies, is a mini form factor (MFF) connector, especially popular for use with Fibre Channel adapters, fast storage area networks, and Gigabit Ethernet adapters (see Figure 1.29).

FIGURE 1.29   Fiber connectors ST, SC, and LC

Single Mode/Multimode

Two types of fiber-optic cable are available: single-mode and multimode. As the name implies, single-mode uses a single direct beam of light, thus allowing for greater distances and increased transfer speeds. With multimode, a lot of light beams travel through the cable, bouncing off the cable walls; this weakens the signal, reducing the length that the data signal can travel.

The most common types of fiber-optic cable include the following:

8.3 micron core/125 micron cladding single mode

50 micron core/125 micron cladding multimode

62.5 micron core/125 micron cladding multimode

Speed and Transmission Limitations

Table 1.1 lists the speed and transmission limitations for the most common fiber-optic implementations.

TABLE 1.1   Fiber speeds and limitations

Characteristic	100BaseFX	1000BaseSX	1000BaseLX	10GBaseER
Speed	100 Mbps	1000 Mbps	1000 Mbps	10,000 Mbps
Distance (multimode)	412 meters	220 to 550 meters	550 meters	(not used)
Distance (single mode)	10,000 meters	(not used)	5 km	40 km

Gigabit

CAT5e cabling transmits data at speeds up to 1 Gbps (1000 Mbps). Category 5e cabling can be used up to 100 meters, depending on the implementation and standard used, and it provides a minimum of 100 MHz of bandwidth. It also contains four twisted pairs of copper wire, but they're physically separated and contain more twists per foot than Category 5 to provide maximum interference protection.

10 GigE

CAT6 cabling transmits data at speed up to 10 Gbps, has a minimum of 250 MHz of bandwidth, and specifies cable lengths up to 100 meters (using CAT6a). It contains four twisted pairs of copper wire and is used in 10GBaseT networks. Category 6 cable typically consists of four twisted pairs of copper wire, but its capabilities far exceed those of other cable types. Category 6 twisted pair uses a longitudinal separator, which separates each of the four pairs of wires from each other and reduces the amount of crosstalk possible.

Small Form-Factor Pluggable (SFP)

The small form-factor pluggable (SFP) is a compact, hot-pluggable transceiver that, though not standardized by any governing body like the IEEE, was created through a multisource agreement (MSA) between competing manufacturers. For this reason, you may find that there is not full compatibility among these from various sources.

These devices allow for adding functionality to a device. For example, you plug in a fiber SFP into an open SFP slot in a device and add a fiber connection where there was none. SFP sockets are found in Ethernet switches, routers, firewalls, and network interface cards. You will find them in storage devices as well. An example of a fiber SFP is shown in Figure 1.30. The example shows a fiber cable plugged into the SFP module, which is then plugged into the SFP slot. The SFP slot is shown removed from a generic slot on a Cisco device.

FIGURE 1.30 Fiber SFP

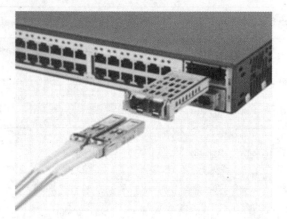

SFP cards can be added to servers if you need to add a connection type currently not present. These cards can be added to a PCI-Express slot. An example of one of these cards is shown in Figure 1.31. This particular model accepts two SFP+ connectors, requiring either Direct Attach Copper Cable (DAC) for copper environments, or fiber transceivers supporting short-haul (SR) optics plus fiber cables for fiber-optic environments.

SFP+

In the previous paragraph we made passing mention of SFP+. So what's the difference between SFP and SFP+? Well, they look the same but at introduction, typical speeds were 1 Gbit/s for Ethernet SFPs and up to 4 Gbit/s for Fibre Channel SFP modules. In 2006, SFP+ specification brought speeds up to 10 Gbit/s, and the SFP28 iteration is designed for speeds of 25 Gbit/s.

FIGURE 1.31   HP two-port server adapter

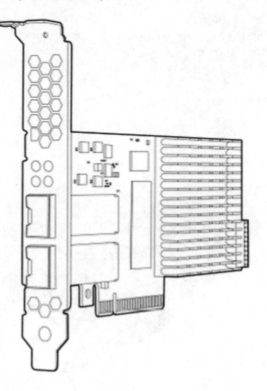

Quad Small Form-Factor Pluggable (QSFP)

The quad small form-factor pluggable (QSFP) transceiver is a version of SFP with four lanes, allowing for speeds 4 times their corresponding SFP. In 2014, the QSFP28 variant was published, allowing speeds up to 100 Gbit/s. In 2019, the closely related QSFP56 was standardized, doubling the top speeds to 200 Gbit/s.

Cable Management

It can be time-consuming to tie cables up, run them in channels, and snake them through walls, but it is time well spent when it keeps one person from harm. It is all too easy to get tangled in a cable or trip over one that is run across the floor. Take the extra time to manage cables, and it will increase your safety as well as that of others who work in that environment. These final sections will discuss cable management in the server room or datacenter.

Cable Channels

Cable channels are used to route cables across floors and other surfaces. They enclose the cables and protect them from damage while also preventing someone from tripping over them. In some cases, these trays may be integrated into the floor of the datacenter as well. An example of a cable channel is shown in Figure 1.32.

FIGURE 1.32 Cable channel

Cable Management Trays

While cable channels are good for floors, in some cases cable must be run up and over racks of equipment. In such instances you can use cable trays, which come in two types: vertical and horizontal.

Vertical

Vertical trays are used to route a group of cables up or down. For example, you may need to get cable from the back of a rack to the ceiling, where it may intersect with horizontal trays that lead the cabling out of the room or to another rack in the room. With vertical installation, cables on cable trays must be fixed by clips or suitable binding materials. An example of a vertical tray is shown in Figure 1.33.

Horizontal

Horizontal trays are used to route cable across the room on the floor, the ceiling, or anywhere in between. A horizontal tray is shown in Figure 1.34.

FIGURE 1.33   Attaching cable to vertical trays

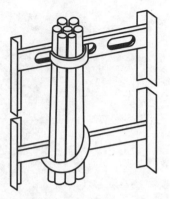

FIGURE 1.34   Horizontal cable tray

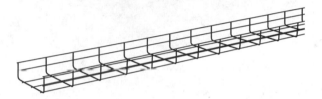

Server Chassis Types

As you learned earlier, servers can come in different form factors, also called chassis types. When we use the term *form factor* when discussing any computing device or component, we are talking about its size, appearance, or dimensions. Form factor is typically used to differentiate one physical implementation of the same device or component from another. In the case of servers, we are talking about the size and dimensions of the enclosure in which the server exists.

In this section we'll look at the major server form factors: the rack mount, the tower, and the blade. Each has its own unique characteristics and considerations you need to take into account when deploying. In this section you'll also learn about chassis security.

Tower

A form factor with which you are likely to be familiar is the *tower server*. This type bears the most resemblance to the workstations you are used to working with. When many of these devices are used in a server room, they reside not in the rack but on shelves. They are upright in appearance, as shown in Figure 1.35.

It is also possible to place a tower server in a rack by using a conversion kit. The issue with this approach is that it wastes some space in the rack. A tower server using a conversion kit is shown in Figure 1.36.

FIGURE 1.35 Tower server

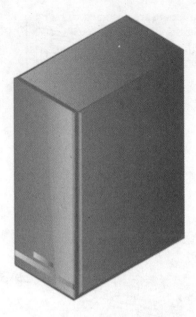

FIGURE 1.36 Tower server in a rack

Rack Mount

Rack-mounted servers are those that are designed to be bolted into a framework called a rack and thus are designed to fit one of several standard size rack slots, or *bays*. They also require *rail kits*, which when implemented allow you to slide the server out of the rack for maintenance. One of the benefits of using racks to hold servers, routers, switches, and other hardware appliances is that a rack gets the equipment off the floor, while also making more efficient use of the space in the server room and maintaining good air circulation. A rack with a server and other devices installed is shown in Figure 1.37.

FIGURE 1.37   Server in a rack

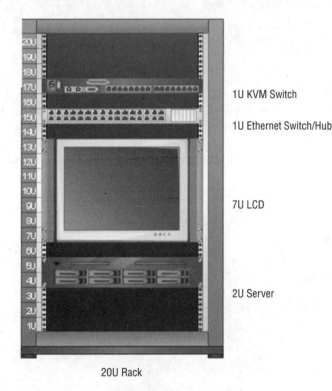

1U KVM Switch

1U Ethernet Switch/Hub

7U LCD

2U Server

20U Rack

Rack-mounted servers may come with locks that prevent removing the server from the rack without opening the lock. Whereas many of these locks are on cabinets that enclose the servers, as discussed in the previous section, others are a part of the server case itself, such as the one shown in Figure 1.38.

FIGURE 1.38   Rack mount lock

Server

You may also have servers you need to physically secure from tampering that are not located in racks or lockable server cabinets. Perhaps you are still using some tower servers. These servers can be secured using a lockable rack such as the one you see in Figure 1.39. A tower server lock connects to a cable that you secure to an immovable object as you would secure a laptop.

FIGURE 1.39   Tower server lock

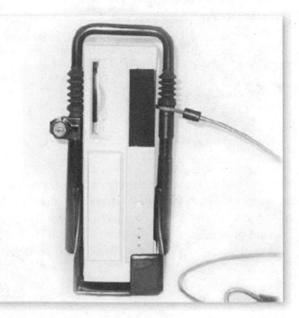

You also can secure a tower in a lockable cabinet made for just such a situation, as shown in Figure 1.40. Usually these come with a ventilation system to keep the server cool.

FIGURE 1.40   Tower cabinet

Blade Technology

Finally, servers may also come in blade form. This technology consists of a server chassis housing multiple thin, modular circuit boards, known as *server blades*. Each blade (or card) contains processors, memory, integrated network controllers, and other input/output (I/O) ports. Servers can experience as much as an 85 percent reduction in cabling for blade installations over conventional 1U or tower servers. Blade technology also uses much less space, as shown in a comparison of a blade system and a rack system in Figure 1.41.

FIGURE 1.41   Rack vs. blade

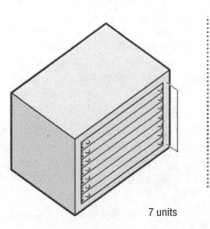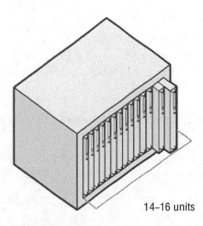

7 units   14–16 units

Blade Enclosure

A blade enclosure is a system that houses multiple blade servers. The chassis of the enclosure provides power and cooling to the blade servers. In Figure 1.42, a blade server is shown being inserted into an enclosure.

FIGURE 1.42   Blade enclosure

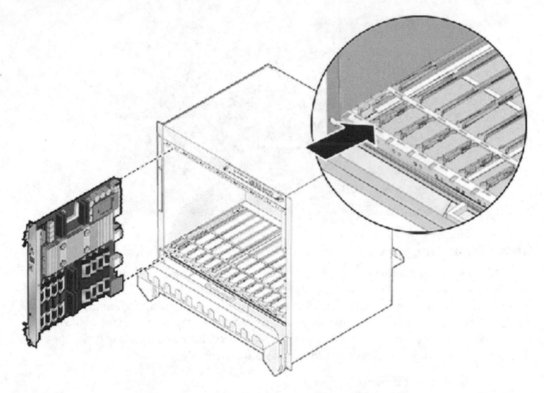

Blade Server

The blade servers are individual cards, each of which acts as a separate physical server. There will be a number of these—for example, 8, 16, or 24. Any blade slots that are not in use should have the blade filler in place. The insertion of both a blade server and a blade filler is shown in Figure 1.43.

Chassis Locks/Intrusion Detection

Although securing the BIOS can keep the server from being accessed by booting to another operating system, it cannot prevent theft of memory or hard drives. You should put locks on the case to prevent it from being opened. You should also use settings in the BIOS to alert you when the case has been opened. These settings are shown in Figure 1 44. Here the open case warning has *not* yet been enabled.

FIGURE 1.43   Inserting a blade server and filler

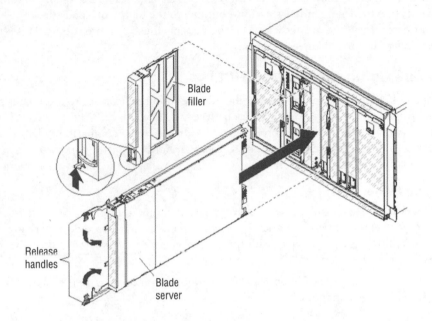

FIGURE 1.44   Open case warning in the BIOS

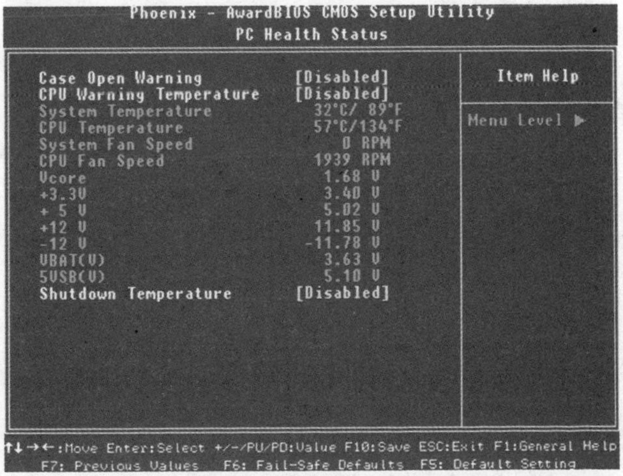

Server Components

Just as an A+ technician needs to be familiar with all of the possible components that may exist inside the box and how to install, maintain, and repair those components, as a Server + technician, you must know the same with regard to servers. Servers have all the same components that are found in workstations, but due to the high workloads they experience as a result of their roles in the network, the components must be more robust. This section explores server versions of key components.

Hardware Compatibility List (HCL)

When deploying a new server or when adding devices and applications to a server, it can be highly beneficial to ensure compatibility between the new addition and the server before spending money. Vendors of both software and hardware create compatibility lists that can be used to ensure that a potential piece of software or hardware will work with the server. These compatibility lists fall into three categories, as covered in the following sections.

Operating Systems

Major operating system vendors issue several types of compatibility lists. Some list the hardware requirements of each operating system. Others list hardware devices that have been tested and are known to work with the operating system. Microsoft calls its list the Windows Compatible Products List. You'll find it here:

```
https://docs.microsoft.com/en-us/windows-hardware/drivers/dashboard/
windows-certified-products-list
```

Hardware

Vendors of the hardware we often connect to our servers also create compatibility lists that describe the operating systems and other pieces of hardware with which their devices are compatible.

Applications

Finally, vendors of software applications also issue compatibility lists that describe the operating systems on which their software will run and the hardware requirements of the system on which the software will be installed.

Central Processing Unit (CPU)

The central processing unit (CPU) in servers must be capable of handling high workloads without overheating. In many cases, this requires the use of both multiple-core processors and multiple CPUs. A multiple-core processor is one with multiple cores, each of which can operate as a separate CPU. In this section we'll look at the types of sockets server CPUs use, the way they use memory, the possible architectures you may encounter, and the various speed values you may see and their meaning. We'll also introduce the concept of CPU stepping.

Socket Type

CPUs are connected to the motherboard via a socket on the board. The most common socket types are listed in Table 1.2.

TABLE 1.2 Server socket types

Socket name	CPU families supported	Package	Pin count	Bus speed
LGA 771/ Socket J	Intel Xeon	LGA	771	1600 MHz
LGA 1366/ Socket B	Intel Core i7 (900 series) Intel Xeon (35xx, 36xx, 55xx, 56xx series), Intel Celeron	LGA	1366	4.8–6.4 GT/s (gigatransfers per second)
LGA 1248	Intel Itanium 9300 series	LGA	1248	4.8 GT/s
LGA 1567	Intel Xeon 6500/7500 series	LGA	1567	4.8–6.4 GT/s
LGA 2011/ Socket R	Intel Core i7 3xxx Sandy Bridge-E Intel Core i7 4xxx Ivy Bridge-E Intel Xeon E5 2xxx/4xxx [Sandy Bridge EP] (2/4S) Intel Xeon E5-2xxx/4xxx v2 [Ivy Bridge EP] (2/4S)	LGA	2011	4.8–6.4 GT/s
Socket F	AMD Opteron 13xs, 2200, 2300, 2400, 8200, 8300, 8400, AMD Athlon 64 FX	LGA	1207	200 MHz
Socket 940	Opteron 100, 200, and 800	PGA-ZIF	940	800 MHz
G34	AMD Opteron 6000	LGA	1974	3.2 GHz
AM3+	AMD Phenom II, Athlon 2, Sempron, Opteron 3xxx	PGA-ZIF	942	3.2 GHz

Notice in Table 1.2 that most of the processors use the land grid array (LGA) package. These types of sockets don't have pins on the chip. Instead, they have bare gold-plated copper that touches pins that protrude from the CPU that goes in the socket. The LGA 2011/ Socket R, however, uses a version of pin grid array (PGA), an alternative design in which the socket has the pins, and they fit into the CPU when it is placed in the socket. A comparison of PGA (on the left) and LGA sockets is shown in Figure 1.45.

FIGURE 1.45 PGA and LGA

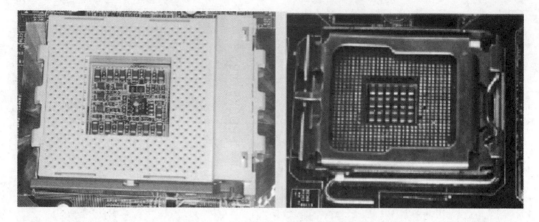

LGA-compatible sockets have a lid that closes over the CPU and is locked in place by an L-shaped arm that borders two of the socket's edges. The nonlocking leg of the arm has a bend in the middle that latches the lid closed when the other leg of the arm is secured.

For CPUs based on the PGA concept, zero insertion force (ZIF) sockets are used. ZIF sockets use a plastic or metal lever on one of the two lateral edges to lock or release the mechanism that secures the CPU's pins in the socket. The CPU rides on the mobile top portion of the socket, and the socket's contacts that mate with the CPU's pins are in the fixed bottom portion of the socket.

Cache Levels: L1, L2, L3

CPUs in servers use system memory in the server, but like most workstation CPUs they also contain their own memory, which is called *cache*. Using this memory to store recently acquired data allows the CPU to retrieve that data much faster in the event it is needed again. Cache memory can be located in several places, and in each instance it is used for a different purpose.

The Level 1 (L1) cache holds data that is waiting to enter the CPU. On modern systems, the L1 cache is built into the CPU. The Level 2 (L2) cache holds data that is exiting the CPU and is waiting to return to RAM. On modern systems, the L2 cache is in the same packaging as the CPU but on a separate chip. On older systems, the L2 cache was on a separate circuit board installed in the motherboard and was sometimes called cache on a stick (COASt).

On some CPUs, the L2 cache operates at the same speed as the CPU; on others, the cache speed is only half the CPU speed. Chips with full-speed L2 caches have better performance. Some newer systems also have an L3 cache, which is external to the CPU die but not necessarily the CPU package.

The distance of the cache from the CPU affects both the amount of cache and the speed with which the CPU can access the information in that cache. The order of distance, with the closest first, is L1, L2, and L3. The closer to the CPU, the smaller the cache capacity, but the faster the CPU can access that cache type.

Speeds

When measuring the speed of a CPU, the values are typically expressed in megahertz (MHz) and gigahertz (GHz). You may sometimes see it (as in Table 1.2) expressed in gigatransfers per second (GT/s). When expressed in GT/s, to calculate the data transmission rate, you must multiply the transfer rate by the bus width.

However, there are two speeds involved when comparing CPUs:

Core   Processors can have one or more *cores*. Each core operates as an individual CPU and each has an internal speed, which is the maximum speed at which the CPU can perform its internal operations and is expressed in either MHz or GHz.

Bus   The bus speed is the speed at which the motherboard communicates with the CPU. It's determined by the motherboard, and its cadence is set by a quartz crystal (the system crystal) that generates regular electrical pulses.

Multiplier

The internal speed may be the same as the motherboard's speed (the external or bus speed), but it's more likely to be a multiple of it. For example, a CPU may have an internal speed of 1.3 GHz but an external speed of 133 MHz. That means for every tick of the system crystal's clock, the CPU has 10 internal ticks of its own clock.

CPU Performance

CPU time refers to the amount of time the CPU takes to accomplish a task for either the operating system or for an application, and it is measured in clock *ticks* or seconds. The CPU *usage* is the total capacity of the CPU to perform work. The CPU time will be a subset of the usage and is usually represented as a percentage.

CPU usage values can be used to assess the overall workload of the server. When CPU usage is high—say 70 percent—there might be a slowing or lag in the system. CPU time values for a specific application or program, on the other hand, represent the relative amount of CPU usage attributable to the application.

We can also monitor CPU usage in terms of which component in the system is being served and in which security domain it is taking place. There are two main security domains in which the CPU operates: user mode and kernel mode. In user mode, it is working on behalf of an application and does not directly access the hardware. In kernel mode, it is working for the operating system and has more privileges.

When you are monitoring CPU performance, the following are common metrics and their meanings you'll encounter:

User Time   Time the CPU was busy executing code in user space.

System Time   Time the CPU was busy executing code in kernel space.

Idle Time   Time the CPU was not busy; measures unused CPU capacity.

Steal Time (Virtualized Hardware)   Time the operating system wanted to execute but was not allowed to by the hypervisor because it was not the CPU's turn for a time slot.

CPU Stepping

When CPUs undergo revisions, the revisions are called *stepping levels*. When a manufacturer invests money to do a stepping, that means they have found bugs in the logic or have made improvements to the design that allow for faster processing. Integrated circuits have two primary classes of *mask sets* (mask sets are used to make the changes): *base layers* that are used to build the structures that make up the logic, such as transistors, and *metal layers* that connect the logic together. A base layer update is more difficult and time-consuming than one for a metal layer. Therefore, you might think of metal layer updates as software versioning. Stepping levels are indicated by an alphabetic letter followed by a numeric number—for example, C-4. Usually, the letter indicates the revision level of a chip's base layers, and the number indicates the revision level of the metal layers. As an example, the first version of a processor is always A-0.

Architecture

Some processors operate on 32 bits of information at a time, and others operate on 64 bits at a time. Operating on 64 bits of information is more efficient but is only available in processors that support it and when coupled with operating systems that support it. A 64-bit processor can support 32-bit and 64-bit applications and operating systems, whereas a 32-bit processor can only support a 32-bit operating system and applications. This is what is being described when we discuss the *architecture* of the CPU. There are three main architectures of CPUs.

x86   Processors that operate on 32 bits of information at a time use an architecture called x86. It derives its name from the first series of CPUs for computers (8086, which was only 16 bits, 286, 386, and 486).

x64   Processors that operate on 64 bits of information at a time use an architecture called x64. It supports larger amounts of virtual memory and physical memory than is possible on its 32-bit predecessors, allowing programs to store larger amounts of data in memory.

ARM   Advanced RISC Machine (ARM) is a family of reduced instruction set computing (RISC) instruction set architectures developed by British company ARM Holdings. Since its initial development, both ARM and third parties have developed CPUs on this architecture. It is one that requires fewer resources than either x86 or x64. In that regard, ARM CPUs are suitable for tablets, smartphones, and other smaller devices.

In Exercise 1.1, you'll replace a CPU in a server.

EXERCISE 1.1

Replacing a CPU in a Server

1.   Shut down and remove power from the entire system.

2.   Remove the server node from the system. (Many systems have multiple servers in bays. To get to each server, you must remove the bay.)

3. Remove the server node cover (follow any instructions included with the documentation).

4. Use the proper type and size of screwdriver (usually a Number 2 Phillips-head) to loosen the screws (usually four) holding the heatsink, and then lift it off the CPU. (Yours may require a different type of screwdriver.)

5. Unclip the first CPU retaining latch and then unclip any remaining (usually there are two) latches.

6. Open the hinged CPU cover plate.

7. Remove the old CPU.

8. Insert the new CPU.

9. Install the heatsink (don't forget to put thermal grease between the CPU and the heatsink).

10. Replace the server node cover.

11. Reinstall the server node.

12. Replace power cords and then power on the system.

Graphics Processing Unit (GPU)

The graphics processing unit (GPU) is a processor dedicated to working on behalf of generating graphic images. They do a better job of this than the system CPU, and they offload some of the work from the CPU, allowing it to operate more efficiently as well.

Memory

Like any computing device, servers require memory, and servers in particular require lots of it. In this section we will discuss the types of memory chips that are used in servers and describe some of the characteristics that differentiate them.

ECC vs. Non-ECC

When data is moved to and from RAM, the transfer does not always go smoothly. Memory chips have error detection features and in some cases error correction functions. A type of RAM error correction is error correction code (ECC). RAM with ECC can detect and correct errors. To achieve this, additional information needs to be stored and more processing needs to be done, making ECC RAM more expensive and a little slower than non-ECC RAM.

In ECC, an algorithm is performed on the data and its check bits whenever the memory is accessed. If the result of the algorithm is all zeroes, then the data is deemed valid and processing continues. ECC can detect single- and double-bit errors and actually correct single-bit errors. This is a now a rarely used type of parity RAM. Most RAM today is non-ECC.

DDR2 and DDR3

Double data rate (DDR) is clock-doubled SDRAM (covered later in this section). The memory chip can perform reads and writes on both sides of any clock cycle (the up, or start, and the down, or ending), thus doubling the effective memory executions per second. So, if you're using DDR SDRAM with a 100 MHz memory bus, the memory will execute reads and writes at 200 MHz and transfer the data to the processor at 100 MHz. The advantage of DDR over regular SDRAM is increased throughput and thus increased overall system speed.

DDR2   The next generation of DDR SDRAM is DDR2 (double data rate 2). This allows for two memory accesses for each rising and falling clock and effectively doubles the speed of DDR. DDR2-667 chips work with speeds of 667 MHz and PC2-5300 modules.

DDR3   The primary benefit of DDR3 over DDR2 is that it transfers data at twice the rate of DDR2 (eight times the speed of its internal memory arrays), enabling higher bandwidth or peak data rates. By performing two transfers per cycle of a quadrupled clock, a 64-bit wide DDR3 module may achieve a transfer rate of up to 64 times the memory clock speed in megabytes per second (MBps). In addition, the DDR3 standard permits chip capacities of up to 8 GB. Selected memory standards, speeds, and formats are shown in Table 1.3.

TABLE 1.3   Selected memory details

Module standard	Speed	Format
DDR-500	4,000 MBps	PC4-000
DDR-533	4,266 MBps	PC4-200
DDR2-667	5,333 MBps	PC2-5300
DDR2-750	6,000 MBps	PC2-6000
DDR2-800	6,400 MBps	PC2-6400
DDR3-800	6,400 MBps	PC3-6400
DDR3-1600	12,800 MBps	PC3-12800

Number of Pins

Memory modules have pins that connect them to the motherboard slot in which they reside. Dual inline memory modules (DIMMs) have two rows of pins and twice the contact with the motherboard, creating a larger interface with it and resulting in a wider data path than older single inline memory modules (SIMMs). DIMMs differ in the number of conductors, or pins, that each particular physical form factor uses. Some common examples are 168-pin (SDR RAM), 184-pin (DDR, DDR2), and 240-pin (DDR3) configurations.

Static vs. Dynamic

RAM can be either static or dynamic. Dynamic RAM requires a refresh signal whereas static RAM does not. This results in better performance for static RAM. A static RAM cell, on the other hand, requires more space on the chip than a dynamic RAM cell, resulting in less memory on the chip. This results in static RAM being more expensive when trying to provide the same number of cells.

In summary, static RAM is more expensive but faster, whereas dynamic RAM is slower but cheaper. The two types are often both used, however, due to their differing strengths and weaknesses. Static RAM is used to create the CPU's speed-sensitive cache, and dynamic RAM forms the larger system RAM space.

Module Placement

Utilizing multiple channels between the RAM and the memory controller increases the transfer speed between these two components. Single-channel RAM does not take advantage of this concept, but dual-channel memory does and creates two 64-bit data channels. Do *not* confuse this with DDR. DDR doubles the rate by accessing the memory module twice per clock cycle.

Using dual channels requires a motherboard that supports dual channels and two or more memory modules. Sometimes the modules go in separate color-coded (not shown in Figure 1.46) banks, as shown in Figure 1.46, and other times they use the same colors. Consult your documentation.

FIGURE 1.46   Dual-channel memory slots

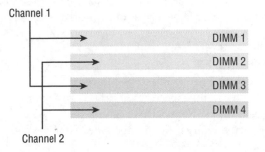

Memory runs in banks, with two slots comprising a bank. The board should indicate which two slots are in the same bank by the color coding. It could be orange and yellow, or it might be some other combination of two colors. When installing the memory, install the same size modules in the same bank. If you don't, the modules will not operate in dual-channel mode. This will impair the performance of the bank.

CAS Latency

Another characteristic that can be used to differentiate memory modules is their CAS latency value. Column access strobe (CAS) latency is the amount of time taken to access a memory module and to make that data available on the module's pins.

The lower the CL value, the better. In asynchronous DRAM, the delay value is measured in nanoseconds and the value is constant, whereas in synchronous DRAM, it is measured in clock cycles and will vary based on the clock rate.

Timing

Memory timing measures the performance of RAM and consists of four components:

CAS Latency   The time to access an address column if the correct row is already open

Row Address to Column Address Delay   The time to read the first bit of memory without an active row

Row Precharge Time   The time to access an address column if the wrong row is open

Row Active Time   The time needed to internally refresh a row

Memory timings are listed in units of clock cycles; therefore, when translating these values to time, remember that for DDR memory, this will be half the speed of the transfer rate. It is also useful to note that memory timing is only part of the performance picture. The memory *bandwidth* is the throughput of the memory. Although advances in bandwidth technology (DDR2, DDR3) may have a negative effect on latency from timing, DDR2 and DDR3 can be clocked faster, resulting in a net gain in performance.

Memory Pairing

Each motherboard supports memory based on the speed of the front-side bus (FSB) and the memory's form factor. If you install memory that is rated at a lower speed than the FSB, the memory will operate at that lower speed, if it works at all. In their documentation, most motherboard manufacturers list which type(s) of memory they support as well as maximum speeds and required pairings.

With regard to adding and upgrading memory, faster memory can be added to a server with slower memory installed, but the system will operate only at the speed of the slowest module present.

Moreover, although you can mix speeds, you cannot mix memory types. For example, you cannot use SDRAM with DDR, and DDR cannot be mixed with DDR2. When looking at the name of the memory, the larger the number, the faster the speed. For example, DDR2-800 is faster than DDR2-533.

Finally, memory pairing also refers to installing matched pairs of RAM in a dual-channel memory architecture.

Replacing RAM

Replacing RAM in a server is not all that different from doing so in a workstation. The box looks different but otherwise the basic steps are the same. In Exercise 1.2 you'll use an IBM blade server.

This exercise applies to an IBM blade server. The procedure for your server may vary, so consult the documentation.

EXERCISE 1.2

Changing RAM in an IBM Blade Server

1. If the blade server is installed in a BladeCenter unit, remove it from the BladeCenter unit.

2. Remove the blade server cover.

3. If an optional expansion unit is installed, remove the expansion unit. This may require an extraction device (thumbscrews or levers) and it may not. If one is not provided, using the blade server cover releases on each side, lift the expansion unit from the blade server, as shown here:

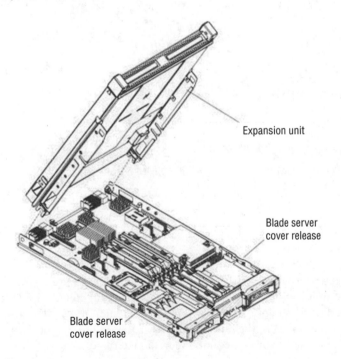

Expansion unit

Blade server cover release

Blade server cover release

EXERCISE 1.2 *(continued)*

4. Locate the DIMM connectors. Determine which DIMM you want to remove from the blade server.

 WARNING   To avoid breaking the retaining clips or damaging the DIMM connectors, handle the clips gently.

5. Move the retaining clips on the ends of the DIMM connector to the open position by pressing the retaining clips away from the center of the DIMM connector. To access DIMM connectors 7 through 12, use your fingers to lift the DIMM access door, as shown here:

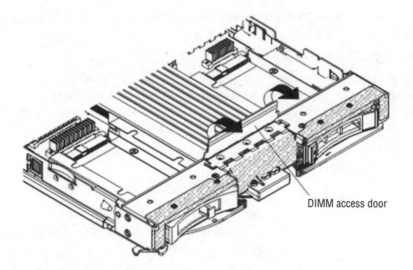

DIMM access door

6. Using your fingers, pull the DIMM out of the connector.

7. Install a DIMM or DIMM filler in each empty DIMM connector.

Note that DIMMs or DIMM fillers must occupy DIMM connectors 1, 2, 13, 14, 15, and 16 for proper cooling on the IBM HS22 blade server.

Bus Types

The motherboard provides the platform to which all components are attached and provides pathways for communication called *buses*. A bus is a common collection of signal pathways over which related devices communicate within the computer system. Expansion buses incorporate slots at certain points in the bus to allow insertion of external devices. In this section we'll look at common server bus types and their characteristics.

Height Differences and Bit Rate Differences

Two major differentiating characteristics of bus types are their bit rates and the form factor of the slot and adapter to which it mates. The dominant bus types in servers are forms of the Peripheral Component Interconnect (PCI) expansion bus. You will learn more about PCI slots in the next section.

Interface Types

In this section we'll look at some internal and external interface types.

PCI

The Peripheral Component Interconnect (PCI) bus is a 33 MHz wide (32-bit or 64-bit) expansion bus that was a modern standard in motherboards for general-purpose expansion devices. Its slots are typically white. You may see two PCI slots, but most motherboards have gone to newer standards. Figure 1.47 shows some PCI slots.

FIGURE 1.47   PCI slots

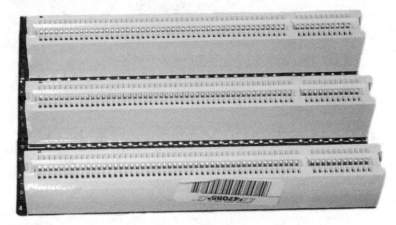

PCI cards that are 32 bit with 33 MHz operate up to 133 MBps, whereas 32-bit cards with 64 MHz operate up to 266 MBps. PCI cards that are 64 bit with 33 MHz operate up to 266 MBps, whereas 64-bit cards with 66 MHz operate up to 533 MBps.

PCI-X

PCI-extended (PCI-X) is a double-wide version of the 32-bit PCI local bus. It runs at up to four times the clock speed, achieving higher bandwidth, but otherwise it uses the same protocol and a similar electrical implementation. It has been replaced by the PCI Express (see the next section), which uses a different connector and a different logical design. There is also a 64-bit PCI specification that is electrically different but that has the same connector as PCI-X. There are two versions of PCI-X: version 1 gets up to 1.06 GBps, and version 2 gets up to 4.26 GBps.

PCIe

PCI Express (PCIE, PCI-E, or PCIe) uses a network of serial interconnects that operate at high speed. It's based on the PCI system; you can convert a PCIe slot to PCI using an adapter plug-in card, but you cannot convert a PCI slot to PCIe. Intended as a replacement for the Advanced Graphics Processor (AGP was an interim solution for graphics) and PCI, PCIe has the capability of being faster than AGP while maintaining the flexibility of PCI. There are six versions of PCIe: version 1 is up to 8 GBps, version 2 is up to 16 GBps, version 3 is up to 32 GBps, version 4 is up to 64 GBps, version 5 is up to 128 GBps, and version 6 is up to 256 GBps. Figure 1.48 shows the slots discussed so far in this section, and Table 1.4 lists the speeds of each. The PCIe speeds shown are per lane. So a 4-lane version of PCIe 2 would operate at 20 GBps.

FIGURE 1.48   Comparison of PCI slot types

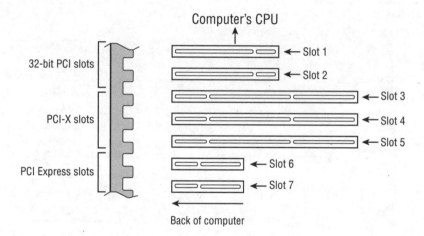

TABLE 1.4   PCI and PCIe slot speeds

Type	Data transfer rate
PCI 33, 32-bit	133 MBps
PCI 33, 64-bit	266 MBps
PCI 66, 32-bit	266 MBps
PCI 66, 64-bit	533 MBps
PCIe version 1	2 GBps
PCIe version 2	5 GBps
PCIe version 3	8 GBps
PCIe version 4	16 GBps

NICs

Network cards do exactly what you would think; they provide a connection for the server to a network. In general, network interface cards (NICs) are added via an expansion slot or they are integrated into the motherboard, but they may also be added through USB. The most common issue that prevents network connectivity is a bad or unplugged patch cable.

Network cards are made for various access methods (Ethernet, token ring) and for various media types (fiber optic, copper, wireless) connections. The network card you use must support both the access method and the media type in use.

The most obvious difference in network cards is the speed of which they are capable. Regardless of other components, the server will operate at the speed of the slowest component, so if the card is capable of 1 Gbps but the cable is only capable of 100 MBps, the server will transmit only at 100 Mbps.

Another significant feature to be aware of is the card's ability to perform auto-sensing. This feature allows the card to sense whether the connection is capable of full duplex and to operate in that manner with no action required.

There is another type of auto-sensing in which the card is capable of detecting what type of device is on the other end and changing the use of the wire pairs accordingly. For example, normally a PC connected to another PC requires a crossover cable, but if both ends can perform this sensing, that is not required. These types of cards are called auto-MDIX.

In today's servers you will most likely be seeing 10 Gb cards and you may even see 40 Gb or 100 Gb cards. Moreover, many servers attach to storage networks and may run converged network adapters (CNAs), which act both as a host bus adapter (HBA) for the storage area network (SAN) and as the network card for the server. This concept is shown in Figure 1.49.

FIGURE 1.49   Traditional and CNA

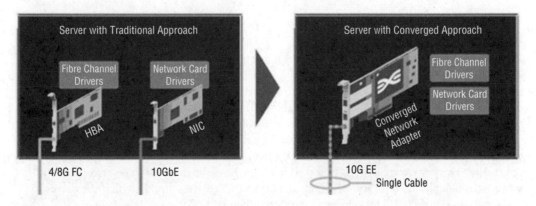

Expansion Cards

Expansion cards allow you to add additional device support to the system. Let's look at some types of these cards.

Riser Cards

Riser cards allow you to add expansion cards to a system. You may already be familiar with their use in low-profile cases where the height of the case doesn't allow for a perpendicular placement of the full-height expansion card. They are also used in rack-mounted and blade servers to allow you to add feature cards in a horizontal position (instead of a standard vertical position).

Typically, a 1U system uses a 1U single-slot riser card whereas a 2U system uses a 2U three-slot riser card. An example of a riser card in a rack server is shown in Figure 1.50.

FIGURE 1.50   Riser card in rack server

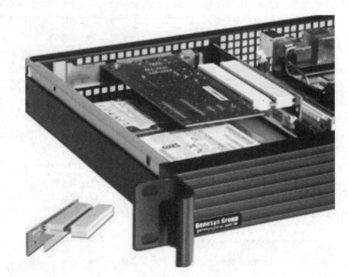

RAID Controllers

Redundant Array of Independent Disks (RAID) is a multiple-disk technology that either increases performance or allows for the automatic recovery of data from a failed hard drive by simply replacing the failed drive. There are several types of RAID that provide varying degrees of increased performance and/or fault tolerance. All of these techniques involve two or more hard drives operating together in some fashion.

RAID can be implemented using software or hardware. The highest levels of protection are provided by using hardware RAID, which requires that the system have a RAID *controller*. This hardware device is used to manage the disks in the storage array so they work as a logical unit. This is a card that fits into a PCI express slot to which the drives in the array are connected. This concept is shown in Figure 1.51.

FIGURE 1.51   RAID controller

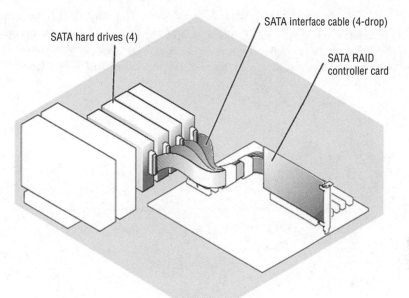

SATA hard drives (4)

SATA interface cable (4-drop)

SATA RAID
controller card

Summary

In this chapter we covered hardware in a server, including the topics in Objective 1 of the exam. This included a discussion of form factors such as the tower, rack, and blade server. We also discussed configuring and maintaining server components such as CPU, memory, NICs, hard drives, riser cards, and RAID controllers. We ended the chapter by exploring methods of satisfying the power and cooling requirements of servers and of the server rooms and datacenters in which they live.

Exam Essentials

Differentiate the server form factors.   These include tower servers; 1U, 2U, 3U, and 4U rack-mounted servers; and blade servers. The U in the rack server notation indicates the number of units in the rack that the servers use.

Describe the components found inside the server.   Inside the server case you will find all of the same components you might find in a workstation, but they will be more robust and there may be more of them. These include CPU, memory, NICs, hard drives, riser cards, and RAID controllers.

Understand the power requirements of servers.   Servers can require from 350 W (for a 1U rack mount) to 4500 W for a chassis with 14 blades in it.

Identify and mitigate cooling issues.   Explain how to use heatsinks, fans, and baffles inside the case to eliminate the heat created by servers. In the server room or datacenter, understand how to deploy baffles and hot/cold aisles to remove heat from the room.

Review Questions

You can find the answers in the Appendix.

1. Which term refers to the size, appearance, or dimensions of a server?
   A. Form factor
   B. Footprint
   C. Physical reference
   D. Outline

2. Which of the following is used to make physical maintenance easier with a rack server?
   A. KVM
   B. Rail kits
   C. Baffles
   D. Rack slot

3. How large is each U in a rack?
   A. 19 inches.
   B. 4.445 inches.
   C. 1.75 inches.
   D. It depends on the rack.

4. What technology consists of a server chassis housing multiple thin, modular circuit boards, each of which acts as a server?
   A. Rack servers
   B. Towers
   C. KVM
   D. Blade technology

5. What type of CPU cache holds data that is waiting to enter the CPU?
   A. L1
   B. L2
   C. L3
   D. L4

6. What term describes the relationship between the internal speed of the CPU and the speed of the system bus?
   A. CPU time
   B. Multiplier
   C. Differential
   D. Coefficient

7. What term describes the time the CPU was executing in kernel mode?

   A. User time

   B. Steal time

   C. System time

   D. Idle time

8. What are revisions in CPUs called?

   A. Service packs

   B. Hot fixes

   C. Base layers

   D. Stepping levels

9. Which CPU architecture was designed for a tablet?

   A. ARM

   B. x86

   C. x64

   D. LGA

10. DDR3 memory is _____ as fast as DDR2.

   A. Three times

   B. Twice

   C. Half

   D. One-third

11. True/False: DDR doubles the rate by accessing the memory module twice per clock cycle.

   A. True

   B. False

12. What statement is true with regard to dual-channel memory?

   A. Installing different size modules in the same bank will result in the modules operating in single-channel mode.

   B. Installing different size modules in the same bank will result in the modules operating in dual-channel mode.

   C. Installing equal size modules in the same bank will result in the modules operating in single-channel mode.

   D. Installing different size modules in the same bank will increase the performance of the bank.

13. Which of the following is the time to access a memory address column if the correct row is already open?

   A. CAS Latency

   B. Row Address to Column Address Delay

    C. Row Precharge Time

    D. Row Active Time

14. Which of the following can be mixed when installing memory? (Choose two.)

    A. Different speeds

    B. Different types

    C. Different form factors

    D. Different manufacturers

15. Which of the following is a double-wide version of the 32-bit PCI local bus?

    A. PCI

    B. PCI-X

    C. PCIe

    D. PCI/2

16. Which type of NIC detects the type of device on the other end and changes the use of the wire pairs accordingly?

    A. Auto-MDIX

    B. Full-duplex

    C. Converged

    D. HBA

17. What type of NIC acts as both a host bus adapter (HBA) for the SAN and the network card for the server?

    A. Auto-MDIX

    B. Full-duplex

    C. Converged

    D. HBA

18. Which of the following supplies power connections to various components?

    A. Cable management arm

    B. Front plane

    C. Midplane

    D. MBP

19. What is the height of a 2U system?

    A. 1.75"

    B. 3.5"

    C. 5.25"

    D. 7"

20. Which of the following is a multiple-disk technology that either increases performance or allows for the automatic recovery of data from a failed hard drive by simply replacing the failed drive?

A. DLP

B. RAID

C. UEFUI

D. SFP

Installing and Configuring Servers

- Template deployment
- Physical to virtual (P2V)

■ Partition and volume types

- Global partition table (GPT) vs. master boot record (MBR)
- Dynamic disk
- Logical volume management (LVM)

■ File system types

- ext4
- New technology file system (NTFS)
- VMware file system (VMFS)
- Resilient file system (ReFS)
- Z file system (ZFS)

✓ **2.3 Given a scenario, configure and maintain server functions and features**

■ Server roles requirements

- Print
- Database
- File
- Web
- Application
- Messaging
- Baselining
  - Documentation
  - Performance metrics

■ Directory connectivity

■ Storage management

- Formatting
- Connectivity
- Provisioning

- Partitioning
- Page/swap/scratch location and size
- Disk quotas
- Compression
- Deduplication
- Monitoring
  - Uptime
  - Thresholds
  - Performance
    - Memory
    - Disk
      - Input output operations per second (IOPS)
      - Capacity vs. utilization
    - Network
    - Central processing unit (CPU)
  - Event logs
    - Configuration
    - Shipping
    - Alerting
    - Reporting
    - Retention
    - Rotation
- Data migration and transfer
  - Infiltration
  - Exfiltration
  - Disparate OS data transfer
    - Robocopy
  - File transfer
  - Fast copy
  - Secure copy protocol (SCP)

- Administrative interfaces
  - Console
  - Remote desktop
  - Secure shell (SSH)
  - Web interface

✓ **2.5 Summarize the purpose and operation of virtualization**

- Host vs. guest
- Virtual networking
  - Direct access (bridged)
  - Network address translation (NAT)
  - vNICs
  - Virtual switches
- Resource allocation and provisioning
  - CPU
  - Memory
  - Disk
  - NIC
  - Overprovisioning
  - Scalability
- Management interfaces for virtual machines
- Cloud models
  - Public
  - Private
  - Hybrid

A server will be of no use unless it has an operating system (OS) that can be used to access and control the hardware you learned about in Chapter 1, "Server Hardware." The OS is a prerequisite to installing any software that runs on the server as well, because in modern systems, applications are not allowed to directly access the hardware and must have an underlying OS to function as a liaison between the hardware and the applications. As you may already know, this is a good thing because it prevents any single application that hangs from hanging up the entire system. In this chapter, we'll look at installing operating systems and some of the preinstallation tasks that are required. We'll also look at securing access to the server for the purpose of managing it. Finally, since in today's networks you'll probably encounter virtualized servers, we'll explore the basics of virtualization components.

Installing Server Operating Systems

You've probably installed an operating system before if you are reading this book. If you have, then you know that the entire process goes much more smoothly when it has been planned correctly and all information required has been gathered ahead of time and all pre-installation tasks have been completed successfully. What you may not know is that when it comes to servers, the stakes are higher because of the significant role they play in the network.

In this section we'll discuss factors in common with those that are taken into account with workstations as well as factors that are unique to servers. We'll also talk about various ways to perform the installation and tasks that should follow the successful installation. Finally, we'll discuss some methods you can use to optimize the performance of the server when it's up and running.

Minimum Operating System (OS) Requirements

Every operating system has a set of requirements with regard to the system resources required to install and run the system. The three main resources are disk space, amount of memory, and CPU capability. For example, Windows Server 2022 requires the following:

- **Processor:** 1.4 GHz 64-bit processor compatible with x64 instruction set
- **Memory/RAM:** 512 MB
- **Disk space:** Minimum 32 GB (Windows Server 2022 using the Server Core installation option)

Hardware Compatibility List (HCL)

There are many different types of hardware, both internal and peripheral, that can be added to a system. But not all hardware plays well with all operating systems. Vendors create what are known as hardware compatibility lists (HCLs) that detail the hardware that is compatible with the system. Always reference that document before investing in hardware to prevent incompatibility.

Installations

There are many different ways to perform an operating system installation. Some are quite simple, and others can get complicated but offer granular control of the process. In this section you'll learn about installation methods.

Graphical User Interface (GUI) (Attended Installation)

During an attended installation, you walk through the installation and answer the questions as prompted. Questions typically ask for the product key, the directory in which you want to install the OS, and relevant network settings.

As simple as attended installations may be, they're time-consuming and administrator-intensive in that they require someone to fill in a fair number of fields to move through the process. Unattended installations allow you to configure the OS with little or no human intervention. You will learn more about them later in this chapter.

Core

When you install Windows Server Core you are installing the part of the operating system shared by all versions. Server Core has a smaller disk footprint and therefore a smaller attack surface due to a smaller code base. There is no desktop in this system. All work is done at the command line, although there will be GUI during the installation process.

To install Windows Server 2022 Server Core, boot to a virtual or physical device using the Windows Server media or mounted ISO file. The out-of-box experience (OOBE) will then run, allowing you to select your regional options, enter a product key, choose between Standard and Datacenter versions, and select a disk to install the operating system on. Finally, you need to set an administrator password.

Bare Metal

A bare-metal installation means that the operating system is installed on an empty drive and requires no software to be there first. For example, you can install Windows Server 2019 on bare metal using the following process:

1. Create a bootable ISO image on a DVD that will be used to access the empty hard drive (instructions for that are here: `https://itproguru.com/expert/2016/05/create-bootable-windows-server-2016-usb-thumb-drive-for-installing-os`).

2. Boot to the bootable DVD ISO image (you may need to change the boot order so that the system boots to the DVD before the hard drive).

3. After booting you will be presented with the first page of the Windows Server 2019 installation program. From this point on, the installation process will be the same as if you were booting to an existing OS. You simply create a partition when that page appears, format it, and chose to install to it.

Virtualized

Typically, when systems are installed virtually (meaning an installation to a VM rather than to a physical machine) an image of the operating system is used rather than running the installation process. The image is simply placed on the virtual drive. Keep in mind that VMs are physical files that represent a physical device, and the OS image is one of them. In most cases, the image that is used has been prepared by running an installation process and saving the resulting image before placing it on the VM.

Remote

A remote or network installation is handy when you have several installations to do and installing by CD is too much work. In a network installation, the installation CD is copied to a shared location on the network. Then individual workstations boot and access the network share.

The workstations can boot either through a boot disk or through a built-in network boot device known as a PXE ROM. Boot ROMs essentially download a small file that contains an OS and network drivers and has enough information to boot the computer in a limited fashion so that it can access the network share and begin the installation.

Slip Streamed/Unattended

Answering the myriad of questions posed by Windows Setup doesn't qualify as exciting work for most people. Fortunately, there is a way to answer the questions automatically: through an unattended installation. In this type of installation, an answer file is supplied with all the correct parameters (time zone, regional settings, administrator username, and so on) so that no one needs to be there to tell the computer what to choose or to hit Next 500 times.

The first step is to create an answer file. This XML file, which must be named `unattend` `.xml`, contains configuration settings specific to the computer on which you are installing the OS, which means that for every installation the answer file will be unique.

Generally speaking, you'll want to run a test installation using that answer file first before deploying it on a large scale because you'll probably need to make some tweaks to it. After you create your answer file, place it on a network share that will be accessible from the target computer. (Most people put it in the same place as the Windows installation files for convenience.)

Boot the computer that you want to install on using a boot disk or CD, and establish the network connection. Once you start the setup process, everything should run automatically.

Scripted Installations

Scripted installations differ from simple image deployment in one way: there is some type of file associated with the deployment that makes changes to the deployment or that provides answers for the installation. In a Windows classic unattended installation, this file is called an *answer file.* When using Windows Deployment Services or any third-party deployment tool, there will be a number of script files that might be used during either an image deployment or a full installation. In an image deployment, the file makes changes to or provides drivers for the image; in a full installation, the full installation process takes place with the file providing answers to the prompts.

Regardless of which type of deployment is taking place, the new system, with no operating system, must be able to:

- Boot up and get an IP configuration
- Locate the deployment server
- Download the image or installation files
- Locate and download any additional scripts that need to run

There are a couple of ways to accomplish this, and we'll look at them now.

PXE BOOT AND TFTP

Preboot Execution Environment (PXE) makes it possible to boot a device with no operating system present and come to a location in the network where the operating system files might be found and installed.

A device that is PXE-enabled will have an additional boot option in its BIOS/UEFI settings called PXE Boot. When the device is set to boot to that option, it will attempt a PXE network boot. The process after that follows these steps:

1. The system begins by looking for a DHCP server. This is referred to as Discover.

2. The DHCP server answers with a packet called the Offer packet, indicating a willingness to supply the configuration. This step is referred to as Offer.

3. The client indicates to the DHCP server that it requires the location of the network boot program (NBP). This step is called the Request.

4. The DHCP server supplies the IP address of this location. This step is called Acknowledge.

5. The client, using Trivial File Transfer Protocol (TFTP), downloads the NBP from the network location specified by the PXE server.

6. The NBP is initialized. At this point, either the full installation occurs with an answer file, or an image is deployed with or without additional script files.

Note that the process is independent of the operating system. Although we have framed this discussion in terms of Windows, the system being deployed can be any operating system. The PXE boot process is shown in Figure 2.1.

FIGURE 2.1   PXE boot process

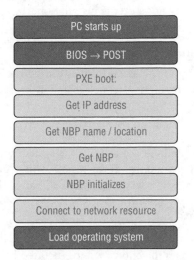

Additional Drivers

Sometimes an installation will fail because the driver used to communicate with the hard drive is not present. If you are running the GUI installation process, at some point you will be offered an option to install mass storage drivers. For example, in Figure 2.2 a Windows Server 2008 installation process is offering that option.

FIGURE 2.2   Add mass storage drivers

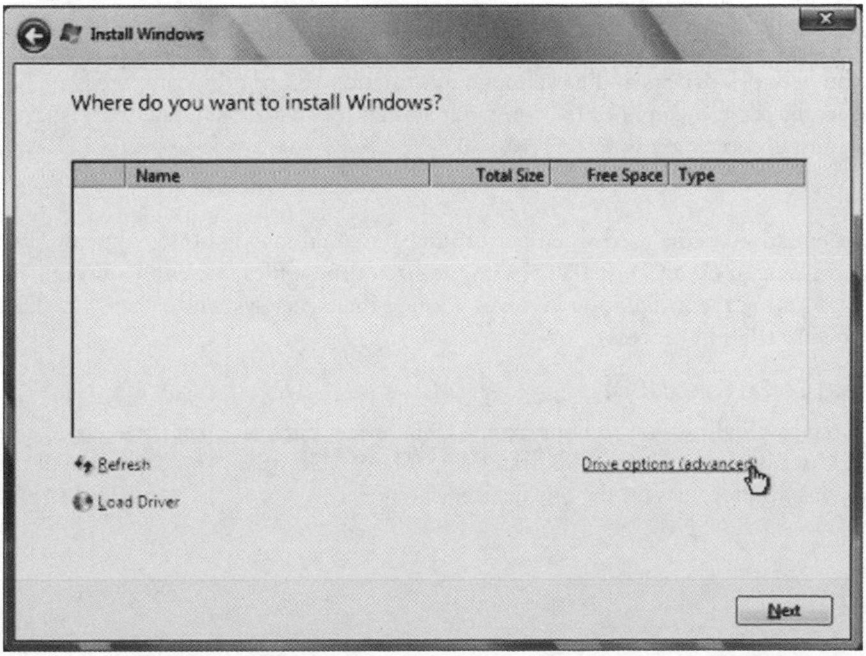

While mass storage drivers must be present to install, there may be other drivers you need later. Although these drivers may not stop the installation, they may cause something like a network interface card (NIC) to not function.

Additional Applications and Utilities

You're not required to add applications and utilities during the installation, but you can choose to do so. This will require an unattended installation. See the earlier section on unattended installations.

Patches

If you run an installation manually, at some point the system will ask you to wait while it downloads and installs the latest updates. If the installation is unattended, you will either need to script this update process or perform it manually after the installation.

Media Installation Type

You have some choices when it comes to the media you use to deliver the installation files or the image, although in most cases the choice will be dictated by the scenario. In this section you'll learn about media options.

Network

Earlier in this chapter you learned that installations can be done remotely. In that case your media will be the network itself. A network installation is handy when you have many installations to do and installing by CD is too much work. In a network installation, the installation CD is copied to a shared location on the network. Then individual workstations boot and access the network share.

The workstations can boot either through a boot disk or through a built-in network boot device known as a PXE ROM. Boot ROMs essentially download a small file that contains an OS and network drivers and has enough information to boot the computer in a limited fashion. At the least, it can boot the computer so that it can access the network share and begin the installation.

Optical

The most common media used when performing a manual installation is optical. This means the files are located on a CD or DVD (with the size of these files, typically a DVD). This means performing the installation involves booting the target system to the DVD. That will invoke the installation process.

Universal Serial Bus (USB)

Most systems will allow you to boot from a USB device, but you must often change the BIOS/UEFI settings to look for USB first. Using a large USB drive, you can store all the necessary installation files on the one device.

Embedded

A Windows Embedded OS brings the same kinds of interface design and functionality to a handheld device. Installing this system is done using an image.

Imaging

One way in which operating systems can be deployed quickly and with consistency is to create images of completed installations and use disk imaging software to copy the image to a drive. Not only does this speed the deployment process, but the image can be preconfigured according to the company policy with regard to the role the server will play.

Cloning

Cloning is the process of making a copy of an existing operating system installation and copying it to another system. This can take several forms. In this section you'll learn more about cloning.

VIRTUAL MACHINE (VM) CLONING

Another of the advantages of a virtualized environment is the ability to maintain an inventory of images for quick use. You can even maintain multiple instances of a VM, all clones of one another, for fault tolerance or in scenarios where high availability is a requirement.

PHYSICAL CLONES

When you make a copy of an existing physical server, it is called a *physical clone*. This copy can be used to deploy another physical server or to create a VM. Typically when an organization decides to create a virtual network, they start by cloning the physical servers and using the clone files to create VMs.

TEMPLATE DEPLOYMENT

A clone is an exact image of a system. VM clones are not suited for mass deployment of virtual machines A template is a more generalized image that is intended for multiple uses. Templates act as a baseline image for a VM. While cloned systems can be turned on, templates cannot. They are used for deployment only.

PHYSICAL TO VIRTUAL (P2V)

Earlier in this section you learned that cloning can be used to copy a physical system and then use the image or clone to set up a VM that can perform the same job. Pleas review that section.

Partition and Volume Types

During the installation, you will be required to create a partition or volume to hold the installation (if it doesn't already exist). Templates act as a baseline image for a VM with the predefined configurations as per your organization's two specifications for managing partitions or volumes and additional issues surrounding setting up the partition or volume.

Global Partition Table (GPT) vs. Master Boot Record (MBR)

There are two specifications for managing partitions and volumes. Devices that use the Unified Extensible Firmware Interface (UEFI) specification instead of a BIOS also use a partitioning standard called GUID Partition Table (GPT). Since 2010, most operating systems support GPT as well as using a master boot record (MBR), which is the alternative method of booting to a legacy BIOS firmware interface. Today, almost all operating systems support it, and many only support booting from a GPT rather than from an MBR.

Moreover, GPT is also used on some BIOS systems because of the limitations of MBR partition tables, which was the original driver for the development of UEFI/GPT. MBR works with disks up to 2 TB in size, but it can't handle larger disks. MBR also supports only up to four primary partitions, so to have more than four, you had to make one of your primary partitions an "extended partition" and create logical partitions inside it. GPT removes both of these limitations. It allows up to 128 partitions on a GPT drive.

Dynamic disk

Partitions can be made dynamic, which—as the name implies—means they can be configured and reconfigured on the fly. The big benefits they offer are that they can increase in size (without reformatting) and can span multiple physical disks. Dynamic partitions can be simple, spanned, or striped.

Dynamic partitions that are simple are similar to primary partitions and logical drives. This is often the route you choose when you have only one dynamic disk and want the ability to change allocated space as needed.

Choosing spanned partitions means that you want space from a number of disks (up to 32) to appear as a single logical volume to users. A minimum of two disks must be used, and no fault tolerance is provided by this option.

Striped partitions are similar to spanned in that multiple disks are used, but the big difference is that data is written (in fixed-size stripes) across the disk set in order to increase I/O performance. Although read operations are faster, a concern is that if one disk fails, none of the data is retrievable (like Spanned, the Striped option provides no fault tolerance).

Logical Volume Management (LVM)

Logical volume management is the use of drive management tools that allow you to create volume structures that are independent of the physical storage devices. For example, in Figure 2.3 you can see that a logical volume on a Linux system might contain data from multiple physical storage systems but will be seen as a single logical volume.

FIGURE 2.3   Logical volume management

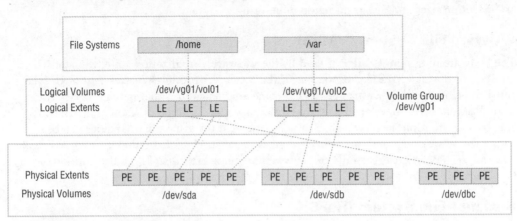

File System Types

You may encounter many different filesystems. In the following sections, we take a brief survey of these filesystem types and see where and when they are used.

ext4

ext2, ext3, and ext4 are Linux filesystems. As you would expect, each version is more capable than the previous one. Although ext4 has the advantages listed here, it should be noted that it is not compatible with Windows. (You can, however, obtain third-party programs that will allow Windows to read ext4.) Here are the strengths of ext4:

- It supports individual file sizes up to 16 TB.

- The overall maximum ext4 filesystem size is 1 EB (exabyte); (1 EB = 1024 PB [petabyte]; 1 PB = 1024 TB [terabyte]).

- The directory can contain 64,000 subdirectories as opposed to 32,000 in ext3.

- You can mount an existing ext3 filesystem as an ext4 filesystem (without having to upgrade it).

- The performance and reliability of the filesystem is improved compared to ext3.

- In ext4, you also have the option of turning off the journaling feature. Journaling is a process where the filesystem records its intention to record a change before the change is made. Although this approach is beneficial when the system crashes before the change is committed, it does take resources.

New Technology File System (NTFS)

Introduced along with Windows NT (and available on all Windows Server and client operating systems), NTFS (NT Filesystem) is a much more advanced filesystem in almost every way than all versions of the previous system (FAT). It includes such features as individual file security and compression, RAID support, and support for extremely large file and partition sizes and disk transaction monitoring.

VMware File System (VMFS)

The VMware filesystem (VMFS) is used by the VMware virtualization suite, vSphere. There are six versions of VMFS, corresponding with ESX Server product releases. Although NFS can also be used with VMware, VMFS has some unique features that make it perfect for virtualization. It was developed to store virtual machine disk images, including snapshots. It allows for multiple servers to access the filesystem at the same time. Volumes can be expanded by spanning multiple VMFS volumes together. The maximum virtual disk size of VMFS is 64 TB, whereas each file can have a maximum size of 62 TB. It also supports long filenames.

Resilient File System (ReFS)

Resilient File System (ReFS) was created by Microsoft to address issues with NTFS, and it brings many improvements. Among them are:

- Improved reliability
- Built-in resiliency (no need to periodically run error-checking tools such as CHKDSK)

   The latest version of ReFS is 3.4.

Z File System (ZFS)

The Zettabyte File System (ZFS) was developed by Sun Microsystems, but it is also an open source project. It is supported on many other operating systems, such as some versions of BSD (BSD, or Berkeley Software Distribution, is a version of Unix). At one point, Apple appeared to be interested in this filesystem but has since dropped that project. ZFS has a focus on integrity of data, which distinguishes it from some of the other filesystems that focus more on performance. ZFS allows for volumes up to 256 ZB (zettabytes) and a maximum file size of 16 EB (exabytes). It also supports filenames up to 255 characters.

Configuring and Maintaining Server Functions and Features

Once you've installed your servers, you must take additional steps to enable them to perform the roles you chose for them in the network. You also need to monitor and maintain the servers so that they continue to perform well. In addition, you want to avoid security-related issues such as malware infections and data breaches by instituting and following best practices with regard to patches, updates, and data security. Finally, you must develop systems that allow you to manage these critical organizational assets in a standardized method throughout the entire asset life cycle.

Server Roles Requirements

Servers exist to serve the network and its users in some form. Each server has a certain role to play, although in small networks a server performs multiple roles. Each of those roles places different types of demand on the hardware and software of the server. Some roles demand lots of memory, whereas others place a heavier load on that CPU. By understanding each server role, you can more appropriately ensure that the proper resources are available to enable the server to successfully serve the network with as little latency and downtime as necessary. In this section we'll explore the major server roles you are likely to encounter and the specific compute resources (CPU, memory, network, and disk) that are stressed in the process of performing those roles.

WARNING When discussing hardware requirements for a server role, we can only speak in general terms based on the typical operation of the software running on the server. The size of your network, the number of servers you have performing a role, and in some cases the exact way you deploy the server role will have a big impact on the requirements. The recommendations in this chapter are simply starting points.

The role of the server will also have an impact on the operating system you install and the services you will enable and configure. It may also impact the amount and type of redundancy you provide for the role the server is playing. For example, if the server will be either a domain controller or a DNS server, you will almost certainly want to have multiple servers for these roles in case one should fail, because the loss of these functions in the network is devastating. The bottom line is that you should have a clear understanding of all the roles the server will be playing before the installation begins.

The role the server will play in the network will dictate what features and roles need to be installed or enabled. With regard to Windows, the same security paradigm that's applied to services has been applied to what are called *features* and *roles* in Microsoft. For example, if the server will be a DNS server, then you must install that role and the related features required to perform that role. This is done in Server Manager, as shown in Figure 2.4, where the FTP role has been added. To navigate to the Add Roles and Features Wizard, open Server Manager and select Manage ➤ Add Roles And Features.

Print

Print servers are used to manage printers, and in cases where that is their only role, they will manage multiple printers. A print server provides the spooler service to the printers that it manages, and when you view the print queue, you are viewing it on the print server. Many enterprise printers come with a built-in print server, which makes using a dedicated machine for the role unnecessary. Here are some of the components that should be maximized to ensure good performance in a print server:

FIGURE 2.4   Adding a role in Server Manager

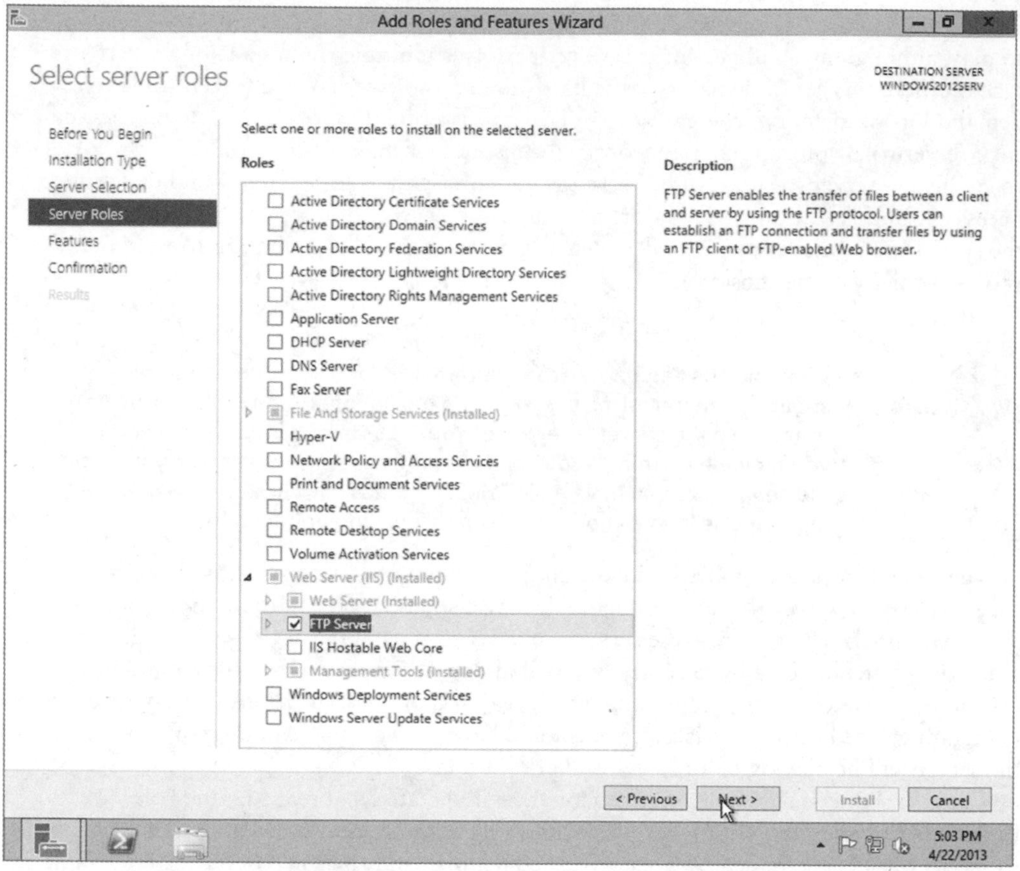

Memory: Print servers need lots of memory to hold the print jobs waiting in the print queue. The exact amount will depend on the number of users assigned to the printers being managed by this print server.

CPU: The number and type of CPUs are impacted by the amount of processing power available on the print devices the server is managing. If they are heavy-duty enterprise printers with plenty of memory and processing power, you'll need less on the server. A physical server will need less processing power than a virtual print server because the physical server can offload some of the print processing to the CPU on the graphics card whereas a virtual print server cannot.

Disk: As is the case with processing power, if there is plenty of disk space on the print device, you will need less on the print server. One thing you should do is move the spool file to a disk other than the one where the operating system is located. If your enterprise requires that completed print jobs be stored, ensure that you periodically remove them to keep them from eating up all the space.

NIC: As always use 1 Gbps NICs, and if the server will be managing many printers and thus many users, you may want to have multiple NICs for fault tolerance and load balancing.

Database

A database server is one that runs database software such as SQL Server or Oracle. It contains information stored in the database, and users can search the database, either directly by issuing commands or by using an application that does this through a GUI. Here are some of the components that should be maximized to ensure good performance in a database server:

CPU: Your CPUs (yes, multiple) should be as fast as you can afford with multiple cores and plenty of cache. The specific number should be driven by the database software recommendations and the number of users.

Memory: With respect to memory, you should fill all available slots with the cheapest memory you can get. That means smaller DIMMs (dual in-line memory modules) but more of them. For example, rather than filling 12 slots with 64 GB of memory, save some money for very little cost in speed by installing 32 GB DIMMs.

Disk: You should use multiple disks in a RAID5 configuration so that you get performance and fault tolerance. The exact number of disks depends on the features you are installing and the size of the database. Review the database software recommendations.

Network: As with all enterprise servers you should use a 1 Gbps card at a minimum. If the server is critical, use multiple cards for fault tolerance and load balancing.

File

File servers are used to store files that can be accessed by the network users. Typically users are encouraged or even required to store any important data on these servers rather than on their local hard drives, because these servers are typically backed up on a regular basis, whereas the user machines typically are not. Here are some of the components that should be maximized to ensure good performance in a file server:

Disk: File servers should have significant amounts of storage space and may even have multiple hard drives configured in a RAID array to provide quicker recovery from a drive crash than could be provided by recovering with the backup.

CPU: The number of processors is driven by the number of concurrent users you expect and whether you will be doing encryption on the server. As the number of users increases, at a certain point it becomes better to use more and slower processors rather than fewer and faster ones. This is because as many concurrent requests come in, multiple slower CPUs will handle the overall load better by spreading the requests among themselves, whereas fewer faster CPUs will try to keep up with a form of multitasking that is not as efficient.

Memory: You should increase RAM in step with the increase in users accessing the file server. Start with the amount designated as a minimum for the operating system and add at least 50 percent to that.

NIC: The same recommendation I gave for all of these roles applies. Use 1 Gbps NICs, and if this server will be very busy, use more than one for fault tolerance and load balancing.

Web

Web servers are used to provide access to information to users connecting to the server using a web browser, which is the client part of the application. A web server uses HTTP as its transfer mechanism. This server can be contained within a network and made so it is only available within the network (called an intranet server), or it can be connected to the Internet where it can be reached from anywhere. To provide security to a web server it can be configured to require and use HTTPS, which uses SSL to encrypt the connection with no effort on the part of the user, other than being aware that the URL must use https rather than http.

Here are some of the components that should be maximized to ensure good performance in a web server:

Disk Subsystem: Disk latency is one of the major causes of slow web performance. The disk system should be as fast as possible. Using high-speed solid-state drives can be beneficial, and if possible, you should deploy either a RAID 0 or RAID 5 configuration, either of which will improve the read performance. If fault tolerance is also a consideration, then go with RAID 5 since RAID 0 will give you no fault tolerance.

RAM: Memory is also critical to a web server. Eighty percent of the web requests will be for the same 20 percent of content. Therefore, plenty of memory may ensure requested pages may still be contained in memory from which access is faster. You can help this situation by deploying web caching. This can be done on the proxy server if you use one.

CPU: CPU is important but not a critical issue for a web server unless the server will be performing encryption and decryption. If that is the case, it may be advisable to use a network card with its own processor for this process.

NIC: The NIC should be at a least 1 Gbps, and using multiple cards would be even better. The amount of traffic you expect will influence this.

Application

An application server is one that users connect to and then run their applications on. This means the server is doing all the heavy lifting while the user machine is simply sending requests to the server and displaying the output. In many cases this server is the middle tier in a three-tier architecture that accepts users' requests to its application and then communicates with a database server where content is stored, as shown in Figure 2.5.

Here are some of the components that should be maximized to ensure good performance in an application server:

CPU: This component is stressed on an application server since it is doing all of the processing on behalf of the clients. Multicore and multiple processors are advisable.

NIC: Considering the traffic the server will be handling (and that could be in two directions if the server is running middleware), the NIC(s) should be 1 Gbps at least.

Disk: The disk system should be fast but it's not the most critical part of the equation for an application server.

Memory: Application servers also require lots of memory, especially if acting as a middle tier to a backend database server.

FIGURE 2.5   Three tiers

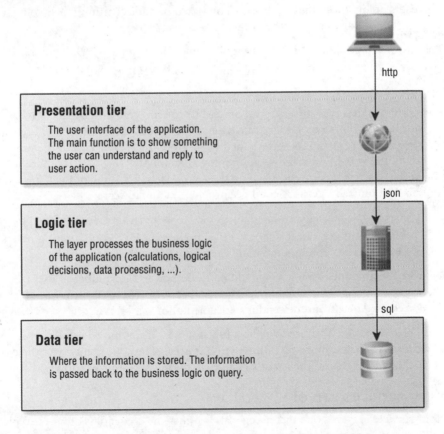

Messaging

Messaging servers run instant messaging software and allow users to collaborate in real time through either chat or video format. Here are some of the components that should be maximized to ensure good performance in a messaging server:

Memory: The amount of memory required is a function of the number of *concurrent* connections. Users have varying habits when it comes to messaging. Some never use it and others use it constantly, so this is hard to predict and you may have to monitor the server usage and adjust memory accordingly.

Disk: Include disk space for the operating system and the instant messaging software. The disk throughput of the system is critical so that the server can keep up, which means you should use faster disks.

CPU: The processing power required is a function of the types of users you have. If most of the users are inactive (that is, they are connected but not chatting), then you will need less CPU than if a high percentage of them are active.

NIC: This resource should be sized using the same guidelines as CPU. If you have many active users, you need faster and/or multiple NICs (as always, 1 Gbps).

Mail Server

Mail servers run email server software and use SMTP to send email on behalf of users who possess mailboxes on the server and to transfer emails between email servers. Those users will use a client email protocol to retrieve their email from the server. Two of the most common are POP3, which is a retrieve-only protocol, and IMAP4, which has more functionality and can be used to manage the email on the server. Here are some of the components that should be maximized to ensure good performance in a mail server:

Disk: The disk system is most often the bottleneck on an email server. It should be high speed, perhaps solid state, and it should be set up in a RAID 5 configuration unless you are using a distributed configuration and the server is not the mail server.

Memory: The amount of memory should be based not on the number of users, but rather on the amount of email they generate and receive. This is an item for which you should seek guidance from the vendor's documentation.

CPU: The amount of CPU used will be a function of the amount of email that is sent and received at a time, meaning if the email traffic is spread out evenly over the day, it will need less CPU than if the email all comes in during a 4-hour window.

Directory services server

A directory services server is one that accepts and verifies the credentials of users. Typically it not only authenticates them but also provides them with access to resources using single sign-on (SSO). SSO allows users to authenticate once and *not* be required to authenticate again to access the resources to which they have been given access. Moreover, these resources may be located across the network on various devices. One of the best examples is a domain controller in a Windows Active Directory domain. These servers are the point to which all users are directed when they need to log in to the network.

Here are some of the components that should be maximized to ensure good performance in a directory services server:

Disks: Use a fast system, and since this function is so important, implement RAID 5 for fault tolerance and performance. Put the Active Directory (AD) database (`ntds.dit`) onto separate disk spindles. Allow at least 0.5 GB per 1,000 users when allocating disk space for the AD database.

Network Connections: Although this will probably not be the bottleneck on the system, it could become one. Ensure you have 1 Gbps cards. If encryption will be involved (which is highly likely), consider offloading this encryption to the network card.

Processor: Multiple-core processors should be used if the server will be performing encryption. If you have not offloaded that encryption to the NIC, you should have multiple CPUs as well. Keep in mind that as the number of users goes up, you may need to add more processing power.

Memory: The memory requirements depend on the size of the AD database or the `ntds.dit` file. You should have enough memory to hold this file or a file with 20 percent additional space added. The `ntds.dit` file is located at `%systemroot%\ntds\ntds.dit`.

Baselining

When all applications have been installed and proper services enabled, you need to create what is called a *performance baseline*. This is a snapshot of the performance of key resources in the server such as the CPU, memory, disk, and network card. This snapshot should be taken during a period of normal activity.

You can use third-party monitoring tools, or you can rely on some that are built into the system, such as the Performance Monitor tool in Windows Server 2022. The Performance Monitor tool can be used to take these snapshots over a period of time as well, so you get a feel for the rise and fall of the workload on the server. In this way, you can better understand the times of day when a higher workload is normal. You may also want to take advantage of tools such as System Center Operations Manager, which allows you to easily do this for a number of servers from a single console. Figure 2.6 shows the seven-day Memory Pages Per Second report for a Windows Server 2012 Datacenter computer.

To navigate to the Performance Monitor in Windows Server 2012 R2, open Server Manager and select Tools ➤ Performance Monitor.

FIGURE 2.6   Seven-day Memory Pages Per Second report

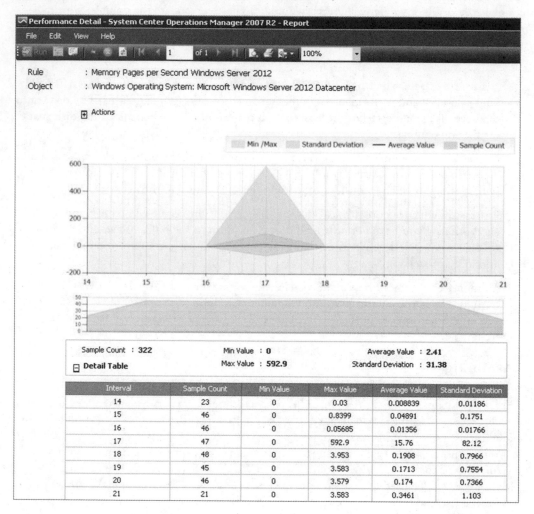

Interval	Sample Count	Min Value	Max Value	Average Value	Standard Deviation
14	23	0	0.03	0.008839	0.01186
15	46	0	0.8399	0.04891	0.1751
16	46	0	0.05685	0.01356	0.01766
17	47	0	592.9	15.76	82.12
18	48	0	3.953	0.1908	0.7966
19	45	0	3.583	0.1713	0.7554
20	46	0	3.579	0.174	0.7366
21	21	0	3.583	0.3461	1.103

Documentation

Save the performance baseline as a reference point for future readings. It is impossible to know when something abnormal is happening unless you know what normal is. That is the function of this baseline. It also helps anticipate a rise in workload over time, so you can take steps to add resources before an issue arises.

Performance metrics

Earlier in this chapter, we covered the resources typically required by certain server roles. As noted, those were only guidelines and starting points in the discussion based on general principles. You should monitor the servers once deployed on a regular basis to determine whether the system is indeed handling the workload. When monitoring resources, you select performance counters that represent aspects of the workload the resource is undergoing. But first you need to know what normal is for your server.

COMPARISON AGAINST PERFORMANCE BASELINE

If you have ever tried to look up a particular performance metric on the Internet to find out what a "normal" value is, you may be quite frustrated that you can't get a straight answer. This is because you have to define what is normal for your network. This is done by creating a set of performance metrics during normal operations when all is working well. While earlier in this chapter we listed some rough guidelines about certain metrics, that is all they are: guidelines.

Only until you have created this set of values called a *performance baseline* can you say what is normal for your network. Creating the set of values should be done during regular operations, not during either times of unusual workload or times of very little workload. After this you can compare the performance metrics you generate later with this baseline.

Directory Connectivity

Enterprise networks join servers, workstations, and other devices in security associations called *domains* or *realms*. These associations are made possible through the use of directory services such as Active Directory. Such associations are what make the concept of single sign-on possible. This means that any user can log into the network using any device that is a domain member and receive all their assigned rights and privileges by using a single logon.

You can join the server to the domain during the installation in some cases, but most administrators do this after the successful installation of the operating system. Figure 2.7 shows an example of how this is done in Windows Server 2012 R2. To navigate to System Properties in Windows Server 2012 R2, open Control Panel and select the System icon (using icon view); then select Advanced System Settings from the menu on the left side of the page. This opens the System Properties dialog box. Select the Computer Name tab and click Change to access the Computer Name/Domain Changes dialog box.

Storage Management

Storage management comprises a set of activities that are designed to ensure that data is always there when you need it. In this section you'll learn about storage management.

Partitioning

When all of the volumes have been configured as you would like them, you must create a partition on one of the volumes to contain the operating system. This can be done during the installation of the operating system using the GUI provided with the installation utility. For example, during the installation of Windows Server 2012 R2 (Figure 2.8), you can create a partition of the desired size. Be mindful of the space required for the operating system and include some additional space.

FIGURE 2.7 Joining the server to the domain

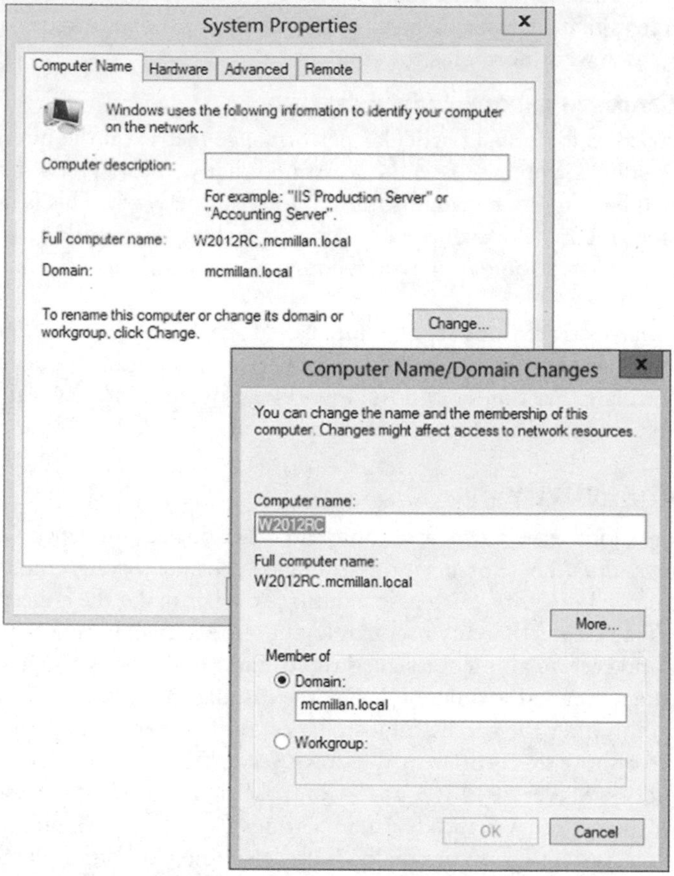

FIGURE 2.8 Creating a partition

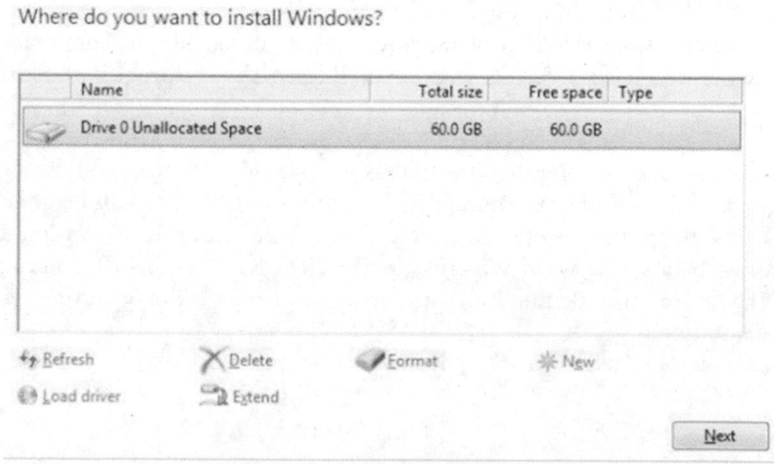

Formatting

Once the partition has been created, it must be formatted with a filesystem. The filesystem choices will be driven by the operating system. Windows, for example, will require using either FAT or NTFS. Other systems, such as Unix and Linux, will use other filesystems. We'll look at filesystems in a bit. You can format the partition during the installation. Using the Windows Server 2012 R2 example, you'd choose the Format option shown in Figure 2.8. Similar options are provided during the installation of many forms of Linux and Unix as well.

Connectivity

Don't forget that you must be able to connect to the storage devices to access data. In data scenarios where high availability or fault tolerance are required, don't forget to take advantage of concepts like multiple NICs and NIC teaming to provide additional bandwidth and/or a backup connection.

Provisioning

The storage provisioning process has several steps and the first several are probably the most important. These steps include:

- Analyze the storage request to determine capacity, security and connectivity requirements.
- Identify the storage solution based on requirements (hard drive, SSD, cloud, storage array).
- Approve the selection and schedule the purchase and deployment.
- Implement the solution.
- Notify requestor that storage is ready.

Partitioning

Partitioning was covered earlier in this chapter in the section "Storage Management".

Page/Swap/Scratch Location and Size

Today's operating systems support the use of swap files, also called page files or scratch files. These are files located on the hard drive that are utilized temporarily to hold items moved from memory when there is a shortage of memory required for a particular function. The running programs believe that their information is still in RAM, but the OS has moved the data to the hard drive. When the application needs the information again, it is swapped back into RAM so that the processor can use it. Providing adequate space for this file is a key disk management issue. Every operating system seems to have its own recommendations as to the optimum size of this file, but in all cases the swap file should be on a different drive than the operating system if possible.

Disk Quotas

One of the ways you make capacity planning easier when dealing with a server where users will be storing their data is to implement disk quotas. These are limits assigned to each user. These limits can be implemented with a warning to users when they are filling their allotted space so that they can delete some data or take some action that keeps them within their limits. This is implemented in Windows Server 2012 R2 in the disk properties, as shown in Figure 2.9. In the figure all users are being given 1 GB of space and will be warned when they get to 50 MB.

FIGURE 2.9 Disk quotas

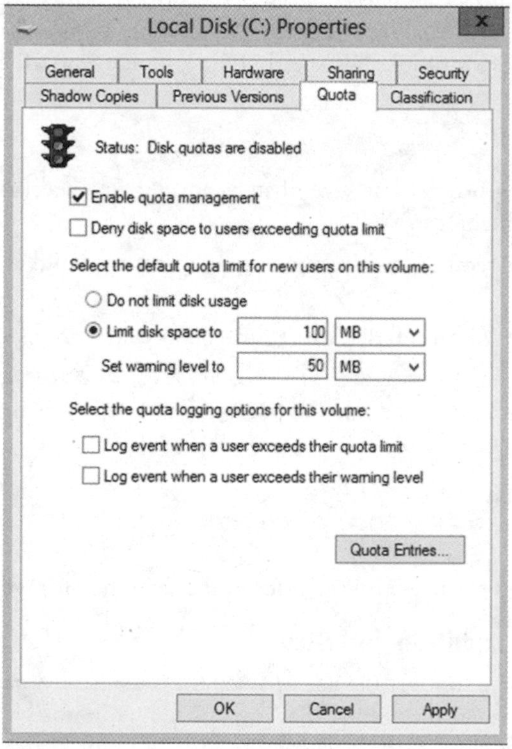

Users that may require a different setting would need to be configured using the Quota Entries button.

The reason this helps with capacity planning is that if you know how much space each user is given, it becomes simple math to determine what you need based on the number of current and prospective users. You should keep in mind that quotas ignore compression and calculate use based on the *uncompressed* space taken.

Compression

Another tactic you can use to better utilize the space you have is to compress files that are used infrequently. This can be done in Windows at both the file and the folder levels. In the advanced attributes of the file or folder properties, select Compress Contents To Save Disk Space, as shown in Figure 2.10.

FIGURE 2.10   Disk compression

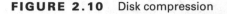

Be aware that when you do this to files and folders that are frequently accessed, you will place a load on the CPU of the server because it decompresses the file to make it available and then compresses it again when saved. For that reason, use this tool with caution.

Deduplication

In many cases, data is located multiple times on the same drive. Deduplication tools remove this redundancy while still making the data available at any location it was previously located by pointing to the single location. This process can be done after the data is on the drive or it can be implemented inline, which means data being written to the drive is examined first to see if it already exists on the drive. These two processes are shown in Figure 2.11.

Monitoring

Earlier in this chapter you learned about performance monitoring and creating baselines to guide the process. In this section you'll learn more about this process and how it relates to various system resources.

FIGURE 2.11 Deduplication techniques

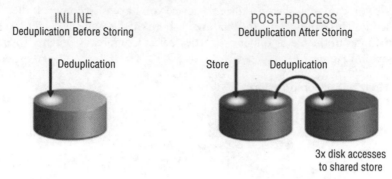

INLINE
Deduplication Before Storing

POST-PROCESS
Deduplication After Storing

Deduplication

Store | Deduplication

3x disk accesses
to shared store

Uptime

Uptime is the description of the ratio of time a system spends up and running as opposed to offline and unavailable. It is represented as a percentage such as 90%, which means that the system was available 90% of the time. The term "number of nine" refers to the number of nines in the percentage. The more nines there are the better the uptime. For example 99.99 % (4 nines) is better than 99.9 % (3 nines). Generally speaking, increasing the number of nines involves spending money to provide the resources necessary to deliver that uptime.

Thresholds

Performance thresholds are used to trigger alerts when system performance or a component's performance falls below a configured level. These alerts are designed to allow technicians to react to a system performance issue before it impacts the business.

Performance

When discussing the performance of system resources such as memory and CPU, you need to know the major metrics that are used to assess performance of each resource. In this section you'll learn about these metrics.

MEMORY

Different server roles place different demands on the memory, so there may be specific metrics (called counters in Windows) of interest you can learn about by consulting the vendor documentation. Common counters monitored by server administrators are as follows:

Memory\% Committed Bytes in Use: The amount of virtual memory in use. If this is over 80 percent, you need more memory.

Memory\Available Mbytes: The amount of physical memory (in megabytes) currently available. If this is less than 5 percent, you need more memory.

Memory\Free System Page Table Entries: The number of entries in the page table not currently in use by the system. If the number is less than 5,000, there may be a memory leak. (Memory leaks occur when an application is issued memory that is not returned to the system. Over time this drains the server of memory.)

Memory\Pool Non-Paged Bytes: The size, in bytes, of the non-paged pool, which contains objects that cannot be paged to the disk. If the value is greater than 175 MB, you may have a memory leak (an application is not releasing its allocated memory when it is done).

Memory\Pool Paged Bytes: The size, in bytes, of the paged pool, which contains objects that can be paged to disk. (If this value is greater than 250 MB, there may be a memory leak.)

Memory\Pages per Second: The rate at which pages are written to and read from the disk during paging. If the value is greater than 1,000 as a result of excessive paging, there may be a memory leak.

DISK

On several of the server roles we discussed, disk was the critical resource. When monitoring the disk subsystem, you must consider two issues: the speed with which the disk is being accessed and the capacity you have available. Let's examine those metrics in more detail.

INPUT/OUTPUT OPERATIONS PER SECOND (IOPS)

Disk input/output operations per second (IOPS) represents the number of reads and writes that can be done in a second. One of the advantages of newer solid-state drives (SSDs) is that they exhibit much higher IOPS values than traditional hard disk drives. For example, a 15,000 rpm SATA drive with a 3 Gb/s interface is listed to deliver approximately 175–210 IOPS, whereas an SSD with a SATA 3 Gb/s interface is listed at approximately 8,600 IOPS (and that is one of the slower SSD drives).

CAPACITY VS. UTILIZATION

The second metric of interest when designing a storage solution is capacity. When planning and managing storage capacity, consider the following questions:

- What do you presently need? Remember that this includes not only the total amount of data you have to store but also the cost to the system for fault tolerance. For example, if data is located on a RAID 1 or mirrored drive, you need twice as much space for the data. Moreover, if the data is located on a RAID 5 array, your needs will depend on the number of drives in the array. As the number of drives in the array go up, the amount of space required for the parity information goes down as a percentage of the space in the drive. For example, with three drives you are losing 33 percent of the space for parity, but if you add another drive, that goes down to 25 percent of the space used for parity. Add another, and it goes down to 20 percent.

- How fast are the needs growing? Remember that your needs are not static. They are changing at all times and probably growing. You can calculate this growth rate manually, or you can use capacity-planning tools. If you have different classes of storage, you may want to make this calculation per class rather than overall because the growth rates may be significantly different for different classes.

- Are there major expansions on the table? If you are aware that major additions are occurring, you should reflect that in your growth rate. For example, if you know you are adding a datacenter requiring a certain amount of capacity, that capacity should be added to the growth rate.

NETWORK

As you learned in the section "Server Roles Requirements," the NIC can become a bottleneck in the system if it cannot keep up with the traffic. Here are some common counters monitored by server administrators:

Network Interface\Bytes Total/Sec: The percentage of bandwidth of which the NIC is capable that is currently being used. If this value is more than 70 percent of the bandwidth of the interface, the interface is saturated or not keeping up.

Network Interface\Output Queue Length: The number of packets in the output queue. If this value is over 2, the NIC is not keeping up with the workload.

CENTRAL PROCESSING UNIT (CPU)

When monitoring the CPU, the specific counters you use depend on the server role. Consult the vendor's documentation for information on those counters and what they mean to the performance of the service or application. Common counters monitored by server administrators include the following:

Processor\% Processor Time: The percentage of time the CPU spends executing a non-idle thread. This should not be over 85 percent on a sustained basis.

Processor\% User Time: Represents the percentage of time the CPU spends in user mode, which means it is doing work for an application. If this value is higher than the baseline you captured during normal operation, the service or application is dominating the CPU.

Processor\% Interrupt Time: The percentage of time the CPU receives and services hardware interrupts during specific sample intervals. If this is over 15 percent, there could be a hardware issue.

System\Processor Queue Length: The number of threads (which are smaller pieces of an overall operation) in the processor queue. If this value is over two times the number of CPUs, the server is not keeping up with the workload.

Event Logs

Servers create log files that record system events, both normal and abnormal. In this section you'll learn about log management issues and how to ensure that event data is there when you need it.

CONFIGURATION

Even if you are using the logs (and you should!), you shouldn't allow them to slowly eat up all the space. You can control the behavior of log files in Windows in several ways:

- You can limit the amount of space used for each log.
- You can determine the behavior when the log is full.
- You can choose to save a log for later viewing.

To set the maximum size for a log file, access the properties of the log in Event Viewer. In the Maximum Log Size option, use the spinner control to set the value you want and click OK, as shown in Figure 2.12.

FIGURE 2.12 Event Log properties

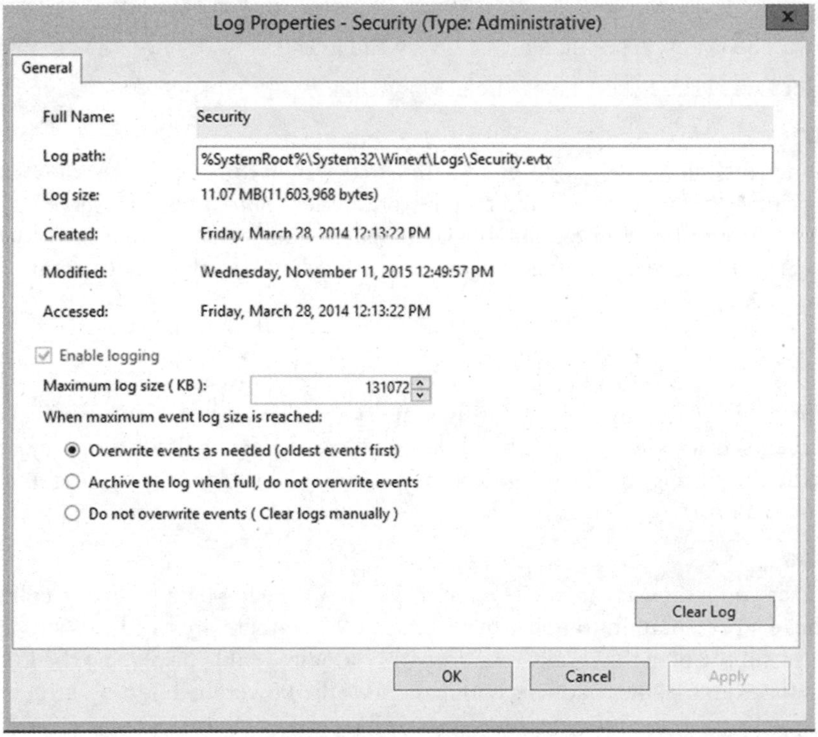

You can also use the command line using the following command, inserting the name of the log file and the maximum size in bytes:

```
wevtutil sl <LogName> /ms:<MaxSizeInBytes>
```

To determine what happens when the log is full, access the same dialog box shown in Figure 2.12 and select one of the three options:

- Overwrite Events As Needed (Oldest Events First)
- Archive The Log When Full, Do Not Overwrite Events
- Do Not Overwrite Events (Clear Logs Manually)

This can also be done at the command line using the following command:

```
wevtutil sl <LogName> /r:{true | false} /ab:{true | false}
```

The r parameter specifies whether you want to retain the log, and the ab parameter specifies whether to automatically back up the log.

Use the following combinations to achieve the desired result:

- Overwrite Events As Needed (Oldest Events First): r = false, ab = false
- Archive The Log When Full, Do Not Overwrite Events: r = true, ab = true
- Do Not Overwrite Events (Clear Logs Manually): r = true, ab = false

SHIPPING

Log shipping is the implementation of an automated system to back up the transaction log files on a primary database server and then restoring them onto a standby server. A transaction log is a history of actions executed by a database management system used to guarantee that updates that have not yet been committed are saved even in the face of an improper shutdown.

ALERTING

Log alerts are used to inform technicians when certain events have occurred. Usually they are created by implementing a query that searches for events of a certain type and then sets an alert when it finds these. In Event Viewer this is done by attaching a task to the log. In Figure 2.13 the alert task is attached to the Security log and is set to the send an email.

REPORTING

In some cases you may want to create a report based off the log data you have collected, perhaps to make a presentation to upper management. While there are third-party tools for this you can also simply pipe the results to a properly formatted table displaying the information you need. For example, the following command uses the PowerShell Get-EventLog cmdlet to dump System event log information to a table. It specifies the last six entries in the log. The command also properly formats the table.

```
PS> Get-EventLog -LogName System -EntryType Error -Newest 6 | Format-Table
-AutoSize -Wrap
```

FIGURE 2.13   Creating an alert

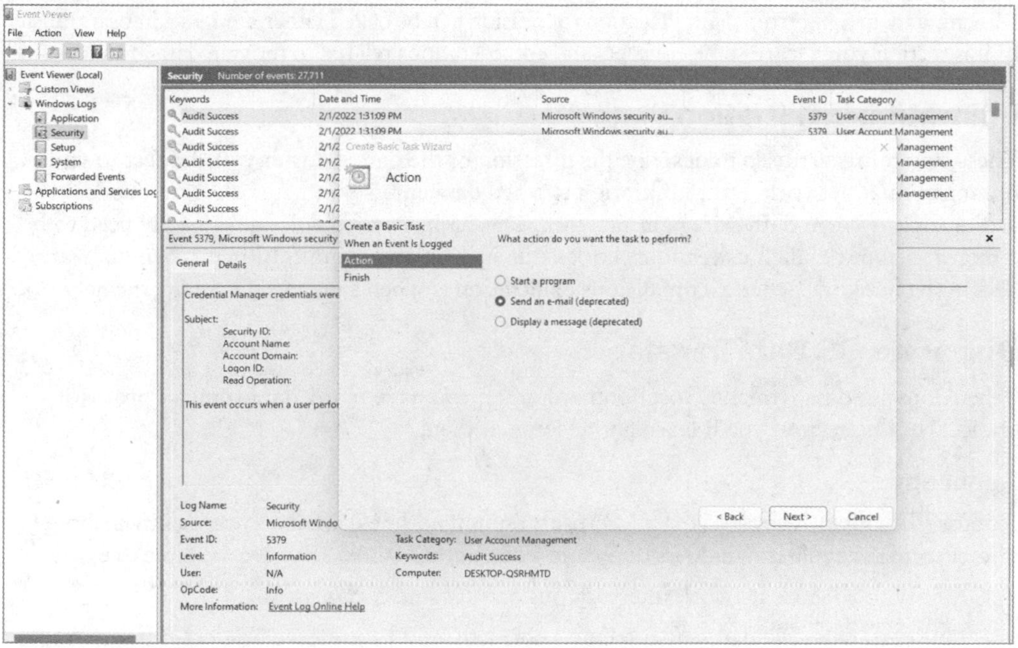

The following is the output of the command with data in the Message column removed due to space limitations:

```
PS C:\Users\TroyMcmillan> Get-EventLog -LogName System -EntryType
Error -Newest 6 | Format-Table -AutoSize -Wrap

Index Time EntryType Source InstanceID Message
----- ---- --------- ------ ---------- -------
20628 Feb 02 09:46 Error DCOM 10010
20627 Feb 02 09:46 Error DCOM 10010
20469 Feb 02 05:55 Error Server 3221227977
20464 Feb 02 05:55 Error Microsoft-Windows-NDIS 10317
20325 Feb 01 17:03 Error DCOM 10010
20324 Feb 01 17:03 Error DCOM 10010
```

RETENTION/ROTATION

As you learned earlier in the section "Configuration," you can control the retention period and the action to be taken when a log is full. Please review that section.

Data Migration and Transfer

Moving data around from digital location to location can be called either a migration or a transfer. In this section you'll learn some concepts and considerations related to moving data around.

Infiltration/Exfiltration

These two terms are used to describe the direction of the data transfer with respect to your organizational network. Data infiltration is when data enters you network from outside. Exfiltration is when data exits your network. This happens all day long. You only need to be concerned about malicious versions. For example, a malicious infiltration is when malware gets in the network, whereas a malicious exfiltration is when sensitive data exits the network.

Disparate OS Data Transfer

When copying data from one location to another, you have many data transfer protocol choices. In this section you'll learn about some of them.

Robocopy

Robust File Copy (Robocopy) is a Microsoft command-line tool. It has capabilities above and beyond the built-in Windows copy and xcopy commands. Here are a couple of examples:

- Ability to tolerate network interruptions and resume copy
- Ability to copy file data and attributes correctly and to preserve original timestamps, as well as NTFS ACLs

The syntax is as follows:

```
robocopy <source> <destination> [<file>[ ...]] [<options>]
```

File Transfer

File Transfer Protocol (FTP) is both a TCP/IP protocol and software that permits the transferring of files between computer systems. Because FTP has been implemented on numerous types of computer systems, files can be transferred between disparate systems (for example, a personal computer and a minicomputer). It uses ports 20 and 21 by default. FTP can be configured to allow or deny access to specific IP addresses and can be configured to work with exceptions. Although the protocol can be run within most browsers, a number of FTP applications are available; FileZilla (http://filezilla-project.org) is one of the most popular.

FastCopy

FastCopy is a file and directory copier that runs under Windows. In 2015 FastCopyV2.11 (BSD License) was ported to Mac OS X. It is sold in the Mac App Store as RapidCopy. In 2016 the Linux version of RapidCopy for Linux was released on GitHub under a BSD 2-Clause license.

Secure Copy Protocol (SCP)

Secure Copy Protocol (SCP) is a secure method of transferring files from one device to another. It is another example of a protocol that runs over SSH, which actually provides the encryption; as such, SCP also uses port 22.

Administrative Interfaces

Managing a system and making changes can be done either sitting at the system physically or from a remote location. In this section you'll learn about administrative interfaces.

Console

By its strictest definition, working from the console means you are physically sitting at the device. In Chapter 3, "Server Maintenance," you will learn that console access can also be provided without physical access to the device. But traditionally the term means sitting at the device, logging in, and working from the desktop of the system.

Remote Desktop

Developed by Microsoft, Remote Desktop Protocol (RDP) allows you to connect to remote computers and run programs on them. When you use RDP, you see the desktop of the computer you've signed into on your screen. The computer at which you are seated is the client, and the computer you're logging into is the server. The server uses its own video driver to create video output and sends the output to the client using RDP. All keyboard and mouse input from the client is encrypted and sent to the server for processing. RDP also supports sound, drive, port, and network printer redirection.

A tool that can be used for this is the Microsoft Remote Desktop Connection Manager (RDCMan). It is a handy console, as shown in Figure 2.14. Note it is *not* limited to managing Microsoft servers, and clients can be found for non-Microsoft systems.

FIGURE 2.14 RDCMan

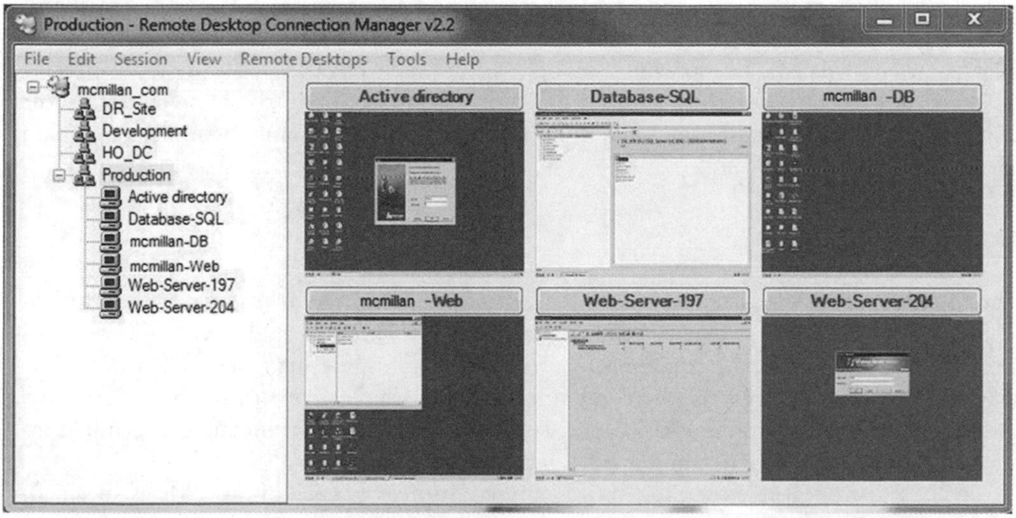

Secure Shell (SSH)

If you don't need access to the graphical interface and you just want to connect to a server to operate at the command line, you have two options: Telnet and SSH. Telnet works just fine, but it transmits all of the data in cleartext, which obviously would be a security issue. Therefore, the connection tool of choice has become Secure Shell (SSH). It's not as easy to set up because it encrypts all of the transmissions and that's not possible without an encryption key.

Although the commands will be somewhat different based on the operating system, you must generate a key, which is generated using some unique information about the server as seed information, so that the key will be unique to the server (the encryption algorithm will be well known). Once configured, the connection process will be very similar to using Telnet, with the exception, of course, that the transmissions will be protected.

Web Interface

It is also possible to use HTTP to connect to a server. When doing so, typically a special port number is configured for the connection rather than port 80. Some remote administration tools, such as Remote Server Administration Tools (RSAT) for Windows, use HTTP and in the case of RSAT, the ports used are 5985 and 5986.

The Purpose and Operation of Virtualization

In today's networks you must understand virtualization. Organizations large and small are moving to take advantage of the benefits of this technology. They are saving power, consolidating, and downsizing (some would say right-sizing) their physical footprint and suffering far fewer bottlenecks caused by resource limitations. This section introduces you to the components that make virtualization work and the specific role each component plays in making these benefits possible.

Host vs. Guest

The foundation of virtualization is the host device, which may be a workstation or a server. This device is the physical machine that contains the software that makes virtualization possible and the containers, or *virtual machines*, for the guest operating systems. The host provides the underlying hardware and computing resources, such as processing power, memory, disk, and network I/O, to the VMs. Each guest is a completely separate and independent instance of an operating system and application software.

The host is responsible for allocating compute resources to each of the VMs as specified by the configuration. The software that manages all of this is called the *hypervisor*. Based on parameters set by the administrator, the hypervisor may take various actions to maintain the performance of each guest as specified by the administrator. Some of these actions may include the following:

- Turning off a VM if not in use
- Taking CPU resources away from one VM and allocating them to another
- Turning on additional VMs when required to provide fault tolerance

The exact nature of the relationship between the hypervisor, the host operating system, and the guest operating systems depends on the type of hypervisor in use. Later on in this section that will be clearer when you learn about hypervisors. The relationship from a high level is shown in Figure 2.15.

FIGURE 2.15   Hosts and guest

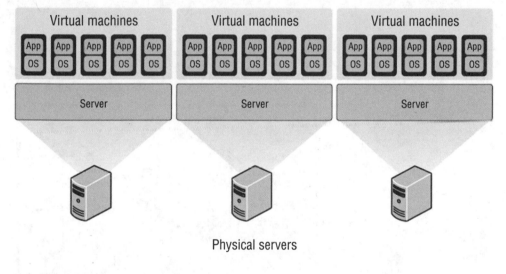

Physical servers

Virtual Networking

It is possible to connect VMs together in a network, and that network can be the same network as the LAN or separate from the LAN. The network can have Internet access or not, depending on how you use the virtual networking components at your disposal. Some of the ways you can connect VMs to the host, to one another, and to devices "outside the box" are covered in this section.

Direct Access (Bridged)

There are two basic options for connecting the VM to the host machine:

- Direct access (bridging), which uses the physical NIC on the host system.
- Network address translation (NAT), which creates a private network on the host system, with the host system acting as a DHCP server. When access to networks beyond this private network is required, the host will perform NAT on the private IP address and use its own IP address.

The easiest configuration is to bridge the VM to use the NIC of the host and use its own IP address. But if you want the IP address of the VM to be hidden, then using NAT will ensure that all packets coming from either the VM or its host will appear to come from the host. You will learn more about NAT in the next section.

If you want to create a network in which the VMs can reach one another, you can use either configuration. Figure 2.16 shows that both methods can be used in the host. You see that some of the hosts are using NAT, which is why they have IP addresses that are used on the LAN, whereas one of the VMs has been bridged and thus does not have an IP address that works on the LAN.

FIGURE 2.16   NAT vs. Bridged

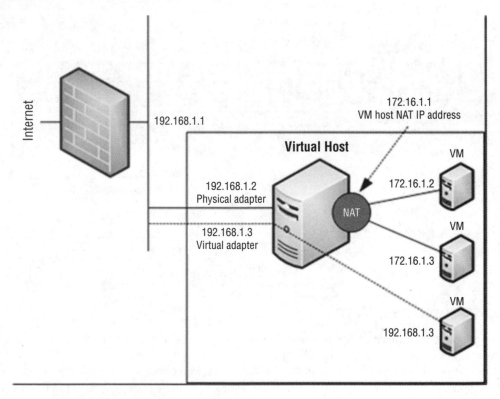

Network Address Translation (NAT)

While not created as a security mechanism, *network address translation* (NAT) provides a unique opportunity to assist in the security of a network.

Originally, NAT extended the number of usable Internet addresses. It translates private IP addresses to public addresses. Now it allows an organization to present a single address to the Internet for all computer connections. The NAT server provides IP addresses to the hosts or systems in the network and tracks inbound and outbound traffic.

A company that uses NAT presents a single connection to the network. This connection may be through a router or a NAT server. The only information that an intruder will be able to get is that the connection has a single address.

NAT effectively hides your network from the world, making it much harder to determine what systems exist on the other side of the router. Most new routers support NAT.

It's important to understand that NAT acts as a proxy between the local area network (which can be using private IP addresses) and the Internet.

Most NAT implementations assign internal hosts private IP address numbers and use public addresses only for the NAT to translate to and communicate with the outside world. The private address ranges, all of which are nonroutable, are 10.0.0.0- 10.255.255.255, 172.16.0.0 –172.30.255.255, and 192.168.0.0. - 192.168.255.255.

In addition to NAT, port address translation (PAT) is possible. Whereas NAT can use multiple public IP addresses, PAT uses a single one for every packet that leaves the network and keeps track of the original sender by recording the dynamic port number that the device used as the source port when the transmission was initiated.

vNICs

You've probably already put this together from the our earlier discussions on virtual networking, but to enable a VM to communicate on either the LAN or a private virtual network you must assign it a virtual NIC (vNIC). Multiple vNICs can be added to the same VM for fault tolerance or load balancing. Once the vNIC is added, you assign it to a network.

Virtual Switches

To create a virtual network as discussed in the previous section, you have to create a virtual switch that will interconnect the VMs and the host. The vNICs of the VMs are connected to the virtual switch, which in turn (if desired) is connected to the physical NIC on the host, as shown in Figure 2.17. Notice that one of the switches is connected to the LAN and the other is not.

When creating a vSwitch, you can choose whether or not to connect the vSwitch to a physical NIC. In Figure 2.18, a vSwitch created in VMware indicates there are two physical adapters available to assign to this switch.

FIGURE 2.17 vSwitch

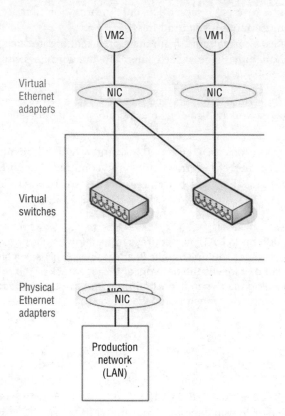

FIGURE 2.18 Assigning a vSwitch to physical adapters

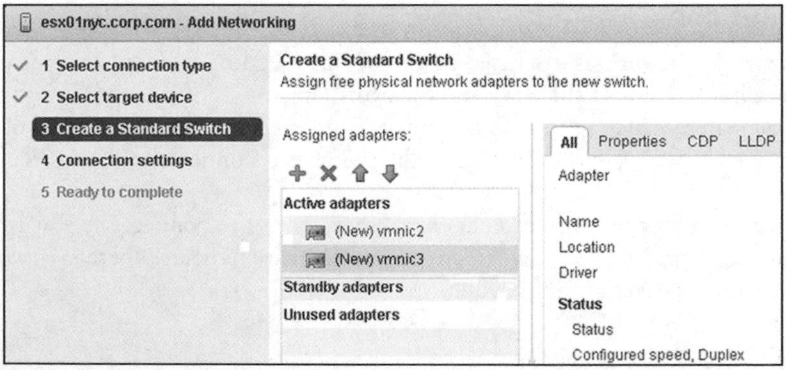

Resource Allocation and Provisioning

One of the issues you need to understand is how the host system and the guest operating systems share resources. Keep in mind that the host and the guests are all sharing the same physical resources (CPU, memory, disk, NIC). This is an advantage of a Type 1, or bare-metal hypervisor. There is no underlying operating system using resources. The resources that are allocated to the VMs are called virtual resources, the number of which need not match the number of physical resources in the host machine. For example, the host may have two processors, yet you could assign four virtual CPUs to the guest. Having said that, according to best practices you probably shouldn't do that. The exact manner in which the resources are assigned and the way in which the administrator uses these assignments to arbitrate use of the physical resource depends on the resources. Let's look at the way the four major resources are allocated in a virtual environment

CPU

You can control the allocation of physical CPU(s) use in one of three ways:

Shares: Values such as Low, Normal, High, and Custom (using VMware as an example) are compared to the sum of all shares of all VMs on the server. Therefore, they define the relative percentage each VM can use.

Reservation: Guaranteed CPU allocation for a virtual machine.

Limit: Upper limit for a virtual machine's CPU allocation.

These settings are used to ensure that the desired VMs have priority to the CPU (shares), that certain VMs are always guaranteed CPU time (reservations), and that no single VM monopolizes the CPU (limits). In Figure 2.19, you can see how this is done in Hyper-V. Although the terminology is slightly different, the concepts are the same. As this figure shows, you can assign multiple virtual CPUs to a VM, which is another way to influence the VMs' performance.

FIGURE 2.19   Setting CPU allocations in Hyper-V

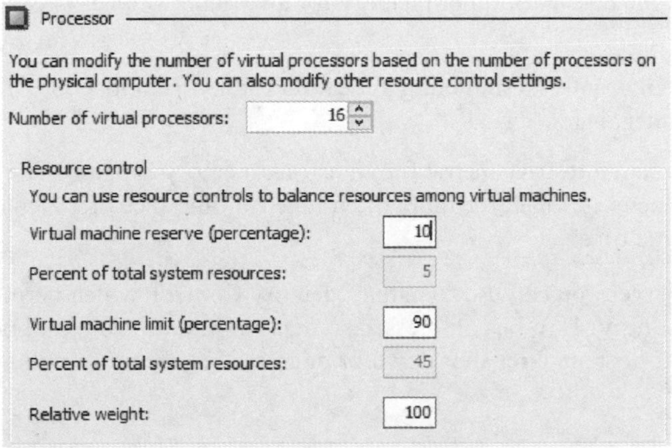

Processor

You can modify the number of virtual processors based on the number of processors on the physical computer. You can also modify other resource control settings.

Number of virtual processors: 16

Resource control
You can use resource controls to balance resources among virtual machines.

Virtual machine reserve (percentage):   10
Percent of total system resources: 5
Virtual machine limit (percentage):   90
Percent of total system resources: 45
Relative weight: 100

CPU Compatibility Support

One of the key issues to consider when reviewing compatibility guides is the CPU. This component plays a critical role in the overall success of the virtualization solution. You should not only ensure that the CPU you are considering or that is present in the candidate host machine is listed on the compatibility list, but you should also make every effort to use a CPU that supports instruction extensions and features designed to enhance virtualization. Let's look at two major vendors and their technologies.

AMD-V and Intel VT

CPUs come with varying abilities to support or enhance virtualization. Intel provides an entire line of processors that support what they call Intel Virtualization Technology. The benefits derived from using a CPU with this technology include the following:

- Acceleration of fundamental virtualization processes throughout the platform
- Reduced storage and network latencies, with fewer potential bottlenecks
- The enhanced security that a solid hardware foundation provides
- Improved short- and long-term value from your software and server investments

AMD has a similar line of processors with a technology they call AMD Virtualization (AMD-V). It adds to the instruction set of the CPU and provides many of the same benefits as the Intel technology.

> Although a server may fully support hardware-assisted virtualization, and the CPU may support virtualization extensions to the instruction set, you may need to enable both of these in the BIOS/UEFI to obtain the benefits.

Memory

Memory resources for a virtual machine are allocated using reservations, limits, and shares, much in the same way as CPU time. A virtual machine can use three user-defined settings that affect its memory resource allocation:

Limit: Limits the consumption of memory for a virtual machine. This value is expressed in megabytes.

Reservation: Guarantees a minimum allocation for a virtual machine. The reservation is expressed in megabytes.

Shares: Represent a relative metric for allocating memory capacity. The more shares a virtual machine is assigned, the more often it gets a time slice of a memory when there is no memory idle time.

In Citrix XenServer, you can use Dynamic Memory Control, which permits the memory utilization of existing VMs to be compressed so that additional VMs can boot on the host. Once VMs on that host are later shut down or migrated to other hosts, running VMs can reclaim unused physical host memory. You enable Dynamic Memory Control by defining minimum and maximum memory settings for virtual machines, as shown in Figure 2.20. In VMware, this concept is called *overcommitting memory*.

FIGURE 2.20   Citrix dynamic memory allocation

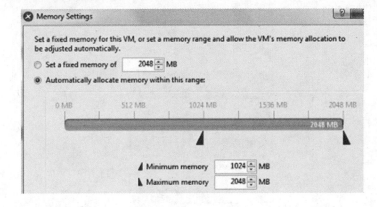

Disk

A benefit of virtualization is the ability of VMs to share storage. This storage can be located in a single storage device or appliance, or it can be located on multiple storage devices. By logically centralizing the storage and managing it centrally, you reduce the waste that formerly occurred when each server used its own storage.

Increasingly, storage is presented to the VMs as local storage but is actually located in either a storage area network (SAN) or on network-attached storage (NAS). A SAN is a high-performance data network separate from the LAN, and NAS is a storage device or appliance that resides on the LAN.

The VMs reside on the host servers and the host servers are attached to the shared storage devices, as shown in Figure 2.21. Conceptually, the shared storage could be either NAS or a SAN, the difference being that, with a SAN, the servers will need to have a host bus controller card installed that can connect the server to the fiber network that typically comprises the SAN.

One of the benefits of shared storage is more efficient use of the storage, with less storage sitting idle while other storage is stressed. When you create VMs, one of the steps involves the creation of a virtual hard drive for the VM. This is space in the shared storage for keeping the image of the VM. There are several types of virtual disks you can create, and some types have unique abilities that aid in this efficient use of space. Every virtualization vendor attaches somewhat different names for these, but they all offer the same basic types. As an example, we'll look at the types offered by VMware, the market leader in virtualization.

FIGURE 2.21 Shared storage

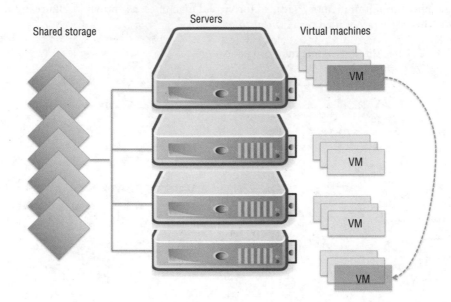

Thick Provision Lazy Zeroed: This is analogous to the classic regular hard drive with one exception. Like the classic disk, space required for the virtual disk is allocated during creation. Unlike with a regular hard drive, if data is present on the disk, it is not deleted until the space is needed for new data.

Thick Provision Eager Zeroed: This is like lazy zeroed but any data on the disk is zeroed out ahead of time. This means it takes longer to create one of these disks.

Thin Provision: This is where the disk efficiency comes in. At first, a thin-provisioned disk uses only as much datastore space as the disk initially needs. If the thin disk needs more space later, it can grow to the maximum capacity allocated to it.

In Figure 2.22, you can see how this is done in Hyper-V, and although the terminology is slightly different, the concepts are the same with most vendors. As this figure shows, you can create what is called a *differencing* disk. This disk type is not unique to Hyper-V. It is used to store changes made to an image when you decide to keep a copy of a previous version of the image. This is what allows for the process of rolling back an image after making changes that you would like to reverse. This makes virtualization perfect for testing changes before an enterprise rollout.

NIC

Earlier in this chapter you learned that VMs and hosts use virtual NICs to communicate. These virtual NICs can be configured to make use of the physical NICs in the infrastructure to communicate beyond the virtual network to the physical network and even to the Internet.

This is how cloud environments, which are built on virtual networks, allow for access to the cloud from the Internet.

FIGURE 2.22   Creating a virtual disk in Hyper-V

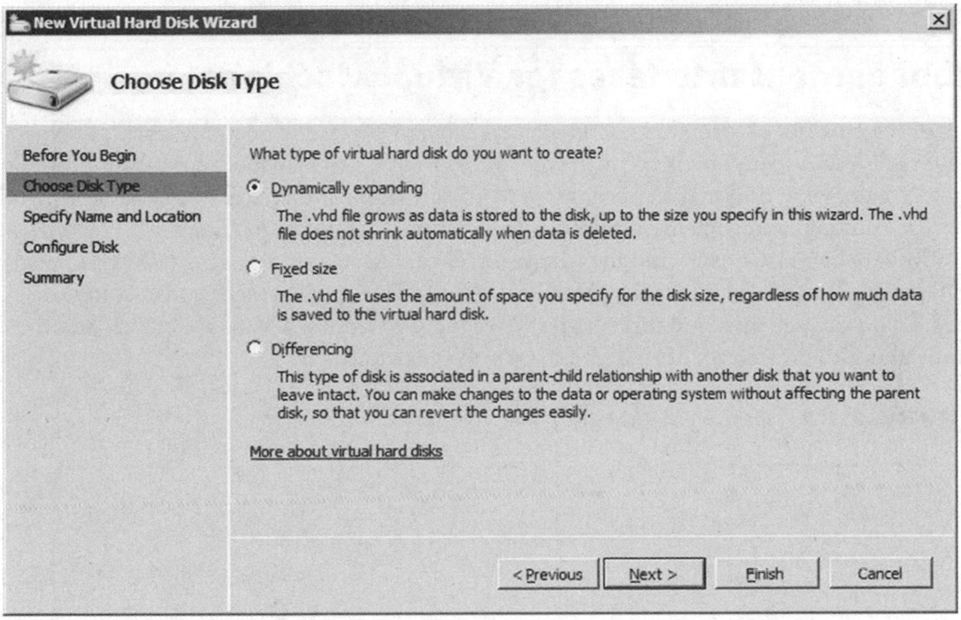

It is also possible to create and combine multiple vNICs together to increase the bandwidth available to a VM in the same way that multiple physical NICS can be combined in a process called NIC teaming. You will learn more about this concept as applied to physical NICs in Chapter 5, "Identifying Fault Tolerance Requirements."

Multiple vNICs can also be created to provide fault tolerance as well. One vNIC can provide backup to a second vNIC and can stand ready to take over in the event of a vNIC failure.

Overprovisioning

Overprovisioning generally means to provide more resources than required for the job to ensure proper performance. For example, you might provision two virtual CPUs rather than one or twice as much memory as you think you may need.

One of the benefits of a cloud environment (virtual in nature) is the ability of the provider to provide additional virtual resources on an as-needed basis. Rather than having additional physical resources (coming at a cost) sitting around idle most the time, you only pay for the additional virtual resources when you need them.

Scalability

Scalability is a characteristic of a device or security solution that describes its capability to cope and perform under an increased or expanding workload. Scalability is generally defined by time factors. Accessing current and future needs is important in determining scalability. Scalability can also refer to a system's ability to grow as needs grow. A scalable system can be expanded, load-balanced, or clustered to increase performance.

In the virtual environment, scalability is easily built in by overprovisioning of resources, as described in the previous sections.

Management Interfaces for Virtual Machines

One of the benefits of virtualization products such as VMware vSphere, Microsoft Hyper-V, and Oracle VM VirtualBox is the management interface they provide. These interfaces allow you to create, view, and make changes to VMs. Some of these changes can be done when the device is running, and some require shutting down the VM. Later in Chapter 3 you will see the VMware Server Console and the Microsoft Virtual Machine Manager (VMM) Console in Hyper-V. Figure 2.23 shows the Oracle VM VirtualBox management console. In this console you can see there are three VMs. We've highlighted the VM named test2, and the details about the resources of that VM appear in the details pane.

FIGURE 2.23   Oracle VM VirtualBox management console

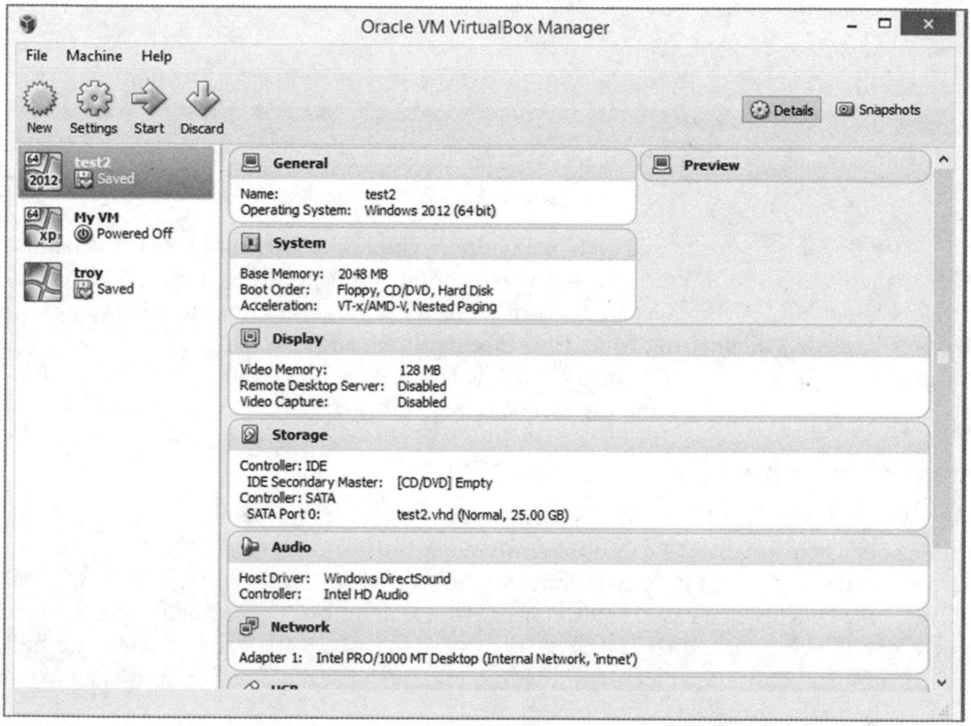

Hypervisor

Earlier you learned that the exact nature of the relationship between the hypervisor, the host operating system, and the guest operating systems depends on the type of hypervisor in use. There are three types of hypervisors in use today. Let's review them now.

Type I

A Type I hypervisor (or native, bare-metal) runs directly on the host's hardware to control the hardware and to manage guest operating systems. A guest operating system runs on another level above the hypervisor. Examples of these are vSphere and Hyper-V.

Type II

A Type II hypervisor runs within a conventional operating system environment. With the hypervisor layer as a distinct second software level, guest operating systems run at the third level above the hardware. VMware Workstation and VirtualBox exemplify Type II hypervisors. A comparison of the two approaches is shown in Figure 2.24.

FIGURE 2.24   Type I and II hypervisors

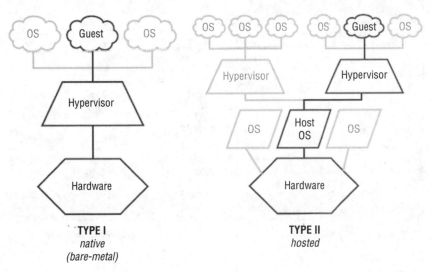

Hybrid

In the datacenter you will most likely encounter Type I hypervisors, but you should be aware of an emerging type of hypervisor: the hybrid. This is basically a Type II hypervisor, but it is integrated with a cloud. The best example of this is VMware Workstation version 12. With this version, it is possible to connect to vCloud Air or to any private cloud and upload, run, and view VMs from the Workstation interface.

Another new approach that might be considered a hybrid is container-based virtualization. Container-based virtualization is also called operating system virtualization. This kind of server virtualization is a technique where the kernel allows for multiple isolated user-space instances. The instances are known as containers, virtual private servers, or virtual environments.

In this model, the hypervisor is replaced with operating system–level virtualization, where the kernel of an operating system allows multiple isolated user spaces or containers. A virtual machine is not a complete operating system instance but rather a partial instance of the same operating system. The containers in Figure 2.25 are the boxes in the top two rows of the container-based example on the right side of the diagram just above the host OS level. Container-based virtualization is used mostly in Linux environments, and examples are the Docker and LXD.

FIGURE 2.25   Container-based virtualization

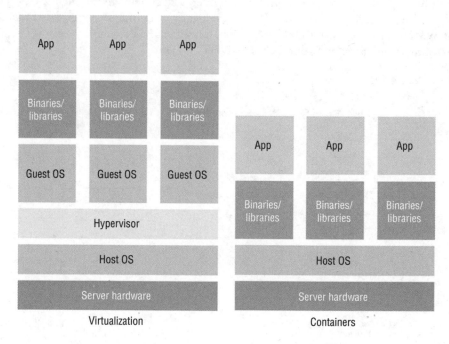

Cloud Models

Increasingly, organizations are utilizing cloud-based storage instead of storing data in local datacenters. The advantages to this approach include the ability to access the data from anywhere, the ability to scale computing resources to meet demand, and robust fault tolerance options. This section will look at various cloud models and some of the concepts that make it a viable option for the enterprise.

Public vs. Private vs. Hybrid vs. Community

When a company pays another company to host and manage this environment, it is called a public cloud solution. If the company hosts this environment itself, it is a private cloud solution.

There is a trade-off when a decision must be made between the two architectures. The private solution provides the most control over the safety of your data but also requires the staff and the knowledge to deploy, manage, and secure the solution. A public cloud puts your data's safety in the hands of a third party, but that party is often more capable and knowledgeable about protecting data in this environment and managing the cloud environment.

When the solution is partly private and partly public, the solution is called a hybrid solution. It may be that the organization keeps some data in the public cloud but may keep more sensitive data in a private cloud, or the organization may have a private cloud that when overtaxed may utilize a public cloud for additional storage space or additional compute resources.

Finally, a community cloud is one that is shared by multiple organizations for some common purpose. This purpose could be to share data for a joint project, for example.

Summary

In this chapter you learned how to install and configure server operating systems, including key steps like updating firmware, configuring the BIOS/UEFI, preparing the disk, and connecting the server to the network. You also learned about the various ways you can manage the server, both locally and across the network. Finally, we covered the basics of virtualization, including the relationship between host and guest, the role of the hypervisor, the types of hypervisors, and how resources are shared by the VMs.

Exam Essentials

Install and configure a server operating system.　Describe the steps in the process and identify which are required and which are optional. Understand the importance of creating a performance baseline.

Identify the components of virtualization and describe their roles.　These components include but are not limited to the host and guest, the management interface, and the hypervisor. You should also be able to describe how CPU, memory, and other resources are shared by the VMs.

Review Questions

You can find the answers in the Appendix.

1. Which of the following is *not* true with respect to UEFI?

    A. It provides better security by helping to protect the preboot process.

    B. It provides faster startup and resuming from hibernation times.

    C. It does not provide support for drives larger than 2.2 terabytes (TB).

    D. It supports modern, 64-bit firmware device drivers.

2. What is the minimum RAM required to run Windows Server 2022?

    A. 128 MB

    B. 256 MB

    C. 512 MB

    D. 1 GB

3. Which of the following is a Microsoft filesystem?

    A. ext2

    B. NTFS

    C. ReiserFS

    D. UFS

4. Which filesystem was created by Sun Microsystems?

    A. ext2

    B. ZFS

    C. ReiserFS

    D. UFS

5. Where is the swap file located?

    A. In memory

    B. In the L1 cache

    C. On the hard drive

    D. Across the network

6. During which type of installation do you walk through the installation and answer the questions as prompted?

    A. Unattended

    B. Attended

    C. Image

    D. Bare-metal

7. What tool is used in Windows Server 2012 R2 to create a baseline?
   A. Performance Monitor
   B. Action Center
   C. System Information
   D. Event Viewer

8. What is another term for a swap file?
   A. vDisk
   B. Pagefile
   C. Transaction log
   D. Checkpoint file

9. How large should the pagefile be on a Windows server that is not a database server?
   A. Half the size of RAM
   B. Equal to the size of RAM
   C. 1.5 times the size of RAM
   D. Twice the size of RAM

10. Which of the following installation types makes use of an answer file?
    A. Unattended
    B. Attended
    C. Image
    D. Bare-metal

11. Which of the following is an industry standard client-server interface that allows networked computers that are not yet loaded with an operating system to be configured and booted remotely by an administrator?
    A. DNS
    B. PXE
    C. iDRAC
    D. NBP

12. The CPU Processor\% Processor Time value should never exceed which value?
    A. 60%
    B. 65%
    C. 70%
    D. 85%

13. Which of the following is an email protocol?
    A. TFTP
    B. IMAP4
    C. PXE
    D. VMM

14. What Microsoft technology allows you to connect to remote computers and run programs on them?

   A. iDRAC

   B. RDP

   C. iDRAC

   D. SSL

15. Which protocol offers an encrypted command line?

   A. Telnet

   B. RDP

   C. SSH

   D. SSL

16. Which of the following is a Linux filesystem?

   A. ext2

   B. NTFS

   C. RFS

   D. UFS

17. Which remote management technology is *not* graphical in nature?

   A. VNC

   B. SSH

   C. RDP

   D. SSL

18. Which statement is true with respect to hypervisors?

   A. Type II is called native.

   B. Type II runs directly on the host's hardware.

   C. A Type II hypervisor runs within a conventional operating system environment.

   D. VMware Workstation and VirtualBox exemplify Type I hypervisors.

19. Which technique is used to allocate relative access to the CPU among VMs?

   A. Reservations

   B. Limits

   C. Shares

   D. Time slots

20. Where are VMs stored in a virtual environment?

   A. On a host

   B. On a guest

   C. In memory

   D. In the virtual box

Chapter

3

Server Maintenance

COMPTIA SERVER+ EXAM OBJECTIVES COVERED IN THIS CHAPTER:

✓ **1.3 Given a scenario, perform server hardware maintenance.**

- Out-of-band management
    - Remote drive access
    - Remote console access
    - Remote power on/off
    - Internet protocol keyboard video-mouse (IP KVM)
- Local hardware administration
    - Keyboard-video-mouse (KVM)
    - Crash cart
    - Virtual administration console
    - Serial connectivity
    - Console connections
- Components
    - Firmware upgrades
- Drives
- Hot-swappable hardware
    - Drives
    - Cages
    - Cards
    - Power supplies
    - Fans
- Basic input/output system (BIOS)/Unified Extensible Firmware Interface (UEFI)

✓ **2.8 Explain licensing concepts.**

- Models
  - Per-instance
  - Per-concurrent user
  - Per-server
  - Per-socket
  - Per-core
  - Site-based
  - Physical vs. virtual
  - Node-locked
  - Signatures
- Open source
- Subscription
- License vs. maintenance and support
- Volume licensing
- License count validation
  - True up
- Version compatibility
  - Backward compatible
  - Forward compatible

Once you've installed your servers, you must take additional steps to enable them to perform the roles you chose for them in the network. You need to monitor and maintain the servers so that they continue to perform well. In addition, you want to avoid security-related issues such as malware infections and data breaches by instituting and following best practices with regard to patches, updates, and data security. Finally, you must develop systems that allow you to manage these critical organizational assets in a standardized method throughout the entire asset life cycle.

Given a Scenario, Perform Server Hardware Maintenance

Like all networked devices, servers need some attention from time to time. If regular maintenance procedures are followed, there will be less downtime, fewer hardware issues, and less frequent headaches for all. Like workstations, servers last longer, perform better, and break down less frequently when they get proper care. In this section we'll list regular hardware maintenance activities you should perform and identify specific areas on which you should concentrate.

Out-of-Band Management

Out-of-band (OOB) management refers to any method of managing the server that does not use the network. This provides some advantages, among them:

- It offers a solution when the network is down or the device is inaccessible.
- It manages devices with no power and remotely reboots devices that have been crashed, turned off, hibernating, or in sleep mode.

There are various ways to connect to a server without using the network, and in this section you'll learn about some of these methods.

Remote Drive Access

One of the things you can do with out-of-band management is to connect to a remote or the drive of a remote server. This is typically done through a serial connection. It can be a DB-9 style connector or a specially wired 8-pin modular (RJ-style) connector. In many cases the drive is connected to an OOB switch that provides OOB remote access to multiple devices or to a remote console server (discussed in the next section).

Many servers come with OOB capability built in. The next two sections are two examples.

iLO

Integrated Lights-Out (iLO) is technology embedded into Hewlett-Packard (HP) servers that allows for out-of-band management of the server. Out-of-band management refers to any method of managing the server that does not use the network.

The physical connection is an Ethernet port that will be on the server and will be labeled iLO. In Figure 3.1, one of these iLO ports is shown in an HP Moonshot chassis (these hold blade servers). HP iLO functions out of the box without additional software installation regardless of the server's state of operation, giving you complete access to the server from any location via a web browser or the iLO Mobile App.

FIGURE 3.1 iLO port

iLO port

iDRAC

A Dell Remote Access Controller (DRAC) card provides out-of-band management for Dell servers. The iDRAC refers to a version of these interface cards that is integrated on the motherboard of the server. There will be a port on the back of the server that looks like an Ethernet port that functions as the iDRAC port. In Figure 3.2 it is labeled the designated system management port.

FIGURE 3.2 iDRAC port

Designated system
management port
(iDRAC)

Once configured, the port will present the technician with an interface on their computer, which is connected to the port when the connection is established. This console interface is shown in Figure 3.3.

FIGURE 3.3   iDRAC console

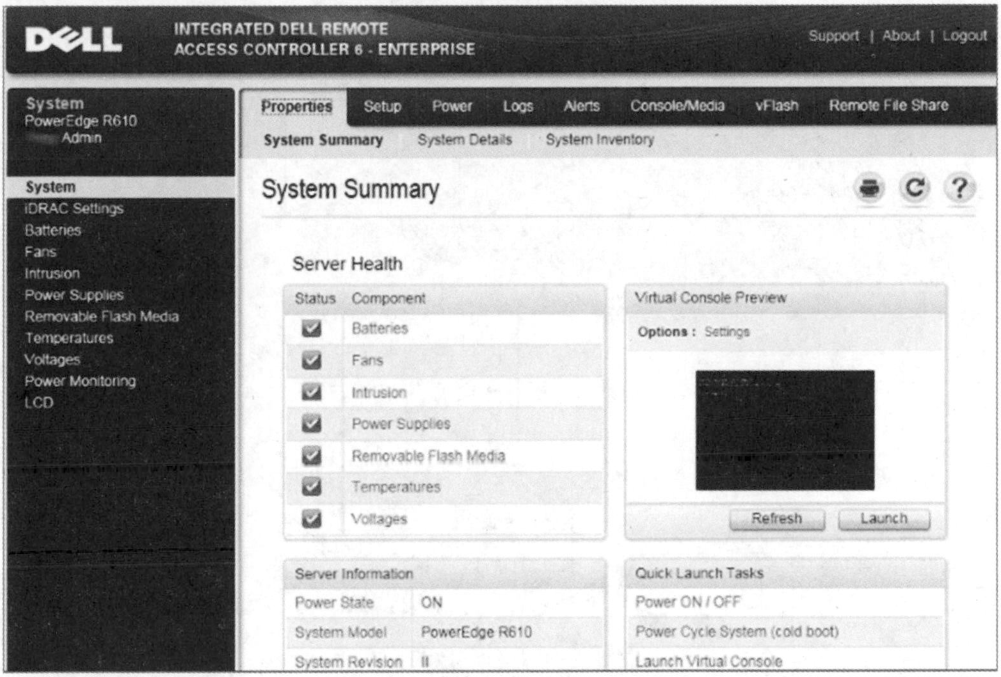

Remote Console Access

In Chapter 1, "Server Hardware," you learned about KVM switches and the advantages of using an out-of-band console server to provide review console access. Please review that section.

Remote Power On/Off

Certain out-of-band connections allow you to power off a device and to power it back on. This is one of the great advantages of OOB. You can also use an OOB connection to manage UPS systems.

Most enterprise-level UPS systems also allow for remote management of the system. In most cases, this will be through the use of a special network card. These cards are installed in slots on the UPS, as shown in Figure 3.4. A slot cover is removed and replaced with the card. Once installed, the card is given an IP address, subnet mask, and gateway. Once the card is on the network, you will be able to use several protocols, such as SMTP, HTTP, SMTP, Telnet, and SSH, to access it.

FIGURE 3.4   Installing the remote management card

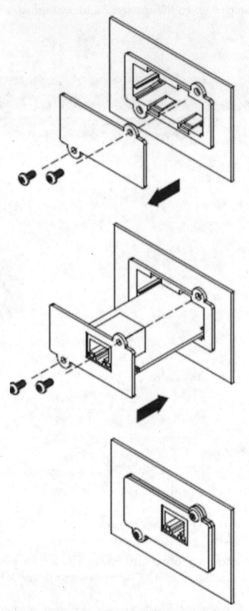

Keep in mind that these cards come with varying levels of functionality. Some give you total control of the device, whereas others may only allow you to monitor the device environment.

On a related note, some network cards offer a feature called Wake on LAN (WOL). This allows the device to be started up from the network by sending a special packet to the NIC (which is not ever actually off). Although this feature can be helpful, it can also be abused by attackers. The magic packets are Layer 2 frames, which can be sent by any device on the same LAN as the target. Although this only allows the startup of the server and does not remove any other authentication required to access the server, it may be a function you want to disable, especially if you don't use it.

This is another configuration that can be done in the BIOS settings in a fashion similar to the way we disabled the USB ports. Figure 3.5 shows where this is done in the BIOS settings. In this case WOL is disabled.

FIGURE 3.5   Disabling WOL

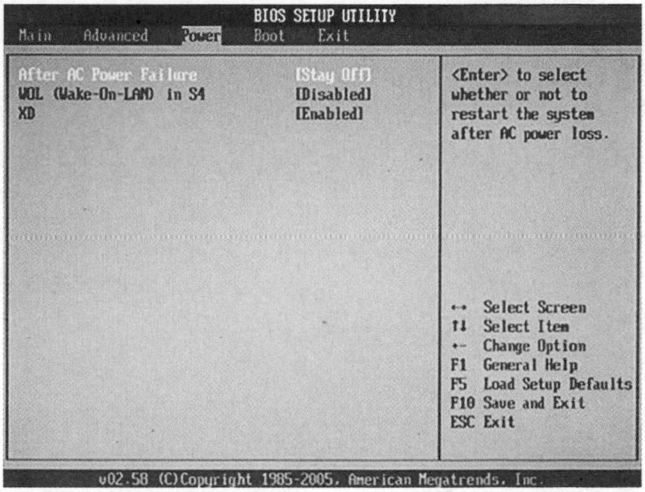

Internet Protocol Keyboard-Video-Mouse (IP KVM)

Earlier you learned about using a basic KVM switch. KVM vendors have responded to the need for a KVM switch that can be accessed over the network. The switch is like the one you saw earlier with one difference—it can be reached through the network, as shown in Figure 3.6. This means it is accessible not only from a workstation in the next room, but from anywhere. In this particular implementation (it can be done several ways), each server has a small device between it and the KVM switch that accepts the serial and keyboard/mouse connections.

FIGURE 3.6 KVM over IP

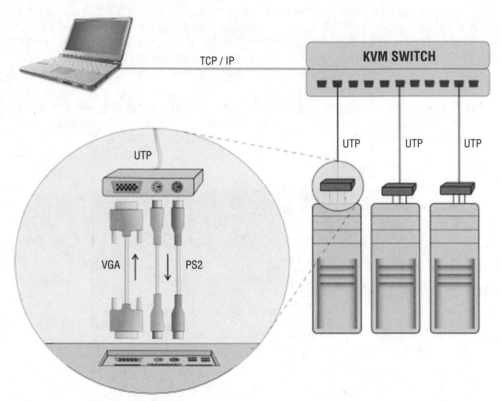

Local Hardware Administration

Managing hardware "locally," used to mean that you will not be connecting to the device over the network—you will be in the server room or datacenter when you do this. Today's definition of local has expanded somewhat to include over the network methods as well. The available options depend on whether the server is a physical device like a rack server, blade server, or tower server, or if it is a virtual server deployed as a virtual machine (VM) on a virtualization host. In this section, we'll explore ways to manage hardware locally.

Keyboard-Video-Mouse (KVM)

You learned all about KVM systems in Chapter 1. Please review that section.

Crash Cart

A crash cart is a mobile server room cart equipped with a secured laptop that is used to provide a direct connection to malfunctioning servers and computers for restoration of crashes. Crash carts should be designed for mobility, versatility, and durability. It should have sturdy casters for ease of movement yet be well balanced in design to protect against tipping. A crash cart is shown in Figure 3.7.

FIGURE 3.7   Crash cart

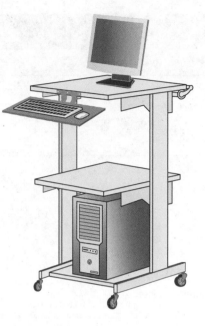

Virtual Administration Console

To manage servers in a virtual environment, vendors of virtualization software provide administration consoles that allow one server to manage another for the purpose of maintenance and administration. Examples include the VMware Server Console and the Virtual Machine Manager Console in Windows Hyper-V.

In Figure 3.8, an example of the VMware Server Console is shown. Here the System Monitor page shows the workload on a specific virtualization host (more on virtualization later, but a host is a physical machine that has multiple virtual machines on it). You can see there are four VMs hosted by the server, all of which are currently powered off. That would explain why only 2 percent of the CPU and only 1.3 GB of memory are being used, none of it by the VMs.

The Virtual Machine Manager (VMM) Console in Hyper-V is shown in Figure 3.9. It also allows for managing the servers centrally from this console. Here ten VMs are shown on the host named LAB-.HV01.

Serial Connectivity

In Chapter 1 you learned that one of the more common ways to make either a local or OOB connection to a server is through a serial connection. Please review that section.

FIGURE 3.8 VMware Server Console

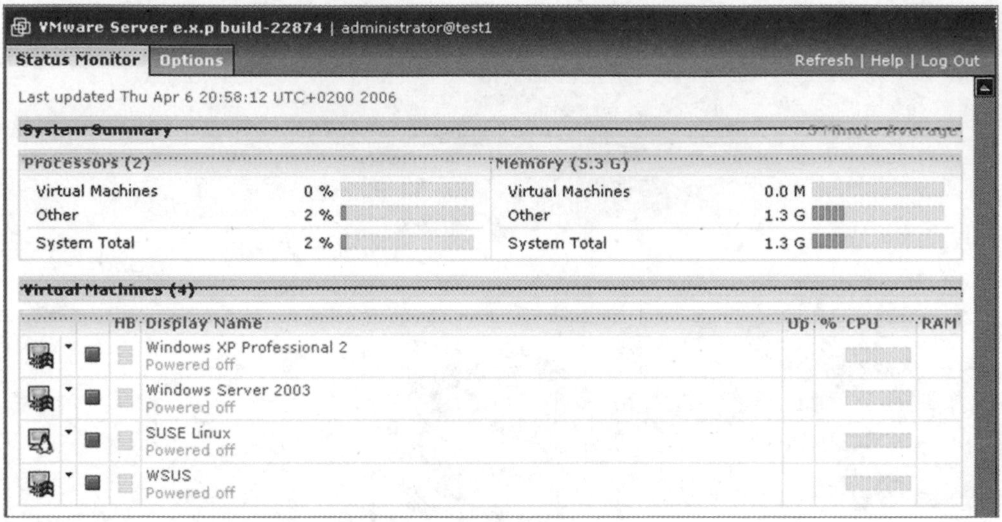

FIGURE 3.9 VMM in Windows Hyper-V

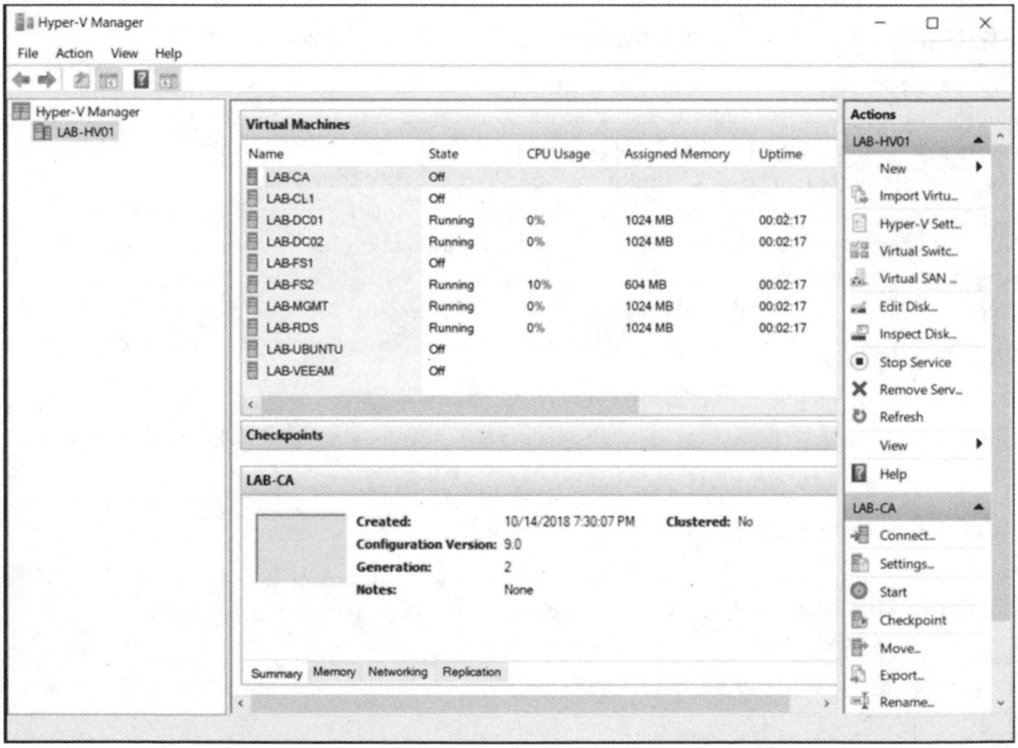

Console Connections

A server may offer the option to connect to it using a special cable called a *console cable*. These cables are also used to connect to and manage routers and switches as well. The port looks like an RJ-45 port, and the cable looks like an Ethernet cable except it's flat and wired differently. Sometimes these cables are called rollover cables. Earlier versions of these cables had a serial connection on one end that connected to a serial port on your laptop, but newer versions have a USB connection on the end since laptops don't have serial ports anymore. When a connection is made with these cables, you will be confined to working at the command line.

Components

Over time, components of a server may need to be upgraded. Physical components are covered later in this chapter, but in this section you'll learn about a software component that may need upgrading from time to time.

Firmware Upgrades

Firmware includes any type of instruction for the server that is stored in nonvolatile memory devices such as ROM, EPROM, or flash memory. BIOS and UEFI code is the most common example for firmware. Computer BIOSs don't go bad; they just become out-of-date or contain bugs. In the case of a bug, an upgrade will correct the problem. An upgrade may also be indicated when the BIOS doesn't support some component that you would like to install—a larger hard drive or a different type of processor, for instance.

Most of today's BIOSs are written to an electrically erasable programmable read-only memory (EEPROM) chip and can be updated through the use of software. Each manufacturer has its own method for accomplishing this. Check out the documentation for complete details. Regardless of the exact procedure, the process is referred to as *flashing* the BIOS. It means the old instructions are erased from the EEPROM chip and the new instructions are written to the chip.

Firmware can be updated by using an update utility from the motherboard vendor. In many cases, the steps are as follows:

1. Download the update file to a flash drive.
2. Insert the flash drive and reboot the machine.
3. Use the specified key sequence to enter the CMOS setup.
4. If necessary, disable Secure Boot.
5. Save the changes and reboot again.
6. Reenter the CMOS settings.
7. Choose boot options and then boot from the flash drive.
8. Follow the specific directions with the update to locate the upgrade file on the flash drive.

9. Execute the file (usually by typing **flash**).

10. While the update is completing, ensure you maintain power to the device.

11. If desired, reenable Secure Boot.

Drives

Servers can contain three different types of hard drive architectures. In this section we'll look at each type.

Magnetic Hard Drives

Magnetic drives were once the main type of hard drive used. The drive itself is a mechanical device that spins a number of disks or platters and uses a magnetic head to read and write data to the surface of the disks. One of the advantages of solid-state drives (discussed in the next section) is the absence of mechanical parts that can malfunction. The parts of a magnetic hard drive are shown in Figure 3.10.

FIGURE 3.10   Magnetic hard drive

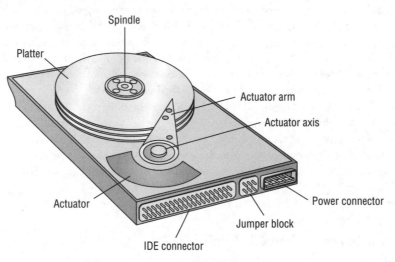

The basic hard disk geometry consists of three components: the number of sectors that each track contains, the number of read/write heads in the disk assembly, and the number of cylinders in the assembly. This set of values is known as CHS (for cylinders/heads/sectors). A *cylinder* is the set of tracks of the same number on all the writable surfaces of the assembly. It is called a cylinder because the collection of all the same-number tracks on all writable surfaces of the hard disk assembly looks like a geometric cylinder when connected together vertically. Therefore, cylinder 1, for instance, on an assembly that contains three platters consists of six tracks (one on each side of each platter), each labeled track 1 on its respective surface. Figure 3.11 illustrates the key terms presented in this discussion.

FIGURE 3.11   CHS

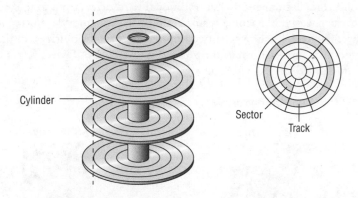

Cylinder

Sector

Track

5400 rpm   The rotational speed of the disk or platter has a direct influence on how quickly the drive can locate any specific disk sector on the drive. This locational delay is called latency and is measured in milliseconds (ms). The faster the rotation, the smaller the delay will be. A drive operating at 5400 rpms will experience about 5.5 ms of this delay.

7200 rpm   Drives that operate at 7200 rpm will experience about 4.2 ms of latency. As of 2022, a typical 7200 rpm desktop hard drive has a sustained data transfer rate up to 1030 Mbps. This rate depends on the track location, so it will be higher for data on the outer tracks and lower toward the inner tracks.

10,000 rpm   At 10,000 rpm, the latency will decrease to about 3 ms. Data transfer rates (about 1.5 Gb/s) also generally go up with a higher rotational speed but are influenced by the density of the disk (the number of tracks and sectors present in a given area).

15,000 rpm   Drives that operate at 15,000 rpm are higher-end drives and suffer only 2 ms of latency. They operate at just under 2 Gb. These drives also generate more heat, requiring more cooling to the case. They also offer faster data transfer rates for the same areal density (*areal density* refers to the number of bits that can be stored in a given amount of space).

Solid-State Drives   Solid-state drives (SSDs) retain data in nonvolatile memory chips and contain no moving parts. Compared to electromechanical hard disk drives (HDDs), SSDs are typically less susceptible to physical shock, are silent, have lower access time and latency, but are more expensive per gigabyte.

Hybrid Drives   A hybrid drive is one in which both technologies, solid-state and traditional mechanical drives, are combined. This is done to take advantage of the speed of solid-state drives while maintaining the cost effectiveness of mechanical drives.

There are two main approaches to this: dual-drive hybrid and solid-state hybrid. Dual-drive systems contain both types of drives in the same machine, and performance is optimized by the user placing more frequently used information on the solid-state drive and less frequently accessed data on the mechanical drive—or in some cases by the operating system creating hybrid volumes using space in both drives.

A solid-state hybrid drive (SSHD), on the other hand, is a single storage device that includes solid-state flash memory in a traditional hard drive. Data that is most related to the performance of the machine is stored in the flash memory, resulting in improved performance. Figure 3.12 shows the two approaches to hybrid drives. In the figure, mSATA refers to a smaller form of the SATA drive, and NAND disk refers to a type of flash memory named after the NAND logic gate.

FIGURE 3.12   Hybrid approaches

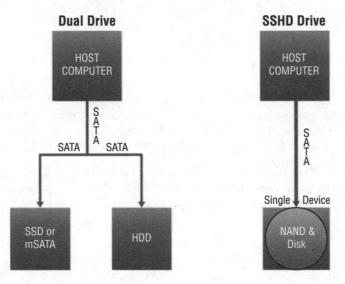

Replacement   At one time, hard disk drives had a higher rate of unexpected failures with respect to the mechanical parts, and SSDs had a shorter normal lifetime. However, this is changing as SSDs become more and more durable. At any rate, you will at some point have to replace a drive. The exact method depends on the type of drives. In Exercise 3.1 you'll use a Dell 1850 rack server and look at changing out a drive.

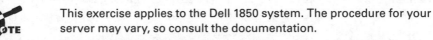

This exercise applies to the Dell 1850 system. The procedure for your server may vary, so consult the documentation.

EXERCISE 3.1

Changing a Drive on a Dell 1850

1.   Shut down the system.

2.   Remove the front bezel.

3.   Use the hard drive handle as shown in this graphic.

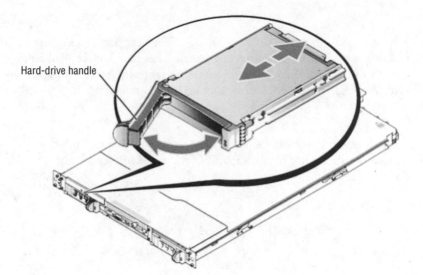

Hard-drive handle

4. Remove the old hard drive from the bay.

5. Insert the new hard drive into the empty bay.

6. Lock the drive in place by closing the hard drive handle.

7. If it was removed in step 2, replace the front bezel.

8. In the system diagnostics, run the SCSI Controllers test.

Hot-Swappable Hardware

A hot-swappable component is one that can be changed without shutting down the server. This is a desirable feature because for many server roles, shutting down the server is something to be minimized. However, just because a component is hot swappable doesn't mean changing the component doesn't require some administrative work before you make that change.

For example, to change a hot-swappable hard drive, in most cases you must prevent any applications from accessing the hard drive and remove the logical software links. Moreover, in many cases drives cannot be hot-plugged if the hard drive provides the operating system, and the operating system is not mirrored on another drive. It also cannot be done if the hard drive cannot be logically isolated from the online operations of the server module. Nevertheless, it is still a great feature. In some high-end servers, it is even possible to hot-swap memory and CPU.

Drives

If a drive can be attached to the server without shutting down, then it is a hot-swappable drive. Drive types that are hot-swappable include USB, FireWire, SATA, and those that connect through Ethernet. You should always check the documentation to ensure that your drive supports this feature.

Cages

A drive cage is an appliance that holds multiple hard drives. When the appliance offers the ability to quickly kick in a replacement hard drive for one that has failed, it is called a hot-swappable cage. The best example of this is a RAID enclosure that can detect a failure, connect a new hard drive, and rebuild the RAID array with no human intervention.

Cards

Some types of cards like memory cards can be hot swappable as well. Keep in mind, however, that many expansion cards are *not* hot swappable. Here are examples of cards that may be (always check documentation):

- Memory
- Video
- PCIE cards

Power Supplies

Some systems also let you swap out a power supply without a shutdown. This requires that the system be provisioned with multiple power supplies to begin with. When one fails, the other will take over. Then you can swap out the failed supply without shutting the system down.

Fans

You can change out the fan on many servers without shutting down. On some of these systems, the challenge is to get the case open and change out the fan before overheating occurs. For this reason, well-designed servers make this easy by providing a way to pull out the old fan module and insert a new one without taking off the case. As fan motors have become more reliable, many servers are going back to power supplies that are not hot swappable. Let's look at changing out a fan.

Servers typically have multiple fans. For example, a Dell PowerEdge has a fan on the chassis back panel and a front fan beneath the drive bays. In Exercise 3.2 you'll change out the one in the back panel.

 This exercise applies to the Dell PowerEdge 2400 system. The procedure for your server may vary, so consult the documentation.

EXERCISE 3.2

Replacing the Back-Panel Fan in a Dell PowerEdge

1. Turn off the system, including peripherals, and disconnect the AC power cable.

2. Remove the right-side computer cover.

3. Remove the cooling shroud.

4. Disconnect the cooling fan cable from the FAN3 (back fan) connector on the system board.

5. Remove the four fasteners that secure the fan to the back of the chassis by pushing the plunger of each back into the fastener barrel, using a coin or flat-tipped screwdriver.

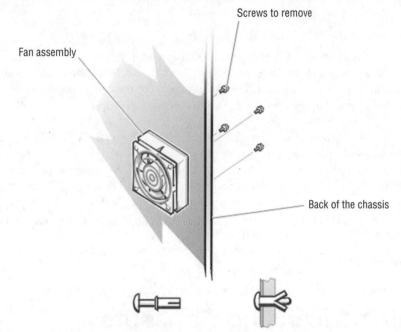

6. On the other side of the back panel, pull the fastener completely out of the back panel.

7. Attach the new fan using the four fasteners you removed.

8. Connect the fan power cord to the system board FAN3 connector.

9. Replace the right-side computer cover and reconnect the power.

10. Turn on the system.

Basic Input/Output System (BIOS)/Unified Extensible Firmware Interface (UEFI)

As you learned earlier in this chapter, servers contain firmware that provides low-level instructions to the device even in the absence of an operating system. This firmware, called either the Basic Input/Output System (BIOS) or the Unified Extensible Firmware Interface (UEFI), contains settings that can be manipulated and diagnostic utilities that can be used to monitor the device.

UEFI is a standard firmware interface for servers and PCs designed to replace BIOS. Here are some advantages of UEFI firmware:

- Better security; protects the preboot process
- Faster startup times and resuming from hibernation
- Support for drives larger than 2.2 terabytes (TB)
- Support for 64-bit firmware device drivers
- Capability to use BIOS with UEFI hardware

At startup, the BIOS or UEFI will attempt to detect the devices and components at its disposal. The information that it gathers, along with the current state of the components, will be available for review in the BIOS settings. Some of the components and the types of information available with respect to these devices and components are covered in this section.

You can view and adjust a server's base-level settings through the CMOS Setup program, which you access by pressing a certain key at startup, such as F1 or Delete (depending on the system). Complementary metal oxide semiconductor (CMOS) refers to the battery type that maintains power to the BIOS settings (also referred to as BIOS Setup). The most common settings you can adjust in CMOS are port settings (parallel, serial, USB), drive types, boot sequence, date and time, and virus/security protections. The variable settings that are made through the CMOS setup program are stored in nonvolatile random access memory (NVRAM), whereas the base instructions that cannot be changed (the BIOS) are stored on an EEPROM chip.

Explain Licensing Concepts

When you purchase software, you are purchasing the right to use it. At any point in time you may face a software audit from one of the major vendors. When this occurs, you will need to be able to provide written proof that you possess a number of licenses for a particular product that is equal to or greater than the number of installations in your network. When that time comes, will you be able to locate them? They should be kept in a safe place where you can put your hand on them at a moment's notice. That does not mean the records can't be digital, but they must be available. In this section you'll learn about licensing concepts.

Models

A licensing model determines how you may use the license. Understanding how different licensing models work is key to choosing the correct model for a scenario. In this section you'll learn about various licensing models.

Per-Instance

A per-instance package is based on the number of permitted installations installed on physical servers and virtual services or in container environments. Multiple instances running on the same physical or virtual hardware are classed as individual instances and are licensed as such.

Per-Concurrent User

This model allows you to have the software installed in as many systems as you would like as long as the number of instances in use does not exceed the amount you paid for. For example, if you have paid for 100 licenses and have the software installed on 200 systems, as long as only 100 are in use concurrently, you are compliant.

Per-Server

With servers running software that users use by connecting to the server and running it from the server, the licensing is based on number of users connecting. In the per-server model, you are allowed a specified maximum number of simultaneous connections to the server. When a user attempts to connect and it causes the user count to exceed that number, the user will be denied access.

Per-Socket

Many server licenses allow you to run one CPU. For example, Windows Server covers up to two processors (sockets) located in one physical server. So if a physical server has more than two processors, you will have to buy one license for each pair of processors.

Per-Core

As you might have expected, this model is based on the number of cores, not processors. This model was created in response to the increasing use of multiple cores in servers, rather than multiple processors or sockets.

Site-Based

A site-based license is one that lets you install the software on multiple systems. Typically, this license has a single installation key, called a volume license key, that will allow for a set number of installations.

Physical vs. Virtual

Vendors have had to react to the use of virtualization in the datacenter and have done so with virtual licensing, which may give you some limited use of a physical license for VMs. Windows Server 2012 R2 Standard edition will entitle you to run one instance in the physical system and two instances in virtual systems with each license. Beyond that, all running instances of a virtual operating system environment (OSE) must be licensed.

Node-Locked

In this model the license is tied to the device on which it is installed. The nodes are identified by a unique hardware ID that is obtained or entered during the product setup or first license validation.

Signatures

Certificate license files used by many licensing platforms often use digital signatures in order to ensure the license files originated from the vendor and are authentic. These signatures can and should be verified to ensure that the files have not been corrupted and that they come from the stated vendor. Digital signatures offer the unique ability to provide assurance of both integrity and proof of origin.

Digital signatures make use of a pair of keys called a private key and a public key. In the following sections you'll learn how these keys are used for digital signatures. In Chapter 7, "Securing Server Data and Network Access," you will learn more about these keys and how they are used in a Public Key Infrastructure (PKI).

Private Key

The private key that is generated as part of the key pair is only made available to the user or device to which it was issued. This key may be stored on software in the user's computer, or it might be stored on a smart card if it is to be used for authentication. At any rate, the key concept here is that it is *only* available to the user or device to which it was issued.

Public Key

The public key that is generated as part of the key pair is made available to anyone to whom the certificate is presented because it is part of the information contained in this digital document. In some cases, public keys may be kept in a repository so that they can be requested by an entity if required. Regardless of the method used to obtain the public key, the thing to remember is that it is available to anyone.

Putting It Together

These keys work together to perform both encryption and digital signatures. To provide encryption, the data is encrypted with the receiver's public key, which results in ciphertext that only the receiver's private key can decrypt. To digitally sign a document, the sender creates what is called a *hash value* of the data being sent, encrypts that value with the sender's private key, and sends this value along with the message. The receiver decrypts the hash using the sender's public key. The receiver then, using the same hashing algorithm, hashes the message. The sender then compares the decrypted hash value to the one just generated. If they are the same, the signature (and the integrity of the data) has been verified.

Open Source

Open source software licenses differ from commercial licenses in that they allow the licensee to view and modify the source code, blueprint, or design. There may be some restrictions on its use and modification. For example, you may not be allowed to distribute it commercially and you may not be able to change its name. There are two main types of open source licenses:

Copyleft   A method for making a software program free while requiring that all modified and extended versions of the program also be free and released under the same terms and conditions.

Permissive   Sometimes called "anything goes" because it guarantees the freedom to use, modify, and redistribute while also permitting proprietary derivative works, permissive open source licenses place minimal restrictions on how others can use open source components.

Subscription

Although all the licenses discussed so far have been what we call perpetual with no end date, with subscription licensing you pay by the month for as long as you want access. This model evolved from the software-as-a-service (SaaS) cloud model where the software is not installed but instead is run from the cloud.

License vs. Maintenance and Support

Your license, warranty, and support plan are three different issues. Let's look at how they differ. The license simply demonstrates that you have paid for the right to use the software and does not imply either a warranty or a promise of help and support. If a warranty is provided, however, it does imply that for the warranty period the software is guaranteed to function properly, and if that is not the case you will get help resolving the issue. A maintenance plan can sometimes be purchased that extends support beyond the normal warranty period.

Warranty information should be readily available to you when equipment breaks. You should never spend time or money repairing items that are still under warranty. It should *not* take you hours to locate this information when that time comes. Keep this paperwork or its digital equivalent close at hand in the same way you would the licensing information.

All service manuals that arrive with new hardware should be kept. They are invaluable sources of information related to the use and maintenance of your devices. They also contain contact information that may make it easier to locate help at a critical time. Many manuals have troubleshooting flowcharts that may turn a 4-hour solution into a 30-minute one. If a paper copy has not been retained, you can usually obtain these service manuals online at the vendor website.

Maintenance plans may include a service level agreement (SLA). SLAs specify the type of support to be provided and the acceptable amount of time allowed to respond to support calls. Typically, these time windows are different for different types of events. For example, they may be required to respond to a server outage in 20 minutes, whereas responding to a user having problems with a browser may only require a response by the end of the day. You will learn more about SLAs in Chapter 4, "Storage Technologies and Asset Management."

Volume Licensing

As you learned earlier site licensing is a form of volume licensing. Volume licensing is the process of purchasing a number of installation instances and then using a single volume license key to demonstrate that you have paid for the installations.

License Count Validation

It is the responsibility of the organization to track both the number of licenses for which they have paid and the number of installations that are live. Vendors perform software audits, and if they discover that you are out of compliance there can be stiff penalties and fines.

Whenever possible you should use license management software to alert you when you get out of compliance (which is easier than you might think). Examples include AssetSonar, Torii, and 10Duke Entitlements.

True Up

A Gartner survey in 2019 found that 85% of organizations have found themselves out of compliance with their licensing agreements. Sometimes they discover it during an internal audit (the lucky ones) and others during a software audit. When an organization finds this to be the case and resolves the issue, either by reducing the number of installations or paying for more licenses, it is called *truing up*. A true-up occurs when a company compares the number of actual software license users to the good-faith estimate of the initial contract.

Version Compatibility

Some software is what we call a *combined work*, meaning it consists of multiple differently licensed parts. This can present an issue when the various parts have very different and incompatible licensing terms. Sometimes projects wind up with incompatible licenses, and the only feasible way to solve it is the relicensing of the incompatible parts. Relicensing is achieved by contacting all involved developers and other parties and getting their agreement for the changed license.

Licenses can also be either forward or backward compatible. In the next two sections you'll learn what this means.

Backward Compatible

A backward-compatible license is one that, though purchased for a newer version of software (for example, Windows Server 2022), can be used to demonstrate license compliance for an older version (such as Windows Server 2019).

Forward Compatible

A forward-compatible license is one that, though purchased for an older version of software (for example, Windows Server 2012), can be used to demonstrate license compliance for a newer version (such as Windows Server 2012 R2). Typically this is limited to minor version upgrades (such as the earlier example from Window Server 2012 to Windows Server 2012 R2) and not to major upgrades, as in going from Windows Server 2019 to Windows Server 2022.

Summary

This chapter covered proper server maintenance techniques such as performance monitoring and hardware maintenance. You also learned about types of hardware that are hot-swappable and the benefits they provide. Finally, you learned about server licensing and the various models that exist.

Exam Essentials

Perform proper server maintenance.   Identify the procedures involved in updating drivers and firmware. Describe how SLAs are used to control the delivery of service to the network.

Describe speeds of magnetic hard drives.   These include 5400 RPM, 7200 RPM, 10000 RPM, and 15000 RPM. Understand how the speed impacts the latency and data rates.

Identify examples of hot-swappable hardware.   These include drives, cages, expansion cards, power supplies, and fans.

Identify licensing models.   These include but are not limited to per-instance, per-concurrent user, per-server, per-socket, per-core, site-based, physical vs. virtual, and node-locked.

Review Questions

You can find the answers in the Appendix.

1. Which of the following refers to any method of managing the server that does not use the network?

   A. Out-of-band

   B. In-band

   C. Direct

   D. Terminal

2. Which of the following licenses is one that though purchased for an older version of software can be used to demonstrate license compliance for a newer version?

   A. Backward compatible

   B. Forward compatible

   C. Side-loaded

   D. Regressive

3. Which of the following is technology embedded into Hewlett-Packard (HP) servers that allows for out-of-band management of the server?

   A. iDRAC

   B. RDP

   C. iLO

   D. SSH

4. Which of the following is software consisting of multiple differently licensed parts?

   A. Rolling manifest

   B. Open source

   C. Backward compatible

   D. Combined work

5. What type of access does a Dell iDRAC card provide?

   A. Out-of-band

   B. In-band

   C. VPN

   D. SSL

6. Which of the following describes the process of correcting software licensing noncompliance.?

   A. Level up

   B. True up

   C. Settle up

   D. Pay up

7. Which of the following allows a device to be started up from the network by sending a special packet to the NIC?

   A. IRL

   B. WOL

   C. iDRAC

   D. iLO

8. Which of the following licensing models use a single license key to demonstrate that you have paid for multiple installations?

   A. Per-user

   B. Open source

   C. Volume

   D. Subscription

9. Which of the following is a mobile server room table equipped with a secured laptop that is used to provide a direct connection to malfunctioning servers and computers?

   A. iDRAC

   B. Response box

   C. Crash cart

   D. Emergency cart

10. Which of the following specifies the type of support to be provided and the acceptable amount of time allowed to respond to support calls?

   A. Rules of engagement

   B. Support scope

   C. MDA

   D. SLA

11. What is a console cable sometimes called?

   A. Rollover cable

   B. Patch cable

   C. Straight-through

   D. Crossover cable

12. Which of the following demonstrates that you have paid for the right to use the software?

   A. SLA

   B. Service plan

   C. Warranty

   D. License

13. Where is WOL support enabled?

    A. BIOS

    B. IOPS

    C. IOS

    D. TIOS

14. In which licensing model do you pay by the month for as long as you want access?

    A. Site-based

    B. Subscription

    C. Per-user

    D. Volume

15. Which of the following includes any type of instruction for the server that is stored in non-volatile memory devices such as ROM, EPROM, or flash memory?

    A. Hardware

    B. Software

    C. Firmware

    D. Shareware

16. Which of the following is the process of updating the firmware?

    A. Burning

    B. Rewriting

    C. Clustering

    D. Flashing

17. Which of the following is a licensing method for making a software program free, while requiring that all modified and extended versions of the program also be free and released under the same terms and conditions?

    A. Copyleft

    B. Permissive

    C. Open source

    D. Node locked

18. What must be maintained during the firmware flashing process?

    A. Network connectivity

    B. Power

    C. Data integrity

    D. Positive magnetic pole

19. To provide encryption, the data is encrypted with the receiver's _____ key, which results in ciphertext that only the receiver's _____ key can decrypt.

  A. Private, private

  B. Public, public

  C. Public, private

  D. Private, public

20. Which of the following is a false statement about hard drives?

  A. The rotational speed of the disk or platter has no influence on how quickly the drive can locate any specific disk sector on the drive.

  B. The faster the rotation, the smaller the delay will be.

  C. The data rate will be higher for data on the outer tracks and lower toward the inner tracks.

  D. A locational delay is called latency.

Chapter

4

Storage Technologies and Asset Management

COMPTIA SERVER+ EXAM OBJECTIVES COVERED IN THIS CHAPTER:

✓ **1.2 Given a scenario, deploy and manage storage.**

- RAID levels and types
  - 0
  - 1
  - 5
  - 6
  - 10
  - Just a bunch of disks (JBOD)
  - Hardware vs. software
- Capacity planning
- Hard drive media types
  - Solid state drive (SSD)
  - Wear factors
    - Read intensive
    - Write intensive
  - Hard disk drive (HDD)
  - Rotations per minute (RPM)
    - 15,000
    - 10,000
    - 7,200
  - Hybrid

- Interface types
  - Serial attached SCSI (SAS)
  - Serial ATA (SATA)
  - Peripheral component interconnect (PCI)
  - External serial advanced technology attachment (eSATA)
  - Universal serial bus (USB)
  - Secure digital (SD)
- Shared storage
  - Network attached storage (NAS)
    - Network file system (NFS)
    - Common Internet file system (CIFS)
  - Storage area network (SAN)
    - Internet small computer systems interface (iSCSI)
    - Fibre Channel
    - Fibre Channel over Ethernet (FCoE)

✓ 2.7 Explain the importance of asset management and documentation.

- Asset management
  - Labeling
  - Warranty
  - Leased vs. owned devices
  - Life-cycle management
    - Procurement
    - Usage
    - End of life
    - Disposal/recycling
    - Inventory
  - Make
  - Model

- Serial number
- Asset tag
- Documentation management
  - Updates
  - Service manuals
  - Architecture diagrams
  - Infrastructure diagrams
  - Workflow diagrams
  - Recovery processes
  - Baselines
  - Change management
  - Server configurations
  - Company policies and procedures
    - Business impact analysis (BIA)
    - Mean time between failure (MTBF)
    - Mean time to recover (MTTR)
    - Recovery point objective (RPO)
    - Recovery time objective (RTO)
    - Service level agreement (SLA)
    - Uptime requirements
- Document availability
- Secure storage of sensitive documentation

Servers, like all computing systems, require a storage system to hold the operating system and all the other files that make a server function, not to mention the data! Moreover, servers like all company assets must be tracked and accounted for. This requires the development and use of certain standard documents, including those that support the business continuity and disaster recovery processes. In this chapter you'll learn about storge and assets management.

Given a Scenario, Deploy and Manage Storage

When designing and deploying a server solution, you need to know some basic information to guide the implementation of the storage system. Naturally one of the drivers will be the amount of storage you need or the capacity of the storage solution. As you will learn in this chapter, this includes what you need now and what additional needs you anticipate in the future.

Perhaps even more important than capacity, however, is the ability to restore data that has been intentionally or unintentionally deleted or lost through hardware failures. Frequent backups are a part of the fault tolerance solution, but in some cases the time it takes to locate the proper tape and perform the restore operation is more than can be tolerated. In that scenario you may want to implement a solution that allows the system to maintain access to the data even with the loss of a drive. In this chapter, we'll look at both capacity considerations and fault tolerance technologies.

RAID Levels and Types

RAID stands for Redundant Array of Independent Disks. It's a way of combining the storage power of more than one hard disk for a special purpose such as increased performance or fault tolerance. RAID can be done with SCSI drives, but it is more often done with Serial Attached SCSI (SAS) drives. Several types of RAID are covered in the following sections. Due to the methods used to provide fault tolerance, the total amount of usable space in the array will vary. Not all versions of RAID provide fault tolerance, and they have varying impacts on performance. Let's look at each type.

RAID 0   RAID 0 is also known as *disk striping*. RAID 0 is illustrated in Figure 4.1.

FIGURE 4.1   RAID 0

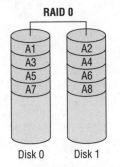

RAID 1   RAID 1 is also known as *disk mirroring*. RAID 1 is illustrated in Figure 4.2.

FIGURE 4.2   RAID 1

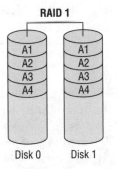

RAID 5   RAID 5 combines the benefits of both RAID 0 and RAID 1 and is also known as *striping with parity*. RAID 5 is illustrated in Figure 4.3.

FIGURE 4.3   RAID 5

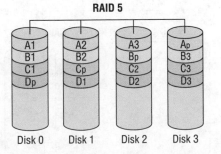

RAID 6   RAID 6 writes parity information across the drives as is done in RAID 5, but it writes two stripes, which allows the system to recover from two drive failures whereas RAID 5 cannot. Because each set of parities must be calculated separately, performance is slowed during writing to the drive. The cost is higher due to the two drives dedicated to parity information.

RAID 6 uses $2/n$ (n = the number of drives in the array) for parity information (for example, two thirds of the space in a three-drive array), and only $1 - (2/n)$ is available for data. So if three 250 GB drives are used in the array (for a total of 750 GB), 250 GB will be the available drive space. In Figure 4.4 you can see that the parity blocks are in pairs and that they are indicated with a small letter next to each. RAID 6 is illustrated in Figure 4.4.

FIGURE 4.4   RAID 6

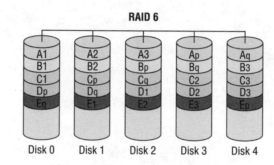

RAID 10   RAID 10 is also known as RAID 1+0. Striped sets are mirrored (a minimum of four drives, and the number of drives must be even). It provides fault tolerance and improved performance but increases complexity. Since this is effectively a mirrored stripe set and a stripe set gets 100 percent use of the drive without mirroring, this array will provide half of the total drive space in the array as available drive space. For example, if there are four 250 GB drives in a RAID 10 array (for a total of 1,000 GB), the available drive space will be 500 GB. RAID 10 is illustrated in Figure 4.5.

FIGURE 4.5   RAID 10

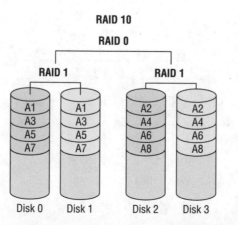

Just a Bunch of Disks (JBOD)

The acronym JBOD refers to "just a bunch of disks." The disks in this "bunch of disks" are independent of one another, unlike disks that participate in a RAID arrangement of some sort. Although the data may be striped across the disks, no fault tolerance is provided. It is a cheaper alternative to a RAID system. JBOD uses a process called concatenation, which is illustrated in Figure 4.6. In the figure you can see that data is concatenated from the end of disk 0 (block 64) to the beginning of disk 1 (block 65). Notice there is no data redundancy, and regardless of the number of disks in the system, if the data is spanned across the disks, the loss of a single disk means the loss of all data, making backup extremely important.

FIGURE 4.6   JBOD

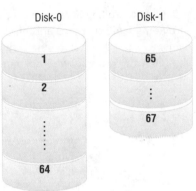

Hardware vs. Software

RAID can be implemented using disk software that comes with an operating system such as Windows Server 2022, but it can also be implemented using hardware, in which case it will be managed, not in the operating system but using a RAID utility built into the drive controller. When using hardware RAID, the disk array is presented to the operating system as a single disk. This has an impact both on performance and on the types of RAID that are available to you in certain situations. Let's look at these issues.

Performance Considerations

Here are the advantages of using software RAID:

- Lower cost
- The ability to implement disk duplexing

- Faster, more reliable performance than software RAID
- Support for online spares
- Support for RAID 10
- Decreased processor load
- User-friendly configuration utilities
- No operating system interface required when starting a rebuild

---

Disk Duplexing

Disk duplexing is the use of separate controller cards for each disk when implementing disk mirroring (RAID 1), thus providing fault tolerance at both the disk level and at the disk controller level, protecting against a single disk failure and a single controller card failure. This concept is illustrated in the following graphic, where a mirrored disk without duplexing is compared to one with duplexing.

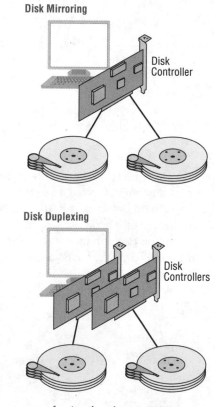

And here are the advantages of using hardware RAID:

If you look at the comparison of the operation of software and hardware RAID shown in Figure 4.7, you can see how much less the operating system is involved in reading and writing both data and parity information with hardware RAID.

FIGURE 4.7   Hardware and software RAID

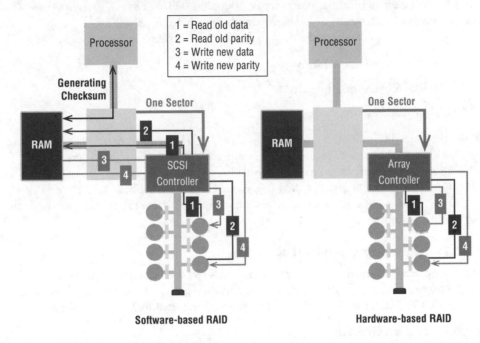

Capacity Planning

Planning for the capacity requirements of a server can be challenging. You must take into account the current needs and those that may occur in the future. Predicting the future is not easy, even when you have data from the past to use as a benchmark. Often you have to factor in somewhat vague assessments of future needs from department managers who may or not be able to do this accurately. At any rate, an attempt must be made to plan for now and the future. In this section we'll look at terms used to discuss capacity, some factors that impact the amount of space you need, and scenarios that may require more space.

Base 10 vs. Base 2 Disk Size Calculation

The question is one that has been asked many times: "Why does the advertised capacity of my drive not equal what I see in Windows?" The answer lies in the way the capacity is calculated. When there is a mismatch of this type, you typically have the vendor using one method and Windows using another.

There are two ways to calculate the space. Vendors typically count using the Base 10 number system, whereas Windows does so using the Base 2 number system. Let's look at how using these two systems can arrive at different answers.

1000 vs. 1024

One gigabyte as defined by a manufacturer is 1,000,000,000,000 bytes. In metric base 10, we define *kilo-* as 1000, *mega-* as 1,000,000, and *giga-* as 1,000,000,000.

Windows, however, calculates the disk size in a Base 2 system. In Base 2:

2^{10} is 1024 bytes, which is 1 kilobyte

2^{20} is 1048576 bytes, or 1 megabyte

2^{30} is 1073741824 bytes, or 1 gigabyte

When the hard disk manufacturer advertises a 120-gigabyte hard drive, they are selling you 120,000,000,000 bytes. Windows divides this number by what it considers a GB (1073741824) and reports the hard disk size as:

120000000000 (bytes) / 1073741824 (bytes per GB) = 111.8 GB.

So just be aware of this and ensure that when comparing drive capacities you are comparing apples to apples.

Capacity Planning Considerations

As you have already learned, capacity planning needs to consider current needs and future needs. A number of things go into making that educated guess about the future. In this section we'll look at issues that impact the amount of space a healthy server requires.

Operating System Growth

Although the number and size of the basic operating system files don't change, the fact is that as you install different sorts of updates, the operating system does in fact take up more space. It also gobbles up space over time monitoring and reporting on the operation of the system. These logs are useful but they take up space. Let's look at three ways in which the operating system can grow over time.

Patches

Patches are the security- or performance-related additions to the operating system code that are issued between service packs. When you add patches, the system may also make a backup or snapshot of the system for rollback purposes. If it doesn't delete these, that's a double whammy on your space.

Service Packs

In the past, all service packs used to be cumulative—meaning you needed to load only the last one. Starting with XP SP3, however, all Windows service packs released, including those for servers, have been incremental, meaning that you must install the previous ones before you can install the new one. Of course, this will never be a consideration if you maintain all of your updates. However, if you are bringing a new server up-to-date on service packs and patches, you need to know this.

One of the things that you can do in Windows to mitigate the amount of space used by constant updates is to manage a folder called the *component store*. This folder, called windows\winsxs, contains all the files that are required for a Windows installation. Any updates to those files are also held within the component store as the updates are installed. This means that over time this directory can get huge.

To reduce the size of the component store directory on a Windows installation, you can elect to install a service pack permanently and reclaim used space from the service pack files. You can also use Disk Cleanup on the directory. Doing either of these actions will make the service pack installation permanent, and not removable.

For complete information on several ways to clean up the component store and/or control the growth of its size, see:

https://technet.microsoft.com/en-us/library/dn251565.aspx.

Hard Drive Media Types

When anticipating the installation or deployment of primary storage devices on servers, consider several factors before you even purchase the drives. First, there are a number of disk specifications to understand, as well as a variety of interfaces that you may be dealing with during the installation. Let's consider both of these issues and then we'll end this section by running through the steps in a typical installation.

Disk Specifications

The number of technical specifications you will find listed when shopping for storage solutions can be bewildering at first. But if you understand what each means and how to compare the values attached to these specifications, the process of choosing the right solution can be much easier. In this section we'll consider the most common characteristics of server storage.

RPM

Revolutions per minute (RPM) is a value that indicates how fast the drive spins. There is an inverse relationship between the RPMs and drive latency. That's means faster spinning drives experience less latency. Disk drives for servers typically have RPM values between 7200 and 15000. Just to be clear, this is a value with meaning only for hard disk drives. SSDs do not spin at all.

Dimensions/Form Factor

It would be pretty embarrassing to buy a drive, get the drive, and then realize it won't fit. Therefore, the size and dimensions (also called the form factor) of the drive must also be considered. The drive must fit into the bay in which it will be installed. The two most common are the 2.5-inch small form factor (SFF) and the 3.5-inch large form factor (LFF). Enterprise-class HDD enclosures typically have a standard length and width. They can vary in height, up to 15 mm for SFF and up to 26.1 mm for LFF. Many SSDs are sized to fit in the same slots used for HDDs. Always consider the bay into which the drive will be installed before purchasing.

Capacity

The capacity of disks can vary widely. The amount of space you need will largely depend on the role the server is playing. Some server roles, such as file servers, require lots of space whereas other roles do not. The latest standard HDDs can hold up to 8 TB of data. Western Digital has a line of helium-sealed drives that go up to 10 TB, and Samsung announced a 2U box with over 700TB of capacity in 2015.

Bus Width

At one time, the width of the bus to which the disk would attach was a key consideration when selecting a disk, but since most drive technology no longer uses parallel communications, bus width is less important. When SCSI and IDE were in use, the wider the bus, the better. But today's serial attached SCSI (SAS) and serial ATA (SATA) use high-speed serial communication.

If you are still using SCSI, then ensuring that you buy a disk drive or drives that make full use of the bus width in the server is essential. So if your SCSI bus will support Ultra 640 SCSI, you should purchase drives that also fully support this.

Seek Time and Latency

Seek time is the time it takes for the actuator arm to arrive at the proper location where the read or write will occur. *Latency* is a measure of the time it takes the platter to spin the disk around so that the actuator arm is over the proper section. Latency is largely a function of the RPMs as a faster spinning disk will arrive at the desired location more rapidly than a slower disk.

Given all this, when it comes to SSDs, there are no moving parts, so seek times and latency times will be much lower and cannot be used in comparison with HDDs. For disks in a datacenter you should look for average seek time between 5 ms and 10 ms.

Solid State Drive (SSD)

One of the advantages of newer SSDs is that they exhibit much higher IOPS values than traditional hard disk drives. In Chapter 3 you learned that though traditional HDDs are less expensive than SSDs, SSDs are faster and suffer fewer failures not due to old age. Also remember that SSDs exhibit much higher IOPS values than traditional HDDs. For example, a 10,000 RPM SATA drive with 3 Gbps is listed to deliver ~125–150 IOPS, whereas an SSD with a SATA 3 Gbps interface is listed at ~8,600 IOPS (and that is one of the slower SSD drives). Finally, one characteristic that you did not learn about in Chapter 3 is that SSDs, unlike HHDs, are unaffected by magnetism, so they cannot be erased using magnetism as you can do with an HDD. In the next section you'll learn about factors that impact wear in an SSD.

Wear Factors

Solid-state drives will wear out like most hardware does at some point. So what are the factors that impact wear? It turns out it depends on what the drive spends most of its time doing. In this section you'll learn about the effects of writing and reading to the drive.

READ INTENSIVE VS. WRITE INTENSIVE

Reading the data on an SSD has little or no impact on the life of the SSD. Writing to the disk is where all the damage that reduces the life of the drive is done. It's the act of writing to the flash memory cell that degrades it. When planning for write-intensive systems that use SSDs, keep in mind your drives may need to be replaced more frequently to avoid issues.

In Exercise 4.1, you will change out a hard drive in an HP ProLiant DL380p Gen8 Server. In the HP ProLiant, both HDDs and SDDs can be changed out without shutting down the server. You server may be different. Consult your vendor documentation.

EXERCISE 4.1

Installing a SATA Drive

1. Remove a drive blank. This is simply a cover over one of the drive bays, as shown here.

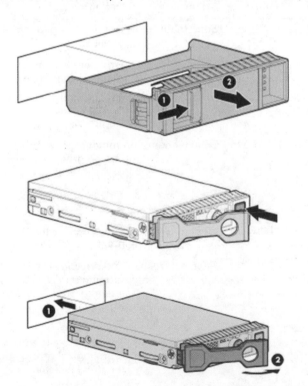

2. Prepare the drive and install the drive back into the slot, as shown in the previous graphic in steps labeled 1 and 2.

3. Observe the status of the LEDs on the front of the drive, as shown here.

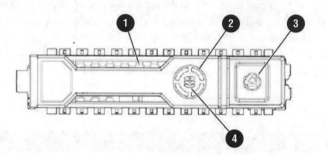

4. Use the following chart to assess the status of the newly installed drive.

LED number	LED name	Status	Definition
1	Locate	Solid blue	Drive is being identified by host application.
		Flashing blue	Firmware is being updated or requires an update.
2	Activity ring	Rotating green	Drive activity.
		Off	No drive activity.
3	Do not remove	Solid white	Do not remove the drive. Removing the drive causes one or more of the logical drives to fail.
		Off	Removing the drive does not cause a logical drive to fail.
4	Drive status	Solid green	The drive is a member of one or more logical drives.
		Flashing green	The drive is rebuilding or performing a RAID migration, stripe size migration, capacity expansion, or logical drive extension, or is erasing.
		Flashing amber/ green	The drive is a member of one or more logical drives and predicts the drive will fail.

LED number	LED name	Status	Definition
		Flashing amber	The drive is not configured and predicts the drive will fail.
		Solid amber	The drive has failed.
		Off	The drive is not configured by a RAID controller.

Hard Disk Drive (HDD)

In Chapter 3 you learned the basics of hard disk drives (HDD). In the next several sections you'll learn about architecture and performance characteristics of HDDs.

Rotations Per Minute (RPM) (15,000, 10,000, 7,200)

In Chapter 3 you learned about the effects of the disk rotation speed on latency. The section "Drives" compared the most common speeds of 15,000, 10,000, and 7200 RPM, among other speeds. Please review that section.

Hybrid

Hybrid drives were covered in Chapter 3. Please review that section.

Interface Types

There are six major drive interfaces you may encounter when installing or swapping out disk drives. We've already discussed a number of these, but just for completeness let's run through them all here in one place.

Serial Attached SCSI (SAS)

Serial Attached SCSI (SAS) is a type of SCSI that uses serial operation rather than parallel as the original SCSI did. There are several other ways in which it differs from parallel SCSI. A SCSI bus is a multidrop bus (one on which multiple points of attachment exist), whereas SAS uses point-to-point communication. Also, SAS requires no termination as in parallel SCSI. The latest version of SAS, SAS-4 operates at 22.5 Gbit/s.

A common SAS setup is shown in Figure 4.8. The cable plugged into the HBA is an external version of the SAS cable using the SFF-8470 connector, and the cable running from the HBA to the drives is an internal variety, also called an octopus cable, using the SFF-8484 connector to the HBA and the SFF-8482 connector to the drives.

FIGURE 4.8   SAS cabling

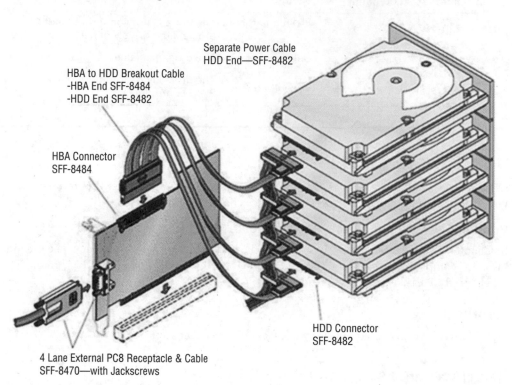

Separate Power Cable
HDD End—SFF-8482

HBA to HDD Breakout Cable
-HBA End SFF-8484
-HDD End SFF-8482

HBA Connector
SFF-8484

HDD Connector
SFF-8482

4 Lane External PC8 Receptacle & Cable
SFF-8470—with Jackscrews

Serial ATA (SATA)

Serial ATA (SATA) is also a serial communication method and began as an enhancement to the original ATA specifications, also known as IDE and, today, PATA. Technology is proving that serial communication is superior to placing multiple bits of data in parallel and trying to synchronize their transmission. Serial transmissions are simpler to adapt to the faster rates than are parallel transmissions. The SAS system receptacle is compatible with both the SAS HDD plug and the SATA HDD plug, as illustrated in Figure 4.9. The opposite is not true; you cannot plug an SAS HDD into a SATA system receptacle.

Peripheral Component Interconnect (PCI)

You learned about peripheral component interconnect (PCI) interfaces in Chapter 1, "Server Hardware." Please review that chapter.

External Serial Advanced Technology Attachment (eSATA)

eSATA provides a form of SATA meant for external connectivity. SATA is used for drive connections internally on many PCs. eSATA uses a more robust connector, longer shielded cables, and stricter (but backward-compatible) electrical standards. The interface resembles that of USB and IEEE 1394 (FireWire), but the cable cannot be as long, and the cable does not supply power to the device. The advantage it has over the other technologies is speed—it is approximately three times as fast as either FireWire or USB 2.0 (although USB 3.0 is faster).

FIGURE 4.9   SAS system receptacle with the SATA HDD plug

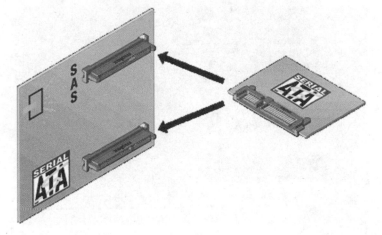

Universal Serial Bus (USB)

Like other computing devices, servers will probably have USB ports. There will likely be at least two, one for a mouse and one for a keyboard (although you will probably use a KVM switch for this when the servers are rack-mounted or blade). These will probably be on the front of the server, although there may be additional ones on the back of the server.

Some specialized server products are able to operate as USB servers in that they allow network devices to access shared USB devices that are attached to the server. This typically requires some sort of USB management software. In this case it may be necessary to use a USB hub connected to one of the USB ports on the server if there are not enough ports provided by the server.

As you already know, USB can provide an interface to practically any type of device, including storage devices. This includes the ability to use special adapter cables to connect a SCSI drive to a USB 3.0 port using the USB Attached SCSI (UAS). One of the cables you would use in such a situation is shown in Figure 4.10.

FIGURE 4.10 USB to SCSI

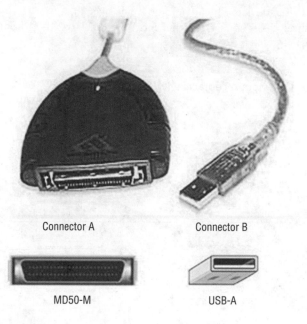

Connector A   Connector B

MD50-M   USB-A

Secure Digital (SD)

Secure Digital (SD) cards are just one type of flash; there are many others. The maximum capacity of a standard SD card is 512 GB, and there are two other standards that go beyond this: Secure Digital High Capacity (SDHC) can go to 32 GB and Secure Digital Extra Capacity (SDXC) to 2 TB. Figure 4.11 shows a Compact Flash card (the larger of the two) and an SD card along with an eight-in-one card reader/writer. The reader shown connects to the USB port and then interacts with Compact Flash, Compact Flash II, Memory Stick, Memory Stick PRO, SmartMedia, xD-Picture cards, SD, and MultiMediaCards. The SD card specification defines three physical sizes, discussed in the following sections.

FIGURE 4.11 SD and Compact Flash

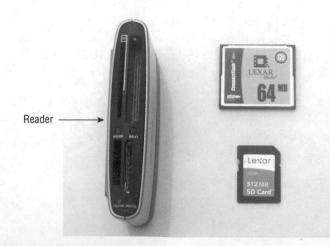

Reader ⟶

Shared Storage

Servers can use several different technologies to reach their storage devices and share their data. Although they can make use of directly attached storage devices in the same way as workstations, the amount of data they sometimes have to store, and the performance and fault tolerance requirements of that data, make it more likely that other types of storage are preferable. In this section three major approaches to providing servers with high-performance, fault-tolerant storage will be covered.

Direct Attached Storage (DAS)

Direct attached storage (DAS) is the type of storage used in workstations. In this approach, the drives are attached to the server locally through a SATA, USB, SCSI, or Serial Attached SCSI (SAS) connection. All these interface types are local interfaces to the server.

Keep in mind that multiple drives or the presence of fault-tolerant technologies such as RAID can still be considered DAS if the interface to the storage is one of these local technologies. One of the key features of DAS is that there is no network connection standing between the server and the storage, as is the case with the other two technologies we'll be discussing. Although DAS has the advantage of being widely understood and simple to deploy, it has the disadvantage of being more difficult to scale than NAS.

Network Attached Storage (NAS)

Network attached storage (NAS), as the name implies, consists of storage devices that are attached to the network and not attached locally to the server or servers that may be accessing the NAS. Although the storage may not be attached locally to the server, it is reachable via the TCP/IP network.

With a NAS, almost any machine that can connect to the LAN (or is interconnected to the LAN through a WAN) can use protocols such as NFS, CIFS, or HTTP to connect to a NAS and share files. The advantages and disadvantages of using NAS are listed in Table 4.1.

TABLE 4.1 Advantages and disadvantages of NAS

Advantages	Disadvantages
A NAS is easily accessed over TCP/IP Ethernet-based networks.	A NAS has higher latency and lower reliability than a SAN.
A NAS is inexpensive to implement.	NAS traffic competes with regular data on the network since it is not on its own network.
A NAS typically supports multiple RAID methods.	
A NAS offers GUI-based management.	Packet drops and congestion are inherent in Ethernet.
A NAS typically contains backup software.	Taking frequent snapshots works better in SAN. (Snapshots are images of operating systems, making a rollback to an earlier state possible.)
Ethernet troubleshooting is well understood.	
A NAS supports high throughput.	

Network File System (NFS)

NFS is one of the protocols that can be used to connect to and share data on a NAS device. Network File System (NFS) is a client/server file-sharing protocol used in Unix/Linux. Version 4 is the most current version of NFS. It operates over TCP port 2049. Secure NFS (SNFS) offers confidentiality using Digital Encryption Standard (DES).

Common Internet File System (CIFS)

Server Message Block (SMB) is an application layer protocol used to provide shared access to resources. The Common Internet File System (CIFS) protocol is a dialect of SMB. It is primarily used in Windows systems. The latest version is 3.1.1, which was released to support Windows 10 and Windows Server 2016. It operates as a client-server application. It uses port 445.

Storage Area Network (SAN)

Classic storage area networks (SANs) consist of high-capacity storage devices that are connected by a high-speed private network (separate from the LAN) using a storage-specific switch. This storage information architecture addresses the collection, management, and use of data. The advantages and disadvantages of a SAN are listed in Table 4.2.

TABLE 4.2 Advantages and disadvantages of SANs

Advantages	Disadvantages
SANs are scalable; it's easy to add additional storage as required.	SANs are expensive.
SANs are available; maintenance can be performed without taking servers offline.	Maintaining SANs requires higher skill levels.
Sharing is made easier by the fact that the SAN is not connected directly to any network or server.	It's not possible to leverage legacy investments.
SANs make it easier to provide physical security. Longer cable runs are made possible because Fibre Channel enables you to access a SAN in a remote location.	There is a relative scarcity of SAN vendors.

Another key difference between the operation of a NAS and that of a SAN is that a SAN provides block-level access to data as opposed to a NAS, which provides file-level access to the data. In file-level access, data is accessed in bulk in the form of a file and the process is controlled by the protocol used by the client. When block-level access is used, data is stored in raw blocks, and each block can be controlled like an individual hard drive.

Each of these systems has advantages, as shown in Table 4.3.

TABLE 4.3   File- and block-level access

File level	Block level
Easy to implement and use.	Better performance.
Stores and presents data as files and folders.	Each block can be treated as an independent disk.
Less expensive.	More reliable.
Well suited for bulk file storage.	Can support external bootup of the systems to which it is connected.

A comparison of the three storage methods we've discussed so far is shown in Figure 4.12. The FC in the diagram refers to Fibre Channel, which we discuss in the section Fibre Channel, later in this chapter.

FIGURE 4.12   Storage technologies

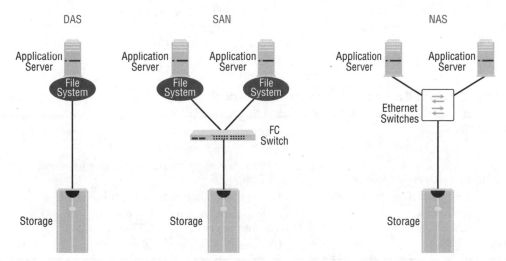

Internet Small Computer Systems Interface (iSCSI)

Internet Small Computer Systems Interface (iSCSI) is an IP-based networking storage standard method of encapsulating SCSI commands (which are used with SANs) within IP packets. This allows you to use the same network for storage that you use for the balance of the network. Whereas iSCSI can also be used in a NAS architecture, we have chosen to include it under SAN as it was first used in a SAN. Figure 4.13 compares a regular SAN and one using iSCSI.

FIGURE 4.13   Classic SAN and SAN with iSCSI

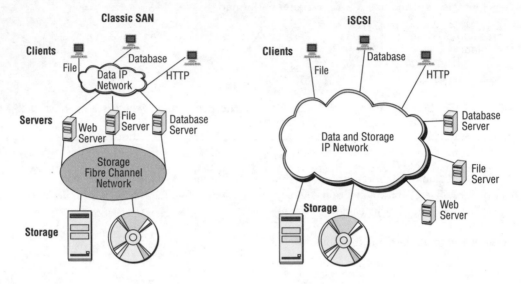

The advantages and disadvantages to using iSCSI are listed in Table 4.4.

TABLE 4.4   Advantages and disadvantages of iSCSI

Advantages	Disadvantages
iSCSI is simple, due to its reliance on Ethernet, which is well known.	Performance issues are possible, due to reliance on software.
iSCSI eliminates distance limitations imposed by SCSI transfers.	iSCSI is susceptible to network congestion.
iSCSI is inexpensive in simple deployments.	In larger deployments, iSCSI can be as expensive as or more expensive than Fibre Channel.

Fibre Channel

A very common interface for storage in servers is a Fibre Channel interface. These are used to connect devices in a high-speed fiber storage network. These networks typically use a fiber switch with devices connected to the switch using Fibre Channel interfaces. Servers will require some implementation of a fiber HBA. Each HBA has a unique World Wide Name (WWN), which like a MAC address uses an organizationally unique identifier (OUI) assigned by the IEEE. An example of a fiber switch to which the cables from the HBAs on the servers would attach is shown in Figure 4.14.

FIGURE 4.14   Fiber switch

SANs can also be implemented in such a way that devices that cannot normally communicate by using the Fibre Channel protocol or SCSI commands can access the storage devices. A technology that makes this possible is covered next.

FIBRE CHANNEL OVER ETHERNET (FCoE)

Fibre Channel over Ethernet (FCoE) encapsulates Fibre Channel traffic within Ethernet frames much as iSCSI encapsulates SCSI commands in IP packets. However, unlike iSCSI, it does not use IP at all. Figure 4.15 shows the structures of iSCSI and FCoE.

FIGURE 4.15   FCoE and iSCSI

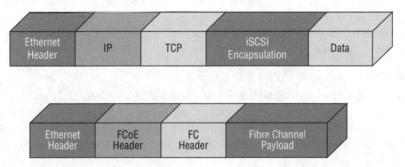

Explain the Importance of Asset Management and Documentation

You would be amazed at how many network administrators can't tell you exactly how many devices of a certain type they have, and if they can, they can't tell you where they all are. This is the result of a combination of poor record keeping and frequent job turnover. While the job turnover may just be an unfortunate characteristic of the business, it should not cause an issue if proper documentation policies are followed. In this section the proper management of assets through the entire asset life cycle will be covered. We'll also talk about the type of documentation you should keep and how it should be handled, especially sensitive information.

Asset Management

Proper asset management is not rocket science. It boils down to knowing exactly what you have, when you got it, where it is, and where the license to use it is. Most server administrators don't set out to intentionally exercise poor asset management; they simply don't assign it the importance it requires to be done correctly. Let's break the process down and talk about its individual parts and why each is important.

Labeling

Labeling servers, workstations, printers, ports on infrastructure devices (routers and switches), and other items is another form of asset documentation that often doesn't receive enough attention. Not only does this make your day-to-day duties easier, but it also makes the process of maintaining accurate records simpler and supports a proper asset management plan. When periodic inventories are taken (you are doing that, right?), having these items labeled makes the process so much quicker. This goes for cables in the server room as well.

In a datacenter, server room, or wiring closet, correct and updated labeling of ports, systems, circuits, and patch panels can prevent a lot of confusion and mistakes when configuration changes are made. Working with incorrect or incomplete (in some cases nonexistent) labeling is somewhat like trying to locate a place with an incorrect or incomplete map. In this section we'll touch on some of the items that should be correctly labeled.

Port Labeling

Ports on switches, patch panels, and other systems should be properly labeled, and the wall outlets to which they lead should match. You should agree on a naming convention to use so that all technicians are operating from the same point of reference. In any case, the labels should be updated where changes are made that dictate an update.

System Labeling

Other systems that are installed in racks, such as servers, firewall appliances, and redundant power supplies, should also be labeled with IP addresses and DNS names that the devices possess.

Circuit Labeling

Circuits entering the facility should also be labeled. Label electrical receptacles, circuit breaker panels, and power distribution units. Include circuit information, voltage and amperage, the type of electrical receptacle, and where in the datacenter the conduit terminates.

Naming Conventions

A naming system or convention guides and organizes labeling and ensures consistency. No matter what name or numbering system you use, be consistent.

Patch Panel Labeling

The key issue when labeling patch panels is to ensure that they're correct. Also, you need to make sure that the wall outlet they're connected to is the same. The American National Standards Institute/Telecommunications Industry Association (ANSI/TIA) 606-B Administration Standard for Telecommunications Infrastructure for identification and labeling approved in April 2012 provides clear specifications for labeling and administration best practices across all electrical and network systems premise classes, including large datacenters.

Warranty

You learned about warranty management in Chapter 3. Please review that chapter.

Leased vs. Owned Devices

When calculating the value of company assets, the treatment of leased assets may be different than that of company-owned assets. Typically the value of leased assets are not considered when calculating total asset value, but in some countries it may depend on the type of lease. There are two types:

Capital Lease   In this type of lease, ownership of the asset is shifted from the lessor to the lessee by the end of the lease period. A capital lease is therefore considered like loan or debt refinancing with interest expensed on the income statement; therefore the assets are considered to already be company property and are counted in totaling asset value.

Operating Lease   Operating lease payments are operating expenses recorded each month. Assets in this type of lease are not counted in calculating total asset value.

Life-Cycle Management

Managing assets becomes easier if you understand that an asset goes through various stages called its life cycle. Consequently, life-cycle management comprises the activities that we undertake with respect to the asset at various points in the life cycle. Let's examine these stages.

Procurement

This includes all activities that might go into purchasing a product. It includes activities such as product research, requests for bids, product selection, and delivery.

Usage

This stage includes day-to-day maintenance tasks that are involved in using the item. This might encompass things like updating the software or firmware or tasks that would be unique to the device type, such as defragmenting a hard drive.

End of Life

End of life can mean a couple of different things. From the vendor perspective, it probably means that they are no longer providing support for a product. From your perspective, it probably means that the product no longer meets your needs or that you have decided to replace the item with a new version. It could also mean that changes in your business process make the item no longer necessary.

Disposal/Recycling

The final stage in the life of an asset is its disposal. Regardless of your approach—whether it is throwing the item away, donating the item to charity, or turning the item in for recycling—you should ensure that all sensitive data is removed. This requires more than simple deletion, and the extent to which you go with this process depends on how sensitive that data is. Degaussing is a way to remove the data for good. With extremely sensitive data, you may find it advisable to destroy the device.

Proactive Life-Cycle Management

Here's a final word of advice: you may find it beneficial to stagger replacement cycles so that your entire server room doesn't need to be replaced all at once. It's much easier to get smaller upgrades added to the budget.

Inventory

As I mentioned at the start of this section, asset management includes knowing what you have. You can't know something is missing until you take inventory, so you should take inventory on a regular basis. So what type of information is useful to record? You may choose to record more, but the following items should always be included:

Make   The manufacturer of the device should be recorded as well as the name they give the device.

Model   The exact model number should be recorded in full, leaving nothing out. Sometimes those dangling letters at the end of the model number are there to indicate how this model differs from another, or they could indicate a feature, so record *the entire number*.

Serial Number   The serial number of the device should be recorded. This is a number that will be important to you with respect to the warranty and service support. You should be able to put your hands on this number quickly.

Asset Tag   If your organization places asset tags on devices, it probably means you have your own internal numbering or other identification system in place. Record that number and any other pertinent information that the organization deems important enough to place on the asset tag, such as region and building.

Documentation Management

Along with a robust asset management plan, you should implement a formal plan for organizing, storing, and maintaining multiple copies in several locations of a wide array of documentation that will support the asset management plan. Just as you should be able to put your hands on the inventory documentation at a moment's notice, you should be able to obtain needed information from any of the following documents at any time.

Updates

You should record all updates made to systems in some sort of log. This will help with addressing issues with updates that break things (which happens all the time). By comparing the time an issue appears with the time and dates of updates, you can determine which update caused the issue and roll back the update. The log should also record updates that you chose not to apply (for whatever reason) and the reasoning behind that. Again, this can help later if you suspect that a missing update might be causing an issue.

Service Manuals

All service manuals that arrive with new hardware should be kept. They are invaluable sources of information related to the use and maintenance of your devices. They also contain contact information that may make it easier to locate help at a critical time. Many manuals have troubleshooting flowcharts that may turn a 4-hour solution into a 30-minute one. If a paper copy has not been retained, you can usually obtain these service manuals online at the vendor website.

Architecture Diagrams

Any diagrams created to depict the architecture of a software program or group of programs should be kept. When the original developers are no longer with the company, these diagrams are invaluable to those left behind to understand the workings of the software. There may be multiple layers of this documentation. Some may only focus on a single piece of software whereas others may depict how the software fits into the overall business process of the company. An example of such a diagram, called an enterprise architecture diagram, is shown in Figure 4.16.

Infrastructure Diagrams

All network or infrastructure diagrams should be kept in both hard copy and digital format. Moreover, these diagrams must be closely integrated with the change management process. The change management policy (covered later in this section) should specifically call for the updating of the diagram at the conclusion of any change made to the network that impacts the diagram and should emphasize that no change procedure is considered complete unless this update has occurred.

FIGURE 4.16 Enterprise architecture diagram

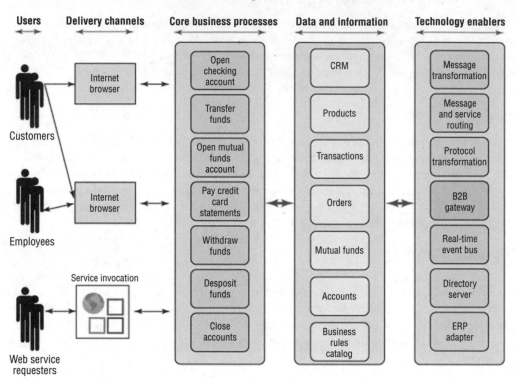

Workflow Diagrams

While some of your network diagrams will focus on the physical pieces of the network, others will be focused on the flow of data in the network in the process of doing business. So these may depict a workflow and how information involved in a single transaction or business process goes from one logical component in the network to another. An example of a dataflow diagram for an order system is shown in Figure 4.17.

Recovery Processes

If your organization has a disaster recovery plan, that plan should call for recovery documentation. It should outline, in detail, the order with which devices should be recovered in the event of a disaster that causes either complete or partial destruction of the facility. It should also cover the steps to be taken in lesser events as well, such as a power outage, the theft of a device, or the failure of a device, and data recovery procedures as well.

FIGURE 4.17   Dataflow for order entry

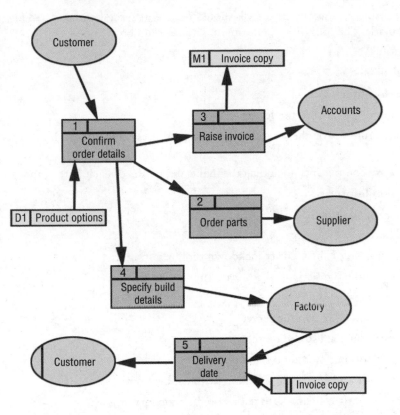

Baselines

Earlier you learned the importance of creating performance baselines for major systems. The baselines will be used as a comparison point to readings taken at regular intervals. This means that the baseline data will need to be available at all times. A plan should be in place to consider at regular intervals whether major changes in the network may require new baselines to be taken.

Change Management

As a part of the overall security policy, the change management policy will outline the steps involved in suggesting, considering, planning, executing, and documenting any change in the server configuration. No change should be made without it undergoing this process. The policy should be available at times for consultation when questions arise about making configuration changes.

Server Configurations

The exact configuration of every server should be fully recorded and updated any time a change is made. The following is information that should be included:

General

- Server name
- Server location
- Function or purpose of the server
- Software running on the server, including operating system, programs, and services

Hardware

- Hardware components, including the make and model of each part of the system

Configuration Information

- Event logging settings
- Services that are running
- Configuration of any security lockdown tool or setting
- Configuration and settings of software running on the server

Data

- Types of data stored on the server
- Owners of the data stored on the server
- Sensitivity of data stored on the server
- Data that should be backed up, along with its location
- Users or groups with access to data stored on the server
- Administrators, with a list of rights of each
- Authentication process and protocols for users of data on the server
- Authentication process and protocols used for authentication
- Data encryption requirements
- Authentication encryption requirements

Users

- Account settings
- List of users accessing data from remote locations and type of media they access data through, such as the Internet or a private network
- List of administrators administering the server from remote locations and type of media they access the server through

Security

- Intrusion detection and prevention method used on the server
- Latest patch to operating system and each service running

- Individuals with physical access to the area the server is in and the type of access, such as key or card access
- Emergency recovery disk and date of last update
- Disaster recovery plan and location of backup data

Company Policies and Procedures

While policies are broad statements of intent, procedures are step-by-step instructions on how something is done in an organization. They are especially relevant in scenarios where users may have performed an operation in a different manner in another organization. These standard operating procedures (SOPs) serve to maintain consistency of operations.

Complying with Company Procedures/Standards

While applying all firmware and operating system patches is a starting baseline for securing the new server, your company's standards and procedures may require that you go further. It may be that upon review of these documents you find that there are additional actions you must take. For example, it could be that according to policy certain server roles require that the network service the server provides (SQL or Project Management Server, for example) be configured to run under the security context of a user account rather than under the context of the system account (a very common safeguard). The bottom line is that no new server should be released to the network until it conforms to all security policies and procedures.

In the following sections you will learn about documents that support the smooth operation of the organization while adhering to company policies and procedures.

Business Impact Analysis (BIA)

A *business impact analysis* (BIA) occurs as part of business continuity and disaster recovery. Performing a thorough BIA will help business units understand the impact of a disaster. The resulting document that is produced lists the critical and necessary business functions, their resource dependencies, and their level of criticality to the overall organization. In essence the following information is assembled with respect to the loss of each function and/or the devices that make that function possible:

Who Is Affected   Identify all users and departments that will be affected if the function or process is lost. Don't forget to consider any other departments that may depend on information generated by any department you have already identified as vulnerable. Unfortunately, in many cases it begets a tidal wave across departments.

What Is Affected   Identify the related processes that may suffer as a result of the loss of each function. For example, if the web commerce server depends on the SQL server and the SQL server is unavailable, the commerce server will also be unable to function.

Severity of Impact   Finally, the impact of the loss of each function must be assigned a severity level. The importance of this is that this information will be used to prioritize the recovery of functions such that the most critical are recovered first.

Mean Time between Failure (MTBF)

This is the estimated amount of time a device will operate before a failure occurs. This amount is calculated by the device vendor. System reliability is increased by a higher MTBF and lower MTTR.

Mean Time to Recover (MTTR)

This is the average time required to repair a single resource or function when a disaster or disruption occurs.

Recovery Point Objective (RPO)

This is the point in time to which the disrupted resource or function must be returned.

Recovery Time Objective (RTO)

This is the shortest time period after a disaster or disruptive event within which a resource or function must be restored in order to avoid unacceptable consequences. RTO assumes that an acceptable period of downtime exists.

Service Level Agreement (SLA)

IT support departments typically have written agreements with the customers they support called service level agreements (SLAs). In some cases these agreements are with other departments of the same company for which they provide support. These agreements specify the type of support to be provided and the acceptable amount of time allowed to respond to support calls.

Typically these time windows are different for different types of events. For example, they may be required to respond to a server outage in 20 minutes, whereas responding to a user having problems with a browser may only require a response by the end of the day. The following sections explore some of the issues that might be covered in a formal SLA as well as other related issues.

Another typical issue requirement in most SLAs is that any schedule downtime should be communicated to all users and that the communication should include the specific parties that will be affected by the downtime and exactly what the impact will be. For example, a notification email describing the scheduled downtime might include the following:

- Departments affected
- Specific applications or service impacted
- Expected length of downtime

CLIENT NOTIFICATION

SLAs should also specify events that require client notification and the time period in which that must occur. It will cover all scheduled downtime but should also address the time period in which notifications should be sent out when unscheduled events occur. It might also discuss parameters for responding to client requests.

Uptime Requirements

An SLA might specify that taking any infrastructure equipment down for maintenance requires prior notification and that the event may only occur during the evening or on the weekend. This type of event is called *scheduled downtime*. It is important that when you schedule this event, you allow enough time in the window to accomplish what you need to, and you should always have a plan in case it becomes obvious that the maintenance cannot be completed in the scheduled downtime.

Unscheduled downtime is the nightmare of any administrator. This is when a device is down or malfunctioning outside of a scheduled maintenance window. Some SLAs might include an unscheduled downtime clause that penalizes the support team in some way after the amount of unscheduled downtime exceeds a predetermined level. If the support is being provided to a customer, there might be a financial penalty. If the SLA applies to another department in the same organization, the penalty might be in a different form.

Document Availability

It goes without saying that there's no use creating all this documentation if no one can find it or it's unavailable to those who need it when they need it. Both digital and hard copies should be created. Finally, use strict version control to ensure that everyone is using the same document version.

Secure Storage of Sensitive Documentation

No discussion of documentation storage would be complete without covering storage of sensitive documents. There should be a system of data classification that extends to cover sensitive documents such as contracts, leases, design plans, and product details. The data protection method accorded each category should reflect its sensitivity label. Any such documents labeled sensitive should be encrypted and stored separately from other categories of data. Here are examples of this sort of information:

- Personally identifiable information, which in part or in combination can be used to identify a person
- Human resources information
- Financial documents that are not public
- Trade secrets and propriety methods
- Plans and designs
- Any other documents that the company deems to be sensitive

Summary

In this chapter you learned about a number of storage technologies, including DAS, NAS, and SAN. We looked at the advantages and disadvantages of each of these techniques. We also discussed various implementations of multiple storage devices such as JBOD.

In the second part of the chapter you learned the importance of proper asset management. We discussed asset management from the perspective of the asset life cycle and the role that proper documentation management plays in proper network management.

Exam Essentials

Describe speeds of magnetic hard drives. These include 5400 RPM, 7200 RPM, 10,000 RPM and 15,000 RPM. Understand how the speed impacts the latency and data rates.

Explain the importance of asset management and documentation. List what should be included when creating an asset inventory. Understand the importance of organizing and maintaining documentation. Describe some of the types of sensitive documents that require special treatment.

Review Questions

You can find the answers in the Appendix.

1. Which RAID type provides no fault tolerance?
   A. RAID 0
   B. RAID 1
   C. RAID 3
   D. RAID 5

2. Which RAID type is also called mirroring?
   A. RAID 0
   B. RAID 1
   C. RAID 3
   D. RAID 5

3. If a hard drive has 120 GB as calculated using the Base 10 number system, what will be the capacity reported by Windows?
   A. 120 GB
   B. 110 GB
   C. 111.8 GB
   D. 122.5 GB

4. Which of the following folders is the Windows component store directory?
   A. `C:\windows`
   B. `C:\windows/winsxs`
   C. `C:\winsxs`
   D. `C:\winnt/winsxs`

5. Which of the following actions can empty temporary directories?
   A. Running wevutil
   B. Running Disk Cleanup
   C. Running defrag
   D. Running Disk Check

6. If three 250 MB disks are present in a RAID 5 array, how much space is actually usable for data?
   A. 125 MB
   B. 200 MB
   C. 250 MB
   D. 500 MB

7. What is the minimum number of disks required for RAID 5?

   A. 2

   B. 3

   C. 4

   D. 5

8. Which of the following licensing models use a single license key to demonstrate that you have paid for multiple installations?

   A. Per-user

   B. Open source

   C. Volume

   D. Subscription

9. RAID 6 writes parity information across the drives as is done in RAID 5, but it writes two stripes. What is the effect of writing two stripes?

   A. Speeds performance

   B. Allows the cable to be longer

   C. Hurts performance

   D. Allows you to use only two drives

10. Which of the following is an advantage of software RAID over hardware RAID?

   A. Better performance

   B. Lower cost

   C. Better security

   D. Faster recovery

11. Which of the following is not an advantage of hardware RAID over software RAID?

   A. Decreased processor load

   B. Ability to do disk duplexing

   C. Support for online spares

   D. Faster performance

12. You have four 500 GB disks in a RAID 10 array. How much space is available for data?

   A. 500 GB

   B. 750 GB

   C. 1000 GB

   D. 2500 GB

13. When separate controller cards are used for each disk, what is it called?

   A. Disk jukebox

   B. JBOD

   C. Disk duplexing

   D. Disk triplexing

14. Which of the following allows a cable to be a maximum of 1 meter in length?

   A. SATA

   B. SCSI

   C. Fibre Channel

   D. iSCSI

15. Which of the following is the costliest to implement?

   A. SATA

   B. SCSI

   C. Fibre Channel

   D. iSCSI

16. Which of the following RPMs will provide the fastest access speed when discussing hard disk drives?

   A. 4800

   B. 5400

   C. 7200

   D. 10000

17. You have three drives that have capacities of 500 MB, 750 MB, and 1000 MB. Setting the cost of parity information aside, what is the total capacity of the array?

   A. 1500 MB

   B. 2250 MB

   C. 3000 MB

   D. 3500 MB

18. Which of the following technologies supports hot swapping inherently?

   A. SAS

   B. SATA

   C. SCSI

   D. Fibre Channel

19. Which of the following is attached to the system but cannot replace a bad disk without manual intervention?

   A. Hot swap

   B. Hot spare

   C. Cold spare

   D. Standby

20. Which of the following describes the average length of time it takes a vendor to repair a device or component?

   A. MTBF

   B. MMTR

   C. MTTR

   D. MTR

Chapter

5

Identifying Fault Tolerance Requirements

COMPTIA SERVER+ EXAM OBJECTIVES COVERED IN THIS CHAPTER:

✓ **2.4   Explain the key concepts of high availability for servers.**

✓ **Clustering**

  ▪ Active-active

  ▪ Active-passive

  ▪ Failover

  ▪ Failback

  ▪ Proper patching procedures

  ▪ Heartbeat

✓ **Fault tolerance**

  ▪ Server-level redundancy vs. component redundancy

✓ **Redundant server network infrastructure**

  ▪ Load balancing

    ▪ Software vs. hardware

    ▪ Round robin

    ▪ Most recently used (MRU)

  ▪ Network interface card (NIC) teaming and redundancy

    ▪ Failover

    ▪ Link aggregation

The ability to restore data that has been intentionally or unintentionally deleted or lost through hardware failures is critical. Frequent backups are a part of the fault tolerance solution, but in some cases the time it takes to locate the proper storage medium and perform the restore operation is more than can be tolerated. In that scenario you may want to implement a solution that allows the system to maintain access to the data even with the loss of a drive.

Since servers are so critical to the operation of the network, in many cases we need to protect ourselves against the negative effects of a server going down. In other cases, we simply need to add more server horsepower to meet a workload. We accomplish these goals through fault tolerance and high availability techniques. In this chapter, we'll look at fault tolerance technologies.

Clustering

Clustering is the process of combining multiple physical or virtual servers together in an arrangement called a cluster, in which the servers work together to service the same workload or application. This may be done to increase performance or to ensure continued access to the service if a server goes down, or its goal could be both. A server cluster is generally recommended for servers running applications that have a long-running in-memory state or frequently updated data. Typical uses for server clusters include file servers, print servers, database servers, and messaging servers. Clustering can be implemented in one of two ways: active–active or active–passive.

Active–Active

In an active–active cluster, both or all servers are actively servicing the workload. That doesn't necessarily mean they are running the same applications at all times, but only that they are capable of taking over the workload of an application running on another cluster member if that member goes down. For example, in Figure 5.1 the server on the left is running two applications prior to failing, whereas the server on the right is running only one of the three applications. After the failure, the server on the right takes over the work of all three applications. With this arrangement you must ensure that the remaining server can handle the total workload.

FIGURE 5.1   Active/active cluster

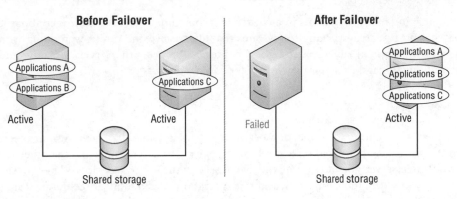

Active–Passive

In an active–passive cluster, at least one of the servers in the cluster is not actively working but simply sitting idle until a failure occurs. This is shown in Figure 5.2. This arrangement comes at the cost of having a server sitting idle until a failure occurs. It has the benefit of providing more assurance that the workload will continue to be serviced with the same level of resources if the servers are alike.

FIGURE 5.2   Active/passive cluster

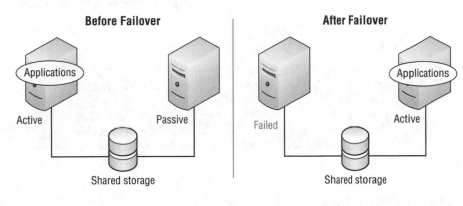

Failover/Failback

Failover is a term that describes when a system fails and the workload is transferred to the backup system. This process is shown in both Figures 5.1 and 5.2. Failback is a term that describes when the original system goes back online and the workload is moved back to the original system.

Proper Patching Procedures

When managing multiple systems in a cluster, it is sometimes very easy to forget about keeping patches up-to-date, especially for systems that are passive and rarely even doing work. While you will learn all about patching in Chapter 6, "Securing the Server," for now understand that one unpatched system in the cluster can wreak havoc.

Heartbeat

A heartbeat connection is a connection between servers in a load balancing scenario across which the servers send a signal (called a heartbeat) used to determine when the other server is down. If one server goes down, the other will service the entire workload. The two servers are typically identical (content-wise), and this is used often as a failover technique. It may be a direct physical connection, as shown in Figure 5.3, or it might be done over the network.

FIGURE 5.3 Heartbeat connection

Fault Tolerance

In Chapter 1, "Server Hardware," you learned about providing power redundancy to the datacenter. But power redundancy is not the only type of fault tolerance with which you need to be concerned. In this section, you'll learn about redundancy at both the sustain level and the component level.

Server-Level Redundancy vs. Component Redundancy

Redundancy can and should be provided at both the server level and the component level. At the server level, servers can be organized into clusters, as you learned earlier in this chapter, and can be set up in a load balancing deployment as well (you will learn more about load balancing later in this chapter).

At the component level, systems can be configured with multiple instances of key components such as power supplies, CPUs, and network cards to provide fault tolerance. By implementing both server-level and component-level redundancy, you can create additional layers of protection.

Redundant Server Network Infrastructure

Providing server-level redundancy can be achieved in two ways. One way, clustering, has been covered. In this section you will learn about another technique called load balancing.

Load Balancing

A second form of fault tolerance that focuses more on providing high availability of a resource is *load balancing*. In load balancing a frontend device or service receives work requests and allocates the requests to a number of backend servers. This type of fault tolerance is recommended for applications that do *not* have long-running in-memory state or frequently updated data. Web servers are good candidates for load balancing. The load balancing device or service can use several methods to allocate the work. Let's look at common allocation methods and two deployment options: hardware and software.

Software vs. Hardware

Load balancing can be done using load balancing software or it can be done with a physical appliance called a load balancer. Figure 5.4 shows the placement of a hardware load balancer. When software is being used, the software operates logically from the same position as with hardware—that is, the software will stand between the work requests and the work servers and will allocate work between the systems using one of the allocation methods covered in the next section.

Round Robin

In a round robin allocation system, the load balancer allocates work requests to each server sequentially, resulting in each getting an equal number of requests. As shown in Figure 5.5, this could mean that a user may make two requests that actually go to two different servers.

FIGURE 5.4   Hardware load balance

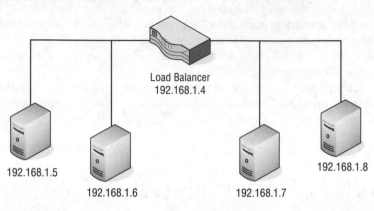

Load Balancer
192.168.1.4

192.168.1.5

192.168.1.6

192.168.1.7

192.168.1.8

FIGURE 5.5   Round robin load balancing

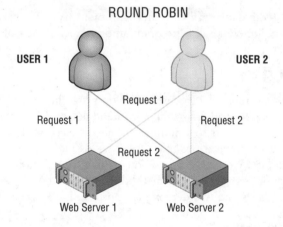

ROUND ROBIN

USER 1   **USER 2**

Request 1

Request 1   Request 2

Request 2

Web Server 1   Web Server 2

Most Recently Used (MRU)

The Most Recently Used algorithm attempts to send clients into running servers, preferably the most recently used server before starting new servers. The goal of this algorithm is to reduce the overhead of starting new servers by using servers that are already running.

Network Interface Card (NIC) Teaming and Redundancy

Redundancy can also be provided at the network interface level. NIC teaming is the process of combining multiple physical network connections into a single logical interface. This process goes by other names as well, including link aggregation and link bonding. Combining these physical links can be done using proprietary methods, and there is also an IEEE standard for the process called 802.3ad, later replaced by 802.1ax-2008. When the standard method is used, a protocol called Link Aggregation Control Protocol (LACP) controls the establishment of the aggregated link based on the proper combination of settings of the ends of the multiple links and on the agreement of certain settings on all physical links in the "bundle" (speed and duplex among them).

The advantages to using a NIC team are increased bandwidth and fault tolerance. You have two physical links, so if one is lost the other is still functional. For links that run between switches, it is better than using two links that are *not* aggregated, because in switch networks that include redundant links (which they should, according to best practices), a switching loop prevention protocol called Spanning Tree Protocol (STP) will disable one of the links. When the links are aggregated, STP considers them to be a single link and does not shut any of the ports in the aggregation.

In Exercise 5.1, you will set up a NIC team on a Windows Server 2012 R2 server.

EXERCISE 5.1

Configuring a NIC Team

Note: This exercise uses Windows Server 2012 R2.

1. Open Server Manager and determine if NIC teaming has been enabled, as shown in the following graphic. If not, double-click the Disabled link.

2. After double-clicking the Disabled link the NIC Teaming window will open, as shown here:

3. Select New Team from the Tasks drop-down menu above the Teams panel on the lower-left side, as shown here:

4. On the next screen, select the network adapters that will be members of the team you are creating. As shown in the following graphic, we are selecting Ethernet 5 and Ethernet 6.

Also note that it is on this page that you can choose whether both adapters are active or if one is only standby. In this example, we have none set for standby, meaning both are functional. From the Teaming Mode drop-down menu, we have chosen Switch Independent, which means that we intend to connect each adapter to a different switch. The Load Balancing drop-down menu allows you to select the method used to distribute the traffic between the two adapters. We set it to Address Hash, which means it will keep all traffic that is part of the same conversation or session on the same adapter.

5. Click OK and the new team is created. You will be returned to the previous dialog box, with the new team listed in the Teams pane.

You can also set up a NIC team in Linux. In Exercise 5.2, you will create a NIC team from two adapters, Ethernet 1 and Ethernet 2, and they will be teamed into an object called Bond0. You will implement round robin, in which both adapters are used.

EXERCISE 5.2

Configuring a NIC Team

 This exercise uses Linux and will only work on Red Hat distributions.

1. Configure Ethernet 1 to be used as a slave by bond0 by opening the ifcfg-eth1 file and editing it as follows:

    ```
    # vi /etc/sysconfig/network-scripts/ifcfg-eth1
    DEVICE="eth1"
    TYPE=Ethernet
    ONBOOT="yes"
    BOOTPROTO="none"
    USERCTL=no
    MASTER=bond0
    SLAVE=yes
    ```

2. Repeat the same procedure on Ethernet 2, as shown here:

    ```
    # vi /etc/sysconfig/network-scripts/ifcfg-eth2
    DEVICE="eth2"
    TYPE=Ethernet
    ONBOOT="yes"
    BOOTPROTO="none"
    USERCTL=no
    MASTER=bond0
    SLAVE=yes
    ```

3. Create the bond0 interface in the /etc/sysconfig/network-scripts/ directory, name it **ifcfg-bond0**, and configure channel bonding:

    ```
    # vi /etc/sysconfig/network-scripts/ifcfg-bond0
    DEVICE=bond0
    ONBOOT=yes
    IPADDR=192.168.246.130
    NETMASK=255.255.255.0
    BONDING_OPTS="mode=0 miimon=100"
    ```

    ```
    Bonding mode=0       means round robin.
    miimon=100           is the polling interval.
    ```

4. Restart the network to make the team functional, as shown here:

    ```
    # systemd: systemctl restart network
    ```

Failover

As you learned earlier in this chapter, failover is when a failed components workload is switched over to a backup component. In this case, when a NIC team is used for fault tolerance this means that the backup NIC takes over for the failing NIC.

Link Aggregation

Link aggregation was discussed in the earlier section "Load balancing."

Summary

In this chapter you learned about methods of providing fault tolerance both at the server and the component levels. These methods included clustering approaches, such as active–active and active–passive deployments.

You also learned about load balancing and methods to allocate the workload such as round robin and most recently used algorithms. Finally we discussed using NIC teaming to provide fault tolerance and high availability to a network connection.

Exam Essentials

Describe clustering deployment options.   Clustering deployment options include active–active and active–passive setups. You also need to know about failover and failback and the function of the cluster heartbeat.

Explain the approaches to load balancing.   Be able to describe the difference between software and hardware load balancing. Also be able to explain the operation of the most recently used (MRU) and round robin allocation methods.

Review Questions

You can find the answers in the Appendix.

1. Which type of fault tolerance is recommended for servers running applications that do not have long-running in-memory state or frequently updated data?

   A. Load balancing

   B. Hot site

   C. Clustering

   D. Cold site

2. Which of the following is a standard method of implementing NIC teaming?

   A. 802.1ax-2008

   B. 802.3

   C. 802.1x

   D. 802.3g

3. What file do you edit in Linux to configure the Ethernet 5 interface to be used in a NIC team?

   A. `ifcfg-eth1`

   B. `ifcfg-bond0`

   C. `ifcfg-eth5`

   D. `ifcfg-bond5`

4. _____ is when a failed components workload is switched over to a backup component.

   A. Failback

   B. Failover

   C. Crossover

   D. Recall

5. Which of the following is a connection between servers in a load balancing scenario across which the servers send a signal used to determine when the other server is down?

   A. Heartbeat

   B. Cluster ID

   C. Magic packet

   D. WOL

6. Which of the following controls the establishment of the aggregated link based on the proper combination of settings of the ends of the multiple links and on the agreement of certain settings on all physical links in the "bundle"?

   A. STP

   B. SSL

   C. LACP

   D. PGP

7. Which of the following is a switching loop prevention protocol?

   A. SSL

   B. STP

   C. SSH

   D. SAG

8. In which clustering deployment are both or all servers actively servicing the workload?

   A. Passive–passive

   B. Active–passive

   C. Active–active

   D. Hybrid

9. Which method of allocating work in a load balancing scenario attempts to send clients into running servers, preferably the most recently used server, before starting new servers?

   A. MRU

   B. FIFO

   C. Hybrid

   D. LIFO

10. Which of the following is the process of combining multiple physical network connections into a single logical interface?

    A. Link bonding

    B. NIC teaming

    C. NIC aggregation

    D. MRU

11. Which of the following is generally recommended for servers running applications that have long-running in-memory state or frequently updated data?

    A. Load balancing

    B. Clustering

    C. RAID

    D. NIC teaming

12. In which load balancing allocation system does the load balancer allocate work requests to each server sequentially, resulting in each getting an equal number of requests?

A. MRU

B. Active–active

C. Round robin

D. Active–passive

13. Which of the following is the process of combining multiple physical or virtual servers together in an arrangement in which the servers work together to service the same workload or application?

A. JBOD

B. Clustering

C. Duplexing

D. NIC team

14. Which of the following types of fault tolerance is recommended for applications that do not have long-running in-memory state or frequently updated data?

A. Clustering

B. Load balancing

C. RAID

D. NIC teaming

15. Which of the following is a term that describes when the original system goes back online and the workload is moved back to the original system?

A. Failover

B. Failback

C. Heartbeat

D. Resumption

16. Which of the following can be done with either software or hardware?

A. Load balancing

B. Clustering

C. Heartbeat

D. Failover

17. What is another name for NIC teaming?

A. Link aggregation

B. NIC tunneling

C. NRP

D. STP

18. Which of the following is also an IEEE standard later replaced by 802.1ax-2008?

   A. 802.11a

   B. 802.1ad

   C. 802.15

   D. 802.3ad

19. In which of the following load balancing algorithms could a user make two requests that actually go to two different servers?

   A. MRU

   B. Active–active

   C. Round robin

   D. Active–passive

20. Which of the following devices will stand between the work requests and the work servers and will allocate work between the systems?

   A. Load balancer

   B. Fiber switch

   C. NIC team

   D. Jump server

Chapter

6

Securing the Server

COMPTIA SERVER+ EXAM OBJECTIVES COVERED IN THIS CHAPTER:

✓ **3.2 Summarize physical security concepts.**

- Physical access controls
    - Bollards
    - Architectural reinforcements
        - Signal blocking
        - Reflective glass
        - Datacenter camouflage
    - Fencing
    - Security guards
    - Security cameras
    - Locks
        - Biometric
        - Radio frequency identification (RFID)
        - Card readers
    - Mantraps
    - Safes
- Environmental controls
    - Fire suppression
    - Heating, ventilation, and cooling (HVAC)
    - Sensors

✓ **3.4 Explain data security risks and mitigation strategies.**

- Security risks
    - Hardware failure
    - Malware
    - Data corruption

- Insider threats
- Theft
  - Data loss prevention (DLP)
  - Unwanted duplication
  - Unwanted publication
- Unwanted access methods
  - Backdoor
  - Social engineering
  - Breaches
    - Identification
    - Disclosure
- Mitigation strategies
  - Data monitoring
  - Log analysis
    - Security information and event management (SIEM)
  - Two-person integrity
    - Split encryption keys tokens
    - Separation of roles
  - Regulatory constraints
    - Governmental
    - Individually privileged information
      - Personally identifiable information (PII)
      - Payment Card Industry Data Security Standard (PCI DSS)
  - Legal considerations
    - Data retention
    - Subpoenas

✓ **3.5 Given a scenario, apply server hardening methods.**

- OS hardening
    - Disable unused services
    - Close unneeded ports
    - Install only required software
    - Apply driver updates
    - Apply OS updates
    - Firewall configuration
- Application hardening
    - Install latest patches
    - Disable unneeded services, roles, or features
- Host security
    - Antivirus
    - Anti-malware
    - Host intrusion detection system (HIDS)/Host intrusion prevention system (HIPS)
- Hardware hardening
    - Disable unneeded hardware
    - Disable unneeded physical ports, devices, or functions
    - Set BIOS password
    - Set boot order
- Patching
    - Testing
    - Deployment
    - Change management

Once you've deployed your server and verified that it is functioning, you must also maintain the server and ensure that the server is secured from attacks from insiders as well as outsiders. Securing the server means that it is capable of providing the three tenets of security: confidentiality, integrity, and availability (CIA). Confidentiality means that the data is accessible only to those who have that right, integrity means that the data has not been altered or corrupted, and availability means that the server is always there as a resource. To provide those three tenets, the server must not only be secured but also maintained so that it is not overloaded or down for service.

Summarize Physical Security Concepts

Although there are many logical security methods that can be used to protect the data on a server, if users can attain physical access to the server, the options available to them to compromise the server increase dramatically. For this reason, servers and other infrastructure equipment should be locked away. In this section we'll look at physical methods used to achieve this.

Physical Access Controls

Measures taken to mitigate physical access attacks are called controls. In this section you'll learn about the types of controls that can be used to prevent or at least mitigate the damage of physical attacks.

Bollards

Barriers called bollards have become quite common around the perimeter of new office and government buildings. These are short vertical posts placed at the building's entrance way and lining sidewalks that help to provide protection from vehicles that might either intentionally or unintentionally crash into or enter the building or injure pedestrians. They can be made of many types of materials. Three types of bollards are shown in Figure 6.1.

FIGURE 6.1   Bollards

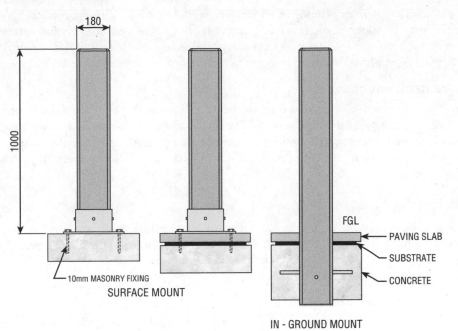

SURFACE MOUNT

IN - GROUND MOUNT

Architectural Reinforcements

Crime Prevention Through Environmental Design (CPTED) refers to designing the facility from the ground up to support security. It is a broad concept that can be applied to any project (such as housing developments, office buildings, and retail establishments). It addresses the building entrance, landscaping, and interior design. It aims to create behavioral effects that reduce crime. In this section you'll learn about measures that can support and enhance CPTED.

Signal Blocking

One technique that can be used to prevent data leakage through radio waves is to use signal blocking materials on walls and windows. This can prevent the reception of any wireless transmissions outside the facility. It is useful to know that by using a high-powered antenna (which is illegal) a hacker can be far away from your building and still receive these signals. While many building materials such as metal and concrete will provide limited protection, you can also use special paint on the walls that will block these signals.

Sometimes emissions coming from the servers themselves can disclose sensitive information. This issue can be addressed by placing the server inside enclosures that can block signals. One example is called a Faraday cage, which implements an outer barrier or coating called a Faraday shield.

Reflective Glass

In areas where sensitive operations are being performed or where sensitive discussions or planning may be taking place, you need to prevent prying eyes from seeing what's going on. When there are windows in the area of concern, you should use reflective glass to prevent the viewing of information that may be written on boards or displayed on screens.

Datacenter Camouflage

Your datacenter should be located in an isolated area if possible and made indistinguishable from other industrial buildings. CPTED calls for using natural landscape elements for camouflage, such as dense trees or even a mountain range. Finally, a datacenter should be enclosed by a wall or metal fence that is difficult to pass through. (More on fences in the next section.)

Fencing

Fencing is the first line of defense in the concentric circle paradigm. When selecting the type of fencing to install, consider the determination of the individual you are trying to discourage. Use the following guidelines with respect to height:

- 3′–4′-tall fences deter only casual intruders.
- 6′–7′-tall fences are too tall to climb easily.
- 8′ and taller fences tend to stop more determined intruders, especially when augmented with razor wire.

Security Guards

Security guards offer the most flexibility in reacting to whatever occurs. Guards can use discriminating judgment based on the situation, which automated systems cannot do. This makes them an excellent addition to the layers of security you should be trying to create. One of the keys to success is adequate training of the guards so that they are prepared for any eventuality. You should create a prepared response for any possible occurrence.

Security Cameras

If you use security guards, you can make them more effective by implementing closed-circuit television (CCTV) systems. These are cameras that can be monitored in real time, allowing guards to monitor larger areas at once from a central location. Even in the absence of guards, these systems can record days of activity that can be viewed as needed at a later time.

Locks

One of the easiest ways to prevent people intent on creating problems from physically entering your environment is to lock your doors and keep them out. A key aspect of access control involves physical barriers. The objective of a physical barrier is to prevent access to computers and network systems. The most effective physical barrier implementations require that more than one physical barrier be crossed to gain access. This type of approach is called a multiple-barrier system. This means a lock to protect the facility, another to protect the server room, and another to open the rack. In this section you'll learn about access control systems that control physical access.

Biometric

For high-security scenarios that warrant the additional cost and administrative effort involved, biometrics is a viable option. Biometric devices use physical characteristics to identify the user. Such devices are becoming more common in the business environment. Biometric systems include hand scanners, retinal scanners, and soon, possibly, DNA scanners. To gain access to resources, you must pass a physical screening process. In the case of a hand scanner, this may include identifying fingerprints, scars, and markings on your hand. Retinal scanners compare your eye's retinal pattern, which are as unique as fingerprints, to a stored retinal pattern to verify your identity. DNA scanners will examine a unique portion of your DNA structure to verify that you are who you say you are.

With the passing of time, the definition of *biometric* is expanding from simply identifying physical attributes about a person to being able to describe patterns in their behavior. Recent advances have been made in the ability to authenticate someone based on the key pattern they use when entering their password (how long they pause between each key, the amount of time each key is held down, and so forth). A company adopting biometric technologies needs to consider the controversy they may face (some authentication methods are considered more intrusive than others). It also needs to consider the error rate and that errors can include both false positives and false negatives.

Radio Frequency Identification (RFID)

An increasingly popular method of tracking physical assets is to tag them with radio frequency identification (RFID) chips. This allows you to track the location of the asset at any time. This technology uses either bar codes or magnetic strips to embed information that can read wirelessly from some distance. Here are the main components:

RFID Reader   This device has an antenna and an interface to a computer.

Transponder   This is the tag on the device that transmits its presence wirelessly.

The reader receives instructions from the human using the software on the computer that is attached to the reader. This causes the reader to transmit signals that wake up or energize the transponder on the device. The device then responds wirelessly, thus allowing the reader to determine the location of the device and display that location to the user on the computer.

The tags can be one of two types: passive and active. Active tags have batteries, whereas passive tags receive their energy from the reader when the reader interrogates the device. As you would expect, the passive tags are cheaper but have a range of only a few meters, whereas the active tags are more expensive but can transmit up to 100 meters.

The drawbacks of this technology are that the tag signal can be read by any reader in range, multiple readers in an area can interfere with one another, and multiple devices can interfere with one another when responding.

Finally, given the distance limitations, once the stolen item is a certain distance away, you lose the ability to track it, so this technology should only be a part of a larger program that includes strong physical security. As you will see later in this section, asset tracking is not the only use for RFID tags.

Card Readers

All users should possess and wear identification cards, but it becomes even more important when those users have access to the server room. A number of different technologies can be used to make these cards part of the authentication process:

Key Fobs   Named after the chains that used to hold pocket watches to clothes. They are security devices that you carry with you that display a randomly generated code that you can then use for authentication. This code usually changes quickly (every 60 seconds is about the average), and you combine this code with your PIN for authentication.

Radio Frequency Identification (RFID)   A wireless, no-contact technology used with these cards and their accompanying reader. The reader is connected to the network and validates against the security system. This increases the security of the authentication process because you must be in physical possession of the smart card to use the resources. Of course, if the card is lost or stolen, the person who finds the card can access the resources it allows.

Smart Card   A type of badge or card that gives you access to resources, including buildings, parking lots, and computers. It contains information about your identity and access privileges. Each area or computer has a card scanner or a reader in which you insert your card. Smart cards are difficult to counterfeit, but they're easy to steal. Once a thief has a smart card, that person has all the access the card allows. To prevent this, many organizations don't put any identifying marks on their smart cards, making it harder for someone to utilize them. Many modern smart cards require a password or PIN to activate the card, and they employ encryption to protect the card's contents.

Physical Tokens   Anything, including key fobs, that users must have on them to access network resources. They are often associated with devices that enable users to generate a one-time password authenticating their identity. SecurID, from RSA, is one of the best-known examples of a physical token; learn more at `www.securid.com`.

KEYPAD

An older technology that is still enjoying widespread use are door keypads, where the user enters a code into the keypad that identifies them, authenticates them, and if allowed, opens the door for them. In many cases these devices can also be configured with an emergency code that can be used when a personal code doesn't work and an alarm code that opens the door but alerts police or other authorities that a hostage scenario is underway.

Mantraps

A *mantrap*, or security vestibule (see Figure 6.2), is a series of two doors with a small room between them. The user is authenticated at the first door and then allowed into the room. At that point additional verification will occur (such as a guard visually identifying the person) and then the user is allowed through the second door. These doors are typically used only in very high security situations. Security vestibules also typically require that the first door be closed prior to enabling the second door to open.

FIGURE 6.2   Mantrap, or security vestibule

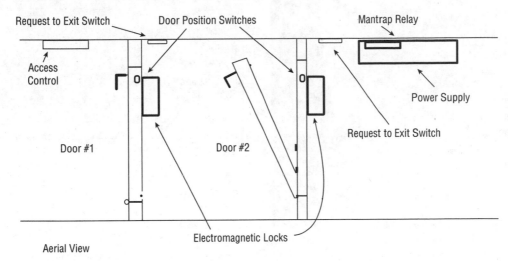

Safes

You also have items that need to be secured that are not servers. Installation CDs and DVDs, network diagrams, disaster recovery plans, and backup tapes are all examples of these items. When considering a safe, you should focus on two items: the ease with which the safe can be compromised, and the ability of the safe to withstand a fire.

In the United States, United Laboratories (UL) assigns ratings to safes that you can use to assess the suitability of the safe. These ratings typically assign a recommended maximum dollar figure that any item you wish to protect with the safe should not exceed. Use these values to guide your choice.

With respect to fire, first understand that no safe is fireproof. Many are fire-resistant and will protect a document from being destroyed, which occurs at a much higher temperature than many of the other items (such as backup tapes and CDs) can tolerate without damage. For this reason, items such as backup tapes should be stored offsite.

Cabinet

Any cabinets that are used to hold spare equipment or tools should be locked and all keys should be accounted for. Any cabinets that enclose racks of servers should be locked as well. This includes all types of equipment enclosures. Some of these locks can be integrated into your access control system, and some also alert you when a cabinet door is opened. An example of one of these locks is shown in Figure 6.3.

FIGURE 6.3   Cabinet lock with alarm

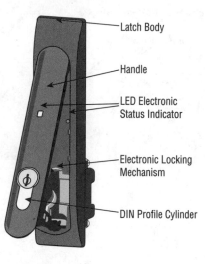

Latch Body

Handle

LED Electronic
Status Indicator

Electronic Locking
Mechanism

DIN Profile Cylinder

Environmental Controls

You might think it a bit off topic to discuss environmental controls in a security chapter. However, it makes perfect sense to do so if you consider what the A in the security triad CIA stands for. CIA is an acronym for the three goals of security: to provide confidentiality (data can be read only by those for which it is intended), integrity (the data has not been altered in any way), and availability (the data is available to those who need it when they need it).

It is the goal of availability that maintaining proper environmental control serves. When proper environmental practices are not in place, servers lock up, shut down, and suffer any number of ailments that make them unable to perform their role or make their resources available. With that said, let's close this section covering best practices.

Fire Suppression

You also must protect yourself and the equipment from fire. While having the proper fire extinguishers handy is important, what happens if no one is there? Fire suppression systems are designed to detect the fire and address the situation. There are several types of systems you can use:

Wet Pipe   Wet pipe systems use water contained in pipes to extinguish the fire. In some areas, the water may freeze and burst the pipes, causing damage. These systems are not recommended for rooms where equipment will be damaged by the water.

Dry Pipe   In this system the water is not held in the pipes but in a holding tank. The pipes hold pressurized air, which is reduced when fire is detected, allowing the water to enter the pipe and the sprinklers. This minimizes the chance of an accidental discharge. A comparison of a wet pipe and dry pipe system is shown in Figure 6.4.

FIGURE 6.4   Wet and dry systems

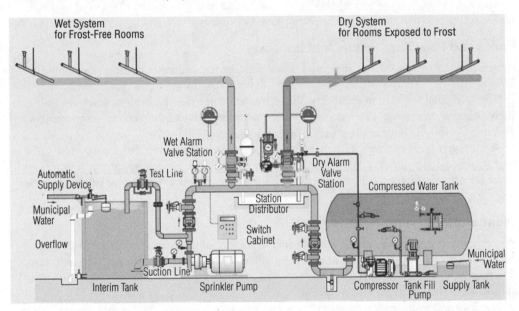

Preaction   This system operates like a dry pipe system except that the sprinkler head holds a thermal-fusible link that must be melted before the water is released. This is currently the recommended system for a computer room.

Deluge   This system allows large amounts of water to be released into the room, which obviously makes this a poor choice for areas where computing equipment is located.

At one time, fire suppression systems used Halon gas, which works well by suppressing combustion through a chemical reaction. However, these systems are no longer used because they have been found to damage the ozone layer.

Environmental Protection Agency (EPA)-approved replacements for Halon include:

- Water
- Argon
- NAF-S-III

Another fire suppression system that can be used in computer rooms that will not damage computers and is safe for humans is FM-200. NAF-S-III shows physical characteristics similar to those of Halon 1301 without the ozone-depleting characteristics. FM-200 is an alternative to Halon from DuPont.

Heating, Ventilation, and Cooling (HVAC)

As stated in the beginning of this chapter, ensuring availability of resources stored on the servers is also a part of the security function. This cannot be done unless the environment in which the servers operate meets certain standards. In this section we'll focus on the heating, ventilation, and air conditioning (HVAC) systems and best practices for ensuring that the server room provides an optimal operational environment to the devices.

Room and Rack Temperature and Humidity

A critical issue that must be considered is maintaining the proper temperate and humidity level for the devices. Maintaining an ambient temperature range of 68° to 75°F (20° to 24°C) is optimal for system reliability. When temperatures rise, bad things start to occur such as server rebooting. Computers can tolerate (and enjoy) slightly colder temperatures without trouble, as long as there aren't huge fluctuations.

A humidity level between 45 percent and 55 percent is recommended for optimal performance and reliability. When the level is too high, it causes condensation, which is bad news for any electronics. When the level is too low, the dry air is conducive to electrostatic discharge (ESD).

Monitoring and Alert Notifications

When either the humidity or the temperature is outside of the recommended range, you need to know it. Even if you are in the room when this occurs, you may not notice it. For this reason, you need to have an environmental monitoring system in place and that system should have the ability to alert someone.

Hardware devices are made (usually rack mountable) that can do this monitoring. Most can also tell you when water is present and when cases or cabinets have been opened. Figure 6.5 shows an example of a monitor in a rack. On the back are connections to various types of sensors. Sensor data can be retrieved from the system using HTTP requests. It can be monitored from a web interface as well. If an event occurs, it can alert you via email, SNMP, or SMS.

Sensors

Alarm systems using sensors can alert you when a physical intrusion has occurred. There are various technologies you can deploy, including these:

- **Passive infrared systems (PIR)** operate by identifying changes in heat waves in an area. Because the presence of an intruder would raise the temperature of the surrounding air particles, this system alerts or sounds an alarm when this occurs.

- **Electromechanical systems** operate by detecting a break in an electrical circuit. For example, the circuit might cross a window or door and when the window or door is opened, the circuit is broken, setting off an alarm of some sort. Another example might be a pressure pad placed under the carpet to detect the presence of individuals.

- **Photoelectric systems** operate by detecting changes in the light and thus are used in windowless areas. They send a beam of light across the area and if the beam is interrupted (by a person, for example), the alarm is triggered.

- **Acoustical detection systems** use strategically placed microphones to detect any sound made during a forced entry. These systems only work well in areas where there is not a lot of surrounding noise. They are typically very sensitive, which would cause many false alarms in a loud area, such as a door next to a busy street.

- **Wave motion detectors** generate a wave pattern in the area and detect any motion that disturbs the wave pattern. When the pattern is disturbed, an alarm sounds.

- **Capacitance detectors** emit a magnetic field and monitor that field. If the field is disrupted, which will occur when a person enters the area, the alarm will sound.

FIGURE 6.5   Rack monitor

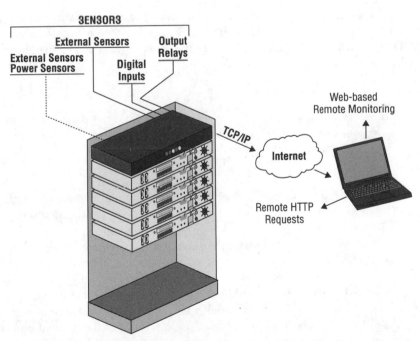

Explain Data Security Risks and Mitigation Strategies

While securing the server from physical access is of immense importance, securing the data that resides on the server is also critical and requires a different approach. Logical or technical controls are used to protect this data. We have to be concerned about the security of the data when it is en route to the user across the network and when it is at rest on the storage media.

Security Risks

Many attacks are made possible because our systems are not secured as well as they could be. When this is the situation, we say a vulnerability exists. In other cases, issues beyond your control may create a security issue. In this section you'll learn about some major vulnerabilities and security risks.

Hardware Failure

In some cases, hardware fails and creates a security issue. For example, if the server goes down and is not available to the users, the effect is the same as if you suffered a denial-of-service (DoS) attack. Keep in mind that one of the goals of security as stated in the CIA model is availability.

Malware

Malware is a category of software that performs malicious activities on a device. It might wipe the hard drive or create a backdoor. In this section we'll look at types of malware and attacks.

Trojan

Trojan horses are programs that enter a system or network under the guise of another program. A Trojan horse may be included as an attachment or as part of an installation program. The Trojan horse can create a backdoor or replace a valid program during installation. It then accomplishes its mission under the guise of another program. Trojan horses can be used to compromise the security of your system, and they can exist on a system for years before they're detected.

The best preventive measure for Trojan horses is not to allow them entry into your system. Immediately before and after you install a new software program or operating system, back it up! If you suspect a Trojan horse, you can reinstall the original programs, which should delete the Trojan horse. A port scan may also reveal a Trojan horse on your system. If an application opens a TCP or IP port that isn't supported in your network, you can track it down and determine which port is being used.

Rootkit

Rootkits have become the software exploitation program du jour. They are software programs that have the ability to hide certain things from the operating system. With a rootkit, there may be a number of processes running on a system that don't show up in Task Manager, or connections may be established/available that don't appear in a Netstat display—the rootkit masks the presence of these items. The rootkit does this by manipulating function calls to the operating system and filtering out information that would normally appear.

Unfortunately, many rootkits are written to get around antivirus and antispyware programs that aren't kept up-to-date. The best defense you have is to monitor what your system is doing and catch the rootkit in the process of installation.

Virus

Viruses can be classified as polymorphic, stealth, retroviruses, multipartite, armored, companion, phage, and macro viruses. Each type of virus has a different attack strategy and different consequences.

Estimates for losses due to viruses are in the billions of dollars. These losses include financial loss as well as lost productivity.

The following sections introduce the symptoms of a virus infection, explain how a virus works, and describe the types of viruses you can expect to encounter and how they generally behave. I'll also discuss how a virus is transmitted through a network.

Symptoms of a Virus/Malware Infection

Many viruses will announce that you're infected as soon as they gain access to your system. They may take control of your system and flash annoying messages on your screen or destroy your hard disk. When this occurs, you'll know that you're a victim. Other viruses will cause your system to slow down, cause files to disappear from your computer, or take over your disk space.

Because viruses are the most common malware, the term *virus* is used in this section.

You should look for some of the following symptoms when determining whether a virus infection has occurred:

- The programs on your system start to load more slowly. This happens because the virus is spreading to other files in your system or is taking over system resources.

- Unusual files appear on your hard drive, or files start to disappear from your system. Many viruses delete key files in your system to render it inoperable.

- Program sizes change from the installed versions. This occurs because the virus is attaching itself to these programs on your disk.

- Your browser, word processing application, or other software begins to exhibit unusual operating characteristics. Screens or menus may change.

- The system mysteriously shuts itself down or starts itself up and does a great deal of unanticipated disk activity.

- You mysteriously lose access to a disk drive or other system resources. The virus has changed the settings on a device to make it unusable.

- Your system suddenly doesn't reboot or gives unexpected error messages during startup.

This list is by no means comprehensive. What is an absolute, however, is that you should immediately quarantine the infected system. It is imperative that you do all you can to contain the virus and keep it from spreading to other systems within your network or beyond.

How Viruses Work

A virus, in most cases, tries to accomplish one of two things: render your system inoperable or spread itself to other systems. Many viruses will spread to other systems given the chance and then render your system unusable. This is common with many of the newer viruses.

If your system is infected, the virus may try to attach itself to every file in your system and spread each time you send a file or document to other users. When you give removable media to another user or put it into another system, you then infect that system with the virus.

Most viruses today are spread using email. The infected system attaches a file to any email that you send to another user. The recipient opens this file, thinking it's something you legitimately sent them. When they open the file, the virus infects the target system. The virus might then attach itself to all the emails the newly infected system sends, which in turn infects the recipients of the emails. Figure 6.6 shows how a virus can spread from a single user to thousands of users in a short time using email.

Types of Viruses

Viruses take many different forms. The following sections briefly introduce these forms and explain how they work. These are the most common types, but this isn't a comprehensive list.

> **NOTE** The best defense against a virus attack is to install and run antivirus software. The software should be on all workstations as well as the server.

Armored Virus

An *armored virus* is designed to make itself difficult to detect or analyze. Armored viruses cover themselves with protective code that stops debuggers or disassemblers from examining critical elements of the virus. The virus may be written in such a way that some aspects of the programming act as a decoy to distract analysis while the actual code hides in other areas in the program.

FIGURE 6.6   An email virus spreading geometrically to other users

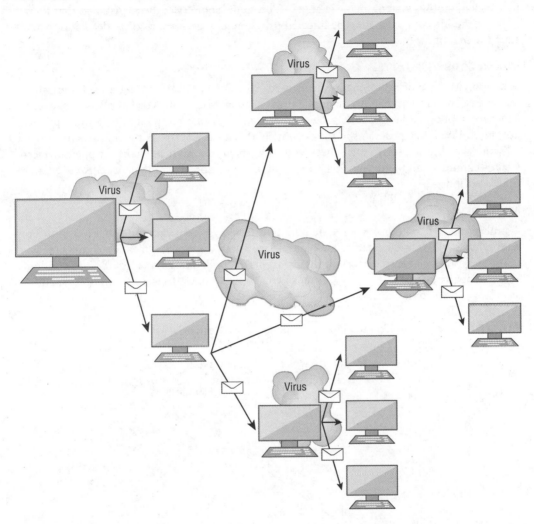

From the perspective of the creator, the more time it takes to deconstruct the virus, the longer it can live. The longer it can live, the more time it has to replicate and spread to as many machines as possible. The key to stopping most viruses is to identify them quickly and educate administrators about them—the very things that the armor intensifies the difficulty of accomplishing.

Companion Virus

A companion virus attaches itself to legitimate programs and then creates a program with a different filename extension. This file may reside in your system's temporary directory. When a user types the name of the legitimate program, the companion virus executes instead of the real program. This effectively hides the virus from the user. Many of the viruses that are used to attack Windows systems make changes to program pointers in the Registry so that they point to the infected program. The infected program may perform its dirty deed and then start the real program.

Macro Virus

A macro virus exploits the enhancements made to many application programs. Programmers can expand the capability of applications such as Microsoft Word and Excel. Word, for example, supports a mini-BASIC programming language that allows files to be manipulated automatically. These programs in the document are called macros. For example, a macro can tell your word processor to spell-check your document automatically when it opens. Macro viruses can infect all the documents on your system and spread to other systems via email or other methods.

Multipartite Virus

A multipartite virus attacks your system in multiple ways. It may attempt to infect your boot sector, infect all your executables files, and destroy your application files. The hope here is that you won't be able to correct all the problems and will allow the infestation to continue. The multipartite virus in Figure 6.7 attacks your boot sector, infects application files, and attacks your Word documents.

FIGURE 6.7   A multipartite virus commencing an attack on a system

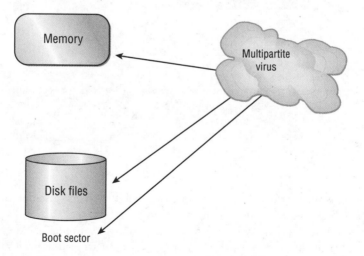

Phage Virus

A phage virus alters other programs and databases. The virus infects all these files. The only way to remove this virus is to reinstall the programs that are infected. If you miss even a single instance of this virus on the victim system, the process will start again and infect the system once more.

Polymorphic Virus

Polymorphic viruses change form in order to avoid detection. The virus will attempt to hide from your antivirus software. Frequently, the virus will encrypt parts of itself to avoid detection. When the virus does this, it's referred to as mutation. The mutation process makes it hard for antivirus software to detect common characteristics of the virus. Figure 6.8 shows a polymorphic virus changing its characteristics to avoid detection. In this example, the virus changes a signature to fool antivirus software.

FIGURE 6.8   The polymorphic virus changing its characteristics

  A signature is an algorithm or other element of a virus that uniquely identifies it. Because some viruses have the ability to alter their signature,
it is crucial that you keep signature files current, whether you choose
to manually download them or configure the antivirus engine to do so
automatically.

Retrovirus

A retrovirus attacks or bypasses the antivirus software installed on a computer. You can consider a retrovirus to be an antivirus. Retroviruses can directly attack your antivirus software and potentially destroy the virus definition database file. Destroying this information without your knowledge would leave you with a false sense of security. The virus may also directly attack an antivirus program to create bypasses for itself.

Stealth Virus

A stealth virus attempts to avoid detection by masking itself from applications. It may attach itself to the boot sector of the hard drive. When a system utility or program runs, the stealth virus redirects commands around itself to avoid detection. An infected file may report a file size different from what is actually present to avoid detection. Figure 6.9 shows a stealth virus attaching itself to the boot sector to avoid detection. Stealth viruses may also move themselves from file A to file B during a virus scan for the same reason.

FIGURE 6.9   A stealth virus hiding in a disk boot sector

← This is a disk.

Boot record   Virus

Present Virus Activity

New viruses and threats are released on a regular basis to join the cadre of those already in existence. From an exam perspective, you need to be familiar with the world only as it existed at the time the questions were written. From an administrative standpoint, however, you need to know what is happening today.

To find this information, visit the Cybersecurity and Infrastructure Security Agency Current Activity web page at www.cisa.gov/uscert/ncas/current-activity. Here you'll find a detailed description of the most current viruses as well as links to pages on older threats.

Spyware

Spyware differs from other malware in that it works—often actively—on behalf of a third party. Rather than self-replicating, like viruses and worms, spyware is spread to machines by users who inadvertently ask for it. The users often don't know they have asked for the spyware but have done so by downloading other programs, visiting infected sites, and so on.

The spyware program monitors the user's activity and responds by offering unsolicited pop-up advertisements (sometimes known as adware), gathers information about the user to pass on to marketers, or intercepts personal data such as credit card numbers.

Ransomware

Ransomware is a type of malware that usually encrypts the entire system or an entire drive with an encryption key that only the hacker possesses. Once they encrypt the machine, the hacker will hold the data residing on the device hostage until a ransom is paid.

The latest version of this attack arrives as an attachment that appears to be a résumé. However, when the attachment is opened, the malware uses software called Cryptowall to encrypt the device. What usually follows is a demand for a large amount of money to decrypt the device. Payments must usually be in cryptocurrency, and paying the ransom is no guarantee that your data will be decrypted.

Keylogger

A keylogger records everything typed and sends a record of this to the attacker. It can be implemented as a malicious software package, maybe even as part of a rootkit, or it may be a hardware device inserted between the keyboard and the USB port.

Boot Sector Virus

Earlier in this section you learned that many viruses can infect the boot sector of floppy disks or the Master Boot Record (MBR) of hard disks (some infect the boot sector of the hard disk instead of the MBR). The infected code runs when the system is booted. If the virus cannot be removed due to encryption or excessive damage to existing code, the hard drive may need reformatting to eliminate the infection.

Cryptominers

Cryptominers are tools that generate new units of a cryptocurrency like Bitcoin. Cryptomining isn't itself malicious in nature. But bad actors are illegally accessing important business assets such as servers to use their processing power to solve the mathematical puzzles required to mine. This consumes CPU cycles and increases the power usage in the datacenter. The result will be slower performance such as you might get from malware.

Data Corruption

Data corruption is also a possibility when data is being written to and read from a drive and when data is being transferred within a system and between systems. If even a single bit in a file is altered at any time, the data will no longer pass the CRC check and will be considered by the system to be corrupted.

So how does corruption occur? There are a number of ways:

- Failure to eject external hard drives and related storage devices before disconnecting them or powering them off
- Power outages or other power-related problems
- Hardware problems or failures, including hard drive failures, bad sectors, bad RAM, and the like
- Bad programming, particularly if it results in either hard restarts or data that is saved incorrectly
- Improper shutdowns, like those caused by power outages or by performing a hard restart, pressing and holding the power button, or on Macs so equipped, the restart button

If the corrupted files are system files, the system may not even boot. If this is the case, try performing one of the system repair processes, which will check the integrity of all system files and replace any bad ones.

In Linux, you can use the `fsck` command to make a repair attempt. For example, the following command will check the sda1 partition:

```
fsck /dev/sda1
```

It is important to note that this command should *not* be used on a mounted drive. If you do so, you run the risk of damaging the filesystem and making the issue worse. If you want `fsck` to attempt to repair any errors it finds, add the `-a` or `-y` parameter after the command, as shown here for the same partition:

```
fsck -a /dev/sda1
```

Of course, if these recovery procedures are not useful, you can restore the data from backup.

Insider Threats

Insider threats should be one of the biggest concerns for security personnel. Insiders have knowledge of and access to systems that outsiders do not have, giving insiders a much easier avenue for carrying out or participating in an attack. An organization should implement the appropriate event collection and log review policies to provide the means to detect insider threats as they occur. These threats fall into two categories: intentional and unintentional.

Intentional

Intentional insider threats are insiders who have ill intent. These folks typically either are disgruntled over some perceived slight or are working for another organization to perform corporate espionage. They may share sensitive documents with others or they may impart knowledge used to breach a network. This is one of the reasons that users' permissions and rights must not exceed those necessary to perform their jobs. This practice helps limit the damage an insider might inflict.

Unintentional

Sometimes internal users unknowingly increase the likelihood that security breaches will occur. Such unintentional insider threats do not have malicious intent; they simply do not understand how system changes can affect security.

Security awareness and training should include coverage of examples of misconfigurations that can result in security breaches occurring and/or not being detected. For example, a user may temporarily disable antivirus software to perform an administrative task. If the user fails to reenable the antivirus software, they unknowingly leave the system open to viruses. In such a case, an organization should consider implementing Group Policies or some other mechanism to periodically ensure that antivirus software is enabled and running. Another solution could be to configure antivirus software to automatically restart after a certain amount of time.

Recording and reviewing user actions via system, audit, and security logs can help security professionals identify misconfigurations so that the appropriate policies and controls can be implemented.

Theft

Data theft sometimes results from theft of a device. In this case, the remote wipe feature can be used to prevent data theft. In many cases, data theft results from transmission of sensitive data in cleartext. Many devices transmit data in cleartext, and sometimes they do it wirelessly. Choosing a device that does not transmit data in cleartext is advised.

There are other ways that data fall into the wrong hands. In this section you'll learn about other ways this can occur and how to prevent this.

Unwanted Duplication

In some cases data that is identical in every way is stored in multiple locations. There are two problems with this scenario:

- This uses storage space needlessly.
- It creates multiple points of potential compromise.

To address this issue, you can use disk deduplication tools to identify and consolidate these duplicates into a single location. This process is illustrated in Figure 6.10.

FIGURE 6.10   Deduplication

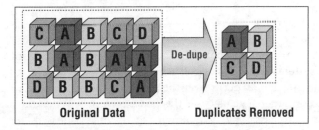

Other techniques for protecting your data will be discussed in the coming sections.

Data Loss Prevention (DLP)

Data loss prevention (DLP) software attempts to prevent data leakage. It does this by maintaining awareness of actions that can and cannot be taken with respect to a document. For example, it might allow printing of a document but only at the company office. It might also disallow sending the document through email. DLP software uses ingress and egress filters to identify sensitive data that is leaving the organization and can prevent such leakage. Ingress filters examine information that is entering the network, whereas egress filters examine information that is leaving the network. Using an egress filter is one of the main mitigations to data exfiltration, which is the unauthorized transfer of data from a network.

Let's look at an example. Suppose that product plans should be available only to the Marketing group. For that document you might create a policy that specifies the following:

- It cannot be emailed to anyone other than Sales group members.
- It cannot be printed.
- It cannot be copied.

Unwanted Publication

In today's world, it is sometimes difficult to keep a lid on the unwanted publication of company data to social media. Users often overshare company data, including plans, designs, and procedures.

- Policies should be developed that address the use of social media, and these policies should be made obvious to the user to prevent this type of data publication. Many times it's not intentional at all and can be corrected with training.

Unwanted Access Methods

There are other scenarios in which data breaches occur in which you and your users are not at fault, at least not directly. In this section you'll learn about ways in which malicious individuals access data without your cooperation.

Backdoor

Earlier in this chapter you learned that a Trojan horse can create a backdoor. These backdoors are also sometimes called Remote Access Trojans (RATs) because they allow the hacker to connect to the machine without going through any sort of authentication process.

Sometimes backdoors are also included in a rootkit, which you also learned about earlier in this chapter. Please review the "Malware" section of this chapter.

Social Engineering

Social engineering is a process in which an attacker attempts to acquire information about your network and system by social means, such as by talking to people in the organization. A social engineering attack may occur over the phone, by email, or by a visit. The intent is to acquire access information, such as user IDs and passwords. When the attempt is made through email or instant messaging, it is known as *phishing* (discussed later) and often is made to look as if it is coming from sites where users are likely to have accounts (Google and Amazon are popular).

These types of attacks are relatively low-tech and are more akin to con jobs. Take the following example. Your help desk gets a call at 4 a.m. from someone purporting to be the vice president of your company. This person tells the help desk personnel that they are out of town to attend a meeting, their computer just failed, and they are sitting in a hotel trying to get a file from their desktop computer back at the office. They can't seem to remember their password and user ID. They tell the help desk representative that they need access to the information right away or the company could lose millions of dollars. Your help desk rep knows how important this meeting is and gives the caller the vice president's user ID and password over the phone.

Another common approach is initiated by a phone call or email from your software vendor, telling you that they have a critical fix that must be installed on your computer system. If this patch isn't installed right away, your system will crash and you'll lose all your data. For some reason, you've changed your maintenance account password and they can't log on. Your system operator gives the password to the person. You've been hit again.

PHISHING

Phishing is a form of social engineering in which you simply ask someone for a piece of information that you are missing by making it look as if it is a legitimate request. An email might look as if it is from a bank and contain some basic information, such as the user's name. In the email, it will often state that there is a problem with the person's account or access privileges. They will be told to click a link to correct the problem. After they click the link—which goes to a site other than the bank's—they are asked for their username, password, account information, and so on. The person instigating the phishing can then use the values entered there to access the legitimate account.

One of the best counters to phishing is to simply mouse over the Click Here link and read the URL. Almost every time it is pointing to an adaptation of the legitimate URL as opposed to a link to the real thing.

The only preventive measure in dealing with social-engineering attacks is to educate your users and staff to never give out passwords and user IDs over the phone or via email or to anyone who isn't positively verified as being who they say they are. In this section you'll learn about some other variants.

SPEAR PHISHING/WHALING

Two other forms of phishing to be aware of are *spear phishing* and *whaling*, and they are similar in nature. With spear phishing, the person conducting it uses information that the target would be less likely to question because it appears to be coming from a trusted source. As an example, instead of Wells Fargo sending you a message telling you to click here to fix a problem with your account, the message that comes in appears to be from your spouse and it says to click here to see a video of your children from last Christmas. Because it appears far more likely to be a legitimate message, it cuts through the user's standard defenses like a spear and has a higher likelihood of being clicked. Generating the attack requires much more work on the part of the miscreant and often involves using information from contact lists, friend lists from social media sites, and so on.

Whaling is nothing more than phishing, or spear phishing, for big users. Instead of sending out a To Whom It May Concern message to thousands of users, the whaler identifies one person from whom they can gain all the data they want—usually a manager or owner—and targets the phishing campaign at them.

VISHING

When you combine phishing with Voice over IP (VoIP), it becomes known as vishing and is just an elevated form of social engineering. While crank calls have been in existence since the invention of the telephone, the rise in VoIP now makes it possible for someone to call you from almost anywhere in the world, without the worry of tracing, caller ID, and other features of the land line, and pretend to be someone they are not in order to get data from you.

SHOULDER SURFING

Shoulder surfing involves nothing more than watching someone when they enter their sensitive data. They can see you entering a password, typing in a credit card number, or entering any other pertinent information. The best defense against this type of attack is to survey your environment before entering personal data. Privacy filters can be used that make the screen difficult to read unless you are directly in front of it.

TAILGATING

Tailgating is the term used for someone being so close to you when you enter a building that they are able to come in right behind you without needing to use a key, a card, or any other security device. Many social-engineering intruders who need physical access to a site will use this method of gaining entry. Educate users to beware of this and other social-engineering ploys and prevent them from happening.

> Mantraps, or security vestibules, are a great way to stop tailgating. A mantrap is a series of two doors with a small room between them that helps prevent unauthorized people from entering a building. For more information, see the "Mantraps" section earlier in this chapter.

IMPERSONATION

Impersonation occurs when an individual pretends to be an IT technician, heating and air repairperson, or other personnel to get in the facility or to convince someone to disclose sensitive information.

DUMPSTER DIVING

It is amazing the information that can be gleaned from physical documents even in the age when there is such a push to go paperless. *Dumpster diving* is a common physical access method. Companies normally generate a huge amount of paper, most of which eventually winds up in dumpsters or recycle bins. Dumpsters may contain information that is highly sensitive in nature (such as passwords after a change and before the user has the new one memorized). In high-security and government environments, sensitive papers should be either shredded or burned. Most businesses don't do this. In addition, the advent of "green" companies has created an increase in the amount of recycled paper, which can often contain all kinds of juicy information about a company and its individual employees.

Breaches

When a hacker finds a vulnerability and exploits it, it can lead to a data breach, which is the exposure of sensitive data. For many attackers this is the goal. They may do this as corporate espionage. In this section you'll learn how your organization can address breaches.

IDENTIFICATION

First, the organization must know when it has been breached. It might surprise you to know that in many cases organizations don't even know that a breach has occurred for weeks or months! Identifying breaches involves deep inspection of log files by experienced technicians to identify that data loss has occurred.

DISCLOSURE

In many highly regulated industries, organizations are required by regulation or law to notify any users whose data has been disclosed. For example, in the healthcare field, the HIPAA Breach Notification Rule, 45 CFR §§ 164.400-414, requires HIPAA-covered entities and their business associates to provide notification following a breach of unsecured protected health information (PHI). As another example, all 50 states, the District of Columbia, Guam, Puerto Rico, and the Virgin Islands have enacted legislation requiring private or governmental entities to notify individuals of security breaches of information involving personally identifiable information (PII).

Mitigation Strategies

While there are many options available to malicious individuals to access, steal, and delete data, there are ways we can fight back. In this section you'll learn about mitigation strategies that can reduce the likelihood or the impact of a data breach.

Data Monitoring

Earlier you learned that in many cases data breaches are not discovered for weeks or months after the breach. How can this happen, you say? It happens because no one is watching. By that I mean that no one is monitoring the data to ensure that it is still there, still has integrity, and is still usable.

This does not have to be a manual and labor-intensive process. There are tools that can alert you when your data is seen on the dark web or in data repositories. For example, Online Protection Solutions (ONSIST) offers a product that does this and generates robust reporting. Another is Troy Hunt's website, ';--have i been pwned? It can be found at:
`https://haveibeenpwned.com`.

Log Analysis

In Chapter 2, "Installing and Configuring Servers," you learned about log files and the proper use of log file analysis. When it comes to data breaches, the key logs are those of the server, the firewall, and any IDSs or IPSs. In the next section you'll learn about a tool that can put all of this data in one place for analysis.

Security Information and Event Management (SIEM)

Security information and event management (SIEM) utilities receive information from log files of critical systems and centralize the collection and analysis of this data. SIEM technology is an intersection of two closely related technologies: security information management (SIM) and security event management (SEM).

Log sources for SIEM can include the following:

- Application logs
- Antivirus logs

- Operating system logs
- Malware detection logs

One consideration when working with a SIEM system is to limit the amount of information collected to what is really needed. Moreover, you need to ensure that adequate resources are available to ensure good performance.

In summary, an organization should implement a SIEM system when:

- More visibility into network events is desired.
- Faster correlation of events is required.
- Compliance issues require reporting to be streamlined and automated.
- It needs help prioritizing security issues.

Two-Person Integrity

Unfortunately, in some cases data breaches are intentionally caused by someone within the organization. While we would like to trust everyone, we know we can't, so the best approach is to TRUST NO ONE. In this section you'll learn about the security principle behind trusting no one and about a process based on this principle.

Split Encryption Keys Tokens

An implementation of the two-person integrity concept is use of split encryption keys tokens. When passphrases are used to create encryption keys for extremely sensitive material, no one person should know the entire passphrase. Rather, two or more people should each know only a part of the passphrase, and all of them would have to be present to create or re-create an encryption key.

Separation of Roles

Separation of duties or roles prescribes that any operation prone to fraud should be broken up into two operations, with different users performing each. For example, the person in charge of accounts payable should not be the same person in charge of accounts receivable. Were this the case, this person could create an invoice to themselves (or their company) and pay it with company money.

Regulatory Constraints

It is your responsibility, as an administrator and a professional, to know (or learn) the regulations that exist for dealing with safety. You should know them from the local level to the federal level and be familiar with the reporting procedures for incidents you are faced with.

If employees are injured, for example, you may need to contact the Occupational Safety and Health Administration (OSHA). On its website (www.osha.gov), you can find links to information about issues of compliance, laws and regulation, and enforcement. In this section you'll learn about the impact of regulatory compliance.

Governmental

Almost all of the regulations discussed in this section are derived from a governmental body (state, local). Those that are not derived from a government come from industry bodies policing themselves in the hope the government will *not* do so. Let's look at some data types that draw attention and a standard designed to address data breaches of that data type.

Individually Privileged Information

Individually privileged information is data about a person. When organizations handle this type of data, they bear a heavy responsibility to protect it. Failure to do so can be very costly. In this section you'll learn about PII and a standard used to protect an example of PII.

PERSONALLY IDENTIFIABLE INFORMATION (PII)

Personally identifiable information (PII) is any piece of information about a user that can be used alone or in combination with other pieces of information to identify that user. While it is the responsibility of all organizations to protect PII that they may possess, it is especially important in certain regulated industries such as healthcare and finance.

The danger of leaking PII is that much of this information, such as address, Social Security number, and place of employment, can be used to perform identity theft, a growing concern worldwide.

PAYMENT CARD INDUSTRY DATA SECURITY STANDARD (PCI DSS)

Credit card data is some of the most sensitive data there is, and users and customers depend on organizations to protect it. PCI-DSS 4.0, the latest version of the Payment Card Industry Data Security Standard, is expected to be released in Q1-2022. It encourages and enhances cardholder data security and facilitates the broad adoption of consistent data security measures globally.

Legal Considerations

Sometimes a security incident involves a crime and the police become involved. In other cases, claims may be made against the organization, or principles of the organization, that require access to data and emails to investigate. In cases like this there may be a requirement placed on the organization to retain access to data and email for a longer period than normal. This is called a *legal hold*. In this section you'll learn about data retention policies and the legal mechanism used to order legal holds.

Data Retention

Once data has reached the end of its life cycle, you should either properly dispose of it or ensure that it is securely stored. Some organizations must maintain data records for a certain number of years per local, state, or federal laws or regulations. This type of data should be archived for the required period. In addition, any data that is part of litigation should be retained as requested by the court of law, and organizations should follow appropriate chain of custody and evidence documentation processes. Data archival and destruction procedures should be clearly defined by the organization.

All organizations need procedures in place for the retention and destruction of data. Data retention and destruction must follow all local, state, and government regulations and laws. Documenting proper procedures ensures that information is maintained for the required time to prevent financial fines and possible incarceration of high-level organizational officers. These procedures must include both the retention period and the destruction process.

Subpoenas

Even if only peripherally involved, the organization may be subpoenaed for emails or data related to a crime. It is interesting to note that if your own data retention polices follow all legal requirements and they call for deleting data prior to the subpoena, that deletion is legal. However, once the subpoena is received you cannot delete any data requested that still exists.

Given a Scenario, Apply Server Hardening Methods

The goal of hardening an operating system is to reduce the attack surface. This involves reducing the available options a hacker or attacker might have to compromise the system. It involves hardening the system logically—that is, hardening the operating system and applications—and hardening the server physically by ensuring the device cannot be tampered with by someone who can touch the server. Both concepts are covered in this section. You'll also learn the steps involved in hardening a server.

OS Hardening

Hardening the server should start with hardening the operating system. This involves a series of steps that should result in a server that offers a minimum of attack points to a hacker. Let's look at six steps that can lead to this result.

Disable Unused Services/Close Unneeded Ports

Any services that are not required on the server should be disabled. Only those required for the server to perform its role in the network should be left on. The easiest way to do this is to install a host firewall on the system and adopt a "disable by default" policy with respect to services by closing the port used for the service. Then manually enable any you need.

Install Only Required Software

It also hardens the system to remove any software the server does not require. Often server operating systems come with certain applications already installed, although this habit has been somewhat discredited in the industry and many vendors are moving away from the practice. You should examine all installed applications and retain only those you need.

Not only does unnecessary software eat resources, but it can also create security loopholes in some cases.

Apply Driver Updates/Apply OS Updates

It almost feels silly at this point in the discussion to have to say this, but I'll say it anyway: always keep the server updated with all operating system patches and service packs. This includes driver updates and OS updates. Arrive at some process or procedure that automates the process such as using a Windows Server Update Services server or at the very least, set the server to check for and download updates. It's not a great idea to install them automatically because you want to test them first and make sure they don't break something on the server.

Firewall Configuration

Although firewalls can be used to keep unwanted and perhaps malicious traffic types out of the network, and port security and network access control (NAC) can help keep intruders out of the network, within the network there will be occasions when you don't want to allow communication between certain devices. Perhaps you want to prevent users in the Sales subnet from accessing data in the Finance subnet. In these scenarios, you can use access control lists (ACLs) on the router.

The inherent limitation of ACLs is their inability to detect whether IP spoofing is occurring. IP address spoofing is one of the techniques used by hackers to hide their trail or to masquerade as another computer. The hacker alters the IP address as it appears in the packet. This can sometimes allow the packet to get through an ACL that is based on IP addresses. It also can be used to make a connection to a system that only trusts certain IP addresses or ranges of IP addresses.

Access control lists are ordered sets of rules that control the traffic that is permitted or denied the use of a path through the router. These rules can operate at Layer 3, making these decisions on the basis of IP addresses, or at Layer 4, when only certain types of traffic are allowed based on a TCP or UDP port number. When this is done, the ACL will typically reference a port number of the service or application that is allowed or denied.

When creating ACL rule sets, keep the following design considerations in mind:

- The order of the rules is important. If traffic matches the first rule, the action specified by the rule will be applied, and no other rules will be read. Place more specific rules at the top of the list and more general ones at the bottom.

- On many devices (such as Cisco routers), an implied deny all rule is located at the end of all ACLs. If you are unsure, it is always best to configure an explicit deny all rule at the end of the ACL list. An implied deny all is a rule that doesn't actually appear in the list but is assumed in all lists. An explicit deny is implemented by specifying "deny all" as the last rule in the list.

- It is also possible to log all traffic that meets any of the rules.

Application Hardening

Application hardening follows the same conceptual process as operating system hardening. Applications can have many features and embedded programs that you may not make use of. Determine which of these you require and, in cases where it is possible, disable all other features. If you have any applications your enterprise has developed, ensure the applications have been developed with security in mind and follow secure coding principles when creating these applications.

Install Latest Patches

Don't forget about the applications that may be running on the server. Applications can also be attacked by hackers. That's why software vendors are also periodically issuing security updates. As security issues are reported, they respond by fixing the software. For Windows applications, these updates can accompany the operating system updates if you choose to enable them.

Other applications may be more of a challenge, but it's hard to find vendors today that don't either automatically send and install the updates or, at the very least, notify you that one is available.

Disable Unneeded Services, Roles, or Features

Server operating systems come with a lot of features, utilities, tools, and roles. In all probability you won't need many of these, even when the server is performing more than one role in the network. In the old days, Windows servers came with many of these roles running. Today, thankfully, that is no longer the case and you can simply refrain from enabling or installing the role or feature rather than uninstalling it.

In Linux and Unix, most versions come with only minimal services installed and running You are required to enable or install these features or services. This makes it easier to restrict the running features to those you desire and trust.

Host Security

When discussing network security, an endpoint or host is any point of entry into the network. A typical example of an endpoint is a laptop connected to the network with a remote access connection. Therefore, the process of providing endpoint security is the process of ensuring that every endpoint (including servers) has been secured in the same way in which you would secure the network gateway. It is based on the assumption that any device that is connected to the network—either permanently, as a server typically is, or temporarily, as when a remote access connection is made—is a potential entryway if the device is compromised. There are two main issues to consider when providing endpoint security: identifying intrusions when they occur and preventing the spread of malware. Let's look at both of these issues.

Antivirus/Antimalware

Although the installation of an HIDS may not be indicated if a network IDS is in place and you want to avoid the issues mentioned in the last section that come along with an HIDS, antimalware software will need to be installed on all endpoints, including servers. Many texts discuss antivirus and antimalware software separately, but for the purposes of our discussion, we are talking about software that addresses all types of malicious software, including viruses, worms, Trojan horses, adware, and spyware.

The primary method of preventing the propagation of malicious code involves the use of antivirus software. Antivirus software is an application that is installed on a system to protect it and to scan for viruses as well as worms and Trojan horses. Most viruses have characteristics that are common to families of virus. Antivirus software looks for these characteristics, or fingerprints, to identify and neutralize viruses before they impact you.

Millions of known viruses, worms, bombs, and other malware have been defined. New ones are added all the time. Your antivirus software manufacturer will usually work very hard to keep the definition database files current. The definition database file contains all known viruses and countermeasures for a particular antivirus software product. You probably won't receive a virus that hasn't been seen by one of these companies. If you keep the virus definition database files in your software up-to-date, you won't be overly vulnerable to attacks.

Host Intrusion Detection System (HIDS)/Host Intrusion Prevention System (HIPS)

An IDS (intrusion detection system) is a system responsible for detecting unauthorized access or attacks. The most common way to classify an IDS is based on its information source: network-based and host-based. A host-based intrusion detection system (HIDS) is installed on the device (for the purpose of our discussion, a server) and the system focuses solely on identifying attacks on that device only. This is in contrast to a network-based system, which monitors all traffic that goes through it looking for signs of attack on any machine in the network.

These systems can use several methods of detecting intrusions. The two main methods are as follows:

Signature-Based   Analyzes traffic and compares patterns, called *signatures*, that reside within the IDS database. This means it requires constant updating of the signature database.

Anomaly-Based   Analyzes traffic and compares it to normal traffic to determine if the traffic is a threat. This means any traffic out of the ordinary will set off an alert.

An HIDS can be configured to also focus on attacks that may be relevant to the role that the server is performing (for example, looking for DNS pollution attacks on DNS servers). But there are drawbacks to these systems, among them:

- A high number of false positives can cause a lax attitude on the part of the security team.

- Constant updating of signatures is needed.

- A lag time exists between the release of the attack and the release of the signature.

- An HIDS cannot address authentication issues.

- Encrypted packets cannot be analyzed.

- In some cases, IDS software is susceptible itself to attacks.

Despite these shortcomings, an HIDS can play an important role in a multilayer defense system.

An IPS is a system responsible for preventing attacks. When an attack begins, an IPS takes actions to contain the attack. An IPS, like an IDS, can be network or host-based. Although an IPS can be signature or anomaly-based, it can also use a rate-based metric that analyzes the volume of traffic as well as the type of traffic. In most cases, implementing an IPS is more costly than implementing an IDS because of the added security needed to contain attacks compared to the security needed to simply detect attacks. In addition, running an IPS is more of an overall performance load than running an IDS.

A host-based IPS (HIPS) monitors traffic on a single system and can take actions to prevent an attack. Its primary responsibility is to protect the system on which it is installed. HIPSs typically work closely with antimalware products and host firewall products. They generally monitor the interaction of sites and applications with the operating system and stop any malicious activity or, in some cases, ask the user to approve changes that the application or site would like to make to the system. An example of an HIPS is SafenSoft SysWatch.

Hardware Hardening

While securing the servers from an attack from across a network is certainly important, you must also harden the servers against any physical attacks that may take place. Some of these issues we have already touched upon in earlier sections, but for completeness, let's cover all physical hardening issues.

Disable Unneeded Hardware/Disable Unneeded Physical Ports, Devices, or Functions

The closing of any software ports that are not in use is part of digital hardening, but the disabling of any physical ports or connections on the server is a part of physical hardening. This encompasses disabling unused devices on the server as well, such as CD drives or DVD burners that may be present. Remember, though, the aim is to do so without preventing the server from performing its role in the network. Some of the items that should be considered for disabling are as follows:

- USB ports

- NICs

- Serial ports
- Firmware ports
- Thunderbolt ports

Most of this work can be done in Device Manager if you are working with Windows. For example, in Figure 6.11 you can see how to disable the USB ports.

FIGURE 6.11   Disabling USB ports in Device Manager

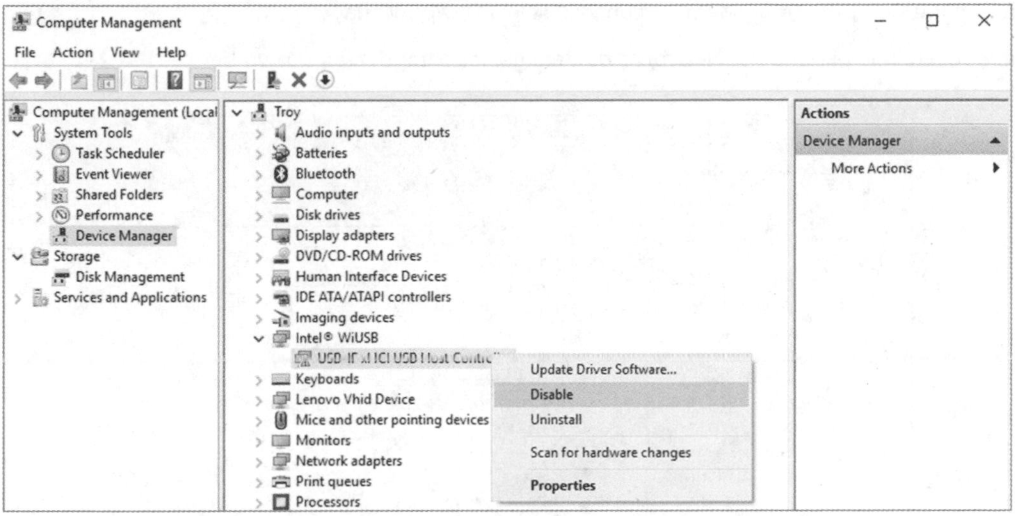

This can also be done in the BIOS or UEFI settings. Figure 6.12 shows disabling the USB ports in the BIOS.

FIGURE 6.12   Disabling USB ports in the BIOS

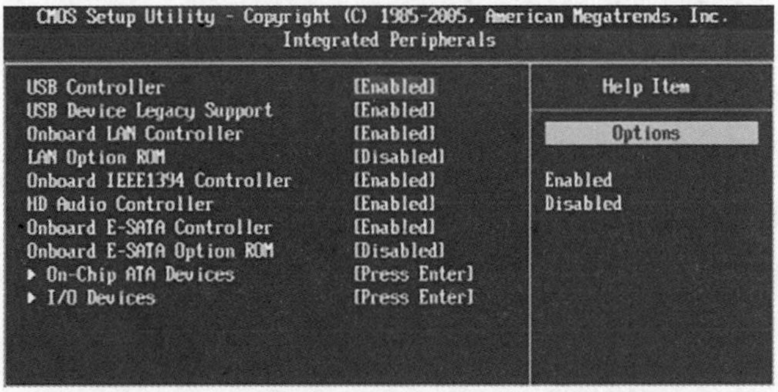

In Exercise 6.1 you will disable the network adapter in Windows Server 2012 R2.

EXERCISE 6.1

Disabling the Network Adapter in Windows Server 2012 R2

1. Open the Server Manager tool if it is not already open.

2. From the Tools menu, select Computer Management.

3. In the Computer Management console, select Device Manager.

4. Locate and expand the Network Adapters device category, as shown here:

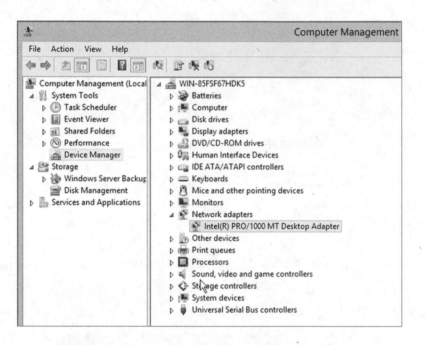

5. Right-click the network adapter you wish to disable (this server has only one, but your server may have more than one) and select Disable from the menu.

6. You can verify your work by looking for the black down arrow next to the adapter, as shown here:

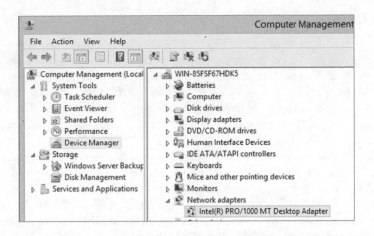

Set BIOS Password

While you are in the BIOS, set a password for it. This will be a password that anyone attempting to boot the device to the BIOS will be required to know. This can prevent someone with physical access to the server from booting to the BIOS, changing the boot order, and enabling a boot device for the purpose of booting to an external OS that they can use to take data off the hard drive.

As you can see in Figure 6.15, you can set one for users and another for the administrator (called the Supervisor password in the BIOS). The critical one is for the administrator because that is the password that allows access to the setup utility.

FIGURE 6.15   Setting a BIOS password

```
                        PhoenixBIOS Setup Utility
    Main      Advanced    Security    Power    Boot     Exit

                                              Item Specific Help

    Set User Password         [Enter]
    Set Supervisor Password   [Enter]         Supervisor Password
                                              controls access to the
                                              setup utility.




    F1   Help    ↑↓  Select Item   -/+   Change Values      F9   Setup Defaults
    Esc  Exit    ←→  Select Menu   Enter Select ► Sub-Menu  F10  Save and Exit
```

Set Boot Order

In either the BIOS setup or by using the UEFI, you can influence the order of the devices where the system will search for boot files. The most common source of boot files is the hard drive, but the files can also be located on DVDs, USB drives, and external drives, or they can be accessed from network locations as well as by using a PXE boot. The system will execute the first boot files (or any executable files) that it encounters in this search. When installing the operating system, you want the system, when booted, to look first in the location where the installation files are located.

If the system already has an operating system, this becomes even more important. This is because normally the first place the system looks is the hard drive. If this order is unaltered, the system will continue to boot to the old operating system, even though you may have the installation DVD in the DVD drive or the installation files located on a USB drive.

This means you must be familiar with entering the BIOS or UEFI and changing this boot order. It also means that when you have completed the installation you need to change it back so that it boots to the operating system you just installed.

Many new servers allow you to use either UEFI or BIOS settings to manage the boot process. In the following exercises, based on a Dell PowerEdge server, you will enter both systems. In either system you can set the boot mode, which tells the server which system to use to manage the boot process.

 WARNING   The operating system that you intend to install must be one that can support UEFI if you plan to use that system. If you set the device to use the UEFI boot mode and the OS does not support that, it could prevent the operating system from booting.

In the first exercise, you will use the traditional BIOS; in the second you will use the UEFI.

EXERCISE 6.2

Changing the Boot Order Using the BIOS

1. Turn on or restart your system.

2. Press F2 after you see the following message:

   `<F2> = System Setup`

3. You will now be on the main system setup screen, as shown here.

```
              Dell Inc. (www.dell.com) - PowerEdge
                          BIOS Version

 Service Tag:                        Asset Tag:

 System Time ...................................... 20:43:30    ▲
 System Date ...................................... Wed Sep 05, 2015

 Memory Settings .................................. <ENTER>
 Processor Settings ............................... <ENTER>

 SATA Settings .................................... <ENTER>

 Boot Settings .................................... <ENTER>

 Integrated Devices ............................... <ENTER>
 PCI IRQ Assignment ............................... <ENTER>

 Serial Communication ............................. <ENTER>
 Embedded Server Management ....................... <ENTER>

 Power Management ................................. <ENTER>    ▼

 Up,Down Arrow to select  |  SPACE,+,- to change  |  ESC to exit  |  F1=Help
```

4. Use the up and down keys to move to the Boot Settings screen.

5. There are two settings related to the boot process on this screen. One is the Boot Mode field, which can be used to set the mode to either BIOS or UEFI, as shown here. The other is the Boot Sequence field; use the arrow keys to focus on and select that field. Then select the device from the list where the boot files are located.

```
              Dell Inc. (www.dell.com) - PowerEdge
                          BIOS Version

 Service Tag:                        Asset Tag:

 System Time ...................................... 05:47:39    ▲
 System Date ...................................... Tue Jun 26, 2015

 Memory  Boot Mode ............................... UEFI
 Proces  Boot Sequence .......................... <ENTER>
         Boot Sequence Retry .................... Disabled
 SATA S

 Boot Settings .................................... <ENTER>

 Integrated Devices ............................... <ENTER>
 PCI IRQ Assignment ............................... <ENTER>

 Serial Communication ............................. <ENTER>
 Embedded Server Management ....................... <ENTER>

 Power Management ................................. <ENTER>    ▼

 Up,Down Arrow to select  |  SPACE,+,- to change  |  ESC to exit  |  F1=Help
```

6. Exit from this screen and choose to save your settings.

7. Reboot the server and it should boot to the installation files.

This exercise demonstrates the process on a Dell PowerEdge. Your system may be different. Consult your documentation.

EXERCISE 6.3

Changing the Boot Order Using the UEFI

1. Turn on or restart your system.

2. Press F11 after you see the following message:

   `<F11> = UEFI Boot Manager`

   You will now be on the UEFI Boot Manager screen.

3. Use the up and down keys to move to the UEFI Boot Settings screen.

4. Use the up and down keys to move to the Change Boot Order screen.

5. Use the arrow keys to focus on and select this field. Then select the device from the list where the boot files are located.

6. Exit from this screen and choose to save your settings.

7. Reboot the server and it should boot to the installation files.

Patching

Earlier you learned the importance of both hardware and security patches or updates. In this section we'll look at some related concepts involved in keeping systems up-to-date.

Testing

We've just finished discussing all kinds of updates that you might apply to a server. Because servers are so important to the function of the network, you must treat updates for them with a dose of caution and skepticism. It is impossible for vendors to anticipate every scenario in which the server might be operating and thus impossible for them to provide assurance that the update won't break something (like a mission-critical operation). With the potential exception of security updates, you should always test the updates and validate their compatibility with your set of hardware and software.

These tests should occur in a test network and not on production servers. One of the benefits of having a virtualization environment is the ability to take images of your servers and test the updates on those images in a virtual environment. Once the updates have been validated as compatible, you can deploy them to the live servers.

Deployment

While in the past patch management in Linux presented more of a challenge than with Windows, today a variation of the same tool used to manage patches with Windows (System Center Configuration Manager) can now be used to patch additional systems such as Linux.

Many of the versions of Linux now make updates much easier than in the past. Both Ubuntu and Fedora offer a GUI tool (shocking!) for this. In Ubuntu, for example, choosing System ➤ Administration and then selecting the Update Manager entry will open Update

Manager. When it opens, click the Check button to see whether there are updates available. Figure 6.18 shows a list of available updates.

FIGURE 6.18   Ubuntu Update Manager

Of course, you can still do this from the command line. Follow these steps:

1. Open a terminal window.
2. Issue the command **sudo apt-get upgrade**.
3. Enter your user's password.
4. Look over the list of available updates and decide whether you want to go through with the entire upgrade.
5. When the desired updates have been selected, click the Install Updates button.
6. Watch as the update happens.

Change Management

The old saying "Too many cooks spoil the broth" applies when it comes to managing servers. When technicians make changes to the servers that are not centrally managed and planned, chaos reigns. In that environment, changes might be made that work at cross purposes. All organizations need a change management process whereby every change goes through a formal evaluation process before it is implemented.

This process ensures that all changes support the goals of the organization and that the impact of each change is anticipated before the change is made. There should be a change management board to which all changes are submitted for review. Only when the change has been approved should it be made.

Summary

In this chapter, you learned concepts related to securing the server. These included physical security methods such as locking cabinets and server rooms and deploying strong authentication methods for accessing those rooms. We also covered server techniques such as stopping unneeded services, installing only needed software, and keeping up-to-date on security patches. Finally, we explored concepts related to ensuring that you can satisfy the availability requirement of the CIA security triad by maintaining the proper environment in which the servers operate.

Exam Essentials

Compare and contrast physical security methods and concepts.   Among these methods are multifactor authentication, mantraps, RFID chips, and access lists. You should also be familiar with all types of locks, including server, rack, and cabinet locks.

Describe what hardening the server entails.   Explain the value of stopping unneeded services, closing unneeded ports, installing only required software, and installing the latest operating system patches. You should also know about physical hardening, including disabling unneeded hardware and physical ports, implementing a BIOS password, and using chassis locks.

List proper environment controls and techniques.   Identify the steps required to ensure availability of the resources on the servers. These include implementing UPS systems, using redundant rack PDUs, and provisioning multiple circuits. It also entails monitoring the temperature and humidity to ensure they are at the recommended levels. Finally, the layout of the server room should be such that it promotes airflow that removes heat.

Review Questions

You can find the answers in the Appendix.

1. Which authentication mechanism is an example of something you have?
   A. Password
   B. Username
   C. Smart card
   D. Retina scan

2. Which of the following is a series of two doors with a small room between them?
   A. Mantrap
   B. Bigate
   C. Holding cell
   D. Visual check door

3. Which of the following is *not* a drawback of using active RFID chips?
   A. The tag signal can be read by any reader in range.
   B. The tag signal can only go a few feet.
   C. Multiple readers in an area can interfere with one another.
   D. Multiple devices can interfere with one another when responding.

4. Which of the following authentication methods is *not* an example of biometrics?
   A. Password
   B. Hand scanners
   C. Fingerprint scan
   D. Retina scan

5. Which of the following offers the most flexibility in reacting to security events?
   A. Cameras
   B. Security guards
   C. Motion sensors
   D. Intrusion prevention systems

6. Which of the following statements is false with respect to safes?
   A. All safes are fireproof.
   B. United Laboratories (UL) assigns ratings to safes that you can use to assess the suitability of the safe.
   C. Those that are fire-resistant might protect a document from being destroyed.
   D. When considering a safe, you should focus on two items: the ease with which the safe can be compromised and the ability of the safe to withstand a fire.

7. Which of the following is a physical hardening technique?

   A. Stopping unneeded services

   B. Closing unneeded ports

   C. Installing only required software

   D. Assigning a BIOS password

8. When discussing security, which of the following is defined as any point of entry into the network?

   A. Access point

   B. Endpoint

   C. Drop point

   D. Access link

9. Which of the following is not true of an HIDS?

   A. A high number of false positives can cause a lax attitude on the part of the security team.

   B. An HIDS cannot address authentication issues.

   C. Encrypted packets cannot be analyzed.

   D. An HIDS monitors all traffic that goes through it looking for signs of attack on any machine in the network.

10. Which CIA goal is supported by using environmental controls?

   A. Availability

   B. Accountability

   C. Integrity

   D. Confidentiality

11. Which of the following is *not* an example of physical hardening of the server?

   A. Disabling USB ports

   B. Implementing strong authentication to log into the server

   C. Installing locks on server racks

   D. Installing locks on the server room door

12. Which of the following utilities receive information from log files of critical systems and centralize the collection and analysis of this data?

   A. RAID

   B. SIEM

   C. JBOD

   D. LANwake

13. Which of the following malware recognition processes analyzes traffic and compares patterns to those that reside within the IDS database?

- **A.** Anomaly-based
- **B.** Heuristics
- **C.** Signature-based
- **D.** Event-based

14. Which fire suppression system is not recommended for rooms where equipment will be damaged by water?

- **A.** Dry pipe
- **B.** Preaction
- **C.** Hybrid
- **D.** Wet pipe

15. Which of the following social engineering attacks can be mitigated by document shredding?

- **A.** Dumpster diving
- **B.** Piggybacking
- **C.** Shoulder surfing
- **D.** Tailgating

16. Which of the following is *not* a physical hardening process?

- **A.** BIOS password
- **B.** Open case alarm
- **C.** Closing unneeded ports
- **D.** Laptop locks

17. Which of the following are short vertical posts placed at the building's entrance way and lining sidewalks that help to provide protection from vehicles that might either intentionally or unintentionally crash into or enter the building or injure pedestrians?

- **A.** Mantrap
- **B.** Bollards
- **C.** PDU
- **D.** Barriers

18. Which of the following refers to designing the facility from the ground up to support security?

- **A.** SIEM
- **B.** OSSINT
- **C.** CPTED
- **D.** WOL

19. Which of the following are enclosures that can block signals?

    A. Bollards

    B. Mantraps

    C. Faraday cage

    D. Security vestibule

20. Which of the following is no longer legal to use in a fire suppression system?

    A. Halon

    B. Water

    C. Argon

    D. NAS-S-III

Chapter

7

Securing Server Data and Network Access

COMPTIA SERVER+ EXAM OBJECTIVES COVERED IN THIS CHAPTER:

✓ **3.1 Summarize data security concepts.**

- Encryption paradigms

    - Data at rest

    - Data in transit

- Retention policies

- Data storage

    - Physical location storage

    - Off-site vs. on-site

- UEFI/BIOS passwords

- Bootloader passwords

- Business impact

    - Data value prioritization

    - Life-cycle management

    - Cost of security vs. risk and/or replacement

✓ **3.3 Explain important concepts pertaining to identity and access management for server administration.**

- User accounts

- User groups

- Password policies

    - Length

    - Lockout

    - Enforcement

- Permissions and access controls
    - Role-based
    - Rule-based
    - Scope-based
    - Segregation of duties
    - Delegation
- Auditing
    - User activity
    - Logins
    - Group memberships
    - Deletions
- Multifactor authentication (MFA)
    - Something you know
    - Something you have
    - Something you are
- Single sign-on (SSO)

✓ **3.6 Summarize proper server decommissioning concepts.**

- Proper removal procedures
    - Company policies
    - Verify non-utilization
    - Documentation
        - Asset management
        - Change management
- Media destruction
    - Disk wiping
    - Physical
        - Degaussing
        - Shredding
        - Crushing
        - Incineration
- Purposes for media destruction

- Media retention requirements
- Cable remediation
  - Power
  - Networking
- Electronics recycling
  - Internal vs. external
  - Repurposing

While securing the server from physical access is of immense importance, securing the data that resides on the server is also critical and requires a different approach. Logical or technical controls are used to protect this data. We have to be concerned about the security of the data when it is en route to the user across the network and when it is at rest on the storage media. In addition, we have to ensure that, when storage media is disposed of, the data that resided on the media is removed completely.

Summarize Data Security Concepts

While controlling access to files and folders is important, it does nothing for you if a device is stolen because it's possible to access the data using an operating system on an external drive. To prevent that, encrypting the data is the solution. In this section, we'll look at various levels of encryption and how they differ.

Encryption Paradigms

A public key infrastructure (PKI) includes systems, software, and communication protocols that distribute, manage, and control public key cryptography. In public key cryptography, two keys are used: a public key and a private key. These two keys are not the same, but they are mathematically related in such a way that if you encrypt data with one of them you can decrypt it with the other. Users and devices are issued public/private key pairs that are bound to a digital document called a digital certificate. This certificate (more specifically, the keys to which it is bound) can be used for a variety of things, including the following:

- Encrypting data
- Authenticating users and devices
- Encrypting email
- Digitally signing software

In this section you'll learn about encryption of data when stored and in transit.

Data at Rest

When using encryption to protect data that resides on storage devices (called *data at rest*), we can apply the encryption at different levels with different results. Let's look at three types of encryption.

File-Level Encryption

Encryption at the file level is performed on each file or on a folder that contains files. In Windows this is done using the Encrypting File System (EFS). EFS is an encryption tool built into all Enterprise versions of Windows. It allows a user to encrypt files that can only be decrypted by the user who encrypted the files. It can only be used on NTFS volumes and is simple to use.

Linux and Unix do not have a system like EFS, but you can encrypt a file using the gpg command. It is an encryption and signing tool for Linux- and Unix-like operating systems such as FreeBSD/Solaris and others. To encrypt a file named Sales.txt, you would execute this command:

```
$ gpg -c Sales.txt
```

This will generate the following output, to which you must respond with a password:

```
Enter passphrase:<YOUR-PASSWORD>
Repeat passphrase:<YOUR-PASSWORD>
```

Disk-Level Encryption

Disk-level encryption encrypts an entire volume or entire disk and may use the same key for the entire disk or, in some cases, a different key for each partition or volume. This can help prevent data loss by the theft of the computer or the hard drive.

Disk-level encryption may also use a Trusted Platform Module (TPM) chip. This chip is located on the motherboard of the system and provides password protection, digital rights management (DRM), and full-disk encryption. It protects the keys used to encrypt the computer's hard disks and provides integrity authentication for a trusted boot pathway. Since the key in the TPM chip is required to access the hard drive, if the drive is removed from the server, decryption of the data on the drive becomes impossible.

In Windows, full-disk encryption is done using BitLocker. In Linux and Unix, open source tools such as TrueCrypt have been used in the past. While development of that tool has been halted, other open source tools such as dm-crypt exist to accomplish full-disk encryption.

Tape Encryption

It is also possible to encrypt data that resides on backup tapes. Starting with version 4 of the Linear Tape-Open tape standard (LTO-4), encryption is a supported feature. You should keep in mind the following issues:

- Choose a product that will perform compression prior to performing encryption. Otherwise, the tape will not compress because encryption effectively scrambles the data, removing the redundancy that compression algorithms rely on.

- All of your tape drives must support the encryption used with LTO-4 drives.

- Ensure that you have a robust key management system; the loss of a key will mean the loss of the data that was encrypted with the key.

Data in Transit

In this section you'll learn about methods to encrypt data when it is traveling across an untrusted network, which we call in transit.

SSL/TLS

Secure Sockets Layer (SSL) is a Transport layer protocol that provides encryption, server and client authentication, and message integrity. It has been replaced by TLS. SSL was developed by Netscape to transmit private documents over the Internet. Transport Layer Security (TLS) is an open-community standard that provides many of the same services as SSL. TLS 1.0 is based on SSL 3.0 but is more extensible. The main goal of TLS is privacy and data integrity between two communicating applications.

SSL is related to a PKI in that a certificate is required on the server end and optionally can be used on the client end of an SSL communication. If the user verifies the server certificate and the server verifies the user certificate, the process is called mutual authentication. In the operation of SSL, the public and private keys of the server are used to encrypt the data and protect its integrity.

VPN

Virtual private network (VPN) connections are remote access connections that allow users to securely connect to the enterprise network and work as if they were in the office. These connections use special tunneling protocols that encrypt the information being transferred between the user and the corporate network. In any case where users, business partners, or vendors are allowed remote access to the network, VPN connections should be used. Examples of tunneling protocol that can be used are as follows:

- Point-to-Point Tunneling Protocol (PPTP)
- Layer 2 Tunneling Protocol (L2TP)

In VPN operations, tunneling protocols wrap around or encapsulate the original packet when this process occurs. PPTP will encrypt the result using Microsoft Point-to-Point Encryption (MPPE). L2TP has no encryption mechanism but is usually combined with IPsec (covered in the next section) to provide the encryption.

IPsec

Internet Protocol Security (IPsec) is a suite of protocols that establishes a secure channel between two devices. IPsec is commonly implemented over VPNs but that is not its only use.

Here are the components of IPsec:

Authentication Header (AH)   Provides authentication and integrity.

Encapsulating Security Payload (ESP)   Provides authentication, integrity, and encryption (confidentiality).

Security Associations (SAs)   A record of a device's configuration needs to participate in IPsec communication.

Security Parameter Index (SPI)   A type of table that tracks the different SAs used and ensures that a device uses the appropriate SA to communicate with another device. Each device has its own SPI.

IPsec runs in one of two modes: transport mode or tunnel mode. Transport mode only protects the message payload, whereas tunnel mode protects the payload, routing, and header information. Both of these modes can be used for gateway-to-gateway or host-to-gateway IPsec communication. IPsec does not specify which hashing or encryption algorithm is used. That choice is up to the designer of the connection, but the parameters must match on both ends.

One of the challenges with IPsec is how to generate an encryption key for the session (each session key is unique). Internet Key Exchange (IKE) is the key exchange method that is most commonly used by IPsec. IKE with IPsec provides authentication and key exchange.

The authentication methods that can be used by IKE with IPsec include preshared keys, certificates, and public key authentication. The most secure implementations of pre-shared keys require a PKI. But a PKI is not necessary if a preshared key is based on simple passwords.

Retention Policies

Once data has reached the end of the life cycle, you should either properly dispose of it or ensure that it is securely stored. Some organizations must maintain data records for a certain number of years per local, state, or federal laws or regulations. This type of data should be archived for the required period. In addition, any data that is part of litigation should be retained as requested by the court of law, and organizations should follow appropriate chain of custody and evidence documentation processes. Data archival and destruction procedures should be clearly defined by the organization.

All organizations need policies and procedures in place for the retention and destruction of data. Data retention and destruction must follow all local, state, and government regulations and laws. Documenting proper procedures ensures that information is maintained for the required time to prevent financial fines and possible incarceration of high-level organizational officers. These procedures must include both retention period and destruction process.

Data Storage

Data must be stored somewhere. In today's world the options include cloud storage, local physical storage, and even tapes, CDs, and DVDs. In this section you'll learn the pros and cons of two approaches to storing data.

Physical Location Storage

When you think about it, *all* storage is physical, even cloud storage and virtual storage, because even in the cloud and in a virtual environment the data is located on a drive somewhere. It's just that the exact location may be abstracted from you. In this context, however, I'm speaking of data stored on physical media owned by the organization. In this section you'll learn about approaches to storing these devices and media.

Off-Site vs. On-Site

Two types of storage mechanisms are available for data storage:

On-Site Storage   *On-site storage* usually refers to a location on the site of the computer center that is used to store information locally. On-site storage containers are available that allow computer cartridges, tapes, and other backup media to be stored in a reasonably protected environment in the building.

On-site storage containers are designed and rated for fire, moisture, and pressure resistance. These containers aren't *fireproof* in most situations, but they're *fire-rated*: a fireproof container should be guaranteed to withstand damage regardless of the type of fire or temperatures, whereas fire ratings specify that a container can protect the contents for a specific amount of time in a given situation.

If you choose to depend entirely on on-site storage, make sure the containers you acquire can withstand the worst-case environmental catastrophes that could happen at your location. Make sure as well that those containers are in locations where you can easily find them after the disaster and access them (near exterior walls, for example).

Off-Site Storage   *Off-site storage* refers to a location away from the computer center where paper copies and backup media are kept. Off-site storage can involve something as simple as keeping a copy of backup media at a remote office, or it can be as complicated as a nuclear-hardened high-security storage facility. The storage facility should be bonded, insured, and inspected on a regular basis to ensure that all storage procedures are being followed.

Determining which storage mechanism to use should be based on the needs of the organization, the availability of storage facilities, and the budget available. Most off-site storage facilities charge based on the amount of space you require and the frequency of access you need to the stored information.

UEFI/BIOS Passwords

You learned about configuring passwords for UEFI/BIOS in Chapter 6, "Securing the Server." Please review that chapter.

Bootloader Passwords

A bootloader is a file that locates the operating system files and loads them into memory so that they can be executed to start the OS. For example, GRUB is the bootloader package in Linux and Unix systems. If it is not present, the system may not boot. You can add a password to GRUB so that the operator must enter the password to interrupt the normal boot sequence.

In Fedora, to set a boot password, select the Use A Boot Loader Password check box. At the command prompt—for example in Red Hat—to set a password of numbskull, use this command:

```
/sbin/grub-md5-crypt
```

and when prompted, type **numbskull** and press Enter. This returns an MD5 hash of the password.

Business Impact

When planning secure storage and backup of data, you should consider each dataset with respect to the importance of the data to your organization. This allows you to focus your attention on the data that is critical without wasting resources on data that is less important. In this section you'll learn what factors you need to consider.

Data Value Prioritization

Determining the relative priority of each dataset cannot be done until all data is classified. There should be a system of data classification that extends to cover sensitive documents such as contracts, leases, design plans, and product details. The data protection method accorded each category should reflect its sensitivity label. Any such documents labeled sensitive should be encrypted and stored separately from other categories of data. Here are examples of this sort of information:

- Personally identifiable information, which in part or in combination can be used to identify a person
- Human resources information
- Financial documents that are not public
- Trade secrets and propriety methods
- Plans and designs
- Any other documents that the company deems to be sensitive

Life-Cycle Management

In Chapter 4, "Storage Technologies and Asset Management," you learned about the life cycle of organizational assets. Since data is considered an asset, this life cycle also applies to data. Please review Chapter 4.

Cost of Security vs. Risk and/or Replacement

Always keep in mind that when considering a security solution (new hardware, different protocol, new procedure) to perform a cost–benefit analysis with respect to the cost of the solution and the potential loss from a vulnerability.

For example, if a new raised floor in the server room costs $50,000 and the anticipated monetary loss from a flood in that room is $30,000, it makes no sense to implement the solution.

Explain Important Concepts Pertaining to Identity and Access Management for Server Administration

Controlling access to data on the server is certainly important, but perhaps even more important is controlling administrative access to the server. In this section you'll learn about access control in general as well as managing access for server administration.

User Accounts

To manage the server, you will need a local account created on the server. A local administrator account is typically created during the process of installing the operating system, but that account will have complete access to everything (called *root access* in some systems), which may be more control than you want technicians to have.

Security best practices recommend that technicians use standard user accounts unless they need to do something that requires administrator access. They can then execute that task using admin credentials. In Windows, this is called running the task *as administrator* (you right-click the icon or app and select Run As Administrator from the context menu), as shown in Figure 7.1. The menu option has a shield next to it, and if you're at the command line, you preface the command with **runas**. This executes the function in an admin security context and ends that context when the process is over. Figure 7.2 shows the use of runas at the command line. After the command executed, Notepad opened a prompt for credentials, which were then provided.

FIGURE 7.1   Running an application as administrator

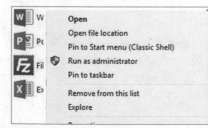

FIGURE 7.2   Using runas

```
C:\Windows\System32>runas /user:troy\pnut ipconfig/all
Enter the password for troy\pnut:
Attempting to start ipconfig/all as user "troy\pnut" ...
RUNAS ERROR: Unable to run - ipconfig/all
2: The system cannot find the file specified.

C:\Windows\System32>runas /user:troy\pnut notepad.exe
Enter the password for troy\pnut:
Attempting to start notepad.exe as user "troy\pnut" ...

C:\Windows\System32>
```

Later, if you join the server to the domain, the domain administrator account will be added to the local administrators group, giving domain administrators full rights to the server. Keep in mind that the same recommendation to use an administrator account *only* when required applies to those in the domain administrators group as well.

Every user is issued an account when hired that is theirs alone. However, there are some default accounts in many operating systems that you should be aware of as well. The most common types of default accounts in an operating system are as follows.

Administrator Account (Root in Linux and Unix)

The Administrator account is the most powerful of all; it has the power to do everything from the smallest task all the way up to removing the operating system. Because of the great power it holds, and the fact that it is always created, many who try to do harm will target this account as the one they try to break into. To increase security, during the installation of a Windows operating system, you are prompted for the name of a user who will be designated as the Administrator. The power then comes not from being truly called "Administrator" (it might now be tmcmillan, mcmillant, or something similar) but from being a member of the Administrators group (notice we use plural for the group and singular for the user).

Guest Account

This account is created in Windows by default (and should be disabled) and is a member of the group called Guests. For the most part, members of Guests have the same rights as users except they can't get to log files. The best reason to make users members of the Guests group is if they are accessing the system only for a limited time.

 As part of operating system security, we usually recommend that you rename the default Administrator and Guest accounts that are created at installation.

Standard User Account

This is the default that standard users belong to. Members of this group have read/write permission to their own profile. They cannot modify systemwide Registry settings or do much harm outside of their own account. Under the principle of least privilege, users should be made a member of the Users group only, unless qualifying circumstances force them to have higher privileges.

User Groups

One of the easier ways to assign permissions to a large number of users with the same needs is to put them all in a group and assign the permissions or rights to the group. There are default groups in Windows operating systems that have standard collections of privileges that you can use if desired, but generally it is better to create your own. One of the best examples is the Administrators group.

Since members of the Administrators group have such power, they can inadvertently do harm (such as by accidentally deleting a file that a regular user could not). To protect against this, the practice of logging in with an Administrator account or as a member of the Administrators group for daily interaction is strongly discouraged. Instead, we suggest that system administrators log in with a user account (lesser privileges) and change to the Administrators group account (elevated privileges) only when necessary.

When creating groups to use for assigning access, you should group users together that need the *same* access. This might be easier if you define roles and create the groups according to these roles. Let's look at roles next.

Roles

When you create a role-based group, you should define what actions this role will be capable of. The choice of permissions or rights you assign to the group that represents this role (for example, customer service rep) should be driven by the tasks required and the resources required to do that job. This is an area where you should exercise a security principle called *least privilege*. This principle states that no user should be given access to any resource that is not required to do the job.

Administrative Rights

Administrative rights should be the most closely controlled rights that exist. There is very little that cannot be done with administrative rights. These rights can be granted as a whole by assigning a user to the Administrators group or by copying the rights assigned to an administrator to the rights assigned to the user. It is also possible to assign only a subset of the rights assigned to the administrator.

When an administrator needs to delegate some of the rights to a user, it can be done two ways. The administrator can directly assign the right to perform certain functions to the user; when done this way, rights are assigned on the object to which those rights apply. For example, to allow a user to manage a printer, the Manage Printer right could be assigned to the user on the printer object in question.

In some cases, however, it may be desirable to assign that right on *all* printer objects. In that case, it will be easier to use the second way to delegate this right: using one of the built-in groups in Windows that exist for such a situation. Placing the user in the Domain Print Operators group ensures that the user will be granted the right to manage all printers in the domain. A number of such built-in groups exist for such a purpose. Here are some additional examples:

- Network configuration operators
- Server operators
- Performance log users
- Event log readers

Each of these groups possesses all rights required to perform the function for which the group was created and allows the right on all relevant objects in the scope of the group.

Distribution Lists

All of the groups we have discussed thus far are *security* groups. Security groups are used to assign rights and permissions. A second type of group is a *distribution* group, also called a distribution list. These are groups used in email. When a distribution group is created, its main function is to serve as a group to which an email can be sent and every member of the group receives the email.

There is an interesting relationship between security groups and distribution groups. While a security group can also be used as a distribution group, a distribution group cannot be used as a security group. To illustrate, if a Sales security group exists, it can also be as a distribution group for the purpose of sending an email to all members of the security group. On the other hand, if a distribution group was created for the members of the Finance department, you cannot assign any rights or permission to that distribution group.

Password Policies

An organization must establish a password management policy. Password management considerations are covered in the following sections.

Length

This specifies the minimum number of characters in the password—the longer, the better.

Lockout

This settings establishes the maximum number of attempts that can be made to submit the correct password. For example, if this number is set to 3, after three failed attempts the user account will be locked and will need to be unlocked by the administrator.

Enforcement

Enforcing these polices in Windows is done by assigning a password policy in AD Group Policy at the proper level in AD. Available policies are shown in Figure 7.3.

FIGURE 7.3   Password policy settings

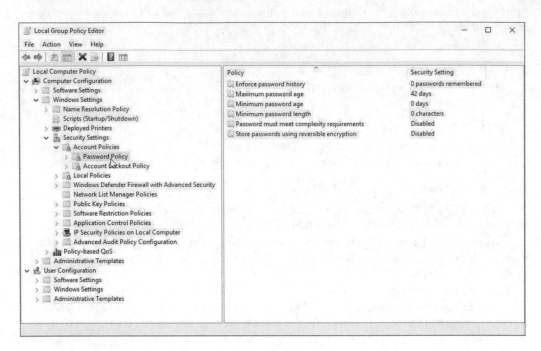

Permissions and Access Controls

A combination of filesystem permissions, user rights, and network access controls is used to define what users can and cannot do. In this section you'll learn more about these techniques.

Permissions

Although some of the names for permissions may be slightly different from one filesystem to another, most filesystems have the same basic permissions that can be applied to resources. In this section we'll look at those basic permissions and also discuss the difference between the operations of file and share permissions. While certainly not the only filesystems you will encounter, Table 7.1 shows the NTFS folder permissions and what these permissions allow, and Table 7.2 shows the NTFS file permissions and what these permissions allow. These tables offer a close approximation of what these permissions allow in any filesystem.

TABLE 7.1 NTFS folder permissions

NTFS permission	Meaning
Full Control	Gives the user all the other choices and the ability to change permission. The user also can take ownership of the directory or any of its contents.
Modify	Combines the Read & Execute permission with the Write permission and further allows the user to delete everything, including the folder.
Read & Execute	Combines the permissions of Read with those of List Folder Contents and adds the ability to run executables.
List Folder Contents	The List Folder Contents permission (known simply as List in previous versions) allows the user to view the contents of a directory and to navigate to its subdirectories. It does not grant the user access to the files in these directories unless that is specified in file permissions.
Read	Allows the user to navigate the entire directory structure, view the contents of the directory, view the contents of any files in the directory, and see ownership and attributes.
Write	Allows the user to create new entities within the folder, as well as to change attributes.

TABLE 7.2 NTFS file permissions

NTFS permission	Meaning
Full Control	Gives the user all the other permissions as well as permission to take ownership and change permission
Modify	Combines the Read & Execute permission with the Write permission and further allows the user to delete the file
Read	Allows the user to view the contents of the file and to see ownership and attributes
Read & Execute	Combines the Read permission with the ability to execute
Write	Allows the user to overwrite the file, as well as to change attributes and see ownership and permissions

Superuser

The term *superuser* applies to any user account that has total control and access to a system. This user will possess the Full Control permission to every resource and object on the device for which the user possesses this account type. Various operating systems attach different names to this account. Windows systems call this the Administrator account; other systems call it root, admin, or supervisor. Whatever this account is called, security best practices call for the account to be used only when required. Users who are members of any group accounts (like the Administrators group) that possess these rights or who are superuser account holders should use standard user accounts for all day-to-day activities and only log on using the superuser account when required.

File vs. Share

The Windows New Technology File System (NTFS) was introduced with Windows NT to address security problems. Before Windows NT was released, it had become apparent to Microsoft that a new filesystem was needed to handle growing disk sizes, security concerns, and the need for more stability. NTFS was created to address those issues.

Although FAT was relatively stable if the systems that were controlling it kept running, it didn't do well when the power went out or the system crashed unexpectedly. One of the benefits of NTFS was a transaction tracking system, which made it possible for Windows NT to back out of any disk operations that were in progress when Windows NT crashed or lost power.

With NTFS, files, directories, and volumes can each have their own security. NTFS's security is flexible and built in. Not only does NTFS track security in ACLs, which can hold permissions for local users and groups, but each entry in the ACL can specify what type of access is given—such as Read, Write, Modify, or Full Control. This allows a great deal of flexibility in setting up a network. In addition, special file-encryption programs encrypt data while it is stored on the hard disk.

Microsoft strongly recommends that all network shares be established using NTFS. Several current OSs from Microsoft support both FAT32 and NTFS. It's possible to convert from FAT32 to NTFS without losing data, but you can't do the operation in reverse (you would need to reformat the drive and install the data again from a backup tape).

 If you're using FAT32 and want to change to NTFS, the convert utility will allow you to do so. For example, to change the E drive to NTFS, the command is convert e: /FS:NTFS.

Share permissions apply only when a user is accessing a file or folder through the network. Local permissions and attributes are used to protect the file when the user is local. With FAT and FAT32, you do not have the ability to assign "extended" or "extensible" permissions, and the user sitting at the console is effectively the owner of all resources on the system. As such, they can add, change, and delete any data or file that they want.

With NTFS as the filesystem, however, you are allowed to assign more comprehensive security to your computer system. NTFS permissions are able to protect you at the file level. Share permissions can be applied to the directory level only. NTFS permissions can affect users logged on locally or across the network to the system where the NTFS permissions are applied. Share permissions are in effect only when the user connects to the resource via the network.

How Do NTFS and Share Permissions Work Together?

Share and NTFS permissions are not cumulative; permission must be granted at both levels to allow access. Moreover, the effective permission that the user has will be the most restrictive of the combined NTFS permissions as compared to the combined share permissions.

Allow vs. Deny

Within NTFS, permissions for objects fall into one of three categories: allow, not allow, and deny. When viewing the permissions for a file or folder, you can check the box for Allow, which effectively allows that group to perform that action. You can also deselect the Allow check box so that group cannot perform that action. Alternatively, you can select the Deny check box, which prevents that group from using that action. There is a difference between not allowing (a cleared check box) and Deny (which specifically prohibits), and you tend not to see Deny used often. Deny, when used, trumps other permissions. This can be a problem for users with permissions derived from multiple groups.

Permissions set at a folder are inherited down through subfolders, unless otherwise changed. Permissions are also cumulative; if a user is a member of a group that has the read permission and a member of a group that has the write permission, the user effectively has both read and write permissions.

Role-Based

You learned about role-based access earlier in this chapter. Please review that section.

Rule-Based

Rule-based access control uses a preconfigured rule to control access, and unlike permissions and user rights, it applies equally to all. An access list is a great example. Access lists can be either a digital list of allowed users that resides on an authentication system or a physical entry roster monitored by a security guard at an entry point. At any physical location where users are arriving and departing the facility or the server room, users should be authenticated through one of the mechanisms discussed in this section. There should be a recording of each user arriving and departing. This can be either a record of all successful and unsuccessful authentications on a log or, in the case of visitors who have no network account, a physical identification process of some sort. In any case, there should be an entry control roster in the form of a physical document that shows when each person entered and left the facility. This will serve as a backup in case the log is lost.

Scope-Based

A scope is a grouping of resources that can be used to restrict the range of an operation or action. Scope-based access control allows you to create a custom set of resources (called a scope) and assign access to them to a user. For example, a datacenter could be organized so that all DNS servers are monitored using one scope and all servers running SQL Server are monitored using another scope.

Segregation of Duties

Segregation of duties is a concept that says when an operation is prone to fraud it should be divided into two operations, with each assigned to a different user. Although this can't guarantee fraud prevention, it makes fraud much less likely as it requires collusion between the two individuals.

Delegation

Whenever you have a distributed application, it means that the application is operating on multiple servers that must talk to one another. This means they require machine-to-machine access to one another. For example, if you install the Microsoft Application Virtualization (App-V) Management Server software using a distributed system architecture (for example, the console on one system, the Management Web Service on one, and the database on another), you must configure the services on each system to be trusted for delegation on the other servers.

This can be done using the following steps on the domain controller for each server's domain:

1. Click Start ➤ Administrative Tools, and then click Active Directory Users And Computers.

2. Expand the domain, and then expand the Computers folder.

3. In the right pane, right-click the computer name for the server, and then click Properties.

4. On the General tab, ensure that the Trust Computer For Delegation check box is selected.

5. Click OK.

Auditing

Someone once said that it is okay to trust but imperative to verify. As it applies to rights, permissions, and access, this means that you must audit the activities of the users to identify and address inappropriate access. In this section we'll look at the types of things you should be auditing.

User Activity

While there are many logs in a server, in Windows, to monitor user activity, the Security log and Event Viewer are the tools of choice. Windows employs comprehensive error and informational logging routines. Every program and process theoretically could have its own logging utility, but Microsoft provides a rather slick utility, Event Viewer, which, through log files, tracks all events on a particular Windows computer. Normally, though, you must be an administrator or a member of the Administrators group to have access to Event Viewer.

With Windows Server 2012 R2, you can access Event Viewer from the Tools menu in Server Manager, as shown in Figure 7.4.

FIGURE 7.4   Tools menu

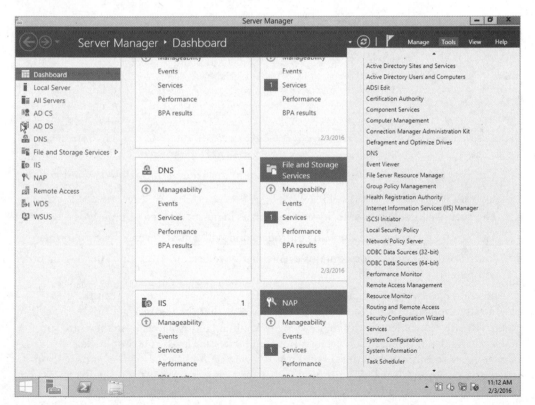

Once Event Viewer is selected, you see the opening page (Figure 7.5):

FIGURE 7.5   The opening interface of Event Viewer

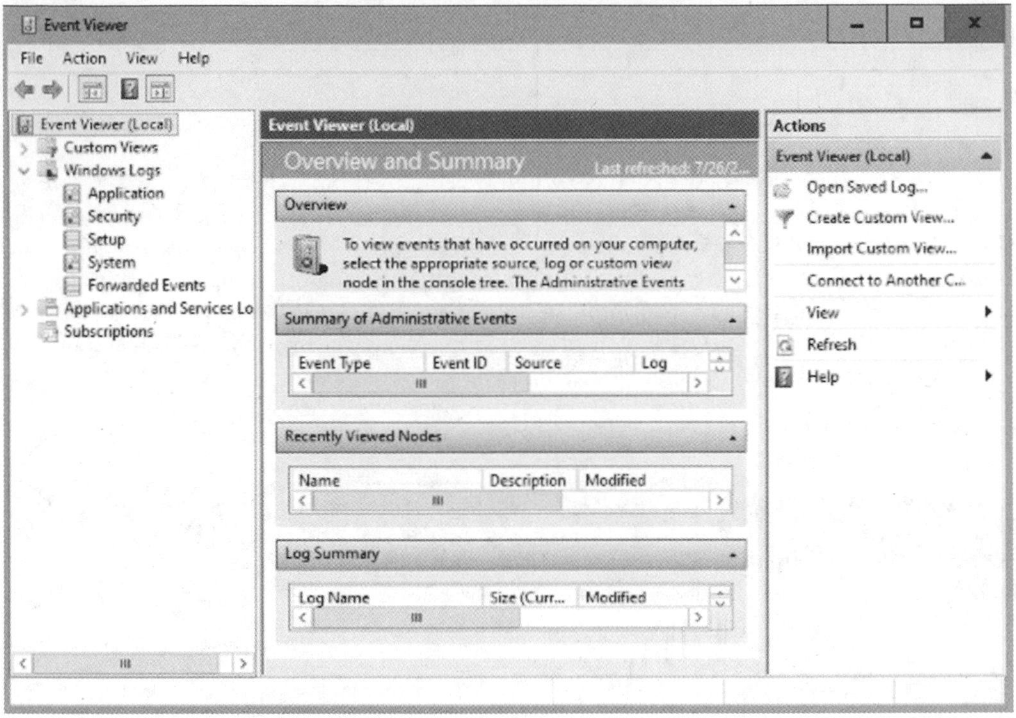

- The System log file displays alerts that pertain to the general operation of Windows.
- The Application log file logs application errors.
- The Security log file logs security events such as login successes and failures.
- The Setup log appears on domain controllers and will contain events specific to them.
- The Forwarded Events log contains events that have been forwarded to this log by other computers.

These log files can give a general indication of a Windows computer's health.

One situation that does occur with Event Viewer is that the log files get full. Although this isn't really a problem, it can make viewing log files confusing because there are so many entries. Even though each event is time- and date-stamped, you should clear Event Viewer every so often. To do this, open Event Viewer, right-click on the log, choose Properties, and click the Clear Log button; in earlier OSs, choose Clear All Events from the Log menu. Doing so erases all events in the current log file, allowing you to see new events more easily when they occur. You can set the maximum log size by right-clicking on the log and choosing Properties. By default, when a log fills to its maximum size, old entries are deleted in first in, first out (FIFO) order. Clearing the log, setting the maximum log size, and setting how the log is handled when full are done on the Log Properties dialog box, as shown in Figure 7.6.

FIGURE 7.6   Event Log Properties

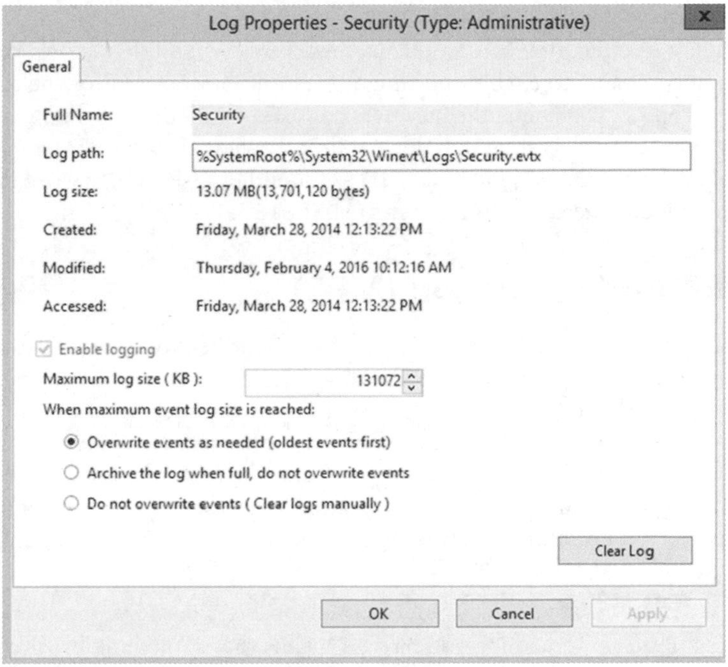

Log Properties - Security (Type: Administrative)   ☒

General

Full Name:	Security
Log path:	%SystemRoot%\System32\Winevt\Logs\Security.evtx
Log size:	13.07 MB(13,701,120 bytes)
Created:	Friday, March 28, 2014 12:13:22 PM
Modified:	Thursday, February 4, 2016 10:12:16 AM
Accessed:	Friday, March 28, 2014 12:13:22 PM

☑ Enable logging

Maximum log size (KB):   131072 ⬍

When maximum event log size is reached:

◉ Overwrite events as needed (oldest events first)

○ Archive the log when full, do not overwrite events

○ Do not overwrite events (Clear logs manually)

[Clear Log]

[OK]   [Cancel]   [Apply]

 You can save the log files before erasing them. The saved files can be burned to a CD or DVD for future reference. Often, you are required to save the files to CD or DVD if you are working in a company that adheres to strict regulatory standards.

In addition to just erasing logs, you can configure three different settings for what you want to occur when the file reaches its maximum size. The first option is "Overwrite events as needed (oldest events first)," and this replaces the older events with the new entries. The second option is "Archive the log when full, do not overwrite events," and this will create another log file as soon as the current one runs out of space. The third option, "Do not overwrite events (Clear logs manually)," will not record any additional events once the file is full.

Logins

Logins are monitored in the Security log of Event Viewer. See the previous section.

Group Memberships

Group memberships can be monitored using a Group Policy setting called Restricted Groups. When this policy is applied to containers in Active Directory, it checks the membership of each group each time the policy is refreshed (at login and startup), removes any members that are not approved, and readds any members that have somehow been deleted.

Deletions

You also configure a setting that can produce a report on demand that shows you all file deletions. You must choose to enable auditing of file and object access for the resource in question. When you do, you can audit successes, failures, or both. At any point after that, you can generate a report that shows all deleted files. To view the report, open the Event Viewer and search the security log for event ID 4656 with a task category of File System or Removable Storage and the string "Accesses: DELETE".

Multifactor Authentication (MFA)

Because attaining access to a server room should be a right held only by a few, the method used to authenticate those attempting to enter the server room should be robust. Names and passwords are simple to create, manage, and use, but you can increase the security of the authentication solution by implementing *multifactor* authentication (MFA).

There are three factors of authentication. When more than one of these factors is required to authenticate, it is called multifactor authentication. It is *not* multifactor if it uses two forms of the same factor of authentication. Let's look at three forms and examples of each.

Something You Have

When the system requires something you have, it means that something in your possession, like a smart card, must be inserted into a reader that will verify that the security credentials on the card are correct and that they correspond to the other factor that you presented.

Something You Know

When the system requires something you know, it means that something that resides in your memory is required such as a password, a username, or a PIN.

Something You Are

When the system requires something you are, it will examine some unique physical feature such as a fingerprint or retina scan. This is called *biometrics*. Although the use of biometrics offers a high level of security, you should know that they are expensive to implement and can be prone to false positives (letting a user in that should not be in) and false negatives (denying a legitimate user).

Remember, when more than one of these factors is required to authenticate it is called multifactor authentication. It is *not* multifactor if it uses two forms of the same factor of authentication such as a username and password (both something you know).

Single Sign-on (SSO)

One of the big problems that larger systems must deal with is the need for users to access multiple systems or applications. This may require a user to remember multiple accounts and passwords. The purpose of a single sign-on (SSO) is to give users access to all the applications and systems they need when they log on. This has become a reality in many environments, including Kerberos, Microsoft Active Directory, Novell eDirectory, and some certificate model implementations.

Single sign-on is both a blessing and a curse. It's a blessing in that once users are authenticated, they can access all the resources on the network and browse multiple directories. It's a curse in that it removes the doors that otherwise exist between the user and various resources.

Summarize Proper Server Decommissioning Concepts

At some point every system will become obsolete, or at the least will be insufficient to do the job. When you decommission a system, security issues can be created if proper removal procedures are not followed. In this section you'll learn proper decommissioning concepts.

Proper Removal Procedures

To be prepared to exercise proper removal procedures, you must take the steps described in this section. Doing so ensures that removal procedures are carried out in a safe and consistent manner.

Company Policies

In Chapter 4 you learned about company policies and how they drive the creation of procedures. You should have a policy addressing the importance of proper decommissioning, and it should lead to the creation of a checklist of procedures that must be followed during any system retirement. This will help prevent the omission of critical steps and other human errors.

Verify Non-Utilization

While it should be obvious to make sure a system is *not* in use before taking it down, CompTIA thinks it needs to be said. A live production system should be replaced, with the replacement successfully accepting and performing work on behalf of the users *before* a system is taken down.

Documentation

During the decommissioning process, certain organizational documents will become relevant. You will need to consult these documents and, in some cases, update them. Let's look at two examples that should be consulted and updated.

Asset Management

In Chapter 4 you learned about asset management and the importance of keeping inventory information current. The inventory document must be updated to reflect both the removal and disposal methods of the old system and the purchase and deployment of the new system.

Change Management

In Chapter 6 you learned about change management and its benefits when performed properly. Whereas you will update the asset inventory document, in the case of the change management document you will be consulting it to ensure that the change management process is followed. This means decommissioning approval must be requested and approved by the change management board.

Media Destruction

At some point in time, storage media must be decommissioned. When that occurs, all sensitive data must be removed. There are a number of ways this can be done, with the results varying widely. We'll discuss data removal methods in this section.

Disk Wiping

There are many approaches to removing sensitive data from a drive. This section covers common methods that stop short of destroying the drive so that it can be reused.

Soft Wipe

A soft wipe describes any method that deletes data in such a way that the data can be recovered later using special data forensics software. The best example of this is the simple file deletion process.

File Deletion

When you right-click on a file and select Delete, the data is not immediately deleted—the area of the hard drive where that data is located is marked for deletion. That means that the filesystem is now given permission to write data over the old data in that location. Until that overwrite occurs, the data is still there on the hard drive. Moreover, even after the data is overwritten, unless the overwriting has occurred many times, the data can be recovered using data recovery software.

Hard Wipe

A *hard wipe* is a term used to describe any deletion process that cannot be reversed using data recovery or forensics software. Most disk management software will provide this type of deletion and may refer to it in various terms, such as "scrubbing" the drive. Let's look at how this process works.

ZERO OUT ALL SECTORS

When a hard wipe is performed, the area where the file is located is zeroed out, meaning all 0s are written to the sectors where the data is located. This is followed by writing all 1s to the same location, followed by another round of all 0s. This process may continue many times. The more times it's done, the more effective the data wipe.

Physical

Ultimately the most effective method of protecting sensitive data located on a hard drive is to destroy the hard drive. While the focus is on hard drives, you can also physically destroy other forms of media, such as flash drives and CD/DVDs.

Degaussing

Degaussing involves applying a strong magnetic field to initialize the media. This process helps ensure that information doesn't fall into the wrong hands.

Since degaussing uses a specifically designed electromagnet to eliminate all data on the drive, that destruction also includes the factory prerecorded servo tracks. (These are tracks put on at the factory.) You can find wand model degaussers priced at just over $500 or desktop units that sell for up to $30,000.

Shredding

When it comes to DVDs and CDs, many commercial paper shredders include the ability to destroy them. Paper shredders, however, are not able to handle hard drives, and you need a shredder created for just such a purpose. Jackhammer makes a low-volume model that will destroy eight drives a minute and carries a suggested list price of just under $18,950.00.

Crushing

Crushing a drive is sometimes easier than shredding the drive and, as you would guess, is just as effective in preventing access to any remaining data.

Incineration

A final option that exists for some forms of storage is to burn the media. Regardless of whether the media is a hard drive, CD, DVD, solid-state drive, or floppy disk, the media must be reduced to ash, or in the case of hard drive platters, the internal platters must be physically deformed from heating.

Purposes for Media Destruction

While hardware repurposing is a good thing and donating legacy computer equipment is laudable, in some cases you just can't take the chance that sensitive data remains in a system. In these scenarios destroying the hardware is the best choice.

Media Retention Requirements

Don't lose sight of the fact that media can also be paper documents. Some of these must be retained and kept safe in hard copy. For example, there are laws and regulations that address record retention for accounting, labor, tax, and contracts records. You should be aware of these requirements and ensure your company is in compliance.

Cable Remediation

When a system is decommissioned, it may be a good time to inspect and remediate any cable issues before bringing the new system online. A quick check and fix now might save a costly outage later.

Power

In Chapter 1, "Server Hardware," you learned about power issues. This would be a good time to look at the device being removed and the neighboring devices and make a quick assessment to ensure that the PDU can supply sufficient wattage to the devices. It might have been some time since this was done.

Networking

This is also a good time to closely inspect the network cable running to the new device, especially if it is the same one that connected to the old device. Does it look worn? Are there crimps in it? Keep in mind that a cable may work but *not* work well, introducing errors and slowing throughput. Test the cable to ensure it does more than just work.

Electronics Recycling

Earlier we talked about reusing hardware in cases where it is safe to do so. Recycling is something that should be done when possible. We'll end this chapter by talking about two ways to recycle.

Internal vs. External

Your organization can recycle hardware internally, externally, or both. Internally it could be that a server that is no longer useful to the IT department might be a great candidate to be a file server in the Content department. Externally, organizations often donate old hardware to schools and nonprofit groups that need equipment but lack funds.

Repurposing

When a decision is made to repurpose a system internally, the system drive should be reviewed to identify any sensitive material that may remain. When this type of data is found, a means to remove it safely must be utilized. If the data cannot be removed, the drive should be destroyed.

Summary

In this chapter, you learned concepts related to securing the server. First, you learned about data security, including encryption paradigms for data at rest and in transit. You also learned about concepts pertaining to identity and access management, including users' groups and permissions. Finally you learned about server decommissioning concepts, including the removal of sensitive data.

Exam Essentials

Describe logical access control methods.   Explain the proper use of access control lists (ACLs) to protect resources. Use groups to apply role-based access control. List common permissions and identify the tasks they enable when working with resources.

Implement secure storage methods and secure data disposal techniques.   Describe various levels at which encryption can be applied and the implications of each. List the techniques for removing sensitive data from storage devices. Understand the advantages and disadvantages of each method.

Review Questions

You can find the answers in the Appendix.

1. Which authentication mechanism is an example of something you have?
   A. Password
   B. Username
   C. Smart card
   D. Retina scan

2. Which of the following types of groups' main function is to serve as a group to which an email can be sent and every member of the group receives the email?
   A. Security
   B. Domain
   C. Distribution
   D. OU

3. Group memberships can be monitored using which Group Policy setting?
   A. Restricted Groups
   B. gpedit.msc
   C. gpresult.msc
   D. Privileged access

4. Which of the following authentication methods is *not* an example of biometrics?
   A. Password
   B. Hand scanners
   C. Fingerprint scan
   D. Retina scan

5. Which of the following is *not* an NTFS file permission?
   A. Read
   B. List Folder Contents
   C. Full Control
   D. Write

6. Which of the following groups have the same rights as standard users except that they can't access log files?
   A. Guests
   B. Administrators
   C. Print Managers
   D. Server Operators

7. Data that resides on storage devices is called which of the following?

   A. Data in transit

   B. Data in use

   C. Data at rest

   D. Data in process

8. Which of the following is an encryption tool built into all Enterprise versions of Windows?

   A. NTFS

   B. AES

   C. EFS

   D. SSL

9. Which of the following is located on the motherboard of the system and provides password protection, digital rights management (DRM), and full-disk encryption?

   A. EEPROM

   B. TPM

   C. EFS

   D. SSH

10. Which of the following is a file that locates the operating system files and loads them into memory so that they can be executed to start the OS?

   A. Bootstrap

   B. Bootloader

   C. BIOS

   D. UEFI

11. Which of the following helps in determining the relative priority of each dataset?

   A. Data encoding

   B. Data classification

   C. Data dictionary

   D. Data print

12. Which of the following is the strongest password?

   A. 0135

   B. PassWord

   C. MyP@$$phraSe

   D. We@kP@$$w0rd

13. Which of the following is sometimes called a superuser account?

   A. Guest

   B. Administrator

   C. Print Manager

   D. Support

14. Which of the following tracks all events on a particular Windows computer?

    A. Event Viewer

    B. Action Center

    C. Security Center

    D. Audit Center

15. Which of the following is *not* an example of something you are?

    A. Fingerprint

    B. Password

    C. Retina scan

    D. Voice recognition

16. Which of the following gives users access to all the applications and systems they need when they log on?

    A. HIDS

    B. PDU

    C. SSO

    D. UPS

17. Which of the following describes any method that deletes data in such a way that the data can be recovered later using special data forensics software?

    A. Degaussing

    B. Shredding

    C. Incinerating

    D. Soft wipe

18. Which of the following is a term used to describe any deletion process that cannot be reversed using data recovery or forensics software?

    A. Deletion

    B. Hard wipe

    C. Soft wipe

    D. Remote Wipe

19. What is the most effective data destruction method?

    A. Degaussing

    B. Hard wipe

    C. Remote wipe

    D. Shredding

20. Which of the following is a grouping of resources that can be used to restrict the range of an operation or action?

A. Realm

B. Domain

C. OU

D. Scope

Chapter

8

Networking and Scripting

COMPTIA SERVER+ EXAM OBJECTIVES COVERED IN THIS CHAPTER:

✓ **2.2 Given a scenario, configure servers to use network infrastructure services.**

- IP configuration
- Virtual local area network (VLAN)
- Default gateways
- Name resolution
    - Domain name service (DNS)
    - Fully qualified domain name (FQDN)
    - Hosts file
- Addressing protocols
    - IPv4
        - Request for comments (RFC) 1918 address spaces
    - IPv6
- Firewall
    - Ports
- Static vs. dynamic
    - Dynamic host configuration protocol (DHCP)
    - Automatic private IP address (APIPA)
- MAC addresses

✓ **2.6 Summarize scripting basics for server administration.**

- Script types
    - Bash
    - Batch

- PowerShell
- Virtual basic script (VBS)
- Environment variables
- Comment syntax
- Basic script constructs
  - Loops
  - Variables
  - Conditionals
  - Comparators
- Basic data types
  - Integers
  - Strings
  - Arrays
- Common server administration scripting tasks
  - Startup
  - Shut down
  - Service
  - Login
  - Account creation
  - Bootstrap

When your server is up and running, you will need to connect it to the network. This task obviously includes connecting a cable to it and then connecting to a switch, but it also includes many other steps that you'll learn about in this chapter. You'll also learn the value of scripting and automating operations.

Given a Scenario, Configure Servers to Use Network Infrastructure Services

Configuring a server to use network infrastructure services goes far beyond simply applying an IP address. In this section you'll learn about various network services, the role they play, and the configuration of a server to use these services.

IP Configuration

Assigning an IP address, subnet mask, and (usually) default gateway is the starting point in connecting the server to the network. Although we typically give servers static IP addresses, it's also possible—and sometimes preferred—to achieve similar stability using a DHCP reservation. DHCP will be covered in detail later in this chapter.

Virtual Local Area Network (VLAN)

Virtual local area networks (VLANs) are logical subdivisions of a switch that segregate ports from one another as if they were in different LANs. VLANs offer another way to add a layer of separation between sensitive devices and the rest of the network. For example, if only one device should be able to connect to the Finance server, the device and the Finance server could be placed in a VLAN separate from the other VLANs. As traffic between VLANs can only occur through a router, access control lists (ACLs) can be used to control the traffic allowed between VLANs.

These VLANs can also span multiple switches, meaning that devices connected to switches in different parts of a network can be placed in the same VLAN regardless of physical location.

VLANs have many advantages and only one disadvantage. These are listed in Table 8.1.

TABLE 8.1   Advantages of VLANs

Advantages	Disadvantages
Cost: Switched networks with VLANs are less costly than routed networks because routers cost more than switches.	Managerial overhead securing VLANs
Performance: By creating smaller broadcast domains (each VLAN is a broadcast domain), performance improves.	
Flexibility: Removes the requirement that devices in the same LAN (or in this case, VLAN) be in the same location.	
Security: Provides one more layer of separation at Layers 2 and 3.	

A VLAN security issue you should be aware of is called *VLAN hopping*. By default, a switch port is an access port, which means it can only be a member of a single VLAN. Ports that are configured to carry the traffic of multiple VLANs, called trunk ports, are used to carry traffic between switches and to routers. A VLAN hopping attack's aim is to receive traffic from a VLAN of which the hacker's port is not a member. It can be done two ways:

Switch Spoofing   Switch ports can be set to use a protocol called Dynamic Trunking Protocol (DTP) to negotiate the formation of a trunk link. If an access port is left configured to use DTP, it is possible for hackers to set their interface to spoof a switch and use DTP to create a trunk link. If this occurs, they can capture traffic from all VLANs. To prevent this, disable DTP on all switch ports.

Double Tagging   Trunk ports use an encapsulation protocol called 802.1q to place a VLAN tag around each frame to identify the VLAN to which the frame belongs. When a switch at the end of a trunk link receives an 802.1q frame, it strips this off and forwards the traffic to the destination device. In a double tagging attack, the hacker creates a special frame that has two tags. The inner tag is the VLAN to which the hacker wants to send a frame (perhaps with malicious content), and the outer tag is the real VLAN of which the hacker is a member. If the frame goes through two switches (which is possible since VLANs can span switches), the first tag gets taken off by the first switch, leaving the second, which allows the frame to be forwarded to the target VLAN by the second switch.

Double tagging is only an issue on switches that use "native" VLANs. A native VLAN is used for any traffic that is still a member of the default VLAN, or VLAN 1. To mitigate double tagging, either move all ports out of VLAN 1 or change the number of the native VLAN from 1 to something else. If that is not possible, you can also enable the tagging of all traffic on the native VLAN. None of these settings are the defaults, so it will require configuration on your part.

Default Gateways

In TCP/IP, a gateway is the address of the machine to send data to that is not intended for a host on this network (in other words, a default gateway). It is the router that allows traffic to be sent beyond the internal network. Hosts are configured with the address of a gateway (called the default gateway), and if they need to correspond with a host outside the internal network, the data is sent to the gateway to facilitate this. When you configure TCP/IP on a host, one of the fields you should provide is a gateway field, which specifies where data not intended for this network is sent in order to be able to communicate with the rest of the world.

Name Resolution

Name resolution services resolve device and domain names (website names) to IP addresses, and vice versa. They make it possible to connect to either without knowing the IP address of the device or the server hosting the website. In this section you'll learn about DNS, the standard for name resolution.

Domain Name Service (DNS)

Every computer, interface, or device on a TCP/IP network needs an *IP address*. Because of the Internet, TCP/IP is the most commonly used networking protocol today. You can easily see that it's difficult for most users to memorize these numbers, so hostnames are used in their place. *Hostnames* are alphanumeric values assigned to a host; any host may have more than one hostname.

For example, the host 192.168.12.123 may be known to all users as Gemini, or it may be known to the Sales department as Gemini and to the Marketing department as Apollo9. All that is needed is a means by which the alphanumeric name can be translated into its IP address. There are a number of methods for doing so, but for this exam, you need to know only one: DNS. On a large network, you can add a server to be referenced by all hosts for the name resolution. Multiple DNS servers can serve an area and provide fault tolerance for one another. In all cases, the DNS servers divide their area into zones; every zone has a primary server and any number of secondary servers. DNS works with any operating system and any version.

Fully Qualified Domain Name (FQDN)

Fully qualified domain names (FQDNs) identify the host and the location of the hostname in the DNS namespace of the organization. FQDNs consists of at least two parts and perhaps more. All FQDNs will have a hostname and a domain name. If the DNS namespace of the organization is subdivided into subdomains, it could have a subdomain section as well. For example, in the FQDN `tmcmillan.acme.com`, *tmcmillan* is the hostname and `acme.com` is the domain name. In the example `tmcmillan.atlanta.acme.com`, *tmcmillan* is the hostname, *atlanta* identifies the subdomain, and `acme.com` is the domain name.

Default Domain Suffix/Search Domain

While `tmcmillan.acme.com` describes a FQDN, if we just consider the hostname portion, *tmcmillan* without the domain name, we would call the name *unqualified* because it is lacking information that fully qualifies or describes its location in the DNS namespace.

In many instances, users make references to unqualified hostnames when accessing resources. When this occurs, DNS needs to know how to handle these unqualified domain names. The treatment of these names by default will be for DNS to append or add domain names (called suffixes) to the unqualified hostname until a match is found in the DNS namespace. If the device has been assigned a domain name, then it uses that as a suffix to unqualified hostnames.

It is also possible to configure a list of domain names for the DNS to append to unqualified hostnames and the order in which they should be tried. In Microsoft this can be done in several ways. It can be done through the use of a Group Policy that is pushed down to the clients, or it can be done manually on the interface of the device. Exercise 8.1 demonstrates the manual method, and Exercise 8.2 demonstrates the use of a Group Policy. This task can also be done with a Registry edit, but Microsoft recommends these two methods as the safest.

EXERCISE 8.1

Configuring a Suffix Search List

Note: While this exercise uses Windows Server 2012 R2, the dialog boxes are basically the same as Windows Server 2022.

1. Access the TCP/IP properties of the network interface. You should be seeing the dialog box as shown below:

2. At the bottom of the screen click the Advanced button.

    Then select the DNS tab and you will be presented with the dialog box as shown below open to the DNS tab.

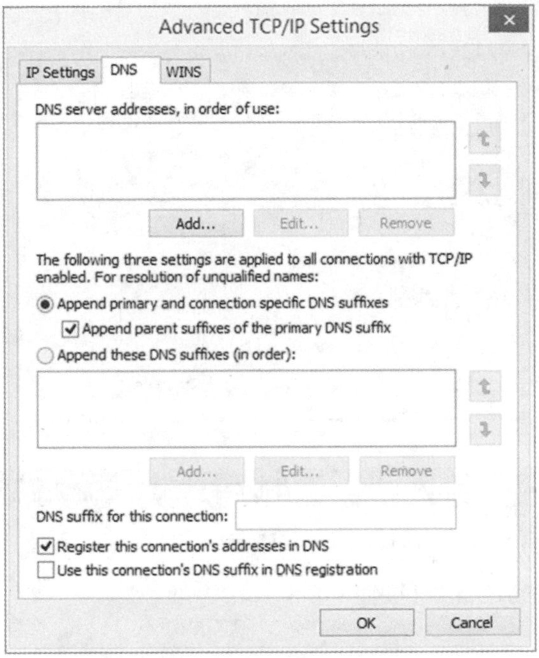

3. In the middle of this page are two radio buttons, one of which is selected by default and tells DNS to append the parent DNS suffix to any unqualified hostnames. The second button, Append These DNS Suffixes (In Order) is the one you select to create a list of domain names to attempt when an unqualified hostname is encountered. Select that radio button.

4. Click the Add button at the bottom of the screen to open a dialog box that allows you to enter a domain suffix to the list, as shown here. You can do this repeatedly until the list is finished. If you need to change the order in which they are attempted, use the up and down arrows next to the list box. Then click OK at the bottom of the page as shown below, to finalize the list.

Configuring a Suffix Search List as a Policy

Note: While this exercise uses Windows Server 2012 R2, the dialog boxes are basically the same as Windows Server 2022.

1. Access the Group Policy Management console by choosing it from the Tools menu in Server Manager as shown below. Right-click the default domain policy in the tree and click Edit.

2. In the Group Policy Management Editor, navigate to Computer Configuration ➢ Administrative Templates ➢ Network ➢ DNS Client, as shown below.

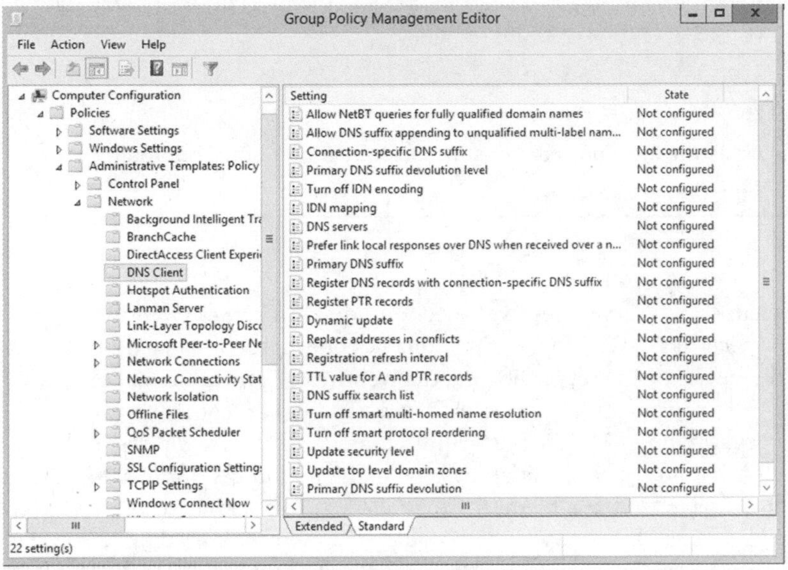

3. Select the Primary DNS Suffix policy, enable it, and in the Enter A Primary DNS Suffix box (shown below), type the suffixes. Use a comma-delimited string to enter multiple addresses, such as acme.com, ajax.com, and then click Apply.

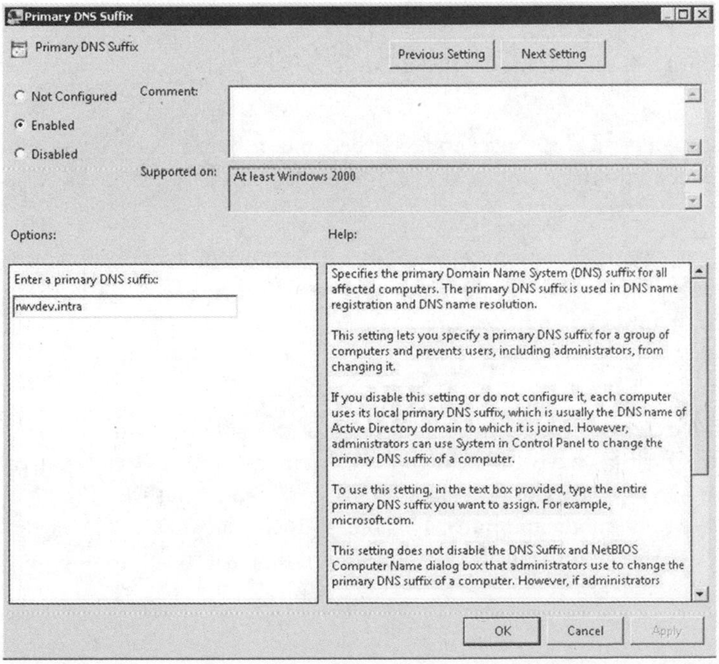

In a Linux environment this can be done by editing a file called `resolv.conf`, which is located in `/etc/resolv.conf`. Open the file using either the `vi` command or the `sudi vi` command. Then simply add search entries to the file. For example, to add the suffix `acme.com`, use the following commands:

```
# vi /etc/resolv.conf
search acme.com
```

Then save and close the file. The search list is currently limited to six domains with a total of 256 characters.

DNS Servers

Domain Name System (DNS) servers resolve device and domain names (website names) to IP addresses, and vice versa. They make it possible to connect to either without knowing the IP address of the device or the server hosting the website. Clients are configured with the IP address of a DNS server (usually through DHCP) and make requests of the server using *queries*. The organization's DNS server will be configured to perform the lookup of IP addresses for which it has no entry in its database by making requests of the DNS servers on the Internet, which are organized in a hierarchy that allows these servers to more efficiently provide the answer. When the DNS servers have completed their lookup, they return the IP address to the client so that the client can make a direct connection using the IP address. Here are some of the components that should be maximized to ensure good performance:

RAM   Memory is the most important resource because the entire DNS zone file will be loaded into memory. As you add zones, or as a zone gets larger, you should add memory. If you expect the server to be answering large numbers of queries concurrently, then that will require additional memory as well.

Disk   The disk is not a critical component, but it does need to be large enough to hold all the zones as well.

NIC   The NIC is not a critical resource unless it becomes a bottleneck during times when there is an overwhelming number of concurrent queries. If you find that to be the case often, add more NICs.

CPU   The CPU is not a critical resource, but if you expect a heavy query load then you should get the fastest processor the budget allows. The CPU can become a bottleneck just as the NIC can in times of high workload.

Hosts File

Most systems rely on DNS for name resolution, but it is not the only method a system can use. Windows and Linux systems have a file called Hosts that can be populated manually with IP address–to-name mappings. The downside to this is the static nature of the file—that is, any changes have to be made manually. This file is always located at `C:\Windows\System32\drivers\etc\hosts`. If this file is misconfigured, it will result in an inability to connect to the destination. To make matters worse, this file is the first place the device looks before it attempts DNS, so if there is an entry in the file for the name, it never uses DNS!

Finally, some forms of malware edit the Hosts file and add entries. So even if you are not aware that anyone has ever edited this file, it is still something to check since malware can add entries.

Addressing Protocols

Servers, like any other network host, require an IP address and a subnet mask to operate on the network. In almost all cases, they require a default gateway and the IP address of a DNS server as well. Moreover, there are a host of networking services that servers typically rely on. To successfully configure a server to operate on the network, you must understand all of these functions and services. First, let's spend time learning and/or reviewing infrastructure services and the configurations required to allow a server to make use of these services.

IPv4/IPv6

IPv4 uses a 32-bit addressing scheme that provides for over 4 billion unique addresses. Unfortunately, a lot of IP-enabled devices are added to the Internet each and every day—not to mention the fact that not all of the addresses that can be created are used by public networks (many are reserved, in classes D and above, and are unavailable for public use). This reduces the number of addresses that can be allocated as public Internet addresses.

IPv6 offers a number of improvements, the most notable of which is its ability to handle growth in public networks. IPv6 uses a 128-bit addressing scheme, allowing a huge number of possible addresses: 340,282,366,920,938,463,463,374,607,431,768,211,456. Table 8.2 compares IPv4 to IPv6.

 In IPv6 addresses, leading zeroes in a hextet can be left out and consecutive hextets consisting of all zeroes can be represented with a double colon, so colons next to each other in the address indicate one or more sets of zeroes for that section. The double colon may only be used once in this fashion, however.

TABLE 8.2 IPv4 vs. IPv6

Feature	IPv4	IPv6
Loopback address	127.0.0.1	0:0:0:0:0:0:0:1 (::1)
Private ranges	10.0.0.0 172.16.0.0 –172.31.0.0 192.168.0.0	FC00::/7 FEC0:: /10
Autoconfigured addresses	169.254.0.0	FE80::

CIDR Notation and Subnetting

Subnetting your network is the process of taking a single network and dividing it into smaller networks. When you configure TCP/IP on a host, you typically need to give only three values: a unique IP address, a default gateway (router) address, and a subnet mask. It is the subnet mask that determines the network on which the host resides. The default subnet mask for each class of network is shown in Table 8.3.

TABLE 8.3   Default subnet values

Class	Default subnet mask
A	255.0.0.0
B	255.255.0.0
C	255.255.255.0

Purists may argue that you don't need a default gateway. Technically this is true if your network is small and you don't communicate beyond it. For all practical purposes, though, most networks need a default gateway.

When you use the default subnet mask, you're requiring that all hosts be at one site and not be subdividing your network. This is called *classful* subnetting. Any deviation from the default signifies that you're dividing the network into multiple subnetworks, a process known as *classless* subnetting.

The problem with classful subnetting is that it only allows for three sizes of networks: Class A (16,777,216 hosts), Class B (65,536 hosts), and Class C (254 hosts). Two of these are too large to operate efficiently in the real world, and when enterprises were issued public network IDs that were larger than they needed, many public IP addresses were wasted. For this reason, and simply to allow for the creation of smaller networks that operate better, the concept of classless routing, or Classless Interdomain Routing (CIDR), was born.

Using CIDR, you can create smaller networks called subnets by manipulating the subnet mask of a larger classless or major network ID. This allows you to create a subnet that is much closer in size to what you need, thus wasting fewer IP addresses and increasing performance in each subnet. The increased performance is a function of the reduced broadcast traffic generated in each subnet.

Request for Comments (RFC) 1918 Address Spaces

Within each of the three major classes of IPv4 addresses, a range is set aside for *private addresses*. These addresses cannot communicate directly with the Internet without using a proxy server or network address translation to do so. Table 8.4 lists the private address ranges for Class A, B, and C addresses.

TABLE 8.4   Private address ranges

Class	Range
A	10.0.0.0/8 to 10.255.255.255/8
B	172.16.0.0/16 to 172.31.255.255/16
C	192.168.0.0/16 to 192.168.255.255/16

Firewall

Firewalls are used to filter out unwanted traffic while allowing desired traffic. They perform this function in a number of different ways. In this section, we'll look at two types of firewalls: network-based and host-based firewalls.

Network-Based

Network-based firewalls are one of the first lines of defense in a network. There are different types of firewalls, and they can either be stand-alone systems, or they can be included in other devices such as routers or servers. You can find firewall solutions that are marketed as hardware only and others that are software only. Many firewalls, however, consist of add-in software that is available for servers or workstations.

Although solutions are sold as "hardware only," the hardware still runs some sort of software. It may be hardened and in ROM to prevent tampering, and it may be customized—but software is present nonetheless.

The basic purpose of a firewall is to isolate one network from another. Firewalls are becoming available as appliances, meaning they're installed as the primary device separating two networks. *Appliances* are freestanding devices that operate in a largely self-contained manner, requiring less maintenance and support than a server-based product.

Firewalls function as one or more of the following:

- Packet filter
- Proxy firewall
- Stateful inspection firewall

To understand the concept of a firewall, it helps to know where the term comes from. In days of old, dwellings used to be built so close together that if a fire broke out in one, it could easily destroy a block or more before it could be contained. To decrease the risk of this happening, firewalls were built between buildings. The firewalls were huge brick walls that separated the buildings and kept a fire confined to one side. The same concept of restricting and confining is true in network firewalls. Traffic from the outside world hits the firewall and isn't allowed to enter the network unless otherwise invited.

The firewall shown in Figure 8.1 effectively limits access from outside networks, while allowing inside network users to access outside resources. The firewall in this illustration is also performing proxy functions.

FIGURE 8.1 A proxy firewall blocking network access from external networks

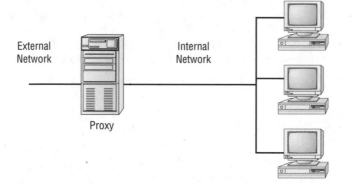

The following list discusses three of the most common functions that firewalls perform:

Although firewalls are often associated with outside traffic, you can place a firewall anywhere. For example, if you want to isolate one portion of your internal network from others, you can place a firewall between them.

Packet Filter Firewalls   A firewall operating as a *packet filter* passes or blocks traffic to specific addresses based on the type of application. The packet filter doesn't analyze the data of a packet; it decides whether to pass it based on the packet's addressing information. For instance, a packet filter may allow web traffic on port 80 and block Telnet traffic on port 23. This type of filtering is included in many routers. If a received packet request asks for a port that isn't authorized, the filter may reject the request or simply ignore it. Many packet filters can also specify which IP addresses can request which ports and allow or deny them based on the security settings of the firewall.

Packet filters are growing in sophistication and capability. A packet filter firewall can allow any traffic that you specify as acceptable. For example, if you want web users to access your site, then you configure the packet filter firewall to allow data on port 80 to enter. If every network were exactly the same, firewalls would come with default port settings hard-coded, but networks vary, so the firewalls don't include such settings.

Proxy Firewalls   A *proxy firewall* can be thought of as an intermediary between your network and any other network. Proxy firewalls are used to process requests from an outside network and those outbound from inside the network. The proxy firewall examines the data and makes rule-based decisions about whether the request should be forwarded or refused. The proxy intercepts all the packages and reprocesses them for use internally. This process includes hiding IP addresses.

The proxy firewall provides better security than packet filtering because of the increased intelligence that a proxy firewall offers. Requests from internal network users are routed through the proxy. The proxy, in turn, repackages the request and sends it along, thereby isolating the user from the external network. The proxy can also offer caching, should the same request be made again, and can increase the efficiency of data delivery.

A proxy firewall typically uses two network interface cards (NICs). Any type of firewall that has two NICs is referred to as a *dual-homed* firewall. One of the cards is connected to the outside network, and the other is connected to the internal network. The proxy software manages the connection between the two NICs. This setup segregates the two networks from each other and offers increased security.

Figure 8.2 illustrates a dual-homed firewall segregating two networks from each other.

FIGURE 8.2   Dual-homed firewall

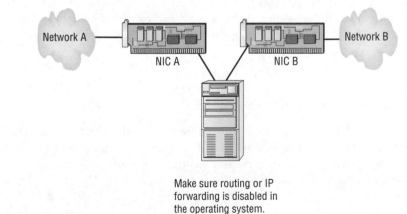

Network A   NIC A   NIC B   Network B

Make sure routing or IP
forwarding is disabled in
the operating system.

The proxy function can occur at either the application level or the session level of the OSI model. *Application-level proxy* functions read the individual commands of the protocols that are being served. This type of server is advanced and must know the rules and capabilities of the protocol used. An implementation of this type of proxy must know the difference between GET and PUT operations (these are HTTP commands used to read and write to a web page), for example, and have rules specifying how to execute them. A *circuit-level proxy* creates a circuit between the client and the server and doesn't deal with the contents of the packets that are being processed.

A unique application-level proxy server must exist for each protocol supported. Many proxy servers also provide full *auditing*, *accounting*, and other usage information that wouldn't normally be kept by a circuit-level proxy server.

Stateful Inspection Firewalls   This last section on firewalls focuses on the concept of stateful inspection. *Stateful inspection* is also referred to as *stateful packet filtering*. Most of the devices used in networks don't keep track of how information is routed or used. After a packet is passed, the packet and path are forgotten. In stateful inspection (or stateful packet filtering), records are kept using a state table that tracks every communications channel. Stateful inspections occur at all levels of the network and provide additional security, especially in connectionless protocols such as *User Datagram Protocol (UDP)* and *Internet Control Message Protocol (ICMP)*. This adds complexity to the process. Denial-of-service (DoS) attacks present a challenge because flooding techniques are used to overload the state table and effectively cause the firewall to shut down or reboot.

Host-Based

Host-based firewalls are software installed on a single device that protects only that device from attacks. Many operating systems today come with personal firewalls or host-based firewalls. Many commercial host-based firewalls are designed to focus attention on a particular type of traffic or to protect a certain application.

On Linux-based systems, a common host-based firewall is iptables, replacing a previous package called ipchains. It has the ability to accept or drop packets. Firewall rules are created, much like creating an access list on a router. An example of a rule set follows:

```
iptables -A INPUT -i eth1 -s 192.168.0.0/24 -j DROP
iptables -A INPUT -i eth1 -s 10.0.0.0/8 -j DROP
iptables -A INPUT -i eth1 -s 172. -j DROP
```

This rule set blocks all incoming traffic sourced from either the 192.168.0.0/24 network or from the 10.0.0.0/8 network. Both of these are private IP address ranges. It is quite common to block incoming traffic from the Internet that has a private IP address as its source because this usually indicates IP spoofing is occurring.

Ports

In Chapter 2, "Installing and Configuring Servers," you learned the port numbers for FTP and SCP. Port numbers can be used to identify protocols that need to be blocked at the firewall. Communication across a TCP/IP-based network takes place using various protocols, such as FTP to transfer files, HTTP to view web pages, and POP3 or IMAP to work with email. Each of these protocols has a default port associated with it, and CompTIA expects you to be familiar with them for this exam.

Both TCP and UDP use port numbers to listen for and respond to requests for communication using various protocols. There are a number of protocols and their port numbers that you must know for this exam, as well as the differences between TCP and UDP.

TCP vs. UDP

There are two transport layer protocols in the TCP/IP stack. TCP provides guaranteed, connection-oriented delivery, whereas UDP provides nonguaranteed, connectionless delivery. Each protocol or service uses one of the two transport protocols (and in some cases both). There will be additional information later in this chapter on TCP and UDP.

TCP and UDP both use port numbers to listen for and respond to requests for communications. RFC 1060 defines common ports for a number of services routinely found in use, and these all have low numbers—up to 1,024. You can, however, reconfigure your service to use another port number (preferably much higher) if you're concerned about security and you don't want your site to be available to anonymous traffic.

SNMP 161

Simple Network Management Protocol (SNMP) is a protocol that facilitates network management functionality. It is not, in itself, a network management system (NMS) but is simply the protocol that makes an NMS possible. It operates over port 161.

SMTP 25

Simple Mail Transfer Protocol (SMTP) is a protocol for sending email between SMTP servers. Clients typically use either IMAP or POP to access their email server and use SMTP to send email. SMTP uses port 25 by default.

FTP 20/21

The File Transfer Protocol (FTP) is both a TCP/IP protocol and software that permits the transferring of files between computer systems. Because FTP has been implemented on numerous types of computer systems, files can be transferred between disparate systems (for example, a personal computer and a laptop). It uses ports 20 and 21 by default. FTP can be configured to allow or deny access to specific IP addresses and can be configured to work with exceptions. Although the protocol can be run within most browsers, a number of FTP applications are available; FileZilla (`http://filezilla-project.org`) is one of the most popular.

SFTP 22

Secure File Transfer Protocol over SSH (SFTP) is a version of FTP that is encrypted by SSH. Since it operates over an SSH session and SSH uses port 22, SFTP uses port 22.

SSH 22

Secure Shell is a remote administration tool that can serve as a secure alternative to using Telnet to remotely access and configure a device like a router or switch. Although it requires a bit more setup than Telnet, it provides an encrypted command-line session for managing devices remotely. As you learned in the section on SFTP, it is used to provide security to a number of other protocols as well. It uses port 22.

SCP 22

Secure Copy (SCP) is a secure method of transferring files from one device to another. It is another example of a protocol that runs over SSH, which actually provides the encryption; as such, SCP also uses port 22.

NTP 123

Network Time Protocol (NTP) is used to keep all of the devices in the network synced to the same time source. This helps keep the timestamps of all network events that may be sent to a central server synchronized so that the events can be placed in the order in which they occurred. Time synchronization of all devices is also critical for proper function of digital certificates and services such as Active Directory. It operates on port 123.

HTTP 80

Hypertext Transfer Protocol (HTTP) is the protocol used for communication between a web server and a web browser. It uses port 80 by default.

HTTPS 443

Hypertext Transfer Protocol over Secure Sockets Layer (HTTPS), or HTTP Secure, is a protocol used to make a secure web connection. It uses port 443 by default.

Telnet 23

Telnet is a protocol that functions at the Application layer of the OSI model, providing terminal-emulation capabilities. Telnet runs on port 23, but it has lost favor to SSH due to the fact that Telnet sends data—including passwords—in plain-text format.

IMAP 143

Internet Message Access Protocol (IMAP) is a protocol with a store-and-forward capability. It can also allow messages to be stored on an email server rather than downloaded to the client. The current version of the protocol is 4 (IMAP4), and the counterpart to it is Post Office Protocol (POP). IMAP runs on port 143.

POP3 110

The Post Office Protocol (POP) is a protocol for receiving email from a mail server. The alternative to POP (which runs on port 110) is IMAP.

RDP 3389

The Remote Desktop Protocol (RDP) is used in a Windows environment to make remote desktop communications possible. It uses port 3389.

FTPS 989/990

File Transfer Protocol over TLS/SSL (FTPS) secures the FTP file transfer process as SFTP does but does so in a different way. Whereas SFTP is version of FTP that is encrypted by SSH, FTPS uses SSL for the encryption. Therefore, unlike all of the protocols secured by SSH that use port 22, FTPS uses ports 989 and 990.

LDAP 389/3268

Lightweight Directory Access Protocol (LDAP) is a protocol that provides a mechanism to access and query directory services systems. These directory services systems are most likely to be Microsoft's Active Directory but could also be Novell Directory Services (NDS). Although LDAP supports command-line queries executed directly against the directory database, most LDAP interactions are done via utilities such as an authentication program (network logon) or by locating a resource in the directory through a search utility. LDAP uses ports 389 and 3268.

DNS 53

As mentioned earlier, DNS is the Domain Name Service, and it is used to translate hostnames into IP addresses. DNS is an example of a protocol that uses both UDP and TCP ports.

DHCP 68

DHCP has been discussed a few times already in this chapter. It serves the useful purpose of issuing IP addresses and other network-related configuration values to clients to allow them to operate on the network. DHCP uses port 68 as well as port 67.

Static vs. Dynamic

The two methods of entering address information for a host are *static* and *dynamic*. Static means that you manually enter the information for the host and it does not change. Dynamic means that Dynamic Host Configuration Protocol (DHCP) is used for the host to lease information from a DHCP server.

DHCP issues IP configuration data. Rather than administrators having to configure a unique IP address for every host added on a network (and *default gateway* and *subnet mask*), they can use a DHCP server to issue these values. That server is given a number of addresses in a range that it can supply to clients.

For example, the server may be given the IP range (or *scope*) 192.168.12.1 to 192.168.12.200. When a client boots, it sends out a request for the server to issue it an address (and any other configuration data) from that scope. The server takes one of the numbers it has available and leases it to the client for a length of time. If the client is still using the configuration data when 50 percent of the lease has expired, it requests a renewal of the lease from the server; under normal operating conditions, the request is granted. When the client is no longer using the address, the address goes back in the scope and can be issued to another client.

DHCP is built on the older Bootstrap Protocol (BOOTP) that was used to allow diskless workstations to boot and connect to a server that provided them with an operating system and applications. The client uses broadcasts to request the data and thus—normally—can't communicate with DHCP servers beyond their own subnet (broadcasts don't route). A DHCP relay agent, however, can be employed to allow DHCP broadcasts to go from one network to another. The relay agent can be one of the hosts on the local network or a router that the hosts in the local network use as their gateway. The positioning of the relay agent is shown in Figure 8.3.

FIGURE 8.3   DHCP relay agent

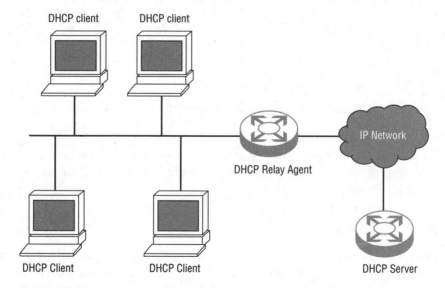

While the primary purpose of DHCP is to lease IP addresses to hosts, when it gives the IP address, it also often includes the additional configuration information as well: DNS server, router information, and so on.

Dynamic Host Configuration Protocol (DHCP)

Dynamic Host Configuration Protocol (DHCP) servers are used to automate the process of providing an IP configuration to devices in the network. These servers respond to broadcast-based requests for a configuration by offering an IP address, subnet mask, and default gateway to the DHCP client. While these options provide basic network connectivity, many other options can also be provided, such as the IP address of a Trivial File Transfer Protocol (TFTP) server that IP phones can contact to download a configuration file. Here are some of the components that should be maximized to ensure good performance:

CPU   Processing power is not one of the critical resources on a DHCP server. Ensure you have the recommended speed for the operating system with the DHCP service installed as indicated by the operating system documentation.

Memory   RAM is one of the critical components on the DHCP server. You should provide plenty of RAM. After deployment you may discover you need to add more if you find the server's usage of memory to be exceeding its capacity.

Disk   The disk is the second critical component. If you intend to host a large number of scopes (scopes are ranges of IP addresses) on the server, keep in mind that each time you add a scope you need more disk space.

NIC   Although this is not a component that's critical to the operation of DHCP, the NIC could become a bottleneck in the system if it is not capable enough or if there are not enough NICs. Use at least 1 Gbps NICs and consider the option of using multiple NICs.

Automatic Private IP Address (APIPA)

Automatic Private IP Addressing (APIPA) is a TCP/IP feature Microsoft added to their operating systems. If a DHCP server cannot be found and the clients are configured to obtain IP addresses automatically, the clients automatically assign themselves an IP address, somewhat randomly, in the 169.254.*x.x* range with a subnet mask of 255.255.0.0. This allows them to communicate with other hosts that have similarly configured themselves but are unable to connect to the Internet. If a computer is using an APIPA address, it will have trouble communicating with other clients if those clients do not use APIPA addresses.

In IPv6, there is a type of address called a *link local address* that is like an APIPA address in many ways in that the device will generate one of these addresses for each interface with no intervention from a human—as is done with APIPA. The scope of the address is also the same in that it is not routable and is only good on the segment on which the device is located.

As is the case with APIPA addresses, if two devices connected to the same segment generate these addresses, they will be in the same network and the two devices will be able to communicate. This is because the devices always generate the address using the same IPv6 prefix (the equivalent of a network ID in IPv4), which is FE80::/64. The remainder of the address is created by spreading the 48-bit MAC address across the last 64 bits, yielding an IPv6 address that looks like this:

```
FE80::2237:06FF:FECF:67E4/64
```

MAC Addresses

Each network interface card (NIC) has a unique hardware address, called a Media Access Control (MAC) address. If two NICs or interfaces on the same network have the same hardware address, neither one will be able to communicate. For this reason, the IEEE has established a standard for hardware addresses and assigns blocks of these addresses to NIC manufacturers, who then hardwire the addresses into the cards.

MAC addresses, also called *physical addresses*, which reside on the Network Access layer of the TCP/IP model, are applied to network interface adapters of various types. These permanent addresses, sometimes called *burned-in addresses (BIAs)*, are assigned to the adapters by the manufacturer.

MAC addresses use the hexadecimal numbering system and follow standard formats that identify both the manufacturer and the individual device. Two formats are set forth by the IEEE; the more common is the MAC-48 format. A newer format, the EUI-64 format, is used with IPv6. As the use of IPv6 increases in North America (still lagging behind the rest of the world), the use of the EUI-64 format will increase. Even when EUI-64 is used, it doesn't actually change the format of the physical 48-bit MAC address. It is a method of spreading the 48-bit MAC address across 64 bits so that it can be used as the last 64 bits of the 128-bit IPv6 address. It does so by ensuring 16 bits in the middle of the MAC address are always set to FF:FE in hex.

Some examples of items that have MAC addresses using the MAC-48 identifier are as follows:

- Wired Ethernet adapters
- Wireless network adapters
- Router interfaces
- Bluetooth devices
- Token Ring network adapters
- FDDI network adapters

The standard format for these addresses is six groups of two hex digits separated by a hyphen or a colon. It is also sometimes displayed in the three groups of four hex digits separated by a period. It's important to note that although we view and discuss these MAC addresses in their hexadecimal format, they are transmitted over the medium (cabling or wireless) in binary. Figure 8.4 shows an example of a MAC address as displayed by executing the `ipconfig/all` command on a computer at the command prompt. This command will display information about the network interfaces of the computer, including the MAC address.

Each part of this address communicates information. The address is divided into two sections, as shown in Figure 8.5. The left half of the address is called the *organizationally unique identifier (OUI)*. The right half is called the *universally administered address (UAA)*. Together they make a globally unique MAC address.

FIGURE 8.4   MAC address output

```
C:\Users\tmcmillan>ipconfig/all

Ethernet adapter Local Area Connection:

    Connection-specific DNS Suffix  . : alpha.kaplaninc.com
    Description . . . . . . . . . . . : Broadcom NetXtreme 57xx Gigabit Controlle

    Physical Address. . . . . . . . . : 00-1A-A0-E1-95-AB
    DHCP Enabled. . . . . . . . . . . : Yes
    Autoconfiguration Enabled . . . . : Yes
    Link-local IPv6 Address . . . . . : fe80::ada3:8b73:a66e:6bc0%11(Preferred)
    IPv4 Address. . . . . . . . . . . : 10.88.2.177(Preferred)
    Subnet Mask . . . . . . . . . . . : 255.255.254.0
    Lease Obtained. . . . . . . . . . : Friday, April 08, 2011 7:05:01 PM
    Lease Expires . . . . . . . . . . : Friday, May 06, 2011 7:08:43 AM
    Default Gateway . . . . . . . . . : 10.88.2.6
    DHCP Server . . . . . . . . . . . : 10.88.10.55
```

FIGURE 8.5   OUI and UAA

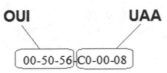

Depending on the manufacturer of the device, and the tool in which you are viewing the MAC address, this MAC address may be represented in the following formats:

```
00-50-56-C0-00-08
00:50:56:C0:00:08
0050.56C0.0008
```

Summarize Scripting Basics for Server Administration

Scripts are used to automate anything that can be accomplished at the command line. You don't have to manually type the commands, and you can schedule a script file to run at a certain time. In this section you'll learn the basics of scripting.

Script Types

Script files can come in various file types. In this section we'll look at these file types.

Bash

Bash is a command shell or interface used in Linux. Scripts can be constructed using the following method:

1. Open a text editor (either vi or nano). Type **vi** or **nano** and press Enter.

2. Declare the interpreter with the following:

   ```
   #!/bin/bash
   ```

   `#!` is called a shebang or hashbang and the remaining part is the path to the interpreter (to get the path to your interpreter, run the command `which bash`).

3. Put in all the commands you want to execute when you run this script.

4. Save the file with a name and the `.sh` extension. (An SH file is a script programmed for Bash.)

5. Make the file executable with the following command:

   ```
   chmod +x <file_name>
   ```

6. Run the script with the following command:

   ```
   ./<file_name>
   ```

Batch

Batch file or files with a `.bat` extension are used to automate a command or set of commands each time you execute the batch file. To create a batch file in Windows, do the following:

1. Open a text editor (such as Notepad) and enter the commands you want to be run when the batch file is executed.

2. Save the file with a `.bat` extension.

3. To execute the file, use the following command:

   ```
   C:\PATH\TO\FOLDER\BATCH-NAME.bat
   ```

While batch files typically use the `.bat` file extension, you can also find them using the `.cmd` or `.btm` extension.

PowerShell

PowerShell is a powerful tool built into all Windows systems. It can automate tasks and be used to script configuration changes. This system works by creating what are called cmdlets and then referencing them in commands. Windows PowerShell can also execute:

- PowerShell scripts (files suffixed by `.ps1`)
- PowerShell functions
- Stand-alone executable programs

Virtual Basic Script (VBS)

The VBScript scripting language contains code that can be executed within Windows or Internet Explorer via the Windows-based script host. Scripts created with this language have the .vbs extension. This language was extensively used by Microsoft administrators, but this is changing with the widespread adoption of PowerShell.

Environment Variables

Variables are used in scripts to hold values that you have assigned to them. This value can be a number, a piece of text, or a mathematical formula, among other things. Environmental values are used to set certain defaults for a user's environment or a system environment. For example, it might set the location of a temp folder or a path to an executable file. There are several types of environmental variables:

- **System:** Defined for any users that use the system (for all)
- **User:** Defined only for a specific user and only used when they log in
- **Program:** Defined for an application or script and is only used within that application or script

Comment Syntax

All scripting languages have a command syntax you must follow. The syntax describes how commands must be constructed and in what order parameters (supporting commands that alter the way a major command is carried out or provide additional information or values to the command) are used.

Comments can be inserted into scripts to identify the purpose of a command or to make the scripts more understandable to someone reviewing the script. Each language has a way of identifying comments as such so that the system does not attempt to execute them. Here are some examples:

- In JavaScript, single-line comments start with //. Any text between // and the end of the line will be ignored by JavaScript (will not be executed).
- In Python, comments starts with a #, and Python will ignore them.
- In Bash, comments starts with a #, unless it is accompanied by the ! as in #! (review the previous section on Bash).
- In PowerShell, comments starts with a #, and the system will ignore them.

Basic Script Constructs

Within scripts there are certain types of character sets that are used to guide the script processing in a way that allows the script to react to the data it is processing that is beneficial to the purpose of the script. For example, it might tell the script to perform an operation over and over until a condition is met. In this section you'll learn about basic script constructs.

Loops

Loops are used to tell the script to perform an operation over and over. There are two types of loops: for and while loops.

for loops have definite start and stop points, and each step in the loop is defined. For example, the following PowerShell script counts starting at 1 and incrementing by 1 until it gets to 10 and then displays the results:

```
For ($count=1; $count -le 5; $count++) {Write-Host "Number $count"}
```

Variables

As you learned earlier, variables are used in scripts to hold values that you have assigned to them. This value can be a number, a piece of text, a or a mathematical formula, among other things. When you declare a variable to the system, you are telling the system that from now on when you use this variable you mean the value that you declared the variable to have. For example, we could declare the letter A to mean the number 50. Some examples are:

VAR=10   This is a user-defined variable that is storing the integer value.

STR=" Hello"   This is a user-defined variable that is storing the string.

Numbers="1 2 3"   This is a user-defined variable that stores a list of values separated by spaces.

Conditionals

Conditions can be used within a script or automation to prevent further execution. A script can also test for multiple conditions at a time, and the ending of the execution can either be based on all conditions being true (an and condition) or any of them being true (an or condition). Finally, conditions can be based on something being true or on something being false.

Comparators

Comparators, or comparison operators, are used to tell the system to look at two things, compare them, and make a decision based on the comparison. Some examples of comparison operators are shown in Table 8.5.

TABLE 8.5   Comparators

Operator	Means	Syntax example
eq	Is equal to	if [$1 -eq 200]
-ne	Is not equal to	if [$1 -ne 1]
-gt	Is greater than	if [$1 -gt 15]
-ge	Is greater than or equal to	if [$1 -ge 10]

Basic Data Types

There are several types of data that are used with scripts. In this section we'll define basic data types used in scripts.

Integers

Integers are simply whole numbers. Earlier you learned that this data type can be used to:

- Assign a value to a variable
- Set the parameters of a loop
- Define a condition to be met

Strings

A string is essentially a sequence of characters. Every string value must start and begin with either a single or a double quotation mark. You must use the same type of quotation mark (single or double) at the beginning and at the end of the string.

Examples of strings include:

```
"This is a string is bookended by double quotation marks."
'This string prefers single quotation marks.'
"Strings can contain any type of character. Example: $%$(*^&^^%%$#$1230___~."
```

Arrays

Sometimes you need to perform an operation or operations on a large set of numbers (say 50). If we use simple variables, then we have to create 50 variables and then perform operations on them. A better option is to store the numbers in a structure called an array and perform operations on the array. For example, the following command declares that the array called MYARRAY contains the values 100, 200, and 300.

```
MYARRAY=(100 200 300)
```

Common Server Administration Scripting Tasks

Scripting makes the scheduling and automation of any function possible. In this section you'll learn about some of the use cases for creating and scheduling scripts to run.

Startup

Many systems benefit from a restart from time to time. Rather than putting this task on a checklist and dedicating a technician's time to walking over to the machine and manually restarting the system, you can schedule the process to occur on a regular basis.

Shut Down

As you may have put together from the last section, rebooting a system requires shutting it down and then starting it up, so you obviously can script a shutdown alone. Maybe you want certain systems to shut down at night when they aren't needed to save power.

Service

Services can either be started or stopped. While this can be done manually, it can also be scripted. Some services seem to benefit from restarting from time to time. You can even set a service to restart automatically when it suffers an error condition in the Windows Services console. When you do so in the GUI, a script is built in the background (and you can build your own) that does one of the following based on your choice:

- Take No Action (default)
- Restart The Service
- Run A Program
- Restart The Computer

Login

Login scripts can be used to apply settings to a system based on the user who logs in. While each user can have their own script, many times an administrator will use the same script for users to map the same drives, etc. for all. The nice thing about this approach is that if you change a setting (such as a drive mapping), you make the change in the script once rather than editing many individual scripts or making the change manually on each device.

Account Creation

You may someday find yourself in a scenario where you need to create 200 new accounts for 200 new employees. While you could perform this mind-numbing task manually (and probably make some mistakes along the way), you can script the process.

Bootstrap

In computing, a bootstrap loader is the first piece of code that runs when a machine starts and is responsible for loading the rest of the operating system. A bootstrap script tells the system additional items to load at that time (perhaps code dependencies). It can even look for updates.

Summary

In this chapter, you learned about networking servers. Topics included configuring the server with an IP address, default gateway, subnet mask, and DNS server—the essential settings in most cases. We covered the use of private IP addressing to enable Internet access while saving public IP addresses. You also learned the basics of scripting and the value of auto-mating certain operations.

Exam Essentials

Identify the most common and important network settings.   A server usually requires an IP address, a subnet mask, a default gateway, and the address of a DNS server to function on a network. Also understand the purpose of private IP addressing and the function of APIPA.

Compare and contrast protocols and ports numbers.   List the port numbers used by well-known network protocols and services, including but not restricted to, FTP, SNMP, DNS, SMTP, HTTP, and SSH. Describe the functionality provided by each.

Review Questions

You can find the answers in the Appendix.

1. Which of the following is the loopback address in IPV6?
   A. 127.0.0.1
   B. FE80::
   C. ::1
   D. FEC0:

2. Which of the following is the IPv6 prefix of an autoconfigured address?
   A. 127.0.0.1
   B. FE80::
   C. ::1
   D. FEC0:

3. When implementing CIDR, what configuration setting is manipulated to size the subnet as desired?
   A. IP address
   B. Subnet mask
   C. Default gateway
   D. Duplex

4. Which of the following is *not* a private IP address?
   A. 10.0.0.5
   B. 172.16.5.9
   C. 192.168.5.9
   D. 172.32.63.4

5. Which of the following is an APIPA address?
   A. 168.254.3.3
   B. 172.16.5.9
   C. 192.168.5.9
   D. 169.254.5.6

6. Which of the following is an example of a link local IPv6 address?
   A. FE80::2237:06FF:FECF:67E4/64
   B. FE80::1/64
   C. ::1
   D. FEC0: 2237:06FF:FECF:67E4/64

7. Which of the following is *not* a FQDN?

    A. tmcmillan

    B. tmcmillan.acme.com

    C. ws5.ajax.com

    D. smitht.smithcorp.com

8. When does a device use a DNS suffix search list?

    A. At all times

    B. When an unqualified hostname is encountered

    C. When an FQDN is encountered

    D. When the users select to use the list

9. Which of the following is a file type used to automate a command or set of commands?

    A. JPG

    B. BAT

    C. TXT

    D. SFX

10. Which of the following are freestanding devices that operate in a largely self-contained manner, requiring less maintenance and support than a server-based product?

    A. VMs

    B. Appliances

    C. Rack systems

    D. Modules

11. Which of the following is a method of spreading the 48-bit MAC address across 64 bits so that it can be used as the last 64 bits of the 128-bit IPv6 address?

    A. TACACS

    B. EIU-64 format

    C. TACACS+

    D. MAC-48 format

12. Which of the following parts of a MAC address identify the manufacturer of the interface?

    A. UAA

    B. BAA

    C. OUI

    D. EUI-64

13. Which of the following attacks' aim is to receive traffic from a VLAN of which the hacker's port is not a member?

  A. SYN flood

  B. VLAN hopping

  C. DoS

  D. Teardrop

14. Which of the following is the address of the machine to send data to that is not intended for a host on this network?

  A. Subnet mask

  B. Default gateway

  C. Management port

  D. Secondary address

15. What is the most important resource for a DNS server?

  A. CPU

  B. Disk

  C. NIC

  D. Memory

16. Which of the following is the port number for SMTP?

  A. 21

  B. 161

  C. 25

  D. 20

17. Which of the following services uses port number 22?

  A. SFTP

  B. NTP

  C. HTTP

  D. HTTPS

18. Which of the following has lost favor to SSH because it sends data—including passwords—in plain-text format?

  A. POP3

  B. Telnet

  C. RDP

  D. IMAP

19. Which of the following is the default Class C subnet mask?

   A. 255.255.0.0

   B. 255.255.255.0

   C. 255.0.0.0

   D. 255.255.255.240

20. Which of the following is a remote administration tool that can serve as a secure alternative to using Telnet to remotely access and configure a device like a router or switch?

   A. SSL

   B. SSH

   C. STP

   D. SCP

Chapter

9

Disaster Recovery

✓ 3.8 **Explain the importance of disaster recovery.**
- Site types
    - Hot site
    - Cold site
    - Warm site
    - Cloud
    - Separate geographic locations

✓ **Replication**
- Constant
- Background
- Synchronous vs. asynchronous
- Application consistent
- File locking
- Mirroring
- Bidirectional

✓ **Testing**
- Tabletops
- Live failover
- Simulated failover
- Production vs. non-production

Despite all of our planning and efforts to prevent them, disasters still occur. Although their level of devastation may vary, their occurrence is inevitable. What is not inevitable is that these events, ranging in seriousness from a single file deletion to the complete loss of an office or location, cripple the organization or prevent it from continuing to do business. What separates organizations that survive the same disaster from those that do not is preparation. In large measure, the success of that preparation is determined by the selection and implementation of appropriate backup techniques.

Explain the Importance of Backups and Restores

The goal of regular backups is to provide the organization with the ability to restore the data in the event of a replication issue or in cases where there is no second site. In this section we'll explore the various types of backup, the media options available for storing the backup, and best practices for managing the backup process. Finally, we'll look at options for storing the backup media and the implications of each option.

Backup Methods

There are many types of backup that you can choose from, and the difference between the methods lies in how each method handles a property of each file called the *archive bit*. This is a bit that is used to communicate to the backup system whether a particular file has changed since the last backup. When the archive bit is cleared (0), it communicates that the file has been backed up already and has not changed since. When the bit is on (1), it communicates that the file has had changes since the last backup and should be backed up again. Its value lies in its ability to prevent an unchanged file from being backed up again needlessly. Next we'll compare various methodologies with respect to the handling of the archive bit and the implications for your backup schedule.

Full

With a full or normal backup, all data is backed up. During the full backup, the current status of the archive bit is ignored, everything is backed up, and the archive bit for each file is cleared. A full backup takes the longest time and the most space to complete. However, if an organization only uses full backups, then only the latest full backup needs to be restored, meaning it is the quickest restore. A full backup is the most appropriate for off-site archiving.

Synthetic Full

A synthetic backup is a full backup performed by synthesizing (combining) the data from the previous full backup (either a regular full backup for the first backup, or the previous synthetic full backup) and the periodic incremental backups. The incremental backups are the only files that need to be transferred during replication, greatly reducing the bandwidth needed for off-site replication.

Incremental

In an incremental backup, all files that have been changed since the last full or incremental backup will be backed up. During the incremental backup process, the archive bit for each file is cleared. An incremental backup usually takes the least amount of time and space to complete. In an organization that uses a full/incremental scheme, the full backup and each subsequent incremental backup must be restored. The incremental backups must be restored in order. For example, if your organization completes a full backup on Sunday and an incremental backup daily Monday through Saturday, you will need the last full and every incremental backup created since.

Differential

In a differential backup, all files that have been changed since the last full backup will be backed up. During the differential backup process, the archive bit for each file is not cleared. Each differential backup will back up all the files in the previous differential backup if a full backup has not occurred since that time. In an organization that uses a full/differential scheme, the full and only the most recent differential backup must be restored, meaning only two backups are needed to perform a restoration.

Archive

Earlier in this section you learned about the archive bit, which is used to communicate to the backup system whether a particular file has changed since the last backup. Please review that section.

Open File

Typically, when a file is open during a backup, the backup system will skip that file. Normally, open files are locked by the application or operating system. However, backup programs that use the Windows Volume Shadow Copy Service (VSS) can back up open files. But you should know that when you back up open files in this manner, changes that may have been made to the file while it was open and the backup job was proceeding will not be present in the backup of the open file and will not be recorded until the next backup.

Snapshot

Using special backup utilities, you can also perform what are called snapshot backups. These are lists of pointers or references to the data and are somewhat like a detailed table of contents about the data at a specific point in time. They can speed the data recovery process when it is needed. There are two types of snapshots: copy-on-write and split mirror.

Keep in mind that snapshots are not a replacement for regular backups. In many cases the snapshot is stored on the same volume as the data, so if the drive goes bad you will also lose the snapshot.

Copy-on-Write

This type of snapshot is taken every time a user enters data or changes data, and it only incudes the changed data. It allows for rapid recovery from a loss of data, but it requires you to have access to all previous snapshots during recovery. As changes are made, multiple copies of snapshots will be created. Some will contain changes not present in others. There will also be some data that remains unchanged in all of them.

Split Mirror

This type of snapshot also is created every time a change is made, but it is a snapshot of everything rather than just the changes. However, as you can imagine it takes significant storage space and the restore process will be slower.

Backup Frequency

The frequency of backups and backup testing should depend on the sensitivity and value of the data involved. For example, extremely mission-critical data might be backed up daily and tested after every backup, whereas the backup of less critical data might be only every 4 days and verified once every four backups.

Media Rotation

Cost and storage considerations often dictate that backup media be reused after a period of time. You should adopt a system of rotating the media you are using, especially when that media is tape, which can only be used a certain number of times reliably. If this reuse is not planned in advance, media can become unreliable due to overuse. Two of the most popular backup rotation schemes are grandfather/father/son and first in, first out:

Grandfather/Father/Son (GFS)   In this scheme, three sets of backups are defined. Most often these three definitions are daily, weekly, and monthly. The daily backups are the sons, the weekly backups are the fathers, and the monthly backups are the grandfathers. Each week, one son advances to the father set. Each month, one father advances to the grandfather set.

First In, First Out (FIFO)   In this scheme, the newest backup is saved to the oldest media. Although this is the simplest rotation scheme, it does not protect against data errors. If an error in data occurs, this system over time may result in all copies containing the error.

Figure 9.1 displays a typical five-day GFS rotation using 21 tapes. The daily tapes are usually differential or incremental backups. The weekly and monthly tapes must be full backups.

FIGURE 9.1 Grandfather/father/son

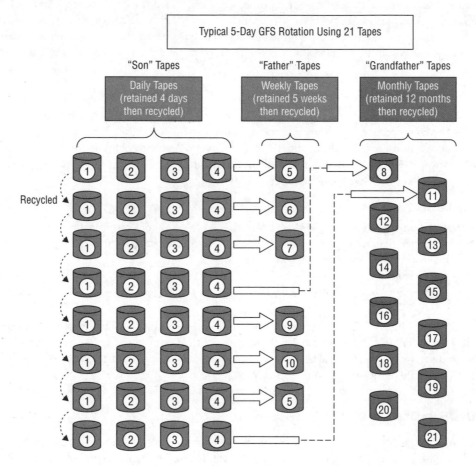

The amount of time you should retain tapes or other backup media will be driven by several issues:

- Any regulations that apply to the industry in which your company operates
- The criticality of the data
- Your company's policies

Backup Media Types

When choosing backup media, it is important to understand the advantages and disadvantages of various technologies. In general backup media, you should allow for two types of access to the data stored on the media: linear and random access. In this section we'll look at the difference between these access methods as well as types of media that use the two methods.

Tape

Tapes have been the default backup media for many years and only recently have been replaced by other media types like CDs, DVDs, and external drives. Although younger technicians may be unfamiliar with the task of rewinding or fast-forwarding a music tape or cassette to access a particular song, it illustrates the way linear access works. A song cannot be played until the tape head (reader) is positioned over the location where that song resides.

Tapes cannot provide instant access (also called random access) to any location on the tape (as can be done with CDs, DVDs, and external drives), but they are the most economical media. They are also still the most widely used media, although that is changing. The lack of random access has been a shortcoming that technicians were willing to accept until recently when technologies that provide random access have become more widespread.

Tapes are also less durable than CDs and DVDs. They are more susceptible to damage from temperature extremes and provide a limited number of times you can record data to them. While the maximum capacity of a standard tape drive has been 10 TB, Sony released a new cassette tape in 2014 that will hold 185 TB of data by storing the data very densely on the tape.

In 2010, IBM introduced the Linear Tape File System (LTFS), which allows you to access files on tape in the same way as on a disk filesystem, meaning random access is available using tapes.

Drive

Tape drives can come in several formats and have ever-increasing capacities. Linear Tape-Open (LTO), IBM, and Oracle are some of the major formats available. The LTO drives have been through a number of generations, the latest of which, LTO-9, has a maximum capacity of 18 TB and operates at 400 MBps uncompressed. One interesting feature with respect to the various versions of LTO is use of colors to indicate a specific cartridge type. For example, though not a standard, LTO-6 cartridges are typically black whereas LTO-5 cartridges are red (unless they are from HP, which has its own color scheme).

One of the historical shortcomings of tape, its sequential access method, was the driver of the introduction of media partitioning in LTO-5. This has enabled tape to be accessed in a new way, using IBM's LTFS. It allows access to files on a tape in a similar fashion to the way files are accessed on a disk or flash drive. Keep in mind that although it may make the tape drive appear to behave like a hard drive, the data is still sequential.

Libraries

A tape library is a storage device that contains multiple tape drives. It also contains a number of slots to hold tape cartridges and a barcode reader that is used to identify the cartridges. A tape library typically contains a robotic method for loading the tapes. As shown in Figure 9.2, it can be connected to the backup device via SCSI, Fibre Channel, or iSCSI.

FIGURE 9.2   Tape library

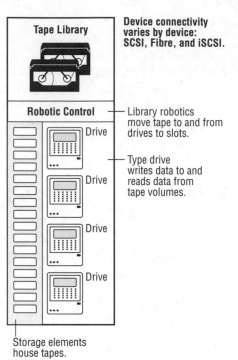

Cloud

Another option gaining favor is to back up to cloud storage. This saves the administrative overhead of management of backup media and rotation schemes. It also is (usually) available over the Internet from anywhere. The disadvantage is that if there are network issues the backups may not be available to you. You should also note that large archives can still take days or longer to upload even using fast connections.

Disk

You can also back up to an external disk. This is typically done for data that is not expected to be needed for some time as locating the media and attaching it to a system and accessing the data will take more time than when recovering data from other media types.

Print

When upgrading a system from one edition of a server to another, if incompatible printer queues are found, all printer queues may be deleted during the upgrade process. You may want to back up the printers so that when the upgrade is over you can just restore them without reconfiguration. To do in Server 2008:

1. Click Start ➢ Administrative Tools, and then click Print Management.
2. On the Print Management screen, right-click Print Management, and then click Migrate Printers.

3. Make sure that Export Printer Queues And Printer Drivers To A File is selected, and then click Next.

4. On the Select A Print Server page, select A Print Server On The Network, type the remote print server name, and then click Next.

5. On the Review The List Of Items To Be Exported page, click Next.

6. On the Select The File Location page, type the location to which you want to back up the printers, such as **system_drive:\backup\remoteservername.printerExport**.

7. Click Finish.

To restore, follow this procedure:

1. Click Start ➢ Administrative Tools, and then click Print Management.

2. On the Print Management screen, right-click Print Management, and then click Migrate Printers.

3. Click Import Printer Queues And Printer Drivers From A File, and then click Next.

4. On the Select The File Location page, type the location to which you want to restore the printers, such as **system_drive:\backup\remoteservername.printerExport**.

5. Click Next twice.

6. On the Select A Print Server page, make sure that the print server that is listed is the print server that hosts the printers, and then click Next.

7. On the Select Import Options page, click Next.

8. Click Finish.

File-Level vs. System-State Backup

In Chapter 2, "Installing and Configuring Servers," you learned about bare metal backup. This is a great example of a system level backup. This is one in which everything, the files and the operating system, are backed up. Also called an image backup, think of it as a snapshot of the entire contents of the drives.

Restore Methods

When it comes time to restore the backup, whether it is a system restoration or recovery of a single deleted file, there are several approaches. In this section you'll learn about several types of restorations.

Overwrite

When you recover using this method, you are writing over a previous version of the file. In the case of a system restore, if there is anything on the drive where you are restoring it will be wiped out.

Side by Side

In a side-by-side scenario, data is backed up from one device and restored to a different device. You might also see this term used to describe a form of replication between databases as well. In that side-by-side scenario, there are two separate database systems with the data replicated between them.

Alternate Location Path

When you restore a file you don't have to restore it to the same location where the file was previously located. You may want to move the file—for example, when the owner of the file has changed or to move it to a more secure location.

Backup Validation

Verifying the integrity of a backup is an optional but important procedure. It verifies that the backup completed successfully. If you create the backup using checksums (which is an option with many utilities), it will allow you to check that the data has not changed since it was made or that it has been corrupted or damaged. It is important to perform a verification after you back up and again before you restore so that you don't restore any damaged data.

Media Integrity

You learned about media integrity in Chapter 1, "Server Hardware," but a review is helpful. The amount of time you should retain tapes or other backup media will be driven by several issues:

- Any regulations that apply to the industry in which your company operates
- The criticality of the data
- Your company's policies

Equipment

If you are using a backup appliance rather than software, you must ensure that the device is in good condition and that it receives all the maintenance required to keep it working correctly. Make sure you take advantage of all service options before the warranty expires.

Regular Testing Intervals

Test if the backup process should be done on a regular basis, even if no issues are occurring. Although many backup utilities offer a "verification process," nothing beats actually attempting to restore the data. Test restorations may not be appropriate after every backup, but they should be done often to ensure that you have not been creating corrupted backups for days on end.

Media Inventory Before Restoration

With some backup appliances, inventory is a process used when you physically change tapes in your tape drive or library and you'd like to inform the device of the change. If you don't do this, the backup appliance may not know which tape is in which slot of the tape drive or library.

Explain the Importance of Disaster Recovery

Disaster recovery principles are based on accepting the inevitability of these events and taking steps to ensure that when they do occur the organization can, in a timely manner, recover both its data and the underlying infrastructure on which it depends. This may entail the establishment of a second site from which the enterprise might operate in severe events that destroy an office. In any case you should have created several plans *before* an event occurs that are used to guide your organization through every type of event. In this section we'll explore types of backup sites, methods of replicating data to backup sites, and the type of plans and documents you need to ensure both disaster recovery and business continuity.

Site Types

Although a secondary site that is identical in every way to the main site with data kept synchronized up to the minute would be ideal, the cost cannot be justified for most organizations. Cost–benefit analysis must be applied to every business issue, even disaster recovery. Thankfully, not all secondary sites are created equally. They can vary in functionality and cost. We're going to explore three types of sites in this section.

Hot Site

A *hot site* is a leased facility that contains all the resources needed for full operation. This environment includes computers, raised flooring, full utilities, electrical and communications wiring, networking equipment, and uninterruptible power supplies (UPSs). The only resource that must be restored at a hot site is the organization's data, usually only partially. It should only take a few minutes to bring a hot site to full operation.

Although a hot site provides the quickest recovery, it is the most expensive to maintain. In addition, it can be administratively hard to manage if the organization requires proprietary hardware or software. A hot site requires the same security controls as the primary facility and full redundancy, including hardware, software, and communication wiring.

Cold Site

A *cold site* is a leased facility that contains only electrical and communications wiring, air conditioning, plumbing, and raised flooring. No communications equipment, networking hardware, or computers are installed at a cold site until it is necessary to bring the site to full operation. For this reason, a cold site takes much longer to restore than a hot or a warm site.

A cold site provides the slowest recovery, but it is the least expensive to maintain. It is also the most difficult to test.

Warm Site

A *warm site* is somewhere between the restoration time and cost of a hot site and a cold site. It is the most widely implemented alternate leased location. Although it is easier to test a warm site than a cold site, a warm site requires much more effort for testing than a hot site.

A warm site is a leased facility that contains electrical and communications wiring, full utilities, and networking equipment. In most cases, the only thing that needs to be restored is the software and the data. A warm site takes longer to restore than a hot site but less time than a cold site.

Cloud

Another option is to provision a site in the cloud with a cloud provider. This offers the same advantages and disadvantages as a backup site in the cloud. That is, it will be available from anywhere with an Internet connection but will not be available if either you or the cloud provider lose your Internet connection.

Separate Geographic Locations

When choosing the location for a secondary site, consider spreading the sites out geographically. This will prevent the same disaster event (flood, fire, riot, earthquake) from impacting both. Balance this consideration against the need to keep the secondary location as close as possible to the main location so that employees don't have so far to go to work at the secondary location if necessary.

Replication

When multiple sites are implemented for fault tolerance, the current state of the data in the main site must be replicated to the secondary site. This is especially critical when using hot sites or what are called mirrored sites, where the two sites are kept up-to-date with each other constantly.

There are several methods you can use to implement this replication. In this section we'll look at three common replication methods.

Constant

When constant replication is in use, each time a change is made (data addition, deletion, change, etc.) at the primary site, the same change is written to the secondary site. This results in the secondary site being constantly up-to-date and is generally an expensive option.

Background

Background replication simply means that the replication process is performed as a background operation. A background operation is processing that occurs "in the background" while a user is performing other tasks in the system. This might be done if the system to which the replication is occurring is also performing work on behalf of users and you prefer that the users' work be carried out in the foreground, where more resources are dedicated to that job.

Synchronous vs. Asynchronous

The difference between these two methods lies in the process of changes or writes. With asynchronous replication, the write operation to the primary system is acknowledged by the primary system before the write is sent to the secondary, whereas with synchronous replication, the write is sent to the secondary system without waiting for acknowledgment from the primary. This two processes are shown in Figure 9.3.

FIGURE 9.3   Synchronous vs. asynchronous

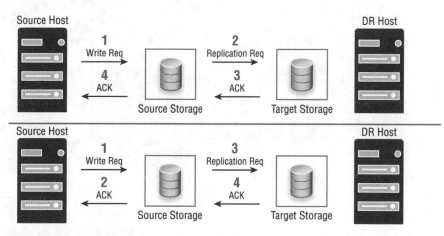

Application Consistent

Any database replication process that is application consistent causes running applications to complete all their operations and flush their buffers to disk (application quiescing) before replication. This is important because portions of data are kept in memory and some transactions may be incomplete when replication occurs. If no actions are taken to flush memory and I/O operations, some transactions could be lost.

File Locking

File locking restricts access to a computer file, or to a region of a file, by allowing only one user or process to modify or delete it at a specific time and to prevent reading of the file while it's being modified or deleted. With respect to databases, this means that when any user is making a change, the object to which the change is being made will be locked until the operation is complete or fails.

Mirroring

While replication is considered to be from database to database, mirroring is from machine to machine or server to server. In server-to-server replication, also called host-based replication, software on the servers handle the replication process. Server-to-server replication is typically less costly than disk- (array-) based, but it will impact the performance of the servers on which it is running. The replication software may also require updating from time to time as patches and service packs are installed. This process is shown in Figure 9.4.

FIGURE 9.4   Server to server

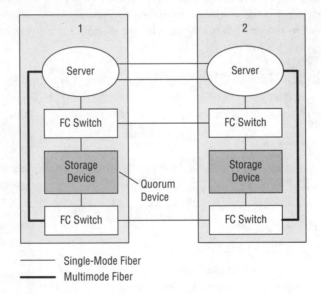

In Figure 9.4, the server and the storage device are connected to a Fibre Channel (FC) switch. The connections are therefore fiber cables. The cables from the servers to the local switches use multimode (which means they can carry more data but a shorter distance), and the cables between the offices are single mode (which means they carry less data but can go long distances).

Bidirectional

Bidirectional replication means that the two databases are both accepting work and therefore making changes to the same database. The two systems must replicate to each other, resulting in bidirectional transfer.

Testing

While developing a disaster recovery plan is a key to ensuring continuity of operations, the time to find out the plan is flawed is *not* when you are standing knee deep in water in the server room. In this section you'll learn about testing approaches to ensure that your disaster recovery plan is sound.

Tabletops

Conducting a tabletop exercise is the most cost-effective and efficient way to identify areas of vulnerability before moving on to more involved testing. A tabletop exercise is an informal brainstorming session that encourages participation from business leaders and other key employees. In a tabletop exercise, the participants agree to determine a particular attack scenario upon which they then focus.

Live Failover

A live failover test is one in which the primary site is taken down and operations are completely switched over to the secondary site. This is the riskiest test to perform, but it will also generate the best data about the sufficiency of your disaster recovery plan.

Simulated Failover

If you're not feeling confident enough to shut down the primary site, you can hedge your bets somewhat and perform a simulated failover. This is one in which you operate as if the primary site is down without actually taking it down. Then if something goes wrong, it's a quicker rollback of the plan.

Production vs. Nonproduction

Another approach is to perform a test of all recovery functions on a nonproduction part of the network. This prevents an issue with the plan causing problems with the production network while still allowing you to identify problems with your plan.

Summary

In this chapter you learned the importance of implementing proper disaster recovery principles. This included a discussion of various types of alternate sites and the replication methods used to synchronize data between the main and backup site.

You also learned about various backup methodologies, such as full, incremental, and differential backups. We also covered the types of media that can be used to store data that has been backed up, both those that supply linear access (tape) and those that supply random access (optical). Managing the media was also discussed, including topics on media storage, labeling, and retention. Finally, the advantages and disadvantages of on-site and off-site storage of backup media ended the chapter.

Exam Essentials

Differentiate backup site types   Describe the pros and cons of various alternate site types, such as hot, warm, and cold sites. Differentiate replication methodologies, including constant, background, synchronous, asynchronous, and file locking.

Implement appropriate backup techniques   Differentiate backup methodologies, including but not limited to full, incremental, and differential backups. Describe the access techniques of various backup media such as tape and optical media. Identify best practices for media storage and labeling. Discuss the security and environmental considerations of storing media off-site and on-site.

Review Questions

You can find the answers in the Appendix.

1. Which of the following site types contains only electrical and communications wiring, air conditioning, plumbing, and raised flooring?
   A. Mirrored
   B. Warm
   C. Cold
   D. Hot

2. Which of the following replication methods results in the secondary site being constantly up-to-date?
   A. Asynchronous
   B. Bidirectional
   C. Constant
   D. Synchronous

3. In which replication method is the write operation to the primary system acknowledged by the primary system before the write is sent to the secondary?
   A. Asynchronous
   B. Bidirectional
   C. Constant
   D. Synchronous

4. Which of the following replication methods is advisable if the system to which the replication is occurring is also performing work on behalf of users?
   A. Bidirectional
   B. Synchronous
   C. Constant
   D. Background

5. Which tape format uses colors to indicate a specific cartridge type?
   A. IBM
   B. Oracle
   C. BIA
   D. LTO

6. Which type of snapshot is a snapshot of everything rather than just the changes?

   A. Copy-on-write

   B. Shadow

   C. File lock

   D. Split mirror

7. What file attribute is used to communicate to the backup system whether a particular file has changed since the last backup?

   A. Read only

   B. Archive

   C. System

   D. Hidden

8. Which backup methods do *not* clear the archive bit? (Choose two.)

   A. Full

   B. Differential

   C. Incremental

   D. Copy

9. Which of the following always requires exactly two tapes to restore?

   A. Full

   B. Differential

   C. Incremental

   D. Copy

10. You do a full backup every Saturday at 1 a.m. and an incremental backup every other day of the week at 1 a.m. A drive failure occurs on Thursday afternoon at 5:30. How many backup tapes do you need to restore?

    A. 1

    B. 3

    C. 4

    D. 6

11. Which snapshot type is taken every time a user enters data or changes data and includes only the changed data?

    A. Site-to-site

    B. Copy-on-write

    C. Array-based

    D. Split mirror

12. Which of the following is required to be supported to perform an open file backup?

   A. VSS

   B. BAA

   C. OUI

   D. EUI-64

13. Which disaster test type is the riskiest test to perform but will also generate the best data about the sufficiency of your disaster recovery plan?

   A. Live failover

   B. Simulated failover

   C. Tabletop

   D. Staged

14. Which backup media type provides linear access to the data?

   A. CD

   B. Tape

   C. DVD

   D. External hard drive

15. What is the purpose of creating a backup using checksums?

   A. For integrity verification

   B. To encrypt the data

   C. To speed restoration

   D. To deduplicate the data

16. Which of the following is from machine to machine or server to server?

   A. Mirroring replication

   B. Asynchronous replication

   C. Synchronous replication

   D. Background replication

17. Which of the following uses three sets of backup tapes?

   A. GFS

   B. Tower of Hanoi

   C. FIFO

   D. LIFO

18. Which of the following rotation schemes does not protect against data errors?

    A. GFS

    B. Tower of Hanoi

    C. FIFO

    D. LIFO

19. Which of the following is a storage device that contains multiple tape drives?

    A. Jumpbox

    B. Tape library

    C. Content library

    D. Jukebox

20. Which type of disaster plan testing is the most cost-effective and efficient way to identify issues?

    A. Live failover

    B. Simulated failover

    C. Tabletop

    D. Staged

Troubleshooting Hardware and Software Issues

COMPTIA SERVER+ EXAM OBJECTIVES COVERED IN THIS CHAPTER:

✓ **4.1 Explain the troubleshooting theory and methodology.**

- Identify the problem and determine the scope

    - Question users/stakeholders and identify changes to the server/environment.

    - Collect additional documentation/logs

    - If possible, replicate the problem as appropriate

    - If possible, perform backups before making changes

    - Escalate, if necessary

- Establish a theory of probable cause (question the obvious)

    - Determine whether there is a common element or symptom causing multiple problems

- Test the theory to determine the cause

    - Once the theory is confirmed, determine the next steps to resolve the problem

    - If the theory is not confirmed, establish a new theory

- Establish a plan of action to resolve the problem

    - Notify impacted users.

- Implement the solution or escalate

    - Make one change at a time and test/confirm the change has resolved the problem

    - If the problem is not resolved, reverse the change, if appropriate, and implement a new change

- Verify full system functionality and, if applicable, implement preventive measures
- Perform a root cause analysis
- Document findings, actions, and outcomes throughout the process

✓ **4.2 Given a scenario, troubleshoot common hardware failures.**

- Common problems
    - Predictive failures
    - Memory errors and failures
        - System crash
            - Blue screen
            - Purple screen
            - Memory dump
        - Utilization
        - Power-on self-test (POST) errors
        - Random lockups
        - Kernel panic
    - Complementary metal- oxide-semiconductor (CMOS) battery failure
    - System lockups
    - Random crashes
    - Fault and device indication
        - Visual indicators
    - Light-emitting diode (LED)
    - Liquid crystal display (LCD) panel readouts
        - Auditory or olfactory cues
        - POST codes
    - Misallocated virtual resources
- Causes of common problems
    - Technical
        - Power supply fault
        - Malfunctioning fans

- Improperly seated heat sink
- Improperly seated cards
- Incompatibility of components
- Cooling failures
- Backplane failure
- Firmware incompatibility
- CPU or GPU overheating
- Environmental
  - Dust
  - Humidity
  - Temperature
- Tools and techniques
  - Event logs
  - Firmware upgrades or downgrades
  - Hardware diagnostics
  - Compressed air
  - Electrostatic discharge (ESD) equipment
  - Reseating or replacing components and/or cables

✓ **4.4 Given a scenario, troubleshoot common OS and software problems.**
- Common problems
  - Unable to log on
  - Unable to access resources
  - Unable to access files
  - System file corruption
  - End of life/end of support
  - Slow performance
  - Cannot write to system logs
  - Service failures
  - System or application hanging

- Reload OS
- Snapshots
- Proper privilege escalations
  - runas/Run As
  - sudo
  - su
- Scheduled reboots
- Software firewalls
  - Adding or removing ports
  - Zones
- Clocks
- Network time protocol (NTP)
- System time
- Services and processes
  - Starting
  - Stopping
  - Status identification
  - Dependencies
    - Configuration management
  - System center configuration manager (SCCM)
  - Puppet/Chef/Ansible
  - Group Policy Object (GPO)
- Hardware compatibility list (HCL)

Just as surely as it is a given that devices and device components will fail from time to time, it is also a given that hardware and software will malfunction or at least appear to be malfunctioning from time to time as well. In some cases, it is a true failure and in others it is simply the result of misconfiguration, human error, a misunderstanding of how the hardware or software operates, or an unrealistic expectation of what the hardware or software can deliver. In this chapter we are going to discuss a general troubleshooting approach that has proven effective and specific troubleshooting approaches to specific issues.

Explain the Troubleshooting Theory and Methodology

If you type the term *troubleshooting methodology* in a search engine, you will find that there are many approaches. Most of them follow the same basic steps with some variation because years of experience have taught us what works and what doesn't work. CompTIA has a specific methodology that you should know for the exam. In this first section of the chapter we'll cover the steps involved.

Identify the Problem and Determine the Scope

Although it may sound obvious, you can't troubleshoot a problem without knowing what the problem is. In some cases, the problem will be obvious. But in others, especially when relying on the description of the problem by the user, it will appear to be one thing on the surface when in actuality the issue the user is experiencing is a symptom of a different, possibly larger problem.

One of the first things you should attempt to do when a user reports an issue is to determine the scope the problem. By that I mean "how widespread is the issue?" Is this the only user experiencing the issue, or is it everyone in that user's subnet or department or VLAN? Is it everyone in an office? Is it the entire network? When the issue is affecting other users, it becomes less likely that the issue is the reporting user's machine and more likely that the source is an infrastructure device or service that many are depending on.

If you do determine that the issue is widespread, have a clear understanding of the potential impact of any changes you make, and always ensure that a rollback plan has been established in advance. Whenever you determine that a change has the potential to cause widespread issues, try to make the change in a test environment or on a small, low-impact section of the network.

In this section, processes that can help bring clarity to the situation are discussed.

Question Users/Stakeholders and Identify Changes to the Server/ Environment

Identify the problem by questioning the user and identifying user changes to the computer. Before you do anything else, ask the user the following:

- What the problem is
- When the last time was that the problem didn't exist
- What has changed since

When performing this step, be wary of accepting the user's diagnosis of the problem at face value. For example, a user may start the conversation with the statement, "The email server is down." At this point, ask the question, "Is there anything else you cannot do besides open your email?" Ask them to try accessing a shared folder or the Internet. If either of those tasks fails, the problem is probably not the email server but basic network connectivity of their computer.

If in fact you do find that the issue lies in the server environment, then you may ask yourself or the system owner of the suspected server the same questions you asked the reporting user—that is, what is the problem, when was the last time the problem didn't exist, and what has changed since then?

Collect Additional Documentation/Logs

One of your best sources of information when answering some of these questions are the logs that the servers produce and any support documentation that may have been developed over time in the process of solving earlier issues. This is one of the reasons that best practices call for keeping a record in some format for every server that lists issues that have occurred and what was done to resolve them.

Creating and maintaining this documentation not only can help to speed the resolution of issues that have already been solved but can also identify trends that may indicate that earlier solutions only treated symptoms and not the root problem when an issue reoccurs over and over.

When you combine this with information gleaned from the server logs, it can help map the appearance of the issue to events that occurred in the logs and changes that may have been made. If you make these connections, it can suggest theories of probable cause and possible solutions.

If Possible, Replicate the Problem as Appropriate

Once you have examined the logs and the documentation, you may attempt to replicate the issue. In many cases, attempting to replicate the issue may be desirable from a troubleshooting standpoint but impossible or inadvisable because of the mayhem that may ensue.

For example, you shouldn't re-create a DNS failure, which typically will bring the entire network down, no matter how valuable the resulting information may be.

However, when appropriate, if you can re-create the issue, it means that you have a very good handle on what's happening and what to do to fix the problem. Unfortunately, in many cases you can't do that (or at least not at first) and the problem may appear to be intermittent, a type of issue that can prove to be the most difficult to solve.

If Possible, Perform Backups before Making Changes

You may find yourself making significant changes on a server in an attempt to locate and/or solve the issue. Be sure that you do a backup before you make any changes so that all your actions can be undone, if necessary. If you have virtual servers or if you have the ability to make a disk image of a physical server, you may want to do the troubleshooting on a restored image of the live server (or a snapshot in the case of a virtual server) to prevent making the issue worse in the production network.

Escalate, if Necessary

It could be that at this point the responding technician may realize that the issue is beyond their expertise. When this is the case, they should be encouraged to escalate the issue to another more experienced technician. Ensure that this avenue is spelled out in procedures so that the responding technician does not spend significant time on an issue they ultimately will not be able to address.

Establish a Theory of Probable Cause (Question the Obvious)

As you get answers to your initial questions, theories will begin to evolve as to the root of the problem.

Once you have developed a list of possible causes, develop a list of tests you can perform to test each to narrow the list by eliminating each theory one by one. Don't forget to consider the obvious and make no assumptions. Just because the cable has worked every day for the last five years doesn't mean the person cleaning the office may not have caught the vacuum cleaner on the cable and damaged its connector last night.

Determine Whether There Is a Common Element or Symptom Causing Multiple Problems

In some cases, it may appear that several issues are occurring at once. While it is possible that multiple unrelated issues are occurring at the same time, always treat that possibility with distrust. Often there is a single element that is causing what may appear to be unrelated issues. The more you know and understand about the details of the innerworkings of a device or piece of software, the easier it will be for you to look at a set of issues and have that "a-ha" moment where you realize what could cause all the issues to occur.

For this reason, never hesitate to seek the counsel of others who may be subject matter experts. That might mean others in your organization or it might mean colleagues in other organizations. Finally, you may want to consult blogs and discussion groups that address the issue. The bottom line is it's not cheating or a sign of weakness to ask for help!

Test the Theory to Determine the Cause

Test related components, including connections and hardware and software configurations; use Device Manager; and consult vendor documentation. Whatever the problem may be, the odds are good that someone else has experienced it before. Use the tools at your disposal—including manuals and websites—to try to zero in on the problem as expeditiously as possible.

Once the Theory Is Confirmed, Determine the Next Steps to Resolve the Problem

If your theory is confirmed, then determine the next steps you need to take to resolve the problem. In cases where you have determined the device where the problem lies but you have no expertise in that area, escalate the problem to someone as needed. For example, if you have narrowed down the problem to the router and you don't understand or manage the router, escalate the problem to the router administrator.

If the Theory Is Not Confirmed, Establish a New Theory

If your theory is not confirmed, then come up with a new theory, or bring in someone with more expertise (escalate the problem). If you make changes to test one theory, make sure you reverse those changes before you test another theory. Making multiple changes can cause new problems and make the process even more difficult.

Establish a Plan of Action to Resolve the Problem

Evaluate the results and develop an action plan of steps to fully resolve the problem. Keep in mind that it's possible that more than one thing is causing the problem. If that is the case, you may need to solve one problem and then turn your attention to the next.

Once you have planned your work, work your plan. Methodically make the required changes while always having a backout plan if your changes cause a larger problem.

Notify Impacted Users

If your plan of action includes any changes that may impact users, you should notify them of the time when the change will be made, the possible impact, and when any limitations caused by the change will be lifted.

Implement the Solution or Escalate

Remember that if a solution evades you because of lack of experience with an issue, escalate the problem to someone who has the skills to address the issues. Don't forget that if no such person is available in the organization, you need to make full use of documentation, online resources, and any other sources of expertise. If all else fails, consider involving any vendors or third-party experts available.

Make One Change at a Time and Test/Confirm the Change Has Resolved the Problem

Throughout the troubleshooting process, make a single configuration change at a time and at every step, stop to test and analyze the results. When you make multiple changes at a time, those changes might interact with one another and make the picture even muddier. If any change resolves the problem, proceed to verifying that the change didn't introduce new issues and that there is full functionality (see this step later in this section).

If the Problem Is Not Resolved, Reverse the Change, if Appropriate, and Implement a New Change

If a change does not solve the issue, roll that change back before making any additional changes. Only by operating in this manner can you truly judge the effects of each configuration change. Remember, making multiple changes at a time not only makes it impossible to correctly assess the effect of each change, but may result in making the issue worse!

Verify Full System Functionality and, if Applicable, Implement Preventive Measures

When the problem is believed to be resolved, verify that the system is fully functional. If there are preventive measures that can be put in place to keep this situation from recurring, take those measures on this machine and on all others where the problem exists. Also keep in mind that times like this are great learning moments to teach users what role they may have played and what actions they may be able to take on their own in the future to prevent the problem, if that is appropriate.

Perform a Root Cause Analysis

While solving the immediate issue is certainly satisfying, and it is tempting to assume the issue is resolved, keep in mind that in many cases you may have treated the symptom and not the root cause. If you have any lingering doubts that the issue is solved, continue to work at finding the root cause. This is one of the benefits of keeping track of all issues and all changes made in attempts to resolve issues for every server. When you see an issue continues to rear its head time and again, it's a pretty good indication that your changes are treating a symptom and not a root cause.

Document Findings, Actions, and Outcomes Throughout the Process

Document your activities and outcomes. Experience is a wonderful teacher, but only if you can remember what you've done. Documenting your actions and outcomes will help you (or a fellow administrator) troubleshoot a similar problem when it crops up in the future.

In some cases, you may think that you have solved a problem only to find that it occurs again later because you only treated the symptom of a larger problem. When this type of thing occurs, documentation of what has occurred in the past can be helpful in seeing patterns that otherwise would remain hidden.

Given a Scenario, Troubleshoot Common Hardware Failures

While problems can occur with the operating system with little or no physical warning, that is rarely the case when it comes to hardware problems. Your senses will often alert you that something is wrong based on what you hear, smell, or see. This section discusses common issues with the main players.

Common Problems

Once you have performed troubleshooting for some time, you will notice a pattern. With some exceptions, the same issues occur over and over and usually give you the same warnings each time. This section covers common symptoms or warning signs. When you learn what these symptoms are trying to tell you, it makes your job easier.

Predictive Failures

Some issues will issue a warning that a failure is in the future. An example of such a device is a hard drive that has support for Self-Monitoring, Analysis and Reporting Technology (SMART). This technology is built into most drives to determine if the device is still physically healthy or failing due to hardware issues.

When the drive supports SMART, you can assess the status of the drive at the command prompt. Use the following procedure:

1. Type the following command to determine if the hard drive is failing and press Enter:

```
wmic diskdrive get status
```

2. In the Status column, confirm that the result is OK, as shown in Figure 10.1.

FIGURE 10.1   Checking drive status

```
Command Prompt                              —     □     ×
Microsoft Windows [Version 10.0.22000.556]
(c) Microsoft Corporation. All rights reserved.

C:\Users\TroyMcmillan>wmic diskdrive get status
Status
OK


C:\Users\TroyMcmillan>
```

You'll see an OK status for each internal drive installed on your device.

Memory Errors and Failures

Memory problems include a bad or failing memory chip, using memory whose speed is incompatible with the motherboard, or using applications that require more memory than is present in the server. These issues typically manifest themselves with system freezes or lockups. If the issue is serious enough, the server may fail the power-on self-test (POST). Replace and upgrade the memory as required.

System Crash

A system crash is when the system shuts itself down. When this occurs, there may be an accompanying warning screen of some sort. In this section you'll learn about these crash screens.

BLUE SCREEN

A serious issue is a STOP message or Blue Screen of Death (BSOD) message. Once a regular occurrence when working with Windows, blue screens have become less common. Occasionally, systems will lock up; you can usually examine the log files to discover what was happening when this occurred and take steps to correct it. Remember, when dealing with a blue screen, always ask yourself, "What did I just install or change?" In many cases, the change is involved in the BSOD. Also keep in mind that (as the instructions on the blue screen will tell you) a simple reboot will often fix the problem. Retaining the contents of the BSOD can help troubleshoot the issue. In most instances, the BSOD error will be in Microsoft's knowledge-base to help with troubleshooting

PURPLE SCREEN

Purple screens of death always appears when there is a critical error on the VMkernel of an ESX/ESXI host. Additionally, your computer screen turns purple due to outdated drivers, unstable GPU, external hardware, or other misconfigured computer settings. Possible solutions include:

- Unplug all external devices and hardware.
- Upgrade your graphics card driver.

- Remove overclock settings.
- Clean the heat sink.
- Memory dump.

When a system performs a memory dump, it is saving the contents of memory (including information about the error and the failure) to a file. Some errors are unrecoverable because they require a reboot to regain functionality, but the information stored in RAM at the time of a crash contains the code that produced the error. Memory dumps save information that might otherwise be lost due to RAM overwriting.

Utilization

Memory leaks occur when an application is issued some memory to use and does not return the memory and any temporary file to the operating system after the program no longer needs it. Over time the available memory for that application or that part of the operating system becomes exhausted and the program can no longer function. This is caused by poor coding practices. While the application that is causing this should be investigated and perhaps updated, a quick solution is to reboot the server. Make sure when you do this it is a cold boot. Many of the latest operating systems don't actually reboot when you restart; they just sleep.

Power-On Self-Test (POST) Errors

During the bootup of the system, a power-on self-test (POST) occurs, and each system-critical device is checked for functionality. If the system boots to the point where the video driver is loaded and the display is operational, any problems will be reported with a numeric error code.

If the system cannot boot to that point, problems will be reported with a beep code. Although each manufacturer's set of beep codes and their interpretation can be found in the documentation for the system or on the website of the manufacturer, one short beep almost always means everything is okay. Here are some examples of items tested during this process:

- RAM
- Video card
- Motherboard

 To interpret the beep codes if you cannot read the error codes on the screen, use the chart provided at www.computerhope.com/beep.htm.

During startup, problems with devices that fail to be recognized properly, services that fail to start, and so on are written to the system log and can also be viewed with Event Viewer. If no POST error code prevents a successful boot, this utility provides information about what's been going on system-wise to help you troubleshoot problems. Event Viewer shows warnings, error messages, and records of things happening successfully. You can access it through Computer Management, or you can access it directly from the Administrative Tools in Control Panel.

Another way to determine a problem during the POST routine is to use a *POST card*. This is a circuit board that fits into an Industry Standard Architecture (ISA) or Peripheral Component Interconnect (PCI) expansion slot in the motherboard and reports numeric codes as the boot process progresses. Each of those codes corresponds to a particular component being checked. If the POST card stops at a certain number, you can look up that number in the manual that came with the card to determine the problem.

 BIOS Central (www.bioscentral.com) is a website containing charts detailing the beep codes and POST error codes for many different BIOS manufacturers.

Most server vendors also include a hardware diagnostic utility in what Dell calls the pre-operation system. As this utility has a physical (as opposed to logical) view of the attached hardware, it can identify hardware problems that the operating system and other online tools cannot identify. You can use the hardware diagnostics utility to validate the memory, I/O devices, CPU, physical disk drives, and other peripherals.

Random Lockups

Lockups can be caused by many issues. Memory-related errors you may find in the log files include:

Data_Bus_Error   This error is usually a hardware issue. It could include the installation of faulty hardware or the failure of existing hardware. In many cases it is related to defective memory of some sort (RAM, L2 cache, or video RAM). If you just added something, remove it and test the results.

Unexpected_Kernel_Mode_Trap   Several items can cause this error. One of them is overclocking the CPU. Try executing the hardware diagnostics provided with the system, especially the memory system. Again, if you just added hardware, remove it and test the result.

Page_Fault_in_Nonpaged_Area   This is another message that can be the result of adding faulty hardware or of hardware (usually memory of some type) going bad. Use the hardware diagnostics provided with the system to gain more information about the error. And as always, if you just added something, remove it and test the results.

Kernel Panic

In the previous section you learned about an error related to the kernel. A kernel panic is an action taken by a system's kernel upon detecting an internal error in which either (1) it is unable to safely recover or (2) continuing to run the system would have a higher risk of major data loss. This can be a cause of blue and purple screens and memory dumps.

Complementary Metal-Oxide-Semiconductor (CMOS) Battery Failure

The CMOS chip must have a constant source of power to keep its settings. To prevent the loss of data, motherboard manufacturers include a small battery to power the CMOS memory. On modern systems, this is a coin-style battery, about the diameter of a dime and about as thick. One of these is shown in Figure 10.2.

FIGURE 10.2   CMOS battery in a server

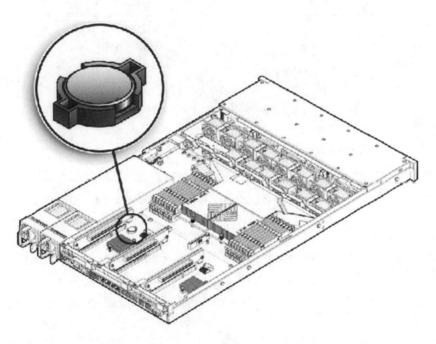

When the server is not keeping correct time or date when turned off, it is usually a CMOS battery issue and a warning that the battery is soon going to die. In the absence of the server receiving time and date updates from a time server such as a Network Time Protocol (NTP) server, the time kept in the CMOS is the time source for the computer.

Always use the type of battery recommended by the vendor. In Exercise 10.1 you'll use an IBM System x3250 M4.

 This exercise applies to an IBM server. The procedure for your server may vary, so consult the documentation.

EXERCISE 10.1

Replacing the Battery in an IBM Server

1. After powering down the server, remove the cover.

2. If necessary, lift the air baffle out of the way. It is over the fans in the middle of the server, as shown in this graphic.

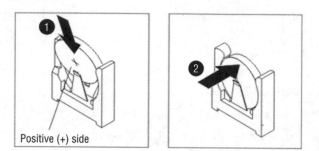

Positive (+) side

3. Remove the old battery.

4. Insert the new battery:

   a. Position the battery so that the positive (+) symbol is facing toward the power supply.

   b. Tilt the battery so that you can insert it into the socket on the side opposite the battery clip.

   c. Press the battery down into the socket until it snaps into place, as shown in this graphic:

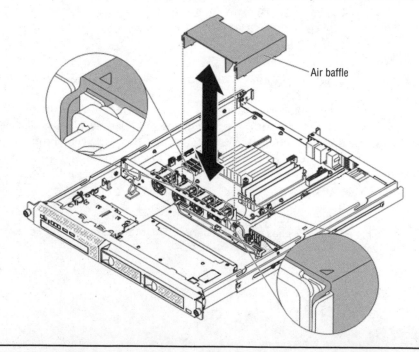

Air baffle

System Lockups

System lockups can be caused by a runaway process. A *runaway process* is one that has taken control of the server and may lock the system up or at least lock up a service or application. Keep in mind that some forms of malware can cause this issue, but we are going to focus on legitimate processes that become runaway.

In Windows you can use Task Manager to stop runaway processes. To do so access the Processes tab and click the CPU and Memory columns to sort the list of running process according to CPU and memory usage. This will allow you to identify the process using all the CPU or memory. Highlight the process and select End Now.

In Linux you can use the `kill` command to stop the process. To do so, you must identity the guilty process using the `ps` command. To list and sort the processes by CPU usage, use this command (the `head-5` option limits it to the top five processes):

```
$ ps aux --sort=-pcpu | head -5

USER    PID %CPU  %MEM    VSZ   RSS TTY  STAT  START TIME COMMAND

root      1 2.6   0.7  51396  7644 ?    Ss    02:02 0:03 /usr/lib/systemd/systemd --switched-root --system --deserialize 23

root   1249 2.6   3.0 355800 30896 tty1 Rsl+  02:02 0:02 /usr/bin/X -background none :0 vt01 -nolisten tcp

root    508 2.4   1.6 248488 16776 ?    Ss    02:02 0:03 /usr/bin/python /usr/sbin/firewalld --nofork

silver 1525 2.1   2.3 448568 24392 ?    S     02:03 0:01 /usr/bin/python /usr/share/s
```

Once you have identified the process, locate the PID and use the `kill` command to stop it as follows (we are killing process 1249):

```
kill -SIGKILL 1249
```

Random Crashes

Throughout this section we've discussed many things that can cause random crashes. Please review the previous sections on system crashes and memory failures.

Fault and Device Indication

There are some indicator mechanisms that will be provided by the vendor of the hardware and the software that can give you an early warning that something is amiss or is about to go bad. You should always react to these indicators in the same way you would react to a warning that your car is overheating, because they typically don't come into play until the situation is getting serious.

Visual Indicators

Many servers come with integrated diagnostics that will generate error codes. These are usually text-based interfaces that you can access even when the server is having significant issues. In other cases, you receive error code messages when you reboot the server (which is often done when issues occur). For example, Dell servers issue these messages and provide tables on their website to help you not only interpret the problem, but in many cases, tell you exactly what to do to resolve the issue.

For example, if you receive the following message when rebooting, it indicates that something has changed and it suggests that if this is unexpected (you neither added nor removed memory), you have a piece of bad memory that is not now being included in the memory amount:

```
Amount of memory has changed
```

Light-Emitting Diode (LED)

Most network devices, including servers, have LEDs on them that indicate certain things. The LED diagram for a Sun Blade X6250 Server Module is shown in Figure 10.3.

FIGURE 10.3   LEDs

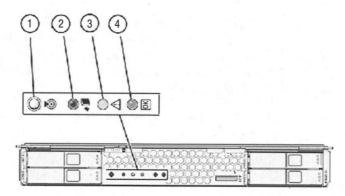

The purpose of the LEDs and buttons is as follows:

#1: LED that helps you identify which system you are working on

#2: Indicates whether the server module is ready to be removed from the chassis

#3: Service action required

#4: Power/OK

Liquid Crystal Display (LCD) Panel Readouts

Many hardware devices like servers also have small LCD screens on the front that may be a source of messages that are helpful during troubleshooting. The Dell PowerEdge has the panel shown in Figure 10.4.

FIGURE 10.4   Dell LCD

Not only is this panel used to make configurations, but it also displays error messages. When it does this, it changes the backlight color from blue to amber so that you notice it quicker. The types of alerts covered are as follows:

- Cable and board presence
- Temperature
- Voltages
- Fans
- Processors
- Memory
- Power supplies
- BIOS
- Hard drives

IBM calls their system *light path diagnostics*. This is a system consisting of an LED panel on the front and a series of LEDs inside the box near various components. One of the LEDs is the Information LED, and when it indicates there is an error, you can open the box, and LEDs inside the box might be lit near the problem component, as shown in Figure 10.5.

FIGURE 10.5   IBM light path diagnostics

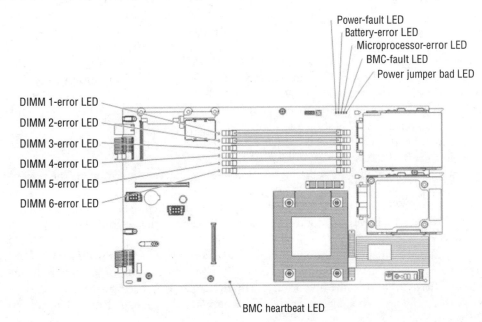

AUDITORY OR OLFACTORY CUES

When the system makes noises, you should listen. A grinding or clicking noise can be a failing drive. A whining sound could be a fan on its way to failing. The point is that when the system makes any noises that are not normal, if you don't check it out you are asking for system failure.

When the system smells like something is burning, it is. Shut the system down and start looking for signs of burnt spots on the motherboard. If the system overheats it can burn and destroy components. Most overheating problems are caused by dust buildup inside the box.

POST CODES

Another possible source of information when troubleshooting server issues are the beep codes heard when rebooting the server. Like workstations, servers emit beep codes that indicate the status of the POST during boot. For example, an IBM blade server emits two long beeps followed by a short beep when a microprocessor register test fails. By using the online list of code descriptions (or the documentation), you will find that the document not only lists the meaning of the pattern but also tells you exactly what to do (in this instance, reseat the processor). It goes on to tell you that if reseating the processor doesn't work, you should change out the processor, and if that doesn't work, change out the board.

Misallocated Virtual Resources

Virtual memory is a portion of the hard drive to which data is temporarily moved when the current available memory is insufficient for the task at hand. Earlier you learned that when the hard drive fills, it limits the amount of space that can be used for this, reducing performance.

The system should properly set the size of the file automatically based on the amount of memory present, but you can increase the size of the file and change its location using the System tools in Control Panel. Keep in mind that if this is a continual situation you need to add more RAM.

This utility allows you to view and configure various system elements. The System applet in Windows Server 2012 R2 is shown in Figure 10.6.

Note while this procedure is in Windows Server 2012 R2 the process is the same on all systems up to Server 2022.

Selecting the Advanced System Settings option in the menu on the left opens the screen in Figure 10.7.

Next, select the Settings button next to Performance and when the next screen opens, select the Advanced tab (yes, a second Advanced tab) to access the options shown in Figure 10.8.

Finally, click the Change button in the Virtual Memory section. As shown in Figure 10.9, you can change the location of the file and adjust its size. Earlier you learned that moving the file to a drive other than the operating system drive may help performance. To make either of these changes, you have to deselect the Automatically Manage Paging File Size For All Drives option.

FIGURE 10.6   System applet in Windows Server 2012 R2

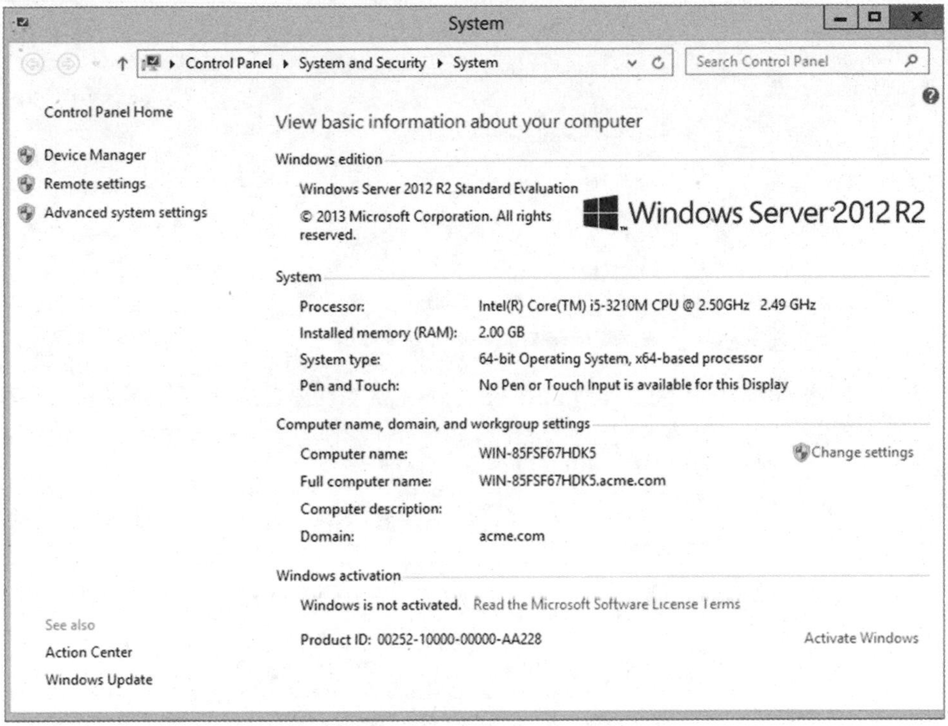

FIGURE 10.7   System Properties, Advanced tab

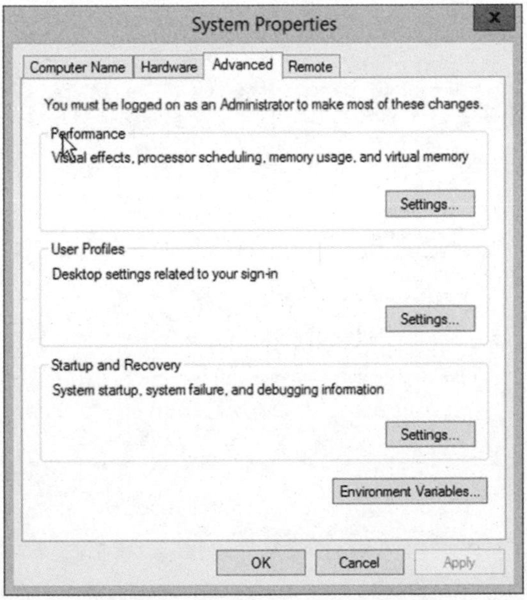

FIGURE 10.8   Performance Options

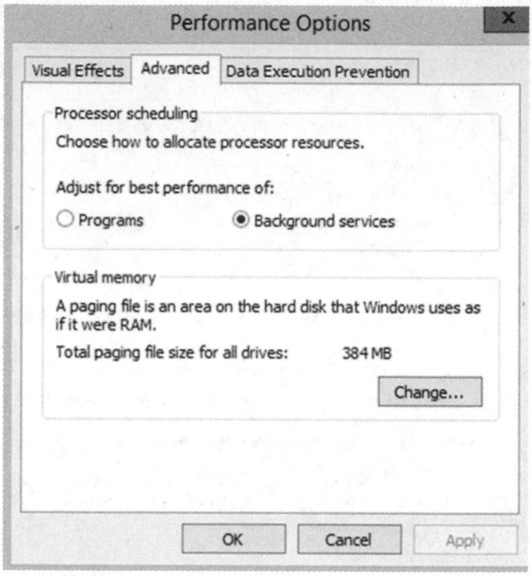

FIGURE 10.9   Virtual Memory settings

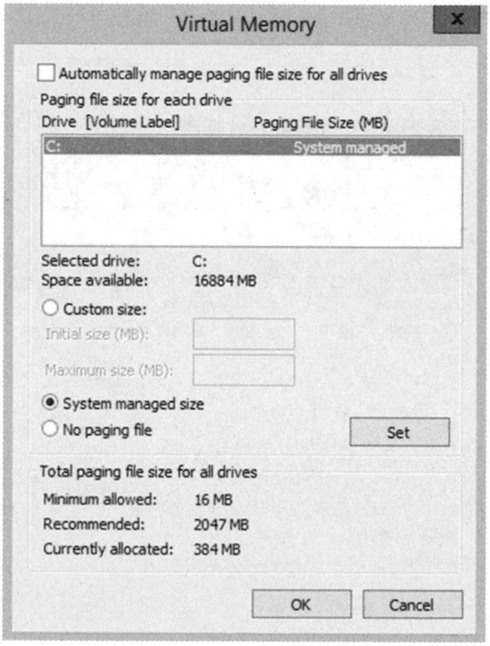

Causes of Common Problems

While incompatible programs and drivers are a possible cause of problems, they are not the only causes of some of the issues raised in this section. We'll look at some other issues that can plague any computer and some that are specific to servers in the datacenter.

Technical

While some issues are caused by environmental issues (such as heat, humidity, and static electricity), others are unavoidable and are just a matter of something breaking. In this section you'll learn about such technical issues.

Power Supply Fault

Although power supply failures do occur, power problems usually involve the following issues and scenarios:

- Check the power cord, and if it's plugged into a power strip or UPS, ensure the strip is plugged in (and if it has a breaker, check to see whether it was tripped by a surge or whether the switch that turns off the entire strip has been inadvertently turned to the off position). In the case of a UPS, check whether the UPS battery is dead and if the outlet is still receiving power.

- Try replacing the power supply with a known good unit to see whether the power supply failed.

- Power supply problems can cause reboots as well. The power supply continually sends a Power_Good signal to the motherboard, and if this signal is not present momentarily, the system will reset.

- Power supplies can also provide too much power, which will fry components in the path—for example, you replace fried memory and the new memory is fried immediately. It could be the power supply is providing too much power.

Malfunctioning Fans

In Chapter 1, "Server Hardware," you learned about fan failures and the replacement of fans. Please review that section.

Improperly Seated Heat Sink

Under normal conditions, the server cools itself by pulling in air. That air is used to dissipate the heat created by the processor (and absorbed by the heat sink). When the heat sink is not properly seated, it will not absorb heat as efficiently and the CPU may overheat and fail. When CPU overheating is occurring, always check the seating of the heat sink.

Improperly Seated Cards

When an expansion card fails in a server, the solution is to replace the card with a new one. However, you should always make sure the card is the culprit first. Check to ensure the card is seated properly. If it is, many servers come with onboard hardware diagnostics that can help you determine if it is the card or the slot in which it resides. While each server's documentation might provide different steps to determine this, the steps in Exercise 10.2 serve as a guide for using the diagnostic tools.

Exercise 10.2 applies to a Dell PowerEdge T110. Your server may differ. Consult the documentation.

EXERCISE 10.2

Troubleshooting Expansion Cards in a Dell PowerEdge T110

1. Run an online diagnostic test. As the system boots, press F10.

2. Click Hardware Diagnostics in the left pane and click Run Hardware Diagnostics in the right pane.

3. When the screen changes, select Run Diags, as shown in this graphic:

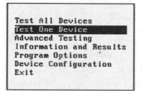

4. Select Test One Device, as shown here:

```
Test All Devices
Test One Device
Advanced Testing
Information and Results
Program Options
Device Configuration
Exit
```

5. When the test has completed, view the results for both the slot and the card in question.

Incompatibility of Components

While vendors of both server hardware and software attempt to cram as much functionality as they can into their products, inevitably customers want systems to do things for which they were not designed or to exhibit functionality not currently present in the product. To meet this demand, third parties often enter the picture and create components that when added to the system deliver that functionality or something close to it.

While these components will certainly find a market, the vendors of these products cannot always ensure that these add-ons will play nice with every operating system or with all your hardware. In their defense, though it is to their benefit to test the component with as many potential interfacing systems (hardware and software) as possible, there is no way they can anticipate every combination of these variables.

For this reason, always consult the websites of your server hardware manufacturer and the operating system and those of any applications that may be installed on the server for guidance regarding supported third-party components. Then, you should still test these components for compatibility as there could be some unusual quirks in your specific configuration that render the component incompatible.

Cooling Failures

CPUs produce heat, and the more powerful the CPU, the more heat it produces. Heat is an enemy to the server in general since it causes problems such as random reboots. Methods of cooling the CPU and in turn the overall interior of the case have evolved with the increasing need to remove this heat.

When cooling fails, it is usually a fan or airflow issue. If the scope of the issue is such that many servers are involved, the issue may be the cooling in the datacenter itself. Always have the contact information of an HVAC expert close at hand for those situations.

When airflow is restricted by clogged ports, a bad fan, and so forth, heat can build up inside the unit and cause problems. Chip creep—the unseating of components—is one of the more common byproducts of a cycle of overheating and cooling inside of the system.

Since the air is being pulled into the machine, excessive heat can originate from outside the server as well because of a hot working environment. The heat can be pulled in and cause the same problems. Take care to keep the ambient air within normal ranges (approximately 60–90 degrees Fahrenheit) and at a constant temperature.

Replacing slot covers is vital. Servers are designed to circulate air with slot covers in place or cards plugged into the ports. Leaving slots on the back of the computer open alters the air circulation and causes more dust to be pulled into the system.

When you have determined that a single server is involved, consider the following possible causes:

- Dead fan
- Blockage from dust or debris of front or back panel vents
- Improperly installed components or cables that can block the flow of air through the server
- Dividers, baffles, component filler panels, and server top covers that may be missing or installed improperly

Backplane Failure

Servers have backplanes that abut the drives and make a connection with the drive so that no cables are required. Backplanes are advantageous in that they provide data and control signal connectors for the hard drives. They also provide the interconnection for the front I/O board, power and locator buttons, and system/component status LEDs.

Unfortunately, this creates a serious single point-of-failure because if the backplane fails, we lose communication with the servers to which it is connected. While this generally is considered a highly unlikely event, that won't make you feel better when it happens to you! If the servers using the backplane are mission critical, you may want to invest in both a spare backplane and the spare cables required to connect the backplane. Before you connect the backplane, make sure you have considered a cable failure as well.

In Exercise 10.3, you'll do this on a Dell PowerEdge 2650.

 This exercise applies to a Dell 2650 server. The procedure for your server may vary, so consult the documentation.

EXERCISE 10.3

Replacing the SCSI Backplane

1. After powering down the server, remove the bezel using the key to unlock it.

2. Loosen the three thumbscrews that secure the cover to the chassis.

3. Slide the back cover backward and grasp the cover at both ends.

4. Carefully lift the cover away from the system.

5. Press the release tab on the control-panel cable cover and lift the cable cover straight up to clear the chassis, as shown in this graphic.

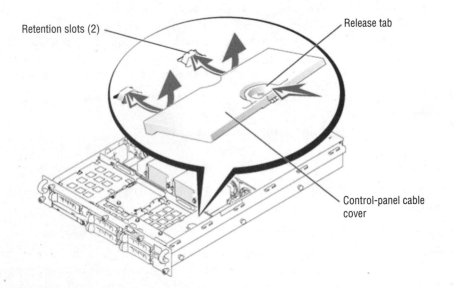

6. Rotate the system board tray levers up simultaneously until the tray releases from the chassis.

7. Pull the system board tray straight back until it stops.

8. Lift the front of the system board tray upward slightly and then pull the tray straight back until it clears the chassis.

9. If the system has a SCSI backplane daughter card, remove it by pulling the retention lever to slide the daughter card away from the SCSI backplane connector.

10. Lift the card up and away from the tabs on the card guide above the drive bay.

11. Grasp the CD/diskette drive tray release handle and pull the tray out of the system, as shown in this graphic.

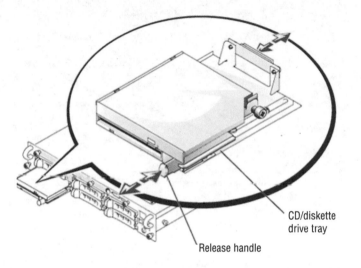

CD/diskette
drive tray

Release handle

12. Open the hard drive carrier handle to release the drive(s). Slide them out so they are not connected to the backplane.

13. Loosen the thumbscrew that secures the SCSI backplane board in the system.

14. Slide the backplane board toward the right-side chassis wall about 0.5 inch.

15. Lift the backplane board off its grounding tabs.

16. Lift the backplane board and disconnect the control-panel cable from the board.

17. Lift the backplane board out of the system board tray, as shown in the following graphic:

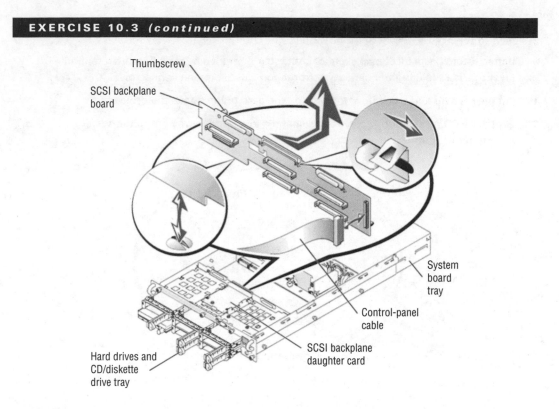

18. Reverse your steps to install the new SCSI backplane and to bring the system back up.

Firmware Incompatibility

At startup, the BIOS will attempt to detect the devices and components at its disposal. The information that it gathers, along with the current state of the components, will be available for review in the BIOS settings. It is required that the BIOS support the devices that it discovers during this process. Otherwise the system will either fail the POST or fail to start, or the component will fail to function after the server starts.

In some cases, you can solve this problem by performing a BIOS upgrade, also called flashing the BIOS. Server BIOSs don't go bad; they just become out-of-date or contain bugs. In the case of a bug, an upgrade will correct the problem. An upgrade may also be indicated when the BIOS doesn't support some component that you would like to install—a larger hard drive or a different type of processor, for instance.

Most of today's BIOSs are written to an Electrically Erasable Programmable Read-Only Memory (EEPROM) chip and can be updated through the use of software. Each manufacturer has its own method for accomplishing this. Check out the documentation for complete details. It means the old instructions are erased from the EEPROM chip and the new instructions are written to the chip.

UEFI (Unified Extensible Firmware Interface) is a standard firmware interface for PCs designed to replace the BIOS. Some advantages of UEFI firmware are as follows:

- Better security—protects the preboot process
- Faster startup times and resuming from hibernation
- Support for drives larger than 2.2 terabytes (TB)
- Support for 64-bit firmware device drivers
- Capability to use BIOS with UEFI hardware

UEFI can also be updated by using an update utility from the motherboard vendor. In many cases the steps are as follows:

1. Download the update file to a flash drive.
2. Insert the flash drive and reboot the machine.
3. Use the specified key sequence to enter the BIOS settings.
4. If necessary, disable Secure Boot.
5. Save the changes and reboot again.
6. Reenter the BIOS settings.
7. Choose Boot Options and boot from the flash drive.
8. Follow the specific directions with the update to locate the upgrade file on the flash drive.
9. Execute the file (usually by typing **flash**).
10. While the update is completing, ensure you maintain power to the device.

CPU or GPU Overheating

Earlier in this section you learned how overheating can damage CPUs. Overheating can damage graphic processing units (GPUs) as well. The same preventive measures apply here: keep slot openings covered, clean the dust out of the system, and make sure fans are functioning properly.

Environmental

Three items closely related to an environmentally friendly computing environment are dust, humidity, and temperature. We will cover the most important elements with all three in this section.

Dust

One of the most harmful atmospheric hazards to a computer is dust. Dust, dirt, hair, and other airborne contaminants can get pulled into computers and build up inside. Because computer fans work by pulling air through the computer (usually sucking it in through the case and then pushing it out the power supply), it's easy for these items to enter and then become stuck. Every item in the computer builds up heat, and these particles are no exception. As they build up, they hinder the fan's ability to perform its function, and the components get hotter than they would otherwise. The dust also serves as insulation to all it covers, causing more heat, and since it can conduct electricity, it can lead to fried parts. Figure 10.10 shows the inside of a system in use for only six months in an area with carpeting and other dusty surroundings.

FIGURE 10.10 Dust builds up inside the system.

You can remove dust and debris from the inside of servers with *compressed air* blown in short bursts. The short bursts are useful in preventing the dust from flying too far out and entering another machine, as well as in preventing the can from releasing the air in liquid form. Compressed air cans should be held 2–3 inches from the system and always used upright so that the content is released as a gas. If the can becomes cold to the touch, discontinue using it until it heats back up to room temperature.

> **WARNING** It's possible to use an air compressor instead of compressed-air cans when you need a lot of air. If you take this approach, make sure you keep the pounds per square inch (PSI) at or below 40, and include measures on the air compressor to remove moisture.

Humidity

Another preventive measure you can take is to maintain the relative humidity at around 50 percent. Be careful not to increase the humidity too much to the point where moisture starts to condense on the equipment! It is a balancing act keeping humidity at the right level since low humidity causes electrostatic discharge (ESD) and high humidity causes moisture condensation. Both extremes are bad but have completely different effects.

Also, use antistatic spray, which is available commercially, to reduce static buildup on clothing and carpets. In a pinch, a solution of diluted fabric softener sprayed on these items will do the same thing.

At the very least, you can be mindful of the dangers of ESD and take steps to reduce its effects. Beyond that, you should educate yourself about those effects so that you know when ESD is becoming a major problem.

Temperature

Heat and computers don't mix well. Many computer systems require both temperature and humidity control for reliable service. The larger servers, communications equipment, and drive arrays generate considerable amounts of heat; this is especially true of mainframe and older minicomputers. An environmental system for this type of equipment is a significant expense beyond the actual computer system costs. Fortunately, newer systems operate in a wider temperature range. Most new systems are designed to operate in an office environment.

If the servers you're responsible for require special environmental considerations, you'll need to establish cooling and humidity control. Ideally, systems are located in the middle of the building, and they're ducted separately from the rest of the heating, ventilation, and air conditioning (HVAC) system. It's a common practice for modern buildings to use a zone-based air conditioning environment, which allows the environmental plant to be turned off when the building isn't occupied. A computer room will typically require full-time environmental control.

Tools and Techniques

There are troubleshooting tools that you should be familiar with that can aid you. This section discusses some of the most important tools.

Event Logs

You learned the value of event logs and event log management in Chapter 2, "Installing and Configuring Servers." Please review that chapter.

Firmware Upgrades or Downgrades

The server hardware on which you will install the operating system already has some basic instructions installed by the manufacturer called firmware, just as a workstation will. This firmware, stored in nonvolatile memory of some sort or on a chip, will be dated as soon as the server leaves the factory where the firmware was installed. If vendors waited until all bugs had been discovered in this firmware, the servers would never ship, so it's understandable that over time, problems are discovered and updates are issued that correct these issues.

It's also true that in some cases these updates don't correct problems—they add functionality or features. As you probably already know, in many cases where you add a new CPU to a system, a firmware update is required for the system to support the new CPU. Another example might be that the firmware update adds support for hardware virtualization.

Regardless of whether you are trying to ensure all issues or bugs have been corrected or you want to ensure all the latest features are available, you should always check for and install any firmware updates that may be available. The place to check for this is the manufacturer's website. Not only will they have the latest update, they also typically have utilities for updating the firmware.

Hardware Diagnostics

Diagnostic utilities are available for troubleshooting hardware issues. Most server vendors also include a hardware diagnostic utility in what Dell calls the pre-operation system. As this utility has a physical (as opposed to logical) view of the attached hardware, it can identify hardware problems that the operating system and other online tools cannot identify. You can use the hardware diagnostics utility to validate the memory, I/O devices, CPU, physical disk drives, and other peripherals.

Compressed Air

You can remove dust and debris from inside servers with compressed air blown in short bursts. Review the "Dust" section earlier in this chapter.

Electrostatic Discharge (ESD) Equipment

Electrostatic discharge (ESD) is one of the most dangerous risks associated with working with computers. Not only does ESD have the potential to damage components of the computer, but it can also injure you. Not understanding the proper way to avoid it could cause you great harm.

Electrostatic discharge is the technical term for what happens whenever two objects of dissimilar charge come in contact—think of rubbing your feet on a carpet and then touching a light switch. The two objects exchange electrons in order to equalize the electrostatic charge between them. If the device receiving the charge happens to be an electronic component, there is a good chance it can be damaged.

The likelihood that a component will be damaged increases with the use of complementary metal-oxide-semiconductor (CMOS) chips because these chips contain a thin metal-oxide layer that is hypersensitive to ESD. The previous generation's transistor–transistor logic (TTL) chips are more robust than the CMOS chips because they don't contain this metal-oxide layer. Most of today's integrated circuits (ICs) are CMOS chips, so ESD is more of a concern lately.

The lowest static voltage transfer that you can feel is around 3,000 volts (it doesn't electrocute you because there is extremely little current). A static transfer that you can *see* is at least 10,000 volts! Just by sitting in a chair, you can generate around 100 volts of static electricity. Walking around wearing synthetic materials can generate around 1,000 volts. You can easily generate around 20,000 volts simply by dragging your smooth-soled shoes across a carpet in the winter. (Actually, it doesn't have to be winter to run this danger; it can occur in any room with very low humidity. It's just that heated rooms in wintertime generally have very low humidity.)

It would make sense that these thousands of volts would damage computer components. However, a component can be damaged with as little as 300 volts. That means if your body has a small charge built up in it, you could damage a component without even realizing it.

Just as you can ground yourself by using a grounding strap, you can ground equipment. This is most often accomplished by using a mat or a connection directly to a ground.

Antistatic Bags

When working with components and when storing them, it is a good idea to store them in antistatic bags. Although you can buy these bags, replacement parts usually come in anti-static bags, and if you keep these bags, you can use them later. These bags also can serve as a safe place to lay a component temporarily when working on a device.

ESD Straps

There are measures you can implement to help contain the effects of ESD. The easiest one to implement is the *antistatic wrist strap*, also referred to as an *ESD strap*.

The ESD that we are speaking about here does not have the capability to kill you since it doesn't have the amperage. What does represent a threat, though, is using a wrist strap of your own design that does not have the resistor protection built into it and then accidentally touching something with high voltage while wearing the wrist strap. Without the resistor in place, the high voltage would be grounded through you!

You attach one end of the ESD strap to an earth ground (typically the ground pin on an extension cord) and wrap the other end around your wrist. This strap grounds your body and keeps it at a zero charge. Figure 10.11 shows the proper way to attach an anti-static strap.

FIGURE 10.11   Proper ESD strap connection

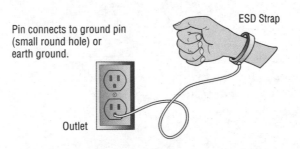

Pin connects to ground pin (small round hole) or earth ground.

ESD Strap

Outlet

If you do not have a grounded outlet available, you can achieve partial benefit simply by attaching the strap to the metal frame of the PC case. Doing so keeps the charge equalized between your body and the case so that there is no electrostatic discharge when you touch components inside the case.

 WARNING   An ESD strap is a specially designed device to bleed electrical charges away safely. It uses a 1 megaohm resistor to bleed the charge away slowly. A simple wire wrapped around your wrist will not work correctly and could electrocute you!

WARNING   Do not wear the antistatic wrist strap when there is the potential to encounter a high-voltage capacitor, such as when working on the inside of a monitor or power supply. The strap could channel that voltage through your body.

ESD Mats

It is possible to damage a device simply by laying it on a benchtop. For this reason, you should have an *ESD mat* (also known as an *antistatic mat*) in addition to an ESD strap. This mat drains excess charge away from any item coming in contact with it (see Figure 10.12). ESD mats are also sold as mouse/keyboard pads to prevent ESD charges from interfering with the operation of the computer.

You can also purchase ESD floor mats for technicians to stand on while performing computer maintenance. These include a grounding cord, usually 6 to 10 feet in length.

FIGURE 10.12   Proper use of an ESD mat

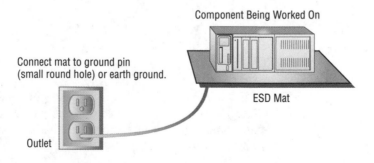

Vendors have methods of protecting components in transit from manufacture to installation. They press the pins of ICs into antistatic foam to keep all the pins at the same potential, and circuit boards are shipped in antistatic bags, discussed earlier. However, keep in mind that unlike antistatic mats, antistatic bags do not drain the charges away—they should never be used in place of antistatic mats.

Self-Grounding

Grounding is the electrical term for providing a path for an electrical charge to follow to return to Earth. This term was mentioned earlier as it relates to ESD straps and mats. Grounding saves you from harm in the event of an electrical discharge as the charge passes to ground. The easiest way to ground yourself is to use a grounding strap.

Reseating or Replacing Components and/or Cables

While it may seem like wasted effort, believe it or not, in many cases simply unplugging a cable or component and plugging it in again can recover functionality. Always try this before assuming the cable or component is bad.

Given a Scenario, Troubleshoot Common OS and Software Problems

Because it's software and there are so many places where things can go wrong, the operating system can be one of the most confusing components to troubleshoot. Sometimes it seems a miracle that they even work at all considering the hundreds of files that work together to make the system function. In this section, common operating system issues and their solutions are covered.

Common Problems

What follows in this section can seem like a daunting list of symptoms the operating system can exhibit. With a proper plan of action and good backup (always have a backup!), you can approach any of these problems with confidence. In many cases today, technicians have ceased to spend significant amounts of time chasing operating system issues since most important data is kept on servers, and computers can be reimaged so quickly that troubleshooting doesn't warrant the effort. Nevertheless, you should know these basic symptoms and the approach to take when they present themselves.

Unable to Log On

When users have difficulty logging on to a server, it can be one of several things:

- User error typing the password
- Incorrect password

- Account disabled
- Account expired
- Inability to contact the domain controller
- DNS server failure
- Incorrect DNS server IP address on the server
- Unauthorized user

If you have verified that the user is using the correct password and typing it correctly, you need to check whether the user's account either has been disabled or has expired. If the server is performing local authentication, you will look in the user account settings on the server. If the server is using domain authentication (more likely) you will check this in Active Directory (AD). It is also possible that in the case where the server is using AD the server may not be able to locate and connect to the AD server. If the DNS settings on the server are incorrect it could cause this, or if there is an issue with AD or if the AD server is down.

Finally, it is possible that the user simply does not have permission to access that server. You can verify this by contacting their department head or superior.

Unable to Access Resources

Your approach to solving resource access issues is not that much different than the approach you take with system logon issues. The possible causes are:

- Unauthorized user
- Error in permission settings
- Inability to connect to the resource server caused by the following issues:
  - Incorrect DNS server address on client
  - DNS server failures
  - Active Directory failure

If the user simply can't connect to the resource server check their DNS server settings. If they are correct, verify that the DNS server is functional. If it isn't, Active Directory won't be functional. If DNS is working, check the domain controller to ensure it is functioning.

If the user can connect but is denied access to the resource, check the permissions applied to the resource. If the user has no permission or the permissions listed do not match what the user tells you, tell the user you must check with their boss and verify permissions. If you need to make changes to the permissions, make sure you tell the user to log out and log back in so those changes will be reflected.

Finally, in Windows, make sure you have checked both the NTFS permissions and the share permissions. The effective permission will be the most restrictive of the combined NTFS permissions (as a user or member of any group) as compared to the combined share permissions (as a user or member of any group).

Users Cannot Print

If you have eliminated a bad cable and users still cannot print, the issue could be located in one of two places:

- The user's computer
- The print device (or print server)

Check to see if others are having an issue, and if so, the problem is probably the print device or print server. Sometimes the printer will not print and all attempts to delete print jobs or clear the print queue fail. It's almost as if the printer is just frozen. When this occurs, the best thing to do is restart the print spooler service on the computer that is acting as the print server. Unfortunately, all users will have to resend their print jobs after this, but at least the printer will be functional again.

Moreover, a printer can have several types of memory errors as well. The most common is insufficient memory to print the page. Sometimes you can circumvent this problem by doing any of the following:

- Turn off the printer to flush out its RAM and then turn it back on and try again.
- Print at a lower resolution. (Adjust this setting in the printer's properties in Windows.)
- Change the page being printed so it's less complex.
- Try a different printer driver if your printer supports more than one Printer Description Language (PDL). (For example, try switching from PostScript to PCL, or vice versa.) Doing so involves installing another printer driver.

Upgrade the memory, if the printer allows.

If only the user is having an issue, check the user's connectivity to the print server. To determine whether it is a connectivity problem to a remote printer, ping the IP address of the printer. If you cannot ping the printer by IP address, that problem must be solved or all other troubleshooting of settings and drivers will be wasted effort.

Finally, printers are considered resources just like files and folders and as such can have permissions attached to them. When a user receives an access denied message, the user lacks the print permission. Typically a printer that has been shared will automatically give all users the print permission, but when permissions have been employed to control which users can print to a particular printer, that default has been altered.

When checking permissions, keep in mind that in Windows, users may have permissions derived from their personal account and from groups of which they are a member. You must ensure that users have not been explicitly denied print permission through their accounts or through any groups of which they are members. A single Deny will prevent them from printing, regardless of what other permissions they may have to the printer.

Also, print availability or print priority can affect access to the printer. Print availability is used to permit certain users to print only during certain times. With print priority, print jobs from certain users or groups are assigned a higher priority than other users or groups. These settings, usually set by an administrator, can prevent or delay successful printing.

Unable to Access Files

Determining why a user may not be able to access files follows the same basic trouble-shooting format as the one covered in the previous section "Unable to Access Resources." Please review that section.

System File Corruption

File can get corrupted, especially when they are being transferred across a network or when the storage where it resides is damaged. In almost all cases a transmitted file that is corrupted will be detected at the destination using a frame check sequence (FCS). However a file gets corrupted, in many cases the file is of no use at that point.

While this is a sad state of affairs for any file, hopefully you have backed up the file if it is important. In the case of corrupted system files, the issue becomes more serious because now something may not work in the operating system. Many times this is caused by malware that alters or changes system files.

Whatever the source of system file corruption, in Windows you can use the System File Checker (SFC) to validate the system files and replace them if required. If you have any doubts about the integrity of important system files, execute the command **sfc / scannow**. The SFC will check the file structure. If the SFC discovers that a protected file has been over-written, it retrieves the correct version of the file from the `systemroot\system32\dllcache` folder, and then replaces the incorrect file.

Another tool you can use in either Linux or Windows is the Tripwire utility. While this requires you to take a hash of all of the system files (and update it each time you update the system), it checks the hash of the files to ensure they have not changed since you took the hash.

End of Life/End of Support

In Chapter 4, "Storage Technologies and Asset Management," you learned about end of life and what that means from a security and support standpoint. Remember that when end of life comes, you will get no more updates for security and you will no longer be able to receive technical support. In some cases issues have their root in the fact that a system has reached end of life and a lack of updates may be causing the issue.

Slow Performance

Slow system performance can result from many issues. For the purposes of this discussion, we are going to focus on performance that deteriorates after being acceptable as opposed to system performance that is poor from the outset (which could be a matter of insufficient resources such as RAM). Here is a list of possibilities:

- Defragment the hard drive. The more fragmented it is, the slower the disk access will be.
- Check the space on the hard drive. When the partition or volume where the operating system is located becomes full, performance will suffer. This is why it is a good idea to store data and applications on a different partition from the one holding the system files.

- Ensure the latest updates are installed. In many cases, updates help to solve performance problems, so make sure they are current.

- Use Task Manager to determine if a process is using too much memory or CPU or is simply locked up (not responding) and, if necessary, end the process.

- Finally, check for the presence of a virus or other malware. If the system seems to have an overabundance of disk activity, scan it for viruses using a virus program that resides externally on a CD/DVD or memory stick.

Cannot Write to System Logs

When the system cannot write to the System log, it is usually because the log is full. In Windows, by default, the System log will overwrite the oldest events with new events, but it is possible to set the log to not do so, which means when it gets full, it stops collecting events. To avoid this issue, you have two choices. First you can set the log to overwrite older events, which means you may lose some older events. Frequent archives of the log can mitigate this loss. The other option is to leave it set as is and increase the size of the log file. Regardless of the solution you choose, you should still archive the log on a regular basis.

Probably the most important log in Linux is the file /var/log/messages, which records a variety of events, including system error messages, system startups, and system shutdowns. To use the logrotate command to manage log files in Linux, visit www.poftut.com/logrotate-command-tutorial-with-examples-for-linux.

Service Failures

Sometimes when the system is started you receive a message that tells you a service failed to start. When that occurs, use the event log to determine the service that failed. Then to interact with the service, access the Administrative Tools section of Control Panel and choose Services. This starts up the Services console. You can right-click any service and choose to start, stop, pause, resume, or restart it. You can also double-click the service to access its properties and configure such things as the startup type, dependencies, and other variables.

If the service refuses to start, it could be that a service on which it depends will not start. To determine what services must be running for the problem service to start, select the Dependencies tab of the service's Properties dialog box, as shown in Figure 10.13.

In the figure you can see that the Remote Desktop Services depend on both the RPC and the Terminal Device Driver to function. Try starting these components first. In some cases, you may need to trace the dependencies up several levels to get things going.

Print Spooler

In some cases, the printer will not print and jobs just seem to be stuck in the queue. The print spooler service controls the print queue. This service can be stopped and started to solve many software-related problems. Locate this service in the Services console and right-click it; you can first start and then stop the service. This can also be done at the command line using the net stop spooler and net start spooler commands.

FIGURE 10.13 Service dependencies

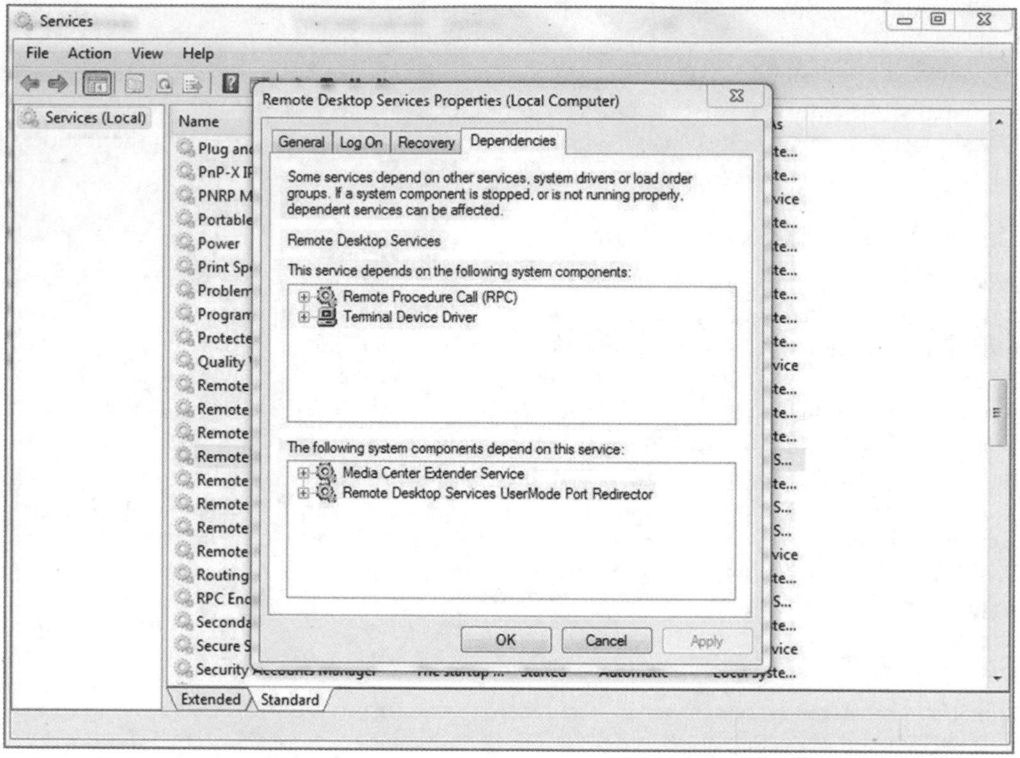

System or Application Hanging

We've already covered many issues that can cause applications and the system in general to hang. Let's take a look at a scenario that we haven't discussed.

In some cases, the system hangs during the shutdown of the system. If the system will not shut down without using the power button, use the button to shut it down and reboot in safe mode. Then attempt to shut down. If this works you should explore driver issues. You can try this:

- Check for a BIOS update.

- Toggle (reverse) the setting of the following Registry entry (make a backup first!):

  `HKEY_LOCAL_MACHINE\SOFTWARE\Microsoft\Windows NT\CurrentVersion\Winlogon`

  - The key you want to change is `PowerdownAfterShutdown`.

    - If it's set to 1, change it to 0.

    - If it's set to 0, change it to 1.

You will need to restart after this change, but the next time you shut down it should stay offline. If not, reverse the change, restart, and it should work from there.

Freezing

Troubleshooting a frozen system follows the same troubleshooting process as application and system hangs since hangs and freezes are basically the same thing and possible solutions come from a common list.

Patch Update Failure

When security and system patches are applied, in some cases they fail. While there have been cases of patches being issued that were problematic in and of themselves, in most cases that is not the issue. If the updates are being installed automatically from either the patch source or from a centralized patch server like Window Server Update Services, the issue could be an interruption of the transfer of the patch to the device. In this case you can either wait until the next scheduled update or you can try performing the update manually and it will succeed if a network issue was the problem. It could also be that there is insufficient drive space to hold the update. It could also be that the patch arrived at the device corrupted. Finally ensure that the firewall is allowing updates.

Causes of Common Problems

While troubleshooting software issues may seem like looking for a needle in a haystack sometimes, there are a number of common causes that you may find yourself coming back to over and over. This is why some experienced technicians say that they sometimes just have a hunch what the issue is. What they really mean is that they have seen so many common issues that they begin to make quicker connections between issues and cause. Although we have covered some of these causes in prior sections, here are some the most common sources of problems.

Incompatible Drivers/Modules

Usually when devices fail to start or are not detected by the system and you have eliminated a hardware issue, the problem involves drivers. Drivers are associated with devices, and you can access them by looking at the properties for the device. The following, for example, are the three most common tabs (in Windows Server 2012 R2 there are five tabs) of an adapter's Properties dialog box in Device Manager (tabs that appear are always dependent on the type of device and its capabilities):

General   This tab displays the device type, manufacturer, and location. It also includes information regarding whether the device is currently working properly.

Driver   This tab displays information on the current driver and digital signer. Five command buttons allow you to see driver details and uninstall or update the driver. It also offers the option to roll back the driver to the previous driver when a new driver causes an issue.

Resources   This tab shows the system resources in use (I/O, IRQ, and so on) and whether there are conflicts.

The most common driver-related device issue is device failure when a new driver is installed. If this occurs, you can use the Roll Back Driver option in Device Manager or boot into the Last Known Good Configuration.

Improperly Applied Patches

Patching issues that are caused by an improper application typically are caused by improperly configured policies that either result in no patch at all or in patches being applied in the wrong order. Examples of policies that when misconfigured can cause issues are:

- Setting restart deadlines (number of days before a device is forced to restart to ensure compliance)

- Automatic Updates (is this enabled?)

- Windows Update service location (is this correct? can the server be found?)

Unstable Drivers or Software

Not all drivers and software are created equally. Some drivers are unstable and even contain malware. While many of the drivers will be already in the operating system, some may not be and you may have to provide them to the server. The best place to obtain these drivers is the vendor website or Windows Update.

For example, in many cases today enterprise printers have a built-in print server, but you still may have a server that is acting as the print server for less capable print devices. When that scenario is in effect, you must make sure that the server has all the drivers required to communicate with the various printers it manages and for all the operating systems that use it as the print server.

Server Not Joined to Domain

In Chapter 2 you learned how to join a server to a domain. If a server is *not* joined to the domain, the domain password that has been issued to users will not work on the server. Moreover, you won't be able to control the server by using domain policies. Please review the section on joining the domain in Chapter 2.

Clock Skew

In an Active Directory environment and in environments where certificates are in use, it's critical that all systems have the same time. It is very important for all clocks to be within 5 minutes of each other (by default) due to the implementation of the Kerberos protocol for authentication. If systems don't have the same time, systems may refuse to accept certificates because they are judged to have expired when they aren't. Later in this chapter you'll learn about a service that can solve this issue: NTP.

Memory Leaks

Memory leaks occur when an application is issued some memory to use and does not return the memory and any temporary file to the operating system after the program no longer needs it. Over time the available memory for that application or that part of the operating system becomes exhausted and the program can no longer function. This is caused by poor coding practices. While the application that is causing this should be investigated and perhaps updated, a quick solution is to reboot the server. Make sure when you do this it is a cold boot. Many of the latest operating systems don't actually reboot when you restart—they just sleep.

Buffer Overrun

Buffers are portions of system memory that are used to store information. A buffer overflow is an attack that occurs when the amount of data that is submitted to memory is larger than the buffer can handle. Typically, this type of attack is possible because of a poorly written application or operating system code. This can result in an injection of malicious code, primarily either a denial-of-service (DoS) attack or a SQL injection.

To protect against this issue, organizations should ensure that all operating systems and applications are updated with the latest service packs and patches. In addition, programmers should properly test all applications to check for overflow conditions.

Hackers can take advantage of this phenomenon by submitting too much data, which can cause an error or, in some cases, execute commands on the machine if the hacker can locate an area where commands can be executed. Not all attacks are designed to execute commands. An attack may just lock the computer such as a DoS attack.

With proper input validation, a buffer overflow attack causes an access violation. Without proper input validation, the allocated space is exceeded, and the data at the bottom of the memory stack is overwritten. The key to preventing many buffer overflow attacks is input validation, in which any input is checked for format and length before it is used. Buffer overflows and boundary errors (when input exceeds the boundaries allotted for the input) are a family of error conditions called input validation errors.

Incompatibility

Earlier in this chapter you learned that incompatible hardware components can cause issues. Problems of incompatibility can extend to other process as well. In this section you'll learn about other incompatibilities that can cause problems.

Insecure Dependencies

The U.S. Department of Homeland Security estimated in 2015 that 90 percent of software components are downloaded from code repositories. These repositories hold code that can be reused. Using these repositories speeds software development because it eliminates the time it would take to create these components from scratch. Organizations might have their own repository for in-house code that has been developed.

In other cases, developers may make use of a third-party repository in which the components are repositories. Many have been documented and disclosed as Common Vulnerabilities and Exposures (CVEs). In many cases these vulnerabilities have been addressed and updates have been uploaded to the repository. The problem is that far too many vulnerabilities have not been addressed, and even in cases where they have, developers continue to use the vulnerable components instead of downloading the new versions.

Developers who rely on third-party repositories must also keep track of the components' updates and security profiles.

Version Management

Everything from operating systems to hardware components comes in versions. Although it is always best to have everyone using the same version of an item, making that happen in a large organization can be a challenge. A formal version management process linked closely with the change management system can help solve this issue.

Architecture

The architecture of a system comprises a set of rules and methods that describe the functionality, organization, and implementation of the system. Not all architectures are compatible with one another. A simple example is CPU architectures. The basic architecture has the CPU at the core with a main memory and input/output system on either side of the CPU (see Figure 10.14).

FIGURE 10.14   Architecture A

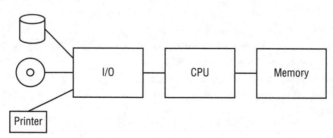

An alternative architecture is shown in Figure 10.15, with the central input/output controller at the core.

FIGURE 10.15   Architecture B

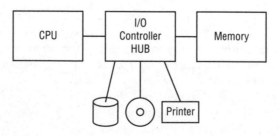

The point is that for systems to be compatible they may need to use the same architecture.

Update Failures

When security and system patches are applied, in some cases they fail. While there have been cases of patches being issued that were problematic in and of themselves, in most cases that is not the issue. If the updates are being installed automatically from either the patch source or from a centralized patch server like Window Server Update Services, the issue could be an interruption of the transfer of the patch to the device. In this case you can wait until the next scheduled update or you can try performing the update manually and it will succeed if a network issue was the problem. The issue could also be that there is insufficient drive space to hold the update or that the patch arrived at the device corrupted. Finally, ensure that the firewall is allowing updates.

Missing Updates

Sometimes a patch was successfully deployed to all systems but you still find some random systems out there without the patch. How did that happen? Keep in mind that a deployment system like SCCM will report a success rate for deployment but it's based on the live systems it sees out there. Systems that are shut down and those that are out of the office may need manual remediation at a later time.

Missing Dependencies

If you remember from our earlier discussion of dependencies, these are items that an application needs that are obtained from a source outside the application, like a code repository. If for some reason the code fragment the application needs from the code repository is no longer there, you will have an issue. This is another reason to use your own code repository rather than a third-party repository, so you will have more control over it and prevent deletions that can cause issues.

Downstream Failures Due to Updates

Applications today are typically written in blocks called components. A downstream component is one that takes values added by the components that are upstream and adds values of its own, as shown in Figure 10.16.

FIGURE 10.16   Downstream components

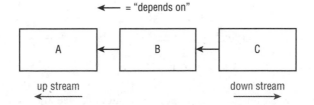

A downstream failure is when a downstream component can't communicate with another component. In open source development, developers sometimes submit patches (that fix a bug or add a feature) and then submit a patch to the original project. When this occurs it can sometimes cause an application based off the open source code to fail.

Inappropriate Application-Level Permissions

In Windows, applications sometimes need to access hardware or software components such as the camera or the location function (GPS). The *app permissions* for an application may be left in an inappropriate setting, creating a security issue. You can control the permissions of every application on the system by selecting Start ➢ Settings ➢ Privacy. Select the app (for example, Calendar) and choose which app permissions are on or off. Check the settings for each application with regard to access to hardware and software components to ensure they are configured correctly.

Improper CPU Affinity and Priority

When you set the processor affinity for an application, you are specifying that the application only use a specific CPU. Processor priority sets the relative workload between multiple processors that may be present.

When affinity or priority settings are incorrect, they can cause performance issues for certain applications. You can set both affinity and priority at the command line. For example, the following command starts Notepad using CPU 10 and CPU 11 at High CPU Priority:

```
cmd.exe /c start "Notepad" /High /affinity C00 "Z:Notepad.exe"
```

The value C00 represents the hex value of 11000000000. In the CPU binary number, 0 means "off" and 1 means "on." For each CPU core that you want to use for the process, change 0 to 1. So this number uses CPUs 10 and 11. To use 10–12, this binary number would be 1110000000 and the hex value would be E0.

OS and Software Tools and Techniques

A number of tools are available for troubleshooting operating system problems, some of which have been mentioned in passing in the earlier sections on common symptoms.

Patching

In Chapter 6, "Securing the Server," you learned about the value of patching and how it should be done. Please review that chapter.

Upgrades

In Chapter 3, "Server Maintenance," you learned about software and hardware upgrades and the value of staggering the upgrade of systems to reduce spending and to facilitate better management of the process. Please review that chapter.

Downgrades

In some cases a patch may break something that worked prior to the patch. It happens all the time. Vendors do their best to test the patch for as many scenarios as possible but perhaps not your scenario. When this occurs you may want to roll back the update. You can roll back Windows 10 Updates from Recovery Settings using the following procedure:

1.   Press Windows key+I to open Settings and then click the Update & Security option.

2.   On the Update & Security screen, switch to the Windows Update tab, and then click the Update History link.

3.   On the View Your Update History screen, click the Uninstall Updates link.

4.   Select the update you would like to remove and click Uninstall.

Package Management

A package-management system is a collection of software tools that automates the process of installing, upgrading, configuring, and removing computer programs in a consistent manner. These tools can make managing updates much easier. Third-party tools are available, but one of the most well-known systems comes free with Windows as a server role.

Windows Server Update Services (WSUS) is a server role that can be added to any server. It requires a policy (Group Policy) that directs all systems to use the local WSUS server as its source for updates. Then you control what updates they receive from the server. An added benefit is that the updates are downloaded from Microsoft only once and then sent to the system locally, saving congestion at the Internet connection.

Recovery

When the system suffers a critical failure—maybe even generates a blue screen—you need to recover the system with as little damaged data as possible. In this section you'll learn about techniques and tools used to make a successful recovery possible.

Boot Options

First let's look at the options available when you boot the system following a failure or crash. Understanding the function of these options will allow you to anticipate what might result.

SAFE MODE

Safe mode starts Windows in a basic state, using a limited set of files and drivers. If a problem doesn't happen in safe mode, this means that default settings and basic device drivers aren't causing the issue. If booting to safe mode solves the issue, the issue lies in your application. It may be outdated or corrupted, so try reinstalling the latest version.

SINGLE USER MODE

Single-user mode is a mode in which a multiuser computer operating system boots into a single superuser security context. There are several reasons you might boot into single-user mode:

- You require exclusive access to shared resources,
- For security purposes; network services are not run, eliminating the possibility of outside interference.
- A lost superuser password can be changed by switching to single-user mode.

Reload OS

Sometimes simply rebooting the system solves issues. This releases resources that might be tied up by frozen functions. It clears out the memory as well. As a matter of fact, there was a time when it was considered regular maintenance to reboot servers to keep them performing well. Rebooting is always worth a shot.

Snapshots

In Chapter 9, "Disaster Recovery," you learned about snapshots. These are lists of pointers or references to the data and are somewhat like a detailed table of contents about the data at a specific point in time. They can speed the data recovery process when needed.

Snapshots can also be made of the entire system, including the data, the OS, and the configuration. Snapshots are used extensively in virtualization. These copies of the system at various points in time can be used to recover a system that is irretrievably damaged.

Proper Privilege Escalations

Privilege escalation is the process of raising your given privileges by changing to another higher privileged account. When this is done improperly, it is an attack on the system and is a standard step in compromising a system. In this section you'll learn about proper privilege escalation.

runas

In Chapter 7, "Securing Server Data and Network Access," you learned that security best practices recommend that technicians use standard user accounts unless they need to do something that requires administrator access. The runas command and the Run As menu option will allow you to raise your privileges to the specified account; then when done with the task requiring the privileges, the security context will return to the original context. You will learn more about runas in Chapter 11, "Troubleshooting Network Connectivity and Security Issues."

sudo

In Linux the same can be done using the sudo command. The sudo command can be added at the front of a command to execute the command using root privileges. For example, to remove a package with root privileges, the command is as follows:

```
sudo apt-get remove {package-name}
```

su

The su command is used to change from one user account to another. When the command is executed, you will be prompted for the password of the account to which you are switching, as shown here:

```
$ su mact
password:
mact@sandy:~$
```

Scheduled Reboots

When shutting down the server for maintenance, make sure you follow proper shutdown procedures. There are two types of reboots:

Soft Reboot   Better for the system than a hard reboot, a soft reboot allows the proper shutdown of all running applications and services yet requires that you be logged in as either administrator or root and that the server be in a responsive state. It is also good to know that since power is not completely removed, memory registers are not cleared.

Hard Reboot   A hard reboot is not good for the system and is equivalent to turning off the power and turning it back on. However, in cases where the server is unresponsive, a hard reboot may be the only option.

Always use a soft reboot whenever possible. A hard reboot does not give the server an opportunity to properly shut down all running applications and services.

Software Firewalls

Host-based firewalls are software installed on a single device that protects only that device from attacks. Many operating systems today come with personal firewalls or host-based firewalls. Many commercial host-based firewalls are designed to focus attention on a particular type of traffic or to protect a certain application.

On Linux-based systems, a common host-based firewall is iptables, replacing a previous package called ipchains. It has the ability to accept or drop packets. Firewall rules are created, much like creating an access list on a router. An example of a rule set follows:

```
iptables -A INPUT -i eth1 -s 192.168.0.0/24 -j DROP
iptables -A INPUT -i eth1 -s 10.0.0.0/8 -j DROP
iptables -A INPUT -i eth1 -s 172. -j DROP
```

This rule set blocks all incoming traffic sourced from either the 192.168.0.0/24 network or the 10.0.0.0/8 network. Both of these are private IP address ranges. It is quite common to block incoming traffic from the Internet that has a private IP address as its source because this usually indicates IP spoofing is occurring.

Adding or Removing Ports

It is possible to block port numbers in addition to IP addresses. In the Windows Defender Firewall with Advanced Security, the software firewall that comes with Windows 11, you can block a port using the following procedure:

1. Open Windows Defender Firewall with Advanced Security, revealing the options shown in Figure 10.17.

FIGURE 10.17   Windows Defender Firewall with Advanced Security

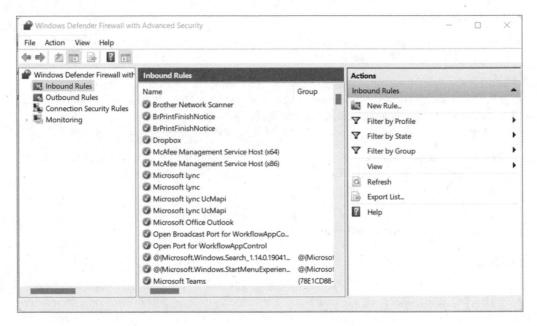

2. Select New Rule in the upper-right side of the screen. On the Rule Type page, select the Port radio button, as shown in Figure 10.18 and click Next.

3. On the Ports And Protocols page, enter the port number, as shown in Figure 10.19. In this case we selected port 80. Click Next.

4. On the Action page, select Block The Connection and click Next, as shown in Figure 10.20.

FIGURE 10.18 Rule Type page

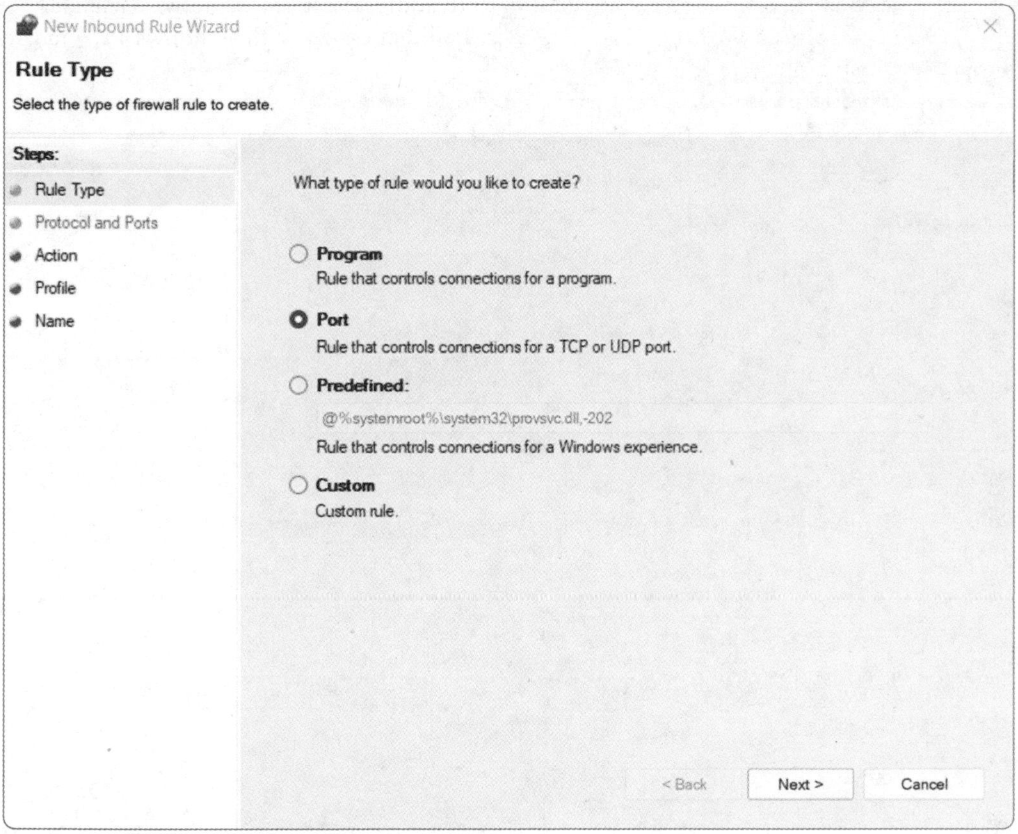

On the Profile page, select the scope of the rules enforcement. In our case we select to enforce it only in the Public network, as shown in Figure 10.21. Click Next.

5. On the Profile page, select the scope of the rules enforcement. In our case we select to enforce it only in the Public network, as shown in Figure 10.21. Click Next.

6. On the Name page, give the rule a name (we're calling it HTTP Rule, as shown in Figure 10.22).

7. Click Finish.

FIGURE 10.19 Ports And Protocols page

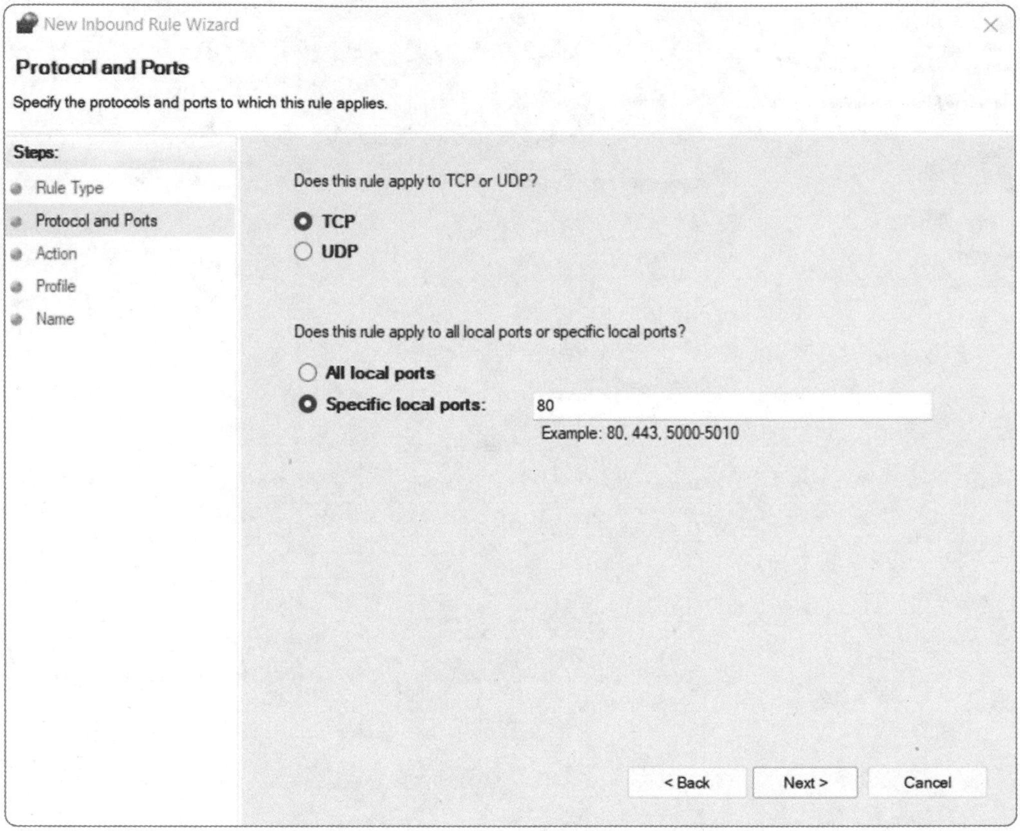

Zones

Some firewalls offer the ability to filter based on zones. A zone is a group of different interfaces that share the same security attributes or the same level of trust. You define which interfaces are in the same zone and then you create rules controlling traffic between the zones. An example grouping into two zones is shown in Figure 10.23.

There is one default zone in every router, known as self, which encompasses the router's own IP addresses. In the absence of creating any rules, default rules apply. The default rules are (this example is for Cisco routers only):

- Inter-zone communication is denied, traffic will be denied between different zones unless we specify a firewall policy.

- Intra-zone is permitted. This is traffic among interfaces in the same zone.

- All Self-Zone traffic is permitted. The self zone is traffic destined to the router (route updates, etc.) and the zone-based firewall will block traffic going through the router unless it is permitted.

FIGURE 10.20   Action page

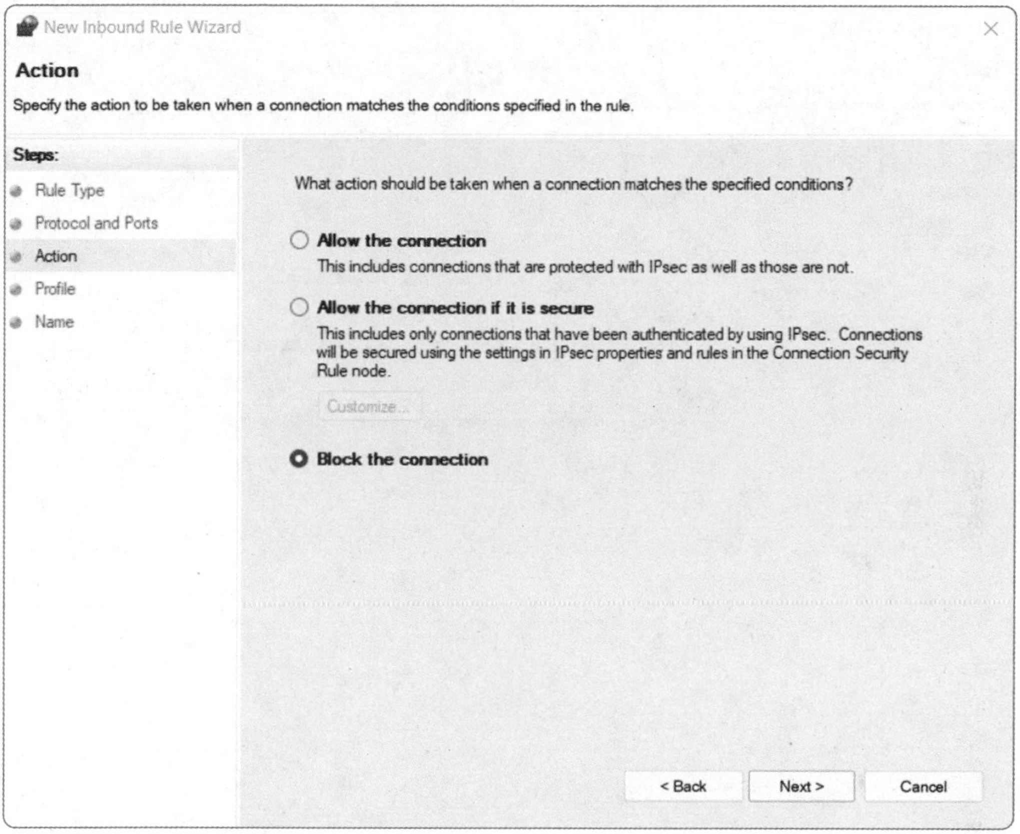

| New Inbound Rule Wizard | ✕ |

Action

Specify the action to be taken when a connection matches the conditions specified in the rule.

Steps:

- Rule Type
- Protocol and Ports
- Action
- Profile
- Name

What action should be taken when a connection matches the specified conditions?

○ **Allow the connection**

This includes connections that are protected with IPsec as well as those are not.

○ **Allow the connection if it is secure**

This includes only connections that have been authenticated by using IPsec. Connections will be secured using the settings in IPsec properties and rules in the Connection Security Rule node.

[Customize...]

◉ **Block the connection**

[< Back]   [Next >]   [Cancel]

Clocks

Some critical functions depend on all systems having the same time. When certificates are in use, time synchronization is critical. Active Directory depends on proper time synchronization. In this section you'll learn about a time synchronization protocol and a bit about the clocks in the system.

Network Time Protocol (NTP)

Network Time Protocol (NTP) servers are used as a time source by the devices in the network. When the devices are configured with the address of an NTP server, they will periodically check in with the server to ensure their time is correct. This service ensures that log entries that are timestamped can be properly interpreted and that digital certificates, which depend heavily on time, continue to function correctly. NTP servers do not typically have high resource requirements, and this service is a good candidate for adding to a server already performing another role.

FIGURE 10.21   Profile page

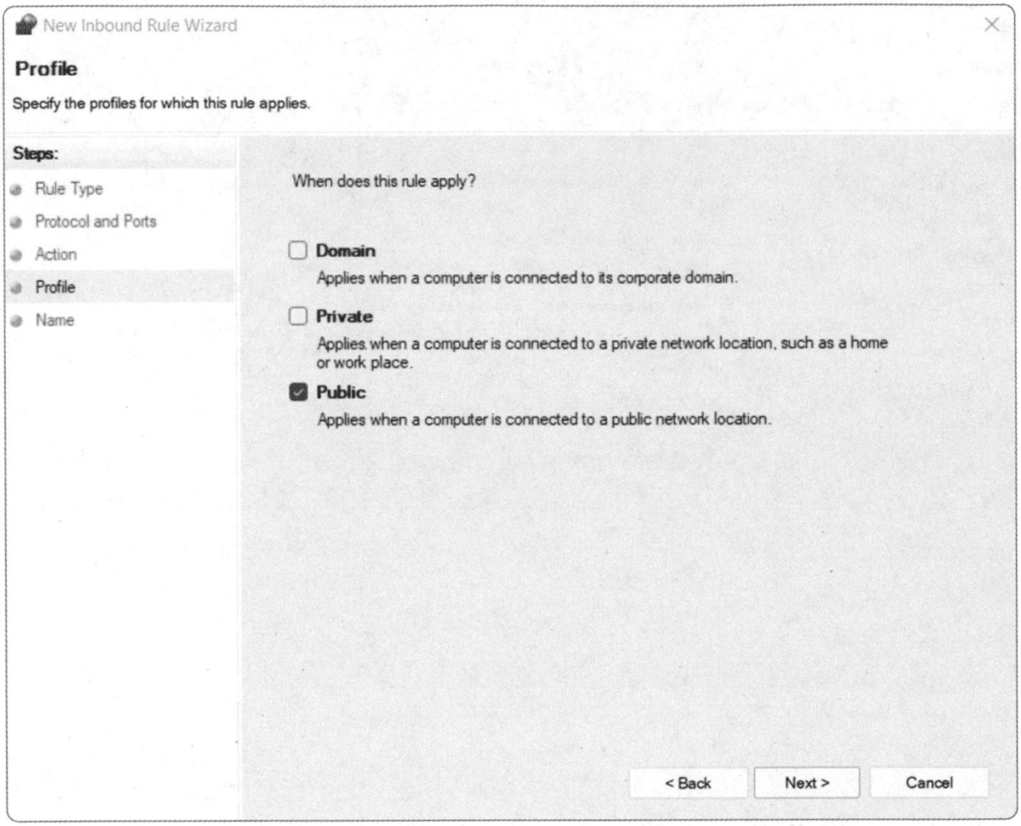

New Inbound Rule Wizard	×

Profile

Specify the profiles for which this rule applies.

Steps:

- Rule Type
- Protocol and Ports
- Action
- Profile
- Name

When does this rule apply?

☐ **Domain**
   Applies when a computer is connected to its corporate domain.

☐ **Private**
   Applies when a computer is connected to a private network location, such as a home or work place.

☑ **Public**
   Applies when a computer is connected to a public network location.

< Back   Next >   Cancel

System Time

System time is the current time and date that the computer system keeps track of so that applications running on the system have ready access to accurate time. This is the time that we want to be synchronized across all systems from a common time source, such an NTP server.

Services and Processes

There are occasions when services and the processes they use to do their job experience issues that slow performance and may even lock up the system. Tools are available that address these issues. In this section you'll learn about using the Services applet in Windows.

FIGURE 10.22   Name page

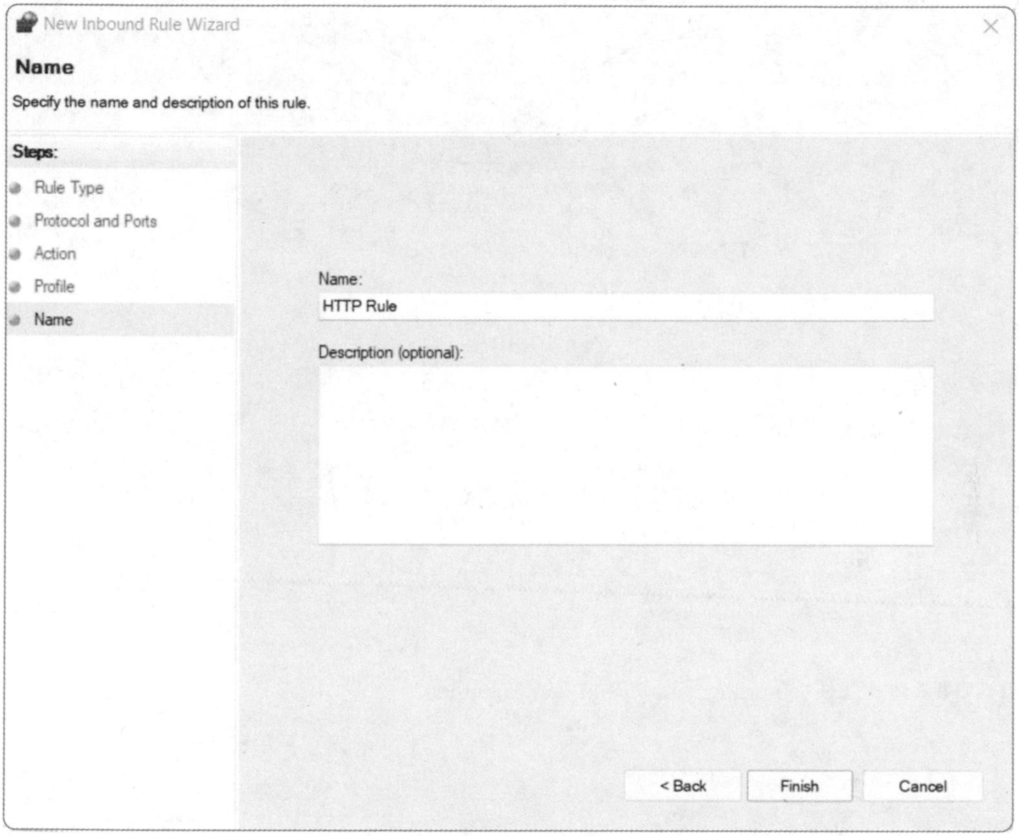

Starting

Services can be started in two places: in Task Manager and at the command line. At the command line use the `net start` command, as shown in Figure 10.24, which starts the print spooler service.

To start the spooler service in Task Manager, open Task Manager, locate the spooler service as shown in Figure 10.25, right-click it, and select Start.

FIGURE 10.23 Zones

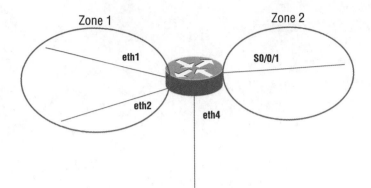

FIGURE 10.24 `net start`

```
C:\WINDOWS\system32>net start spooler
The Print Spooler service is starting.
The Print Spooler service was started successfully.


C:\WINDOWS\system32>
```

FIGURE 10.25 Starting a service in Task Manager

Name	PID	Description	Status	Group
SNMPTrap		SNMP Trap	Stopped	
spectrum		Windows Perception Service	Stopped	
Spooler	27340	Print Spooler	Running	
sppsvc		Software Protection	Stopped	
SSDPSRV	10164	SSDP Discovery	Running	LocalServiceAn...
ssh-agent		OpenSSH Authentication Agent	Stopped	
SstpSvc	4852	Secure Socket Tunneling Protocol Ser...	Running	LocalService
StateRepository	3400	State Repository Service	Running	appmodel
StiSvc	2456	Windows Image Acquisition (WIA)	Running	imgsvc
StorSvc	3756	Storage Service	Running	LocalSystemNe...
SupportAssistAgent	18300	Dell SupportAssist	Running	
svsvc		Spot Verifier	Stopped	LocalSystemNe...
swprv		Microsoft Software Shadow Copy Pro...	Stopped	swprv
SysMain	2968	SysMain	Running	LocalSystemNe...
SystemEventsBroker	1084	System Events Broker	Running	DcomLaunch
TabletInputService	9632	Touch Keyboard and Handwriting Pan...	Running	LocalSystemNe...
TapiSrv	5344	Telephony	Running	NetworkService
TermService		Remote Desktop Services	Stopped	NetworkService
Themes	2980	Themes	Running	netsvcs
TieringEngineService		Storage Tiers Management	Stopped	
TimeBrokerSvc	1868	Time Broker	Running	LocalServiceNe...
TokenBroker	9432	Web Account Manager	Running	netsvcs
TrkWks	4940	Distributed Link Tracking Client	Running	LocalSystemNe...

Stopping

Services can also be stopped in the same two places, in Task Manager and at the command line. At the command line use the `net stop` command, as in Figure 10.26, which stops the print spooler service.

FIGURE 10.26   net stop

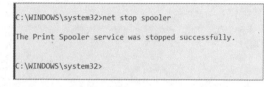

```
C:\WINDOWS\system32>net stop spooler

The Print Spooler service was stopped successfully.


C:\WINDOWS\system32>
```

To stop the spooler service in Task Manager, open Task Manager, locate the spooler service, right-click it, and select Stop.

Status Identification

If you have any doubt as to whether a service is running or not, you can check in two places. In Task Manager it will be stated in the Status column.

At the command line, typing **sc query spooler** will display the status of the spooler service, as shown in Figure 10.27.

FIGURE 10.27   Status at the command line

```
C:\WINDOWS\system32>sc query spooler

SERVICE_NAME: spooler
        TYPE               : 110  WIN32_OWN_PROCESS  (interactive)
        STATE              : 1   STOPPED
        WIN32_EXIT_CODE    : 0   (0x0)
        SERVICE_EXIT_CODE  : 0   (0x0)
        CHECKPOINT         : 0x0
        WAIT_HINT          : 0x0

C:\WINDOWS\system32>
```

Dependencies

Some services depend on other services to function, which means that a service will not start if a service it depends on is not started. To determine what services a service depends on, you can use the Services applet. To determine the dependencies of the BranchCache service, for example, locate BranchCache in Services, right-click it, and select Properties. You will see the properties box shown in Figure 10.28. Select the Dependencies tab and you will see that HHTP must be running for BranchCache to start.

FIGURE 10.28   Properties of BranchCache

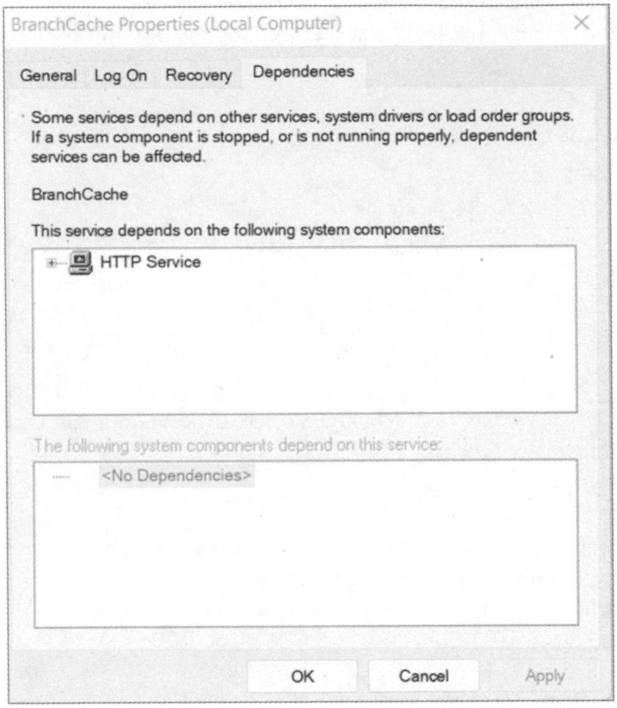

Configuration Management

Managing the configuration of many servers can be daunting. There are tools that can make keeping everything consistent easier. In this section you'll learn about configuration management tools and about tools that automate processes and configurations.

System Center Configuration Manager (SCCM)

SCCM features remote control, patch management, operating system deployment, network protection, and various other services, all in one console. It can even integrate with the Microsoft mobile management tool, Intune, to control mobile devices as well. SCCM is available from Microsoft and can be used on a limited time trial basis. When the trial period expires, you must purchase a license to continue using it.

Puppet/Chef/Ansible

Automating workflows and processes saves time and human resources. One of the best examples is the automation revolution occurring in network management. Automation tools such as Puppet, Chef and Ansible, use scripting to automate once manual tasks such as log analyses, patch application, and intrusion prevention.

These tools and scripts perform the job they do best, which is manual drudgery, thus freeing up humans to do what they do best, which is deep analysis and planning. Alas, with automation comes vulnerabilities. An example is the cross-site scripting (XSS) vulnerability found in IBM workflow systems, as detailed in CVE-2019-4149, which can allow users to embed arbitrary JavaScript code in the web UI, thus altering the intended functionality and potentially leading to credentials disclosure within a trusted session.

Group Policy Object (GPO)

In Chapter 8, "Networking and Scripting," you learned how Group Policies can be used to control devices. When you do, the policy exists as a Group Policy Object (GPO) that can then be applied to a domain, OU, or child OU. By applying the GPO to the proper container (security groups are not containers!) the scope of its enforcement can be set. Policy settings are inherited by child objects by default, although you can alter that behavior if desired.

Hardware Compatibility List (HCL)

Before installing or upgrading an OS, ensure that the system supports all the hardware prerequisites. The Windows Hardware Compatibility List (HCL) is a list of hardware devices compatible with a particular version of Windows. If you don't check ahead of time, the installation or upgrade may fail when you attempt it.

Summary

In this chapter you learned about software troubleshooting, beginning with the CompTIA methodology for troubleshooting. You learned that following the eight steps in the CompTIA troubleshooting method can help you organize your efforts and solve issues in the least amount of time. We also covered hardware troubleshooting, which included discussing the common issues you will see and the likely causes of these issues. Finally, this chapter closed with a discussion of common software issues, their sources, and the tools you use to deal with them.

Exam Essentials

List the eight steps in the CompTIA troubleshooting method.   In order, the steps are identify the problem and determine the scope; establish a theory of probable cause; test the theory to determine cause; establish a plan of action to resolve the problem and notify impacted users; implement the solution or escalate as appropriate; verify full system functionality and, if applicable, implement preventive measures; perform a root cause analysis; and document findings, actions, and outcomes throughout the process.

Identify common hardware issues, their causes, and solutions. Describe common hardware issues, among them failed POST, overheating, memory failure, onboard component failure, processor failure, incorrect boot sequence, expansion card failure, operating system not found, drive failure, power supply failure, and I/O failure.

Identify common software issues, their causes, and their solutions. Describe common software issues, among them: user unable to logon, user cannot access resources, memory leak, BSOD/stop, OS boot failure, driver issues, runaway process, cannot mount drive, cannot write to system log, slow OS performance, patch update failure, service failure, hangs on shutdown, and user cannot print.

Review Questions

You can find the answers in the Appendix.

1. Which of the following steps in the CompTIA troubleshooting method come last?
    A. Verify full system functionality and, if applicable, implement preventive measures.
    B. Document findings, actions, and outcomes throughout the process.
    C. Identify the problem and determine the scope.
    D. Perform a root cause analysis.

2. Which of the following actions should be taken before making changes during troubleshooting?
    A. Reboot the computer in safe mode.
    B. Perform a backup.
    C. Notify the user.
    D. Disable the antimalware.

3. Which of the following statements is true with regard to troubleshooting?
    A. Make one change at a time.
    B. If multiple users are involved, the source is likely their local computers.
    C. You should always try to replicate the issue in the production environment.
    D. Always assume the cabling is good.

4. Which of the following events causes chip creep?
    A. High humidity
    B. Overheating
    C. Dropping the device
    D. Power surges

5. Replacing slot covers helps to prevent which event?
    A. Corrosion
    B. Overheating
    C. Theft
    D. EMI

6. In Linux you can use which of the following commands to stop a process?
    A. `quit`
    B. `kill`
    C. `stop`
    D. `net stop`

7. What operating system generates BSOD error messages?

   A. Mac

   B. Linux

   C. Windows

   D. Android

8. Which of the following is a group of different interfaces that share the same security attributes or the same level of trust?

   A. Zone

   B. Scope

   C. Subnet

   D. Collision domain

9. Which of the following starts by using a preselected minimal set of drivers and startup programs?

   A. Clean boot

   B. Safe mode

   C. Diagnostic boot

   D. Core mode

10. Which of the following servers are used as a time source by the devices in the network.?

    A. WINS

    B. NTP

    C. DNS

    D. Global Catalog

11. Which of the following is *not* a possible reason users are having difficulty logging on to a server?

    A. Incorrect password

    B. Account disabled

    C. SQL server failure

    D. User error typing the password

12. Which of the following is true of server backplanes?

    A. They can be a single point of failure.

    B. They provide data and control signal connectors for the CPU.

    C. Backplane failures are common.

    D. You should implement redundant backplanes.

13. How should you use compressed air inside the case?

    A. Use long sustained bursts.

    B. Use short bursts.

    C. Hold the can 12 inches away from the system.

    D. Hold the can upside down.

14. What should the humidity be in the server room?

    A. 30 percent

    B. 40 percent

    C. 50 percent

    D. 60 percent

15. What can be the result of low humidity?

    A. Corrosion

    B. ESD

    C. RFI

    D. EMI

16. Which tab in Device Manager is used to identify IRQ conflicts?

    A. General

    B. Resources

    C. Driver

    D. Security

17. Which of the following may indicate a failing fan?

    A. Burning smell

    B. Whining sound

    C. Clicking noise

    D. Grinding noise

18. Which of the following could *not* be a reason why a user cannot log on?

    A. User error typing the password

    B. Unauthorized user

    C. Incorrect password

    D. Spyware

19. Which of the following occurs when an application is issued some memory to use and does not return the memory?

   A. Kernel panic

   B. BSOD

   C. Memory leak

   D. Mantrap

20. Which of the following is an attack where the attacker submits too much data?

   A. SQL injection

   B. Buffer overflow

   C. Teardrop attack

   D. VLAN hopping

Chapter

11

Troubleshooting Network Connectivity and Security Issues

COMPTIA SERVER+ EXAM OBJECTIVES COVERED IN THIS CHAPTER:

✓ **4.5 Given a scenario, troubleshoot network connectivity issues.**

- Common problems

    - Lack of Internet connectivity

    - Resource unavailable

    - Receiving incorrect DHCP information

    - Non-functional or unreachable

    - Destination host unreachable

    - Unknown host

    - Unable to reach remote subnets

    - Failure of service provider

    - Cannot reach server by hostname/fully qualified domain name (FQDN)

- Causes of common problems

    - Improper IP configuration

    - IPv4 vs. IPv6 misconfigurations

    - Improper VLAN configuration

    - Network port security

    - Component failure

    - Incorrect OS route tables

    - Bad cables

    - Firewall (misconfiguration, hardware failure, software failure)

- Misconfigured NIC
- DNS and/or DHCP failure
- DHCP server misconfigured
- Misconfigured hosts file
- Tools and techniques
  - Check link lights
  - Confirm power supply
  - Verify cable integrity
  - Check appropriate cable selection
  - Commands
    - ipconfig
    - ip addr
    - ping
    - tracert
    - traceroute
    - nslookup
    - netstat
    - dig
    - telnet
    - nc
    - nbtstat
    - route

✓ **4.6 Given a scenario, troubleshoot security problems.**

- Common problems
  - File integrity
  - Improper privilege escalation
    - Excessive access
  - Applications will not load
  - Cannot access network fileshares
  - Unable to open files

- Causes of common problems
  - Open ports
  - Services
    - Active
    - Inactive
    - Orphan/zombie
  - Intrusion detection configurations
  - Anti-malware configurations
  - Improperly configured local/group policies
  - Improperly configured firewall rules
  - Misconfigured permissions
  - Virus infection
  - Malware
  - Rogue processes/services
  - Data loss prevention (DLP)
- Security tools
  - Port scanners
  - Sniffers
  - Telnet clients
  - Anti-malware
  - Antivirus
  - File integrity
    - Checksums
    - Monitoring
    - Detection
    - Enforcement
  - User access controls
    - SELinux
    - User account control (UAC)

When users are unable to connect to the resources they need, they can't do their job. There are two main sources of connectivity problems. Network issues mean that a misconfigured or malfunctioning device exists somewhere between users and their resources. Security issues mean that a security feature is either correctly or incorrectly denying the user access to the resources. In this chapter, we'll discuss the diagnosis of both of these issues.

Given a Scenario, Troubleshoot Network Connectivity Issues

Users cannot access a resource if a clear and valid path in the network does not exist between their device and the device holding the resource. This means that any network connectivity issue could exist in a number of places between the two. It could be that one of the two end devices is misconfigured, or the problem could be related to one of the infrastructure devices between them (switches and routers). In this section we're going to first look at common network issues and error messages and then follow that discussion up with possible solutions. Finally, we'll look at tools that can aid you in identifying these issues.

Common Problems

As you address networking issues, you'll find a number of common problems seem to appear frequently. The users may not always describe the issues in these terms, but you will learn over time which of these issues are possible causes of their dilemma.

Lack of Internet Connectivity

When users cannot connect to the Internet, you will hear about it and soon. This issue can have a number of sources, such as the following:

- The IP configuration of the user's computer
- The IP configuration of the user's default gateway or router
- The IP configuration of any routers that stand between the gateway and the Internet
- The DNS server
- The ISP
- The DHCP server

Each of these potential sources will yield specific clues that may indicate their involvement. Some of these clues will be covered in the sections that follow. It is always helpful to first determine the scope of the issue as that may eliminate some possibilities. If the user is the only one having the issue, then it is probably the IP configuration of that user's device (or malfunctioning hardware on the device). In that case, check for the correct IP address, subnet mask, default gateway, and DNS server address on the user's device. Don't forget to ask the user about any changes they may have made recently. Recently made changes are frequently found to be the cause of issues.

If multiple users are having this issue, it is probably an infrastructure device that stands between the users and the Internet. If you know where the affected users are located, it may help you to determine what network path these devices share to the Internet. Then you can trace your way from them to the Internet, checking the configuration and functionality of each until you locate the problem.

Resource Unavailable

Network problems, usually manifesting themselves as an inability to connect to resources, can arise from many different sources. This section discusses some common symptoms of networking issues. For many of the issues we will cover, you may find that the user simply has no connectivity. This is as good a time as any to talk about general network troubleshooting for a single device.

No Connectivity

When no connectivity can be established with the network, your troubleshooting approach should begin at the Physical layer and then proceed up the OSI model. As components at each layer are eliminated as the source of the problem, proceed to the next higher layer. A simple yet effective set of steps might be as follows:

1. Check the network cable to ensure it is the correct cable type (crossover or straight-through) and that it is functional and fully plugged in. If in doubt, try a different cable.

2. Ensure that the NIC is functional and the TCP/IP protocol is installed and functional by pinging the loopback address (127.0.0.1 in IPv4 or ::1 in IPv6). If required, install or reinstall TCP/IP and/or replace or reseat the NIC.

3. Check the local IP configuration and ensure that the IP address, subnet mask, and gateway are correct. If the default gateway can be pinged, the computer is configured correctly for its local network, and the problem lies beyond the router or with the destination device. If pings to the gateway are unsuccessful, ensure that the IP configurations of the router interface and the computer are compatible and in the same subnet.

When dealing with a wireless network, ensure that the wireless card is functional. The wireless card is easily disabled with a keystroke on a laptop and should be the first thing to check. If the network uses a hidden SSID, ensure that the station in question is configured with the correct SSID.

Receiving Incorrect DHCP Information

If you have a single DHCP server that is configured correctly, you may be wondering how does one receive incorrect DHCP information (IP address, subnet mask, gateway, etc.)? It could be a rogue DHCP server, one that you do not control. In most instances that is not the only issue. Usually it's a DHCP server in a rogue WLAN access point.

Rogue access points are APs that you do not control and manage. There are two types: those that are connected to your wired infrastructure and those that are not. The ones that are connected to your wired network present a danger to your wired and wireless networks. They may be placed there by your own users without your knowledge, or they may be purposefully put there by a hacker to gain access to the wired network. In either case, they allow access to your wired network. Wireless intrusion prevention system (WIPS) devices can be used to locate rogue access points and alert administrators to their presence. Wireless site surveys can also be conducted to detect such threats.

Non-functional or Unreachable

Always keep in mind that the destination device may not be functional or it may not be reachable even though it is functioning. We'll be looking at the meaning of certain ICMP messages in a moment; they can tell you a lot, but know that although you may be able to ping the destination by both IP address and name, that doesn't mean that the service the destination is providing is working. You can determine this by attempting a Telnet connection to the IP address of the device and adding the port number of the service, as shown here. In this example, the test is meant to test the functionality of HTTP:

```
telnet 192.168.5.5 80
```

If the port is open, you will see a blank screen. This will mean that the connection is successful. If it is not open, you will see this:

```
telnet 192.168.5.5 80
Connecting to 192.168.5.5 ..... could not open connection to the host on port
80: connect failed
```

Keep in mind that this only tests connectivity to the service and does not guarantee the service is configured or functioning correctly.

Destination Host Unreachable

This is an error message you may receive when attempting to ping the destination device. This means that one of the routers along the path to destination does not have a route to the network where the device resides. It does *not* mean that the device is not on or is unavailable. That is a different message.

It will appear as a destination unreachable message (this is a group of message types that all have code numbers) with a code number of 1.

Code numbers do not appear in a destination unreachable message. However, you can use a protocol analyzer to capture one of the packets and view the code number by viewing the packet in the tool. You will do this in Exercise 11.1

Using a Sniffer to Identify the Code Number

This exercise uses Wireshark, a well-known protocol analyzer or sniffer. To get it, go to www
.wireshark.org.

1. If Wireshark is not already installed, follow the directions to install it.

2. Open Wireshark, and from the opening page in the section Interface List, select the
   interface on which you would like to capture packets. When you click it, the capture
   should begin. If it doesn't, open the Capture menu at the top of the screen and select
   Start Capture.

3. Open the command prompt and ping the unreachable destination to generate the ICMP
   messages.

4. Return to Wireshark and from the Capture menu select Stop Capture. You will have
   many captured packets listed, as shown here:

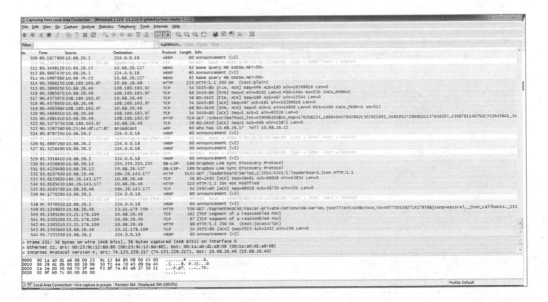

5. In the capture windows, locate one of the ICMP packets and double-click it. The details
   of that packet will appear in a pop-up that looks something like this:

EXERCISE 11.1 *(continued)*

Wireshark · Packet 215 · wireshark_pcapng_AC1C6C97-7351-44DB-96DA-D23A4DAC6D51_20160302165606_a20312

```
> Frame 215: 74 bytes on wire (592 bits), 74 bytes captured (592 bits) on interface 0
> Ethernet II, Src: IntelCor_7e:04:6c (9c:4e:36:7e:04:6c), Dst: CiscoInc_df:a4:70 (a8:0c:0d:df:a4:70)
> Internet Protocol Version 4, Src: 192.168.10.136, Dst: 10.10.10.10
> Internet Control Message Protocol
```

6. Expand the tree structure as shown here. In the ICMP section, you will find the type and code. In this example, the code is 3, which is Port Unreachable.

```
⊞ Frame 7: 70 bytes on wire (560 bits), 70 bytes captured (560 bits) on interface 0
⊞ Ethernet II, Src: c2:02:09:58:00:00 (c2:02:09:58:00:00), Dst: c2:01:1a:18:00:00 (c2:01:1a:18:00:00)
⊟ Internet Protocol Version 4, Src: 192.168.23.3 (192.168.23.3), Dst: 192.168.12.1 (192.168.12.1)
     Version: 4
     Header Length: 20 bytes
  ⊞ Differentiated Services Field: 0xc0 (DSCP 0x30: Class Selector 6; ECN: 0x00: Not-ECT (Not ECN-Capable Transport))
     Total Length: 56
     Identification: 0x000e (14)
  ⊞ Flags: 0x00
     Fragment offset: 0
     Time to live: 254
     Protocol: ICMP (1)
  ⊞ Header checksum: 0x17a2 [validation disabled]
     Source: 192.168.23.3 (192.168.23.3)
     Destination: 192.168.12.1 (192.168.12.1)
     [Source GeoIP: Unknown]
     [Destination GeoIP: Unknown]
⊟ Internet Control Message Protocol
     Type: 3 (Destination unreachable)
     Code: 3 (Port unreachable)
     Checksum: 0xa16b [correct]
  ⊟ Internet Protocol Version 4, Src: 192.168.12.1 (192.168.12.1), Dst: 192.168.23.3 (192.168.23.3)
       Version: 4
       Header Length: 20 bytes
    ⊞ Differentiated Services Field: 0x00 (DSCP 0x00: Default; ECN: 0x00: Not-ECT (Not ECN-Capable Transport))
       Total Length: 28
       Identification: 0x002d (45)
    ⊞ Flags: 0x00
       Fragment offset: 0
    ⊟ Time to live: 1
      ⊞ [Expert Info (Note/Sequence): "Time To Live" only 1]
       Protocol: UDP (17)
    ⊞ Header checksum: 0x1550 [validation disabled]
       Source: 192.168.12.1 (192.168.12.1)
       Destination: 192.168.23.3 (192.168.23.3)
       [Source GeoIP: Unknown]
       [Destination GeoIP: Unknown]
    ⊞ User Datagram Protocol, Src Port: 49173 (49173), Dst Port: 33435 (33435)
```

If the message comes with no source IP address, that means the message is coming from the local router (the default gateway of the sender). If it has the source IP address of the sender, then it is another router in the path. If this is the message you are getting, it's time to start looking at the routing tables of the routers or to escalate the issue if that is outside your realm.

Unknown Host

This message tells you that the host specified is not known. This message is usually generated by a router local to the destination host and usually means a bad IP address. It will appear as a destination unreachable message (this is a group of message types that all have code numbers) with a code number of 7.

Unable to Reach Remote Subnets

When a computer can communicate only on its local network or subnet, the problem is usually one of the following:

Incorrect Subnet Mask   Sometimes an incorrect mask will prevent all communication, but in some cases it results in successful connections locally but not remotely (outside the local subnet). The subnet mask value should be the same mask used on the router interface connecting to the local network.

Incorrect Default Gateway Address   If the computer cannot connect to the default gateway, it will be confined to communicating with devices on the local network. This IP address should be that of the router interface connecting to the local network.

Router Problem   If all users on the network are having connectivity problems, you likely have a routing issue that should be escalated to the proper administrators.

Failure of Service Provider

While it is typically not the cause of Internet issues, always keep in mind that it is possible that the ISP is suffering a failure. If the entire location is suffering an inability to reach the Internet, it is time to consider this possibility. This is simple enough to verify by contacting the ISP, but if you want to verify it yourself, execute a traceroute to an Internet address and then you can determine where the traffic is stopping. The traceroute command will be covered in "Commands" later in this chapter, but for now know that it allows you to identify the last router that was able to route the packet, thus telling you where the path ends.

Cannot Reach Server by Hostname/Fully Qualified Domain Name (FQDN)

When attempting to connect to resources by name, which is the method users employ, the connection is made to a fully qualified domain name (FQDN) in the form of *hostname*.domain.com. As you learned earlier, if this is not possible, it is a name resolution issue or a DNS issue. This means that the problem could be located in several places. Always consider those possibilities:

- The DHCP server may be issuing an incorrect DNS server address.
- The computer may be configured manually with an incorrect DNS server IP address.
- There may be a network issue preventing access to the DNS server.
- The DNS server is malfunctioning.

In some cases, the computer has connectivity to some but not all resources. When this is the case, issues that may reside on other layers of the OSI model should come under consideration. These include the following.

Authentication Issues

Does the user have the permission to access the resource?

DNS Issues

You may be able to ping the entire network using IP addresses, but most access is done by name, not IP address. If you can't ping resources by name, DNS is not functional, meaning either the DNS server is down or the local machine is not configured with the correct IP address of the DNS server. If recent changes have occurred in the DNS mappings or if your connection to the destination device has recently failed because of a temporary network issue that has been solved, you may need to clear the local DNS cache using the `ipconfig` or `flushdns` command.

Remote Problem

Don't forget that establishing a connection is a two-way street, and if the remote device has an issue, communication cannot occur. Always check the remote device as well. Any interconnecting device between the computer and resource, such as a switch or router, should also be checked for functionality.

Causes of Common Problems

While coverage of many of the common causes of these issues is provided in each section as it applies to that issue, we'll go over them again in more detail in this section.

Improper IP Configuration

As you know already, no networking will be possible unless the IP configurations of the computers on both ends of a connection attempt are correct. This includes the following:

- IP address
- Default gateway
- Subnet mask
- DNS server

IP Conflict

IP address conflicts are somewhat rare when DHCP is in use, but they can still happen. DHCP servers and clients both check for IP duplication when the DHCP client receives an IP address, but the process doesn't always work. Moreover, if someone with a statically configured IP address connects to the network with the same address as another machine, a conflict will exist.

Regardless of how the conflict occurs, it must be resolved because until it is, one or possibly both computers with the same address will not be able to network. You can determine the MAC address of the computer with which you are experiencing the conflict by using the `ping` command followed by `arp -a`. In Exercise 11.2 you will identify an IP address conflict.

EXERCISE 11.2

Identifying an IP Address Conflict

1. Begin by pinging the IP address in conflict, as shown here:

```
C:\WINDOWS\system32\cmd.exe                          —    □    ×

C:\WINDOWS\system32>ping 10.200.97.48

Pinging 10.200.97.48 with 32 bytes of data:
Reply from 10.200.97.48: bytes=32 time<1ms TTL=128
Reply from 10.200.97.48: bytes=32 time<1ms TTL=128
Reply from 10.200.97.48: bytes=32 time<1ms TTL=128
Reply from 10.200.97.48: bytes=32 time<1ms TTL=128

Ping statistics for 10.200.97.48:
    Packets: Sent = 4, Received = 4, Lost = 0 (0% loss),
Approximate round trip times in milli-seconds:
    Minimum = 0ms, Maximum = 0ms, Average = 0ms

C:\WINDOWS\system32>
```

2. Use the `arp-a` command to view the ARP cache where the MAC address–to–IP address mapping your computer just created will be located, as shown here. As you can see in the output, the MAC address of the IP address we pinged is 18-67-b0-c3-3d-27.

```
C:\WINDOWS\system32\cmd.exe                          —    □    ×

C:\WINDOWS\system32>arp -a

Interface: 192.168.56.1 --- 0x4
  Internet Address      Physical Address      Type
  192.168.56.255        ff-ff-ff-ff-ff-ff     static
  224.0.0.22            01-00-5e-00-00-16     static
  224.0.0.252           01-00-5e-00-00-fc     static
  229.55.150.208        01-00-5e-37-96-d0     static
  239.255.255.250       01-00-5e-7f-ff-fa     static
  255.255.255.255       ff-ff-ff-ff-ff-ff     static

Interface: 10.200.97.49 --- 0x8
  Internet Address      Physical Address      Type
  10.200.97.1           64-00-f1-b5-d9-03     dynamic
  10.200.97.48          18-67-b0-c3-3d-27     dynamic
  10.200.97.255         ff-ff-ff-ff-ff-ff     static
  224.0.0.22            01-00-5e-00-00-16     static
  224.0.0.252           01-00-5e-00-00-fc     static
  224.0.0.253           01-00-5e-00-00-fd     static
  229.55.150.208        01-00-5e-37-96-d0     static
  239.255.255.250       01-00-5e-7f-ff-fa     static
  255.255.255.255       ff-ff-ff-ff-ff-ff     static

C:\WINDOWS\system32>
```

Default Gateway Misconfigured

Earlier you learned that if the computer cannot connect to the default gateway, it will be confined to communicating with devices on the local network. This IP address should be that of the router interface connected to the local network. You should also ensure that the IP address of the computer is in the same network with the gateway, which means they must share the same network ID. They cannot share the same network ID unless they have the same subnet mask as well. When troubleshooting gateway issues, consider all of these factors. At the end of the day, the device must be able to ping its gateway.

IPv4 vs. IPv6 Misconfigurations

IPv6 is the new version of IP that uses 128-bit IP addresses rather than 32-bit, as in IPv4. Many technicians are still learning IPv6, and it is an area ripe for misconfiguration.

IPv6 offers a number of improvements, the most notable of which is its ability to handle growth in public networks. IPv6's 128-bit addressing scheme allows for a huge number of possible addresses: 340,282,366,920,938,463,463,374,607,431,768,211,456.

Table 11.1 compares IPv4 to IPv6.

TABLE 11.1   IPv4 vs. IPv6

Feature	IPv4	IPv6
Loopback address	127.0.0.1	0:0:0:0:0:0:0:1 (::1)
Private ranges	10.0.0.0/8	FC00:/7
	172.16.0.0/12	FEC0:: /10
	192.168.0.0/24	
Autoconfigured addresses	169.254.0.0/16	FE80::

> In IPv6 addresses, repeating zeroes can be left out so that colons next to each other in the address indicate one or more sets of zeroes for that section.

One common mistake is to configure two ends of a link such that they are not in the same subnet. In IPv6, the number of bits in the prefix is given after the address, as shown here:

```
aaaa.bbbb.cccc.dddd.0000.0000.0000.0000 /64
```

This means that the prefix is 64 bits long, or `aaaaa.bbbbb.ccccc.ddddd`. Therefore, for two IP addresses to be in the same network, the address must be the same across the first 64 bits.

Improper VLAN Configuration

By default, all ports in a switch are in the same Layer 2 network or the same LAN. It is possible to subdivide the switch into separate Layer 2 networks called virtual LANs, or VLANs. When we do this, we also place the devices that are in different VLANs in different Layer 3 networks as well. However, even if we assign devices in different VLANs with IP addresses in the same subnet, they will not be able to communicate because they are also separated at Layer 2.

VLANs can also span switches, meaning that devices connected to different switches can be in the same VLAN. When this is done, you must create special links called trunk links that permit the traffic of multiple VLANs between these switches.

This means that misconfiguration of VLANs can cause communication issues. The types of mistakes that can cause this include:

- Ports assigned to an incorrect VLAN

- Devices in the same VLAN with IP addresses in different IP subnets

- VLANs that have been mistakenly disallowed from crossing a trunk link

When VLANs are in use, always consider these possible misconfigurations on the switch and escalate the problem if that is not your area of expertise.

Network Port Security

Port security applies to ports on a switch, and since it relies on monitoring the MAC addresses of the devices attached to the switch ports, we call it Layer 2 security. While disabling any ports not in use is always a good idea, port security goes a step further and allows you to keep the port enabled for legitimate devices while preventing its use by illegitimate devices.

There are several things you can accomplish with port security. It can be used to:

- Set the maximum number of MAC addresses that can be seen on a port

- Define exactly which MAC addresses are allowed on the port

- Take a specific action when a port violation occurs

The following scenarios can be prevented through the use of port security:

- A malicious individual enters the facility, unplugs a legitimate computer, and plugs in their computer.

- Users in a department violate policy by attaching a hub to one of the switch ports so that they can connect more devices.

- A student in a computer lab disconnects one of the lab computers and connects their laptop to the network.

As you can imagine, this creates a scenario ripe for connectivity issues. Even if the port security configuration is correct, the connection of an unauthorized device to a port might shut down the port, causing an issue for a legitimate device when it is reconnected to the port. If you suspect port security, check the following:

- Is the port listed as err-disabled in the output of the `show port` command? If so, it must be enabled manually.

- Is the port allowing all required legitimate MAC addresses (don't forget the IP phone to which the computer may be connected)?

- Is the port allowing the required number of MAC addresses—for example, if it is only allowing one and there are two attached (IP phone and computer)?

When port security is in use, always consider these possible misconfigurations on the switch and escalate if that is not your area of expertise.

Component Failure

Yes, it's true that the network problem may not be your fault—at least it might not be a misconfiguration. Sometimes components fail. If any router, switch, or firewall in the network fails or one of its components fails, there will be network issues. When this occurs, typically the effect is widespread. It will usually affect an entire subnet or an entire section of the network. These issues should be escalated as soon as they are discovered due to their scope.

Onboard components (also called integrated components) are those that are built into the motherboard. Unfortunately, when these components fail, a replacement of the motherboard is usually required. Although it is possible to make some component replacements, doing so requires soldering and in many cases causes more issues than it solves. Even if you have the skills, always weigh the value of the time taken to attempt the repair (you may waste the time in vain) against the cost of a new motherboard. Having said all this, if the board is a newer board, you may be able to disable the defective onboard component and set the system to use a replacement component installed in one of the expansion slots.

Incorrect OS Route Tables

Routers route packets by consulting a routing table that the router creates by placing all directly connected (or local) networks in the table and then adding remote networks as they become known to the router. The router can learn remote networks in one of two ways: by administrators adding them manually or by learning them from other routers via a common routing protocol. As both of these methods involve human beings making configuration settings, there are always opportunities for misconfigurations.

When you have discovered that the path between two devices ends at a specific router (remember, you can determine this with the `traceroute` command), it is time to suspect the routing table of that router. The `show ip route` command can be used to identify the routes of which the router is aware. If the router is missing the route, it will never be able to forward packets to the destination network. While configuring routers is beyond the scope of this book, consider this possibility when you have identified a router where a path between two devices ends and then escalate as necessary.

Routing and switch issues like firewall issues will typically affect multiple users. This is not a book on routers and switches, but you should be able to connect certain errors with certain devices. You've already learned that if a router has no route in its table to a destination network, it will be unable to send traffic to that network. That will result in a destination unreachable message when you attempt to ping that destination. Here are several messages that indicate a lack of a route or a security issue:

- Destination unreachable with a source address (and a code number of 0): A router in the path other than the local route has no route to that network.

- Destination unreachable with no source address (with a code number of 0): The local router has no route to the network.

- Destination unreachable (with a code number of 9 or 10): The source device is not permitted to send to that network (code 9) or to that device (code 10). This message indicates an ACL is prohibiting the traffic.

Switch issues will only affect those devices attached to the switch unless there are VLANs spanning switches; then the effect may be more widespread. Most issues with switches concern switch port security misconfigurations or speed and duplex mismatches, but problems can also occur when trunk links are misconfigured between switches. While the default setting is to allow the traffic of all VLANs across a trunk link, it is possible to disallow certain VLANs. Obviously a mistake when configuring that setting could cause issues. Always consider that possibility when intra-VLAN issues are occurring.

Bad Cables

While technicians learn at the beginning of their careers to always check the Physical layer first, hours are sometime devoted to troubleshooting upper-layer issues to no avail when a bad cable is the culprit. Keep in mind as well that performance issues also sometimes have their roots in a damaged cable.

In some cases, a cable may function but not well. If the cable has a nick in the outside covering it allows electromagnetic interference (EMI) and radio-frequency interference (RFI) to more easily enter the cable. This "noise" damages packets and causes them to fail the integrity check when they arrive at their destination. This causes the packet to be lost for good in the case of UDP traffic, and it causes it to be retransmitted in the case of TCP traffic. The time spent sending the packet again could have been used to send new packets, so this results in a lower data rate. Always consider a damaged cable first when a server is suffering poor performance.

Though it is beyond the scope of this book, if you examine the performance information on the switch port to which the server is connected you can identify when packets are being dropped due to Cyclic Redundancy Check (CRC) errors.

Firewall (Misconfiguration, Hardware Failure, Software Failure)

As with other infrastructure devices such as routers and switches, when a firewall has issues, multiple users are typically affected. These issues usually are caused by one of three things.

Misconfiguration

Firewalls use rule sets that must be constructed carefully or they will not achieve their goal. In most cases, but not all, access control lists (ACLs) are used to control traffic through an interface. The list of rules is created and then applied either inbound or outbound to an interface. When a packet arrives at an interface on the firewall, the firewall starts at the top of the list of rules and starts comparing the traffic type in the packet to each rule in order. When it finds the first rule that matches the traffic type in the packet, it takes the action (either allow or deny) specified in the rule and stops reading the list. This means the order is very important.

For example, let's say our intent is to prevent a computer at 192.168.5.5/24 from sending traffic through an interface while allowing everyone else in the subnet to send traffic. We create these two rules in this order:

Permit 192.168.5.0/24

Deny 192.168.5.5/24

Can you guess what will happen? Since the devices at 192.168.5.5/24 match both rules and the permit rule is first, the rule that we created designed to deny this traffic will never be denied. So as you can see, incorrect rule order is a common mistake.

Another common characteristic of ACLs is that (in most systems but not all) there is an implied deny all rule at the end of every ACL. You don't see it; it's automatic. This means that if the firewall goes all the way through the list and none of the rules allow the traffic, the traffic is denied. Failing to explicitly allow traffic that should be allowed is another common mistake.

Finally, you can create ACLs until you are blue in the face and if you never apply them to an interface, they never enforce anything. So failure to apply the ACL is another common mistake.

Although most systems use the logic just explained, there are some systems that, rather than applying the first rule that matches, go all the way through the list and select the rule that is the *best* match. So a system that uses that logic would have been able to select the proper rule in our previous example because the second rule in the list is a better match of the sender's IP address than the first rule in the list. You must understand the logic of each system.

Hardware Failure

It is also possible that the firewall may suffer a hardware failure. This can happen regardless of whether the firewall is implemented as an appliance or as software running on a server. Any hardware issue that affects the server on which the software is installed will affect the firewall function. Likewise, any hardware issues with interfaces, memory, or CPU on an appliance will affect the hardware appliance as well.

Software Failure

Software failures can also occur either in the firewall software running on a server or with the firmware or operating system running in an appliance. In many cases, these failures can be avoided by maintaining all patches to the firewall software and firmware as it becomes available. Although these failures are always possible, a more likely threat is a misconfiguration of the software, as discussed earlier.

Misconfigured NIC

Many technicians don't think much about the settings on a NIC; they just plug it in and if it works they are satisfied. A misconfigured NIC, like a damaged cable, may work but not work well if its duplex and speed settings do not match those of the switch port to which it is connected. Although most network cards supposedly "autosense" the setting on the other end and set themselves to match, this function requires a negotiation process that can fail, and when it does the two ends may default to a mismatch.

Just as a damaged cable causes damaged packets that fail the integrity check and must be transmitted again, a speed or duplex mismatch causes packet collisions, which also cause packets to be re-sent and thus lower throughput. This is another behavior you can detect by reviewing errors occurring on the switchport.

Improper Subnetting

Devices that are in the same IP subnet must have an IP address and subnet mask combination that places them in the same subnet. Regardless of whether you are using default subnet masks or you are implementing CIDR (which allows nondefault mask lengths), for two devices to be in the same subnet they must share the same network portion of the IP address. This means that their IP addresses must agree in the bits covered by the mask. For example, consider these two addresses:

192.168.6.5/16

192.168.5.6/16

For these two addresses to be in the same subnet, they must agree in the first 16 bits (the number of bits in the mask). In this case, they both have 192.168 in the first two octets or 16 bits so they are in the same subnet. However, consider these changes:

192.168.6.5/24

192.168.5.6/24

Now they must agree in the first 24 bits, which they do not (192.168.5 and 192.168.6), so they are now not in the same subnet. Regardless of whether CIDR is in use, always consider these possible misconfigurations on the devices.

DNS and/or DHCP Failure

DNS and DHCP failures will affect multiple users, and the damage will depend on several factors. Let's start with DHCP.

Most issues with DHCP result in computers being unable to obtain an IP configuration. That manifests itself to the user as an inability to connect to anything, which may result in all sorts of misdiagnoses by the user (the email server is down, the web server is down, etc.). This can be caused by:

- The DHCP server is out of IP addresses.
- The computer is unable to reach the DHCP server.
- The DHCP server is down.

The first problem is simple enough to solve: add more IP addresses. The second can occur if the computer is located in a different subnet from the DHCP server and *relay agents* are not in use. Since DHCP clients locate the DHCP server with a broadcast packet, they must be in the same subnet or the server will never hear the broadcast. Relay agents can be applied to the router interfaces, and then the router interface can relay these packets to the server. In their absence, an inability to connect will occur. One of the symptoms of this condition is that the device will have a self-generated IP address. If the device is Windows and it is running IPv4, the address will have 169 in the first octet.

DNS issues will also be widespread. Users will be unable to locate resources by name. To them, this issue will appear to be the same as an issue with DHCP in that they can't connect to anything. So you may get some of the same user misdiagnoses. You can easily determine which it is by pinging the destination by name and by IP address. If you can ping by IP address but not by name, the issue is DNS.

DHCP Server Misconfigured

As you learned earlier, if the DHCP server has an issue many users may be affected. Always ensure it has a sufficient number of IP addresses to service each scope. Also make sure that any default gateway and DNS server addresses it is issuing are correct; if they aren't, it will cause the users to be unable to leave their local subnet or perform name resolution.

Misconfigured Hosts File

Most systems rely on DNS for name resolution, but it is not the only method a system can use. Windows and Linux systems have a file called Hosts that can be populated manually with IP address–to-name mappings. The downside to this is the static nature of the file—that is, any changes have to be made manually. This file is always located at C:\Windows\System32\drivers\etc\hosts. If this file is misconfigured, it will result in an inability to connect to the destination. To make matters worse, this file is the first place the device looks before it attempts DNS, so if there is an entry in the file for the name, it never uses DNS!

Finally, some forms of malware edit the Hosts file and add entries. So even if you are not aware that anyone has ever edited this file, it is still something to check since malware can add entries.

Tools and Techniques

A number of tools and techniques are available to help you diagnose network issues, some of which we have already referred to. You should understand how these tools work and in which situations they may help you gather useful diagnostic data.

Check Link Lights

There will be link lights on the switch to which the server is plugged that can impart information about the status of the link. While you should always reference the documentation that comes with the switch, let's look at an example. On a Cisco switch each port has a light that can mean different things based on its color and behavior. The port mode determines the type of information shown by the port LEDs.

To select or change a mode, press the Mode button until the desired mode is highlighted. When you change port modes, the meanings of the port LED colors also change. The only mode we are interested in now is the STAT (port status). That node allows us to identify the state of the link. The possible colors and behaviors and their meaning are in Table 11.2.

TABLE 11.2   STAT mode color meanings

LED color	Meaning
Green	Link present, no activity.
Blinking green	Activity. Port is sending or receiving data.
Alternating green-amber	Link Fault caused by errors, resulting in retransmission of a corrupted frame.
Amber	Port is not forwarding traffic at all. Typically due to STP blocking a switching loop (beyond the scope of this book).

Confirm Power Supply

In Chapter 1, "Server Hardware," you learned that a power supply must be able to supply all the power needs of the server. Power requirements can and will change when you add or remove power drawing components. If some components are not working or only work at certain times, it could be a power issue. Review power capacity planning in Chapter 1.

Verify Cable Integrity

Always check the physical layer first as it is required for any of the other layers in the OSI model to be operational. Check the following:

- Is this the right type of cable? Use crossover cables to run directly from one device to another, but use a straight-through cable to connect to a switch.

- Check the cable with a cable tester. Just because it works doesn't mean it isn't suffering error conditions that can reduce the performance due to the retransmission of frames that have been damaged.

Check Appropriate Cable Selection

While we're talking about cable selection, there is one more consideration beyond type of cable. Does the cable support the top speed that the NIC is capable of? For example, if you are using a CAT 5 cable with a 10 GB NIC you are wasting a lot of speed. The cable can only send at 100 MB, while the NIC is capable of 10 GB. For this you should use a CAT 6e cable.

Commands

A number of command-line tools are available to help you diagnose network issues, some of which we have already referred to. You should understand how these tools work and in which situations they may help you gather useful diagnostic data.

ipconfig

The `ipconfig` command is used to view the IP configuration of a device and, when combined with certain switches or parameters, can be used to release and renew the lease of an IP address obtained from a DHCP server and to flush the DNS resolver cache. Its most common use is to view the current configuration. Figure 11.1 shows its execution with the `/all` switch, which results in a display of a wealth of information about the IP configuration.

FIGURE 11.1 Using `ipconfig`

```
C:\Users\tmcmillan>ipconfig/all

Windows IP Configuration

        Host Name . . . . . . . . . . . . : tmcmillan
        Primary Dns Suffix  . . . . . . . : alpha.kaplaninc.com
        Node Type . . . . . . . . . . . . : Hybrid
        IP Routing Enabled. . . . . . . . : No
        WINS Proxy Enabled. . . . . . . . : No
        DNS Suffix Search List. . . . . . : alpha.kaplaninc.com
                                            kaplaninc.com

Ethernet adapter Local Area Connection:

        Connection-specific DNS Suffix  . : alpha.kaplaninc.com
        Description . . . . . . . . . . . : Broadcom NetXtreme 57xx Gigabit Controlle
r
        Physical Address. . . . . . . . . : 00-1A-A0-E1-95-AB
        DHCP Enabled. . . . . . . . . . . : Yes
        Autoconfiguration Enabled . . . . : Yes
        Link-local IPv6 Address . . . . . : fe80::ada3:8b73:a66e:6bc0%10(Preferred)
        IPv4 Address. . . . . . . . . . . : 10.88.2.103(Preferred)
        Subnet Mask . . . . . . . . . . . : 255.255.254.0
        Lease Obtained. . . . . . . . . . : Monday, January 30, 2012 9:38:37 AM
        Lease Expires . . . . . . . . . . : Tuesday, January 31, 2012 9:38:37 AM
        Default Gateway . . . . . . . . . : 10.88.2.6
        DHCP Server . . . . . . . . . . . : 10.88.10.48
        DHCPv6 IAID . . . . . . . . . . . : 234887840
        DHCPv6 Client DUID. . . . . . . . : 00-01-00-01-14-EE-0F-98-00-1A-A0-E1-95-AB

        DNS Servers . . . . . . . . . . . : 10.88.10.48
                                            10.75.139.18
        NetBIOS over Tcpip. . . . . . . . : Enabled
```

You can use `ipconfig` to release and renew a configuration obtained from a DHCP server by issuing the `ipconfig/release` command, followed by the `ipconfig/renew` command.

It is also helpful to know that when you have just corrected a configuration error (such as an IP address) on a destination device, you should ensure that the device registers its new IP address with the DNS server by executing the `ipconfig/registerdns` command.

It may also be necessary to clear incorrect IP address–to-hostname mappings that may still exist on the devices that were attempting to access the destination device. This can be done by executing the `ipconfig/flushdns` command.

ip addr

The `ip` command in Linux has many subcommands, each of which works on a type of object, such as IP addresses and routes. The `ip address` command shows IPv4 and IPv6 addresses assigned to all network interfaces. If you execute it without switches the output will be as follows:

```
1: lo: mtu 65536 qdisc noqueue state UNKNOWN group default qlen 1000
link/loopback 00:00:00:00:00:00 brd 00:00:00:00:00:00
inet 127.0.0.1/8 scope host lo
valid_lft forever preferred_lft forever
inet6 ::1/128 scope host
valid_lft forever preferred_lft forever
2: wlp58s0: mtu 1500 qdisc mq state UP group default qlen 1000
link/ether 9c:b6:d0:d0:fc:b5 brd ff:ff:ff:ff:ff:ff
inet 192.168.1.20/24 brd 192.168.1.255 scope global dynamic
noprefixroute wlp58s0
valid_lft 5962sec preferred_lft 5962sec
inet6 fe80::bf14:21e3:4223:e5e4/64 scope link noprefixroute
valid_lft forever preferred_lft forever
```

The output shows that the first interface, the loopback interface, has an address of 127.0.0.1, as it always does unless you change it. The second interface has an address of 192.168.1.20. You can see the IPv6 address it has as well (fe80::bf14:21e3:4223:e5e4/64).

ping

The `ping` command makes use of the ICMP protocol to test connectivity between two devices. `ping` is one of the most useful commands in the TCP/IP protocol. It sends a series of packets to another system, which in turn sends a response. The `ping` command can be extremely useful for troubleshooting problems with remote hosts.

The `ping` command indicates whether the host can be reached and how long it took for the host to send a return packet. On a LAN, the time is indicated as less than 10 milliseconds. Across WAN links, however, this value can be much greater. When the `-a` parameter is included, the command will also attempt to resolve the hostname associated with the IP address. Figure 11.2 shows an example of a successful ping.

FIGURE 11.2   The ping command

```
C:\Users\tmcmillan>ping 10.88.2.103

Pinging 10.88.2.103 with 32 bytes of data:
Reply from 10.88.2.103: bytes=32 time<1ms TTL=128
Reply from 10.88.2.103: bytes=32 time<1ms TTL=128
Reply from 10.88.2.103: bytes=32 time<1ms TTL=128
Reply from 10.88.2.103: bytes=32 time<1ms TTL=128

Ping statistics for 10.88.2.103:
    Packets: Sent = 4, Received = 4, Lost = 0 (0% loss),
Approximate round trip times in milli-seconds:
    Minimum = 0ms, Maximum = 0ms, Average = 0ms
```

tracert/traceroute

The tracert command (called traceroute in Linux and Unix) is used to trace the path of a packet through the network. Its best use is in determining exactly where in the network the packet is being dropped. It will show each hop (router) the packet crosses and how long it takes to do so. Figure 11.3 shows a partial display of a traced route to www.nascar.com.

FIGURE 11.3   Using tracert

```
Microsoft Windows [Version 10.0.10586]
(c) 2015 Microsoft Corporation. All rights reserved.

C:\WINDOWS\system32>tracert www.nascar.com

Tracing route to a1269.w7.akamai.net [8.18.43.66]
over a maximum of 30 hops:

  1  2273 ms    <1 ms    <1 ms  10.200.97.1
  2     1 ms    <1 ms    <1 ms  rrcs-24-199-211-193.midsouth.biz.rr.com [24.199.211.193]
  3     1 ms    12 ms     1 ms  70.62.94.106
  4     1 ms     1 ms     1 ms  70.62.94.66
  5     1 ms     1 ms     1 ms  24.27.255.238
  6     7 ms     7 ms     7 ms  ten2-0-0.rlghncrdc-pe-rtr01.southeast.rr.com [24.93.73.78]
  7     7 ms     8 ms     7 ms  ten2-0-0.gnboncsg-p-rtr01.southeast.rr.com [24.93.73.37]
  8    21 ms     7 ms     7 ms  ten2-0-0.gnboncsg-pe-rtr01.southeast.rr.com [24.93.73.74]
  9     7 ms    22 ms     7 ms  ten2-0-0.chrlncsa-p-rtr01.southeast.rr.com [24.93.73.33]
 10    21 ms    11 ms    11 ms  24.93.67.100
 11    16 ms    20 ms    15 ms  bu-ether44.atlngamq46w-bcr00.tbone.rr.com [107.14.19.46]
 12    15 ms    12 ms    12 ms  0.ae1.pr0.atl20.tbone.rr.com [66.109.6.177]
 13    13 ms    12 ms    12 ms  216.156.108.45.ptr.us.xo.net [216.156.108.45]
 14    55 ms    26 ms    26 ms  207.88.13.48.ptr.us.xo.net [207.88.13.48]
 15    31 ms    36 ms    28 ms  te-11-4-0.rar3.washington-dc.us.xo.net [207.88.12.201]
 16    26 ms    26 ms    26 ms  207.88.12.132.ptr.us.xo.net [207.88.12.132]
 17    26 ms    26 ms    29 ms  207.88.14.191.ptr.us.xo.net [207.88.14.191]
 18    26 ms    25 ms    25 ms  be3013.ccr41.iad02.atlas.cogentco.com [154.54.9.5]
 19    26 ms    26 ms    26 ms  be2657.ccr42.dca01.atlas.cogentco.com [154.54.31.109]
 20    37 ms    30 ms    26 ms  be2113.ccr42.atl01.atlas.cogentco.com [154.54.24.222]
 21    25 ms    26 ms    25 ms  be2848.ccr41.atl04.atlas.cogentco.com [154.54.6.118]
 22    31 ms    25 ms    25 ms  38.122.47.42
 23    25 ms    25 ms    25 ms  8.18.43.66

Trace complete.

C:\WINDOWS\system32>
```

nslookup

The nslookup command is a command-line administrative tool for testing and trouble-shooting DNS servers. It can be run in two modes: interactive and noninteractive. Noninteractive mode is useful when only a single piece of data needs to be returned; interactive allows you to query for either an IP address for a name or a name for an IP address without leaving nslookup mode. The command syntax is as follows:

```
nslookup [-option] [hostname] [server]
```

To enter interactive mode, simply type **nslookup**. When you do, by default it will identify the IP address and name of the DNS server that the local machine is configured to use, if any, and then will go to the > prompt. At this prompt, you can type either an IP address or a name, and the system will attempt to resolve the IP address to a name or the name to an IP address.

```
C:\> nslookup
 Default Server: nameserver1.domain.com
 Address: 10.0.0.1
 >
```

The following are other queries that can be run that may prove helpful when you are troubleshooting name resolution issues:

- Looking up different data types in the database (such as Microsoft records)
- Querying directly from another name server (different from the one the local device is configured to use)
- Performing a zone transfer

netstat

The netstat (network status) command is used to see what ports are listening on the TCP/IP-based system. The –a option is used to show all ports, and /? is used to show what other options are available (the options differ based on the operating system you are using). When executed with no switches, the command displays the current connections, as shown in Figure 11.4.

dig

The Linux dig command performs network DNS lookups. It can be used to troubleshoot DNS by interrogating DNS name servers.

The syntax is:

```
dig [@server] [-b address] [-c class] [-f filename] [-k filename] [-m]
[-p port#] [-q name] [-t type] [-x addr] [-y [hmac:]name:key] [-4] [-
6] [name] [type] [class] [queryopt...]
```

For more information on the arguments, visit:
www.computerhope.com/unix/dig.htm

FIGURE 11.4   Using netstat

```
C:\Users\tmcmillan>netstat

Active Connections

  Proto  Local Address          Foreign Address        State
  TCP    10.88.2.103:51273      64.94.18.154:https     ESTABLISHED
  TCP    10.88.2.103:51525      srat1060:microsoft-ds  ESTABLISHED
  TCP    10.88.2.103:51529      gmonsalvatge:microsoft-ds  ESTABLISHED
  TCP    10.88.2.103:51573      sjc-not18:http         ESTABLISHED
  TCP    10.88.2.103:51716      schexv02:2785          ESTABLISHED
  TCP    10.88.2.103:51720      schvoip01:epmap        ESTABLISHED
  TCP    10.88.2.103:51721      schvoip01:1297         ESTABLISHED
  TCP    10.88.2.103:51722      schvoip01:1299         ESTABLISHED
  TCP    10.88.2.103:51824      69.31.116.27:http      CLOSE_WAIT
  TCP    10.88.2.103:51965      dcalpsch2:1026         ESTABLISHED
  TCP    10.88.2.103:53865      cs219p3:5050           ESTABLISHED
  TCP    10.88.2.103:53871      sip109:http            ESTABLISHED
  TCP    10.88.2.103:62522      ord08s08-in-f22:https  ESTABLISHED
  TCP    10.88.2.103:62567      ord08s08-in-f22:https  CLOSE_WAIT
  TCP    10.88.2.103:62682      by2msg3010613:http     ESTABLISHED
  TCP    10.88.2.103:63554      baymsg1020213:msnp     ESTABLISHED
  TCP    10.88.2.103:63770      v-client-2b:https      CLOSE_WAIT
  TCP    10.88.2.103:63771      ec2-174-129-205-197:https  CLOSE_WAIT
  TCP    10.88.2.103:63772      v-client-2b:https      CLOSE_WAIT
  TCP    10.88.2.103:63773      65.55.121.231:http     ESTABLISHED
  TCP    10.88.2.103:63774      168.75.207.20:http     ESTABLISHED
  TCP    10.88.2.103:63777      65.55.17.30:http       ESTABLISHED
  TCP    10.88.2.103:63779      70.37.131.11:http      ESTABLISHED
  TCP    10.88.2.103:63781      65.124.174.56:http     ESTABLISHED
  TCP    10.88.2.103:63788      69.31.76.41:http       ESTABLISHED
  TCP    10.88.2.103:63791      207.46.140.46:http     ESTABLISHED
  TCP    10.88.2.103:63792      64.4.21.39:http        ESTABLISHED
  TCP    127.0.0.1:2002         tmcmillan:51543        ESTABLISHED
  TCP    127.0.0.1:19872        tmcmillan:51571        ESTABLISHED
  TCP    127.0.0.1:51543        tmcmillan:2002         ESTABLISHED
  TCP    127.0.0.1:51549        tmcmillan:51550        ESTABLISHED
  TCP    127.0.0.1:51550        tmcmillan:51549        ESTABLISHED
  TCP    127.0.0.1:51571        tmcmillan:19872        ESTABLISHED
  TCP    127.0.0.1:53869        tmcmillan:53870        ESTABLISHED
  TCP    127.0.0.1:53870        tmcmillan:53869        ESTABLISHED
  TCP    127.0.0.1:63557        tmcmillan:63574        ESTABLISHED
  TCP    127.0.0.1:63574        tmcmillan:63557        ESTABLISHED

C:\Users\tmcmillan>
```

telnet

The Linux telnet command can be used to establish a Telnet connection, but it can also be used to troubleshoot connection issues. If you can make a Telnet connection to a port, the port is open or listening. The following is a successful connection sequence to port 22 on a site named testsite.com:

```
# telnet testsite.com 22
Trying 35.99.2.9&hellip;
Connected to testsite.com.
Escape character is '^]'.
SSH-2.0-OpenSSH_6.6.1p1 Ubuntu-2ubuntu2.13
```

nc

The nc command runs the netcat utility in Linux and is used to set up connections between systems. The syntax is as follows:

```
netcat OPTIONS DESTINATION PORT
```

The options mean:

OPTIONS   Used to set some special behavior like timeout, help, jumbo frame, etc.

DESTINATION   Used to specify the remote system IP or hostname

PORT   The remote system port number

For more information on using netcat, visit:
Netcat – Basic Usage and Overview: `www.geeksforgeeks.org/`
`netcat-basic-usage-and-overview`

nbtstat

Microsoft networks use an interface called Network Basic Input/Output System (NetBIOS) to resolve workstation names with IP addresses. The `nbtstat` command can be used to view NetBIOS information. In Figure 11.5 it has been executed with the `-n` switch, which will display the NetBIOS names that are currently known to the local machine. In this case, this local machine is aware only of its own NetBIOS names.

FIGURE 11.5   Using `nbtstat`

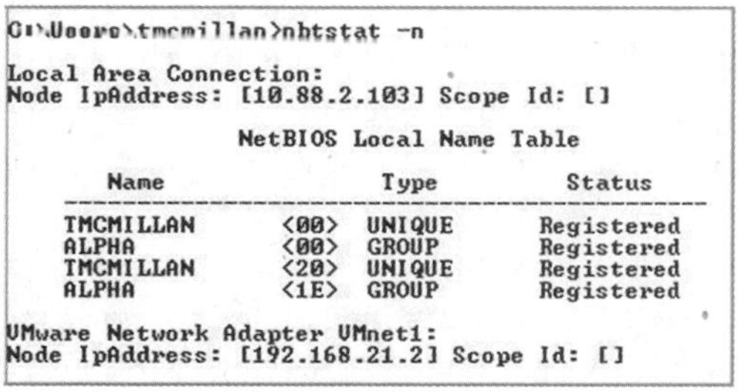

```
C:\Users\tmcmillan>nbtstat -n

Local Area Connection:
Node IpAddress: [10.88.2.103] Scope Id: []

                NetBIOS Local Name Table

      Name            Type          Status
      ----------------------------------------
      TMCMILLAN    <00>  UNIQUE      Registered
      ALPHA        <00>  GROUP       Registered
      TMCMILLAN    <20>  UNIQUE      Registered
      ALPHA        <1E>  GROUP       Registered

VMware Network Adapter VMnet1:
Node IpAddress: [192.168.21.2] Scope Id: []
```

route

The `route` command can be used in both Linux and Windows to view and edit the routing table on computers. To view the routing table in Linux, use the `route` command like this:

```
$ route
Kernel IP routing table
Destination Gateway Genmask Flags Metric Ref Use Iface
192.168.1.0 * 255.255.255.0 U 0 0 0 eth0
```

The output shows that the device is aware of one network (the one to which it is connected).

In Windows, the command requires the print keyword, as shown here:

```
C:\WINDOWS\system32>route print
===============================================================================
Interface List
 18...9c 4e 36 7e 04 6d ......Microsoft Wi-Fi Direct Virtual Adapter
  6...0a 00 27 00 00 00 ......VirtualBox Host-Only Ethernet Adapter
 10...08 9e 01 36 53 73 ......Realtek PCIe FE Family Controller
 14...9c 4e 36 7e 04 6c ......Intel(R) Centrino(R) Wireless-N 2200
 12...e0 06 e6 be cc 7b ......Bluetooth Device (Personal Area Network)
  1...........................Software Loopback Interface 1
  7...00 00 00 00 00 00 00 e0 Microsoft ISATAP Adapter
 17...00 00 00 00 00 00 00 e0 Teredo Tunneling Pseudo-Interface
  5...00 00 00 00 00 00 00 e0 Microsoft ISATAP Adapter #9
===============================================================================

IPv4 Route Table
===============================================================================
Active Routes:
Network Destination Netmask Gateway Interface Metric
 0.0.0.0 0.0.0.0 192.168.0.1 192.168.0.6 20
 127.0.0.0 255.0.0.0 On-link 127.0.0.1 306
 127.0.0.1 255.255.255.255 On-link 127.0.0.1 306
 127.255.255.255 255.255.255.255 On-link 127.0.0.1 306
 192.168.0.0 255.255.255.0 On-link 192.168.0.6 276
 192.168.0.6 255.255.255.255 On-link 192.168.0.6 276
 192.168.0.255 255.255.255.255 On-link 192.168.0.6 276
 192.168.56.0 255.255.255.0 On-link 192.168.56.1 266
 192.168.56.1 255.255.255.255 On-link 192.168.56.1 266
 192.168.56.255 255.255.255.255 On-link 192.168.56.1 266
 224.0.0.0 240.0.0.0 On-link 127.0.0.1 306
 224.0.0.0 240.0.0.0 On-link 192.168.56.1 266
 224.0.0.0 240.0.0.0 On-link 192.168.0.6 276
 255.255.255.255 255.255.255.255 On-link 127.0.0.1 306
 255.255.255.255 255.255.255.255 On-link 192.168.56.1 266
 255.255.255.255 255.255.255.255 On-link 192.168.0.6 276
===============================================================================
Persistent Routes:
 None

IPv6 Route Table
```

```
=============================================================================
Active Routes:
 If Metric Network Destination Gateway
 17 306 ::/0 On-link
 1 306 ::1/128 On-link
 17 306 2001::/32 On-link
 17 306 2001:0:5ef5:79fb:30be:34ca:cd75:ec40/128
On-link
 6 266 fe80::/64 On-link
 10 276 fe80::/64 On-link
 17 306 fe80::/64 On-link
 17 306 fe80::30be:34ca:cd75:ec40/128
On-link
 6 266 fe80::a1f4:3886:392:d218/128
On-link
 10 276 fe80::f098:57fb:c0d7:5e65/128
On-link
 1 306 ff00::/8 On-link
 6 266 ff00::/8 On-link
 17 306 ff00::/8 On-link
 10 276 ff00::/8 On-link
=============================================================================
Persistent Routes:
 None
```

This output lists both the IPv4 and IPv6 routing tables as well as a list of the interfaces. Use the route and route print commands to determine if a device has a route to its default gateway. A route of this type is called the default route, and in Windows it's listed as a destination network of 0.0.0.0 with a mask of 0.0.0.0.

Given a Scenario, Troubleshoot Security Problems

While many connectivity problems are rooted in network issues, others are caused by security features and functions. The end result is the same—the user cannot connect to a resource—but the symptoms are somewhat different. Next, we'll look at diagnosing security issues that cause connectivity issues and other more general security concerns.

Common Problems

Just as certain hardware and software issues seem to happen more often than others, there will be some security issues that are commonplace as well. Many of these are the result of human error in configuration, and others are the result of poorly configured or poorly written applications. In this section we'll look at some common security issues.

File Integrity

When files become altered either through corruption or unauthorized access, we say that the *integrity* of the file has been compromised. When system files are altered (sometimes through the actions of malware), it can cause operating system errors and crashes. In the "Security Tools" section, we'll look at some ways to maintain the integrity of both system files and other critical files that need protection.

Improper Privilege Escalation

When any user is able to attain additional rights and permissions, we say that privilege escalation has occurred. In most cases, this occurs as a result of the user obtaining the login information for a privileged account, logging in as that user, and making use of those additional rights and permissions. If the compromised action is an administrator or root account, the situation becomes worse because then the user may be able to clear the security log and hide their tracks. In the "Causes of Common Problems" section, we'll talk about how this occurs and what can be done to minimize the likelihood of this happening.

Excessive Access

Sometimes when users have excessive access to a resource it is a case of privilege escalation, But in most cases, it is human error in assigning rights and permissions. Periodic account reviews should be conducted to identify situations in which users have more rights or permissions that they need to do the job.

Also, over time as users change jobs, get promoted, and move from one department to another, something called permission creep occurs. This means that while they have attained new permissions as the result of the new job, the old permissions that applied to the previous position are not removed as they should be. This problem can be prevented by performing a formal permission review at the time of the application of the new permissions and also at regular intervals thereafter.

Applications Will Not Load

Another possible symptom of a malware infection is the crashing of applications. While this will occur from time to time for other reasons, when it is occurring repeatedly you should suspect malware. When the application that is crashing is your antivirus software, this is an even stronger indication of malware, as disabling or damaging your antivirus protection is the first thing that some types of malware attempt to do.

It is also a possibility that if your organization makes use of software restriction policies, the user may be trying to run a disallowed application. In that case, you should ensure that the software restriction policies that are controlling the user are correct.

Finally, it is always possible that the application is simply corrupted. In that case, try removing and reinstalling it.

Cannot Access Network Fileshares

Although network issues should be ruled out first, in some cases network file and share permissions may be preventing a user from accessing a share or file. In Windows, you must always consider the effects of multiple permissions users may have as a result of permissions applied to their account and those applied to any groups they may be in. You should have a clear understanding of how these permissions work together.

Unable to Open Files

When files will not open on a machine, there is always the possibility that the file permissions are the cause, but there can be other reasons. If the user lacks the application required to open the file, it will not open. This often occurs when users receive an email attachment in a file format for which they do have the proper application. They may or may not know how to locate and install the application, even if the application is free. If a software restriction policy is preventing the installation of the proper application, the user may have to get assistance and permission to read the document.

Causes of Common Problems

It may be hard to determine, but every issue has a cause. Although it is sometimes tempting to adopt a quick work-around to get things moving (and in some cases that may be the best approach), you should always attempt to determine the root cause. Otherwise, the issue could keep returning. In this section, we'll look at some causes that are worthy of consideration because they are common. We'll also cover common security weaknesses that you should be aware of.

Open Ports

One of the guiding principles of security is to disable all services that are not needed and to close the port of any services not in use. Hackers know common attacks that utilize common port numbers. In most cases, maintaining patches and updates prevents hackers from taking advantage of open ports, but not always. In the "Security Tools" section, we'll talk about how you can use the same tools the hackers do to discover these open ports.

Services

Services that run in the operating system can cause issues when they fail to start or crash. In this section you'll learn about service issues.

Active

While on the surface the presence of active services might appear to be a good thing, in some cases it is not. Following the same principle we followed with respect to open ports, any services or applications that are not required on a device should be disabled. The reason for this is that most services and applications have been compromised at some point. If all patches are applied, these compromises are usually addressed, but any that are not required should be disabled to be safe.

Inactive

When required services are inactive, it's a problem. Sometimes when the system is started you receive a message that tells you a service failed to start. When that occurs, use the event log to determine the service that failed. Then, to interact with the service, access the Administrative Tools section of Control Panel and choose Services. This starts up the Services console. You can right-click any service and choose to start, stop, pause, resume, or restart it. You can also double-click the service to access its properties and configure such things as the startup type, dependencies, and other variables.

If the service refuses to start, it could be that a service on which it depends will not start. To determine what services must be running for the problem service to start, select the Dependencies tab of the service's Properties dialog box, as shown in Figure 11.6.

FIGURE 11.6   Service dependencies

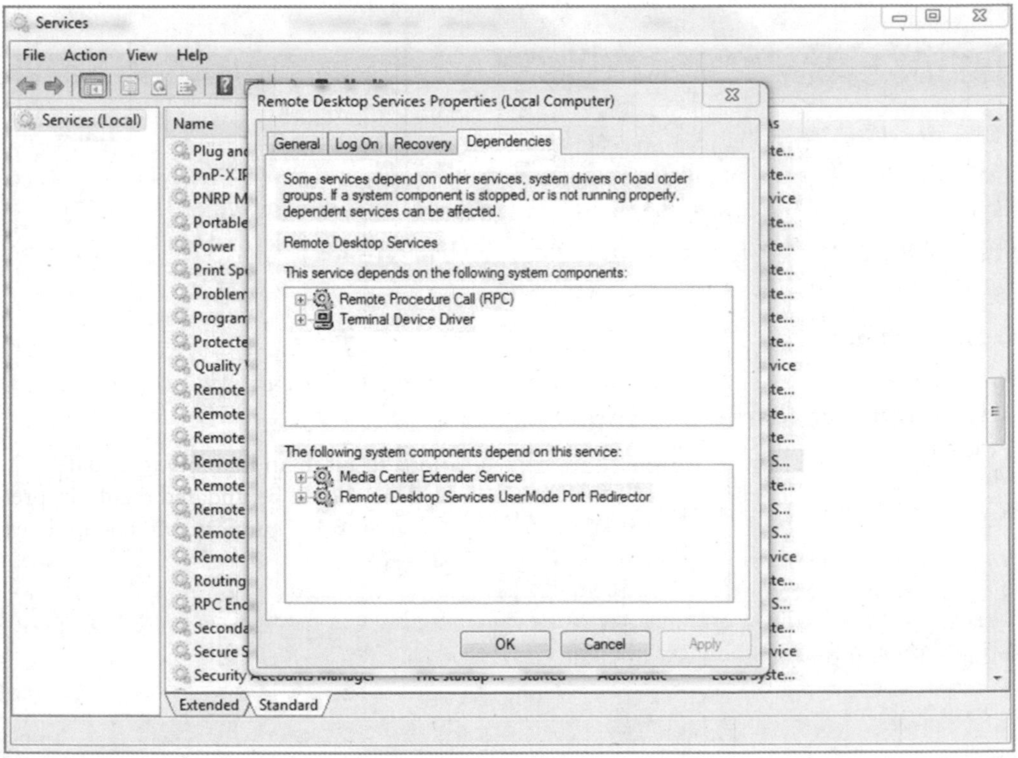

In the figure you can see that the Remote Desktop service depends on both the RPC and the Terminal Device Driver services to function. Try starting these services first. In some cases, you may need to trace the dependencies up several levels to get things going.

Orphan/Zombie

There are two types of service issues that deserve special attention. Let's take a look.

A *zombie* process (work performed on behalf of services is done using processes) is one that is a child of another process. It becomes a zombie when it completes its work but is mistakenly marked as a dead process, preventing it from ending.

An *orphan* process is a child process that remains running even after its parent process is terminated or completed without waiting for the child process to complete.

In either case, the orphan or zombie process will have to be ended manually.

Intrusion Detection Configurations

An intrusion detection system (IDS) is a system responsible for detecting unauthorized access or attacks. It can verify, itemize, and characterize threats from outside and inside the network. Most IDSs are programmed to react in certain ways in specific situations. Event notification and alerts are crucial to IDSs as these devices do not respond to or prevent attacks. These notifications and alerts inform administrators and security professionals when and where attacks are detected. The most common way to classify an IDS is based on its information source: network-based or host-based.

The most common IDS, a network-based IDS (NIDS), monitors network traffic on a local network segment. To monitor traffic on the network segment, the network interface card (NIC) must be operating in promiscuous mode. An NIDS can monitor only the network traffic. It cannot monitor any internal activity that occurs within a system, such as an attack against a system that is carried out by logging on to the system's local terminal. An NIDS is affected by a switched network because generally an NIDS monitors only a single network segment.

When these devices are misconfigured, the result will not be what you desire. Anyone supporting these should be trained in configuring and supporting them. Even when they are configured correctly, there can be errors. A false positive occurs when an event is identified as a threat when it is not. A false negative is even worse; it occurs when a threatening event is not identified. As you see, configuring these can be tricky and requires expert knowledge.

Anti-malware Configurations

Most issues that occur with anti-malware configurations result in an inability to update either the malware definitions or the malware engine. Both should be updated regularly, preferable on an automatic basis, which almost all enterprise products support. Missing updates are one of the biggest causes of malware outbreaks in a network. Although some threats (called zero-day threats) will occur before the vendor has developed a solution, outbreaks that occur due to missing updates should be viewed as a failure of your processes. You should develop procedures to ensure that updates occur.

Improperly Configured Local/Group Policies

When Group Policies are used to control security in an enterprise, an incomplete understanding of how Group Policies operate can result in actions being allowed that should not be allowed and actions being prevented that should not be prevented. Active Directory, the directory service used in Windows, has a hierarchal structure, and policy settings are inherited from one level to another in a specific way. When a machine starts up and is applying Group Policies, it applies them in this order:

- Domain
- Organizational unit (OU)
- Local

This means that policies on the local machine will overrule any at the OU level and any at the OU level will overrule any from the domain level. Further complicating this is the fact the user may have one set of policies applied while their computer may have another. So the system is ripe for misconfiguration by someone with an incomplete understanding of the inheritance process.

Fortunately, there is a tool that can help identity why a particular policy is not being applied to a device or user. The gpresult command is used to show the Resultant Set of Policy (RSoP) report/values for a remote user and computer. Bear in mind that configuration settings occur at any number of places. Often one of the big unknowns is which set of configuration settings takes precedence and which is overridden. With gpresult, it is possible to ascertain which settings apply. An example of the output is shown in Figure 11.7.

Improperly Configured Firewall Rules

When firewall rules are misconfigured, not only can it cause network connectivity issues, it can also create serious security issues. You learned earlier that the order of the rules in an ACL are sometimes critical to the proper operation of the ACL. This is another area where an incomplete understanding of the logic used by a particular firewall product can have disastrous and far-reaching results. Only technicians who have been trained in that product should be allowed to manage these ACLs.

Misconfigured Permissions

Earlier you learned that incomplete understanding of the inheritance of Group Policies can result in the policies either not being applied or being applied incorrectly. Because filesystem permissions also use inheritance, an opportunity also exists for issues with permissions. Most of the confusion when it comes to permissions involves the inheritance process, the interaction of various permissions that a user may have as a result of being a member of groups that may also have permissions, and the fact that there are two systems at work—the NTFS security system and the Share security system.

FIGURE 11.7   gpresult output

Allow vs. Deny

By default, the determination of NTFS permissions is based on the cumulative NTFS permissions for a user. Rights can be assigned to users based on group membership and individually; the only time permissions do not accumulate is when the Deny permission is invoked.

When NTFS permissions and share permissions come in conflict, the system will compare the combined NTFS permissions to the combined share permissions. The system will apply the most restrictive of these two.

Virus Infection

Sometimes despite all efforts a virus outbreak may occur. Even if you maintain all updates, the system will not be able to recognize or mitigate a zero-day attack. When this does occur, you should take certain steps to contain and eliminate the issue:

Recognize   Learn to recognize how a system reacts to malware.

Quarantine   Prevent malware from propagating.

Search and Destroy   Remove malware from infected systems.

Remediate   Return the system to normal after the malware is gone.

Educate   Train users to prevent malware outbreaks.

Malware

Malware is a category of software that performs malicious activities on a device. It might wipe the hard drive or create a backdoor. In this section we'll look at types of malware and attacks.

Trojan

Trojan horses are programs that enter a system or network under the guise of another program. A Trojan horse may be included as an attachment or as part of an installation program. The Trojan horse can create a backdoor or replace a valid program during installation. It then accomplishes its mission under the guise of another program. Trojan horses can be used to compromise the security of your system, and they can exist on a system for years before they're detected.

The best preventive measure for Trojan horses is not to allow them entry into your system. Immediately before and after you install a new software program or operating system, back it up! If you suspect a Trojan horse, you can reinstall the original programs, which should delete the Trojan horse. A port scan may also reveal a Trojan horse on your system. If an application opens a TCP or IP port that isn't supported in your network, you can track it down and determine which port is being used.

Rootkit

Rootkits have become the software exploitation program *du jour*. They are software programs that have the ability to hide certain things from the operating system. With a rootkit, there may be a number of processes running on a system that don't show up in Task Manager, or connections may be established/available that don't appear in a Netstat display—the rootkit masks the presence of these items. The rootkit does this by manipulating function calls to the operating system and filtering out information that would normally appear.

Unfortunately, many rootkits are written to get around antivirus and antispyware programs that aren't kept up-to-date. The best defense you have is to monitor what your system is doing and catch the rootkit in the process of installation.

Virus

Viruses can be classified as polymorphic, stealth, retroviruses, multipartite, armored, companion, phage, and macro viruses. Each type of virus has a different attack strategy and different consequences.

 Estimates for losses due to viruses are in the billions of dollars. These losses include financial loss as well as lost productivity.

The following sections will introduce the symptoms of a virus infection, explain how a virus works, and describe the types of viruses you can expect to encounter and how they generally behave. I'll also discuss how a virus is transmitted through a network.

Symptoms of a Virus/Malware Infection

Many viruses will announce that you're infected as soon as they gain access to your system. They may take control of your system and flash annoying messages on your screen or destroy your hard disk. When this occurs, you'll know that you're a victim. Other viruses will cause your system to slow down, cause files to disappear from your computer, or take over your disk space.

 Because viruses are the most common malware, the term *virus* is used in this section.

You should look for some of the following symptoms when determining whether a virus infection has occurred:

- The programs on your system start to load more slowly. This happens because the virus is spreading to other files in your system or is taking over system resources.

- Unusual files appear on your hard drive, or files start to disappear from your system. Many viruses delete key files in your system to render it inoperable.

- Program sizes change from the installed versions. This occurs because the virus is attaching itself to these programs on your disk.

- Your browser, word processing application, or other software begins to exhibit unusual operating characteristics. Screens or menus may change.

- The system mysteriously shuts itself down or starts itself up and does a great deal of unanticipated disk activity.

- You mysteriously lose access to a disk drive or other system resources. The virus has changed the settings on a device to make it unusable.

- Your system suddenly doesn't reboot or gives unexpected error messages during startup.

This list is by no means comprehensive. What is an absolute, however, is that you should immediately quarantine the infected system. It is imperative that you do all you can to contain the virus and keep it from spreading to other systems within your network or beyond.

How Viruses Work

A virus, in most cases, tries to accomplish one of two things: render your system inoperable or spread itself to other systems. Many viruses will spread to other systems given the chance and then render your system unusable. This is common with many of the newer viruses.

If your system is infected, the virus may try to attach itself to every file in your system and spread each time you send a file or document to other users. When you give removable media to another user or put it into another system, you then infect that system with the virus.

Most viruses today are spread using email. The infected system attaches a file to any email that you send to another user. The recipient opens this file, thinking it's something you legitimately sent them. When they open the file, the virus infects the target system. The virus might then attach itself to all the emails the newly infected system sends, which in turn infects the recipients of the emails. Figure 11.8 shows how a virus can spread from a single user to thousands of users in a short time using email.

FIGURE 11.8 An email virus spreading geometrically to other users

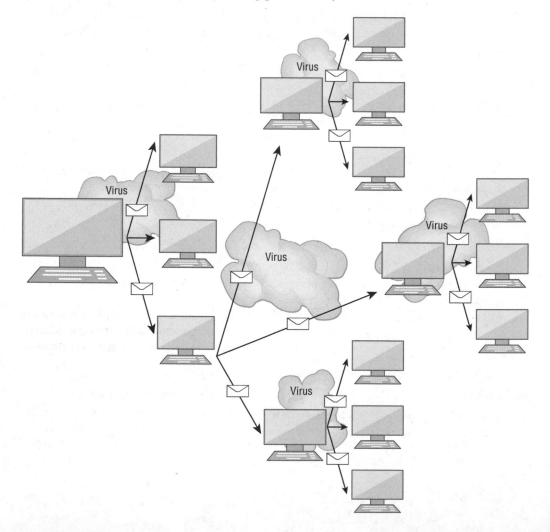

Types of Viruses

Viruses take many different forms. The following sections briefly introduce these forms and explain how they work. These are the most common types, but this isn't a comprehensive list.

> The best defense against a virus attack is to install and run antivirus software. The software should be on all workstations as well as the server.

Armored Virus

An armored virus is designed to make itself difficult to detect or analyze. Armored viruses cover themselves with protective code that stops debuggers or disassemblers from examining critical elements of the virus. The virus may be written in such a way that some aspects of the programming act as a decoy to distract analysis while the actual code hides in other areas in the program.

From the perspective of the creator, the more time it takes to deconstruct the virus, the longer it can live. The longer it can live, the more time it has to replicate and spread to as many machines as possible. The key to stopping most viruses is to identify them quickly and educate administrators about them—the very things that the armor intensifies the difficulty of accomplishing.

Companion Virus

A companion virus attaches itself to legitimate programs and then creates a program with a different filename extension. This file may reside in your system's temporary directory. When a user types the name of the legitimate program, the companion virus executes instead of the real program. This effectively hides the virus from the user. Many of the viruses that are used to attack Windows systems make changes to program pointers in the Registry so that they point to the infected program. The infected program may perform its dirty deed and then start the real program.

Macro Virus

A macro virus exploits the enhancements made to many application programs. Programmers can expand the capability of applications such as Microsoft Word and Excel. Word, for example, supports a mini-BASIC programming language that allows files to be manipulated automatically. These programs in the document are called macros. For example, a macro can tell your word processor to spell-check your document automatically when it opens. Macro viruses can infect all the documents on your system and spread to other systems via email or other methods.

Multipartite Virus

A multipartite virus attacks your system in multiple ways. It may attempt to infect your boot sector, infect all your executable files, and destroy your application files. The hope here is that you won't be able to correct all the problems and will allow the infestation to continue. The multipartite virus in Figure 11.9 attacks your boot sector, infects application files, and attacks your Word documents.

FIGURE 11.9 A multipartite virus commencing an attack on a system

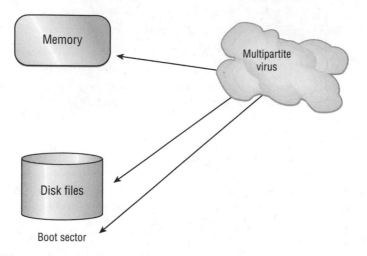

Phage Virus

A phage virus alters other programs and databases. The virus infects all these files. The only way to remove this virus is to reinstall the programs that are infected. If you miss even a single instance of this virus on the victim system, the process will start again and infect the system once more.

Polymorphic Virus

Polymorphic viruses change form in order to avoid detection. The virus will attempt to hide from your antivirus software. Frequently, the virus will encrypt parts of itself to avoid detection. When the virus does this, it's referred to as mutation. The mutation process makes it hard for antivirus software to detect common characteristics of the virus. Figure 11.10 shows a polymorphic virus changing its characteristics to avoid detection. In this example, the virus changes a signature to fool antivirus software.

 A signature is an algorithm or other element of a virus that uniquely identifies it. Because some viruses have the ability to alter their signature, it is crucial that you keep signature files current, whether you choose to manually download them or configure the antivirus engine to do so automatically.

Retrovirus

A retrovirus attacks or bypasses the antivirus software installed on a computer. You can consider a retrovirus to be an anti-antivirus. Retroviruses can directly attack your antivirus software and potentially destroy the virus definition database file. Destroying this information without your knowledge would leave you with a false sense of security. The virus may also directly attack an antivirus program to create bypasses for itself.

FIGURE 11.10   The polymorphic virus changing its characteristics

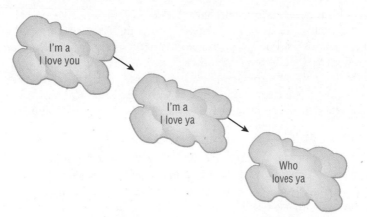

Stealth Virus

A stealth virus attempts to avoid detection by masking itself from applications. It may attach itself to the boot sector of the hard drive. When a system utility or program runs, the stealth virus redirects commands around itself to avoid detection. An infected file may report a file size different from what is actually present to avoid detection. Figure 11.11 shows a stealth virus attaching itself to the boot sector to avoid detection. Stealth viruses may also move themselves from file A to file B during a virus scan for the same reason.

FIGURE 11.11   A stealth virus hiding in a disk boot sector

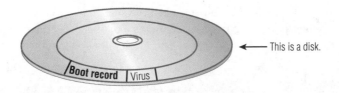

Present Virus Activity

New viruses and threats are released on a regular basis to join the cadre of those already in existence. From an exam perspective, you need to be familiar with the world only as it existed at the time the questions were written. From an administrative standpoint, however, you need to know what is happening today.

To find this information, visit the CERT/CC Current Activity web page at www.cisa.gov/ uscert/ncas/current-activity. Here you'll find a detailed description of the most current viruses as well as links to pages on older threats.

Spyware

Spyware differs from other malware in that it works—often actively—on behalf of a third party. Rather than self-replicating, like viruses and worms, spyware is spread to machines by users who inadvertently ask for it. The users often don't know they have asked for the spyware but have done so by downloading other programs, visiting infected sites, and so on.

The spyware program monitors the user's activity and responds by offering unsolicited pop-up advertisements (sometimes known as adware), gathers information about the user to pass on to marketers, or intercepts personal data such as credit card numbers.

Ransomware

Ransomware is a type of malware that usually encrypts the entire system or an entire drive with an encryption key that only the hacker possesses. Once they encrypt the machine, they will hold the data residing on the device hostage until a ransom is paid.

One version of this attack arrives as an attachment that appears to be a résumé. However, when the attachment is opened, the malware uses software called Cryptowall to encrypt the device. What usually follows is a demand for a large sum of money to decrypt the device.

Keylogger

A keylogger records everything typed and sends a record of this to the attacker. It can be implemented as a malicious software package, maybe even as part of a rootkit, or it may be a hardware device inserted between the keyboard and the USB port.

Boot Sector Virus

Earlier in this section you learned that many viruses can infect the boot sector of floppy disks or the Master Boot Record (MBR) of hard disks (some infect the boot sector of the hard disk instead of the MBR). The infected code runs when the system is booted. If the virus cannot be removed due to encryption or excessive damage to existing code, the hard drive may need reformatting to eliminate the infection.

Cryptominers

Cryptominers are tools that generate new units of a cryptocurrency like Bitcoin. Cryptomining isn't itself malicious in nature, but bad actors are illegally accessing important business assets such as servers to use their processing power to solve the mathematical puzzles required to mine. This consumes CPU cycles and increases the power usage in the datacenter. The result will be slower performance such as you might get from malware.

Rogue Processes/Services

Earlier you learned about orphan and zombie processes. Sometimes processes that normally would not be causing issues suddenly starts to consume large amounts of resources. These processes may be suffering from a leaky memory scenario (where the process refuses to release memory issued to it when a job is over), but it might also be malware. In this case the rogue process is the malware and it may even masquerade as a legitimate process.

When memory utilization goes up without a corresponding known increase in workload, it is usually an indication of malware. It makes complete sense if you think about it. The memory is being used by something and in this case it is the malware. Any instance of excessive memory utilization should be investigated to see if malware is the issue. Otherwise, you could have a faulty application that needs to be patched or replaced.

Data Loss Prevention (DLP)

Data loss prevention (DLP) software attempts to prevent data leakage. It does this by maintaining awareness of actions that can and cannot be taken with respect to a document. For example, DLP software might allow printing of a document but only at the company office. It might also disallow sending the document through email. DLP software uses ingress and egress filters to identify sensitive data that is leaving the organization and can prevent such leakage. Another scenario might be the release of product plans that should be available only to the Sales group. You could set the following policy for that document:

- It cannot be emailed to anyone other than Sales group members.
- It cannot be printed.
- It cannot be copied.

Security Tools

Just as you have many networking tools available to troubleshoot network connectivity issues, you also have an impressive set available to you for security issues. These tools allow you to gain the same visibility a hacker might have so you can make any required changes to maintain a secure network. In this section we'll survey the most common of these tools.

Port Scanners

Internet Control Message Protocol (ICMP) messages can be used to scan a network for open ports. Open ports indicate services that may be running and listening on a device that may be susceptible to attack. An ICMP, or port scanning, attack basically pings every address and port number combination and keeps track of which ports are open on each device as the pings are answered by open ports with listening services and not answered by closed ports. One of the most widely used port scanners is Network Mapper (Nmap), a free and open source utility for network discovery and security auditing. Figure 11.12 shows the output of a scan using Zenmap, an Nmap security scanner GUI. Starting in line 12 of the output shown in this figure, you can see that the device at 10.68.26.11 has seven ports open:

```
Discovered open port 139/tcp on 10.68.26.11
```

Figure 11.13 shows output from the command-line version of Nmap. You can see in this figure that a ping scan of an entire network just completed. You can see that the computer at 172.16.153.242 has three ports open: 23, 443, and 8443. However, the computer at 172.16.153.253 has no open ports. The term *filtered* in the output means that the ports are not open. To obtain this output, the command `Nmap 172.16.153.0/23` was executed, instructing the scan to include all computers in the 172.16.153.0/23 network.

FIGURE 11.12 Zenmap

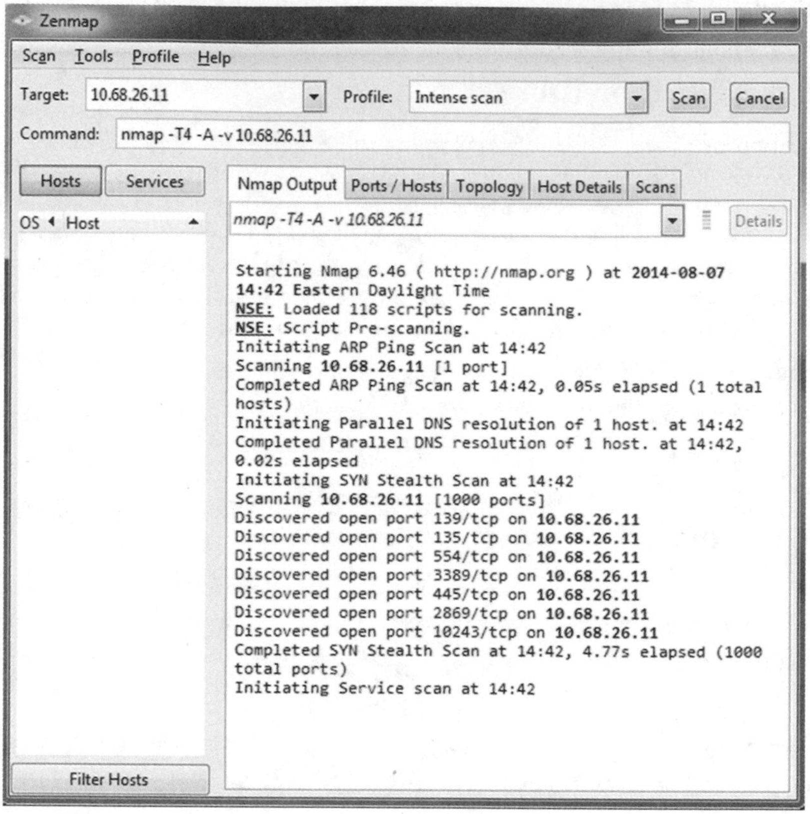

FIGURE 11.13 nmap command line

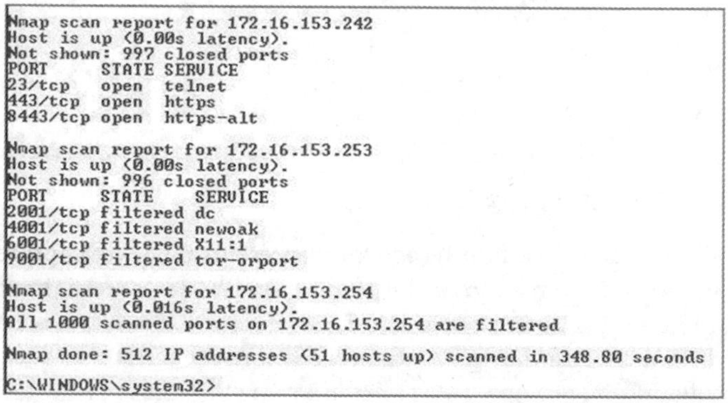

In a scenario where you need to determine what applications and services are running on the devices in your network, a port scanner would be appropriate. It also allows you to identify any open ports that should not be open.

Sniffers

Sniffing is the process of capturing packets for analysis; sniffing used maliciously is referred to as *eavesdropping*. Sniffing occurs when an attacker attaches or inserts a device or software into the communication medium to collect all the information transmitted over the medium. Sniffers, called *protocol analyzers*, collect raw packets from the network; both legitimate security professionals and attackers use them. The fact that a sniffer does what it does without transmitting any data to the network is an advantage when the tool is being used legitimately and a disadvantage when it is being used against you (because you cannot tell you are being sniffed). Organizations should monitor and limit the use of sniffers. To protect against their use, encrypt all traffic on the network.

One of the most widely used sniffers is Wireshark. It captures raw packets off the interface on which it is configured and allows you to examine each packet. If the data is unencrypted, you will be able to read the data. Figure 11.14 shows an example of Wireshark in use.

FIGURE 11.14 Wireshark

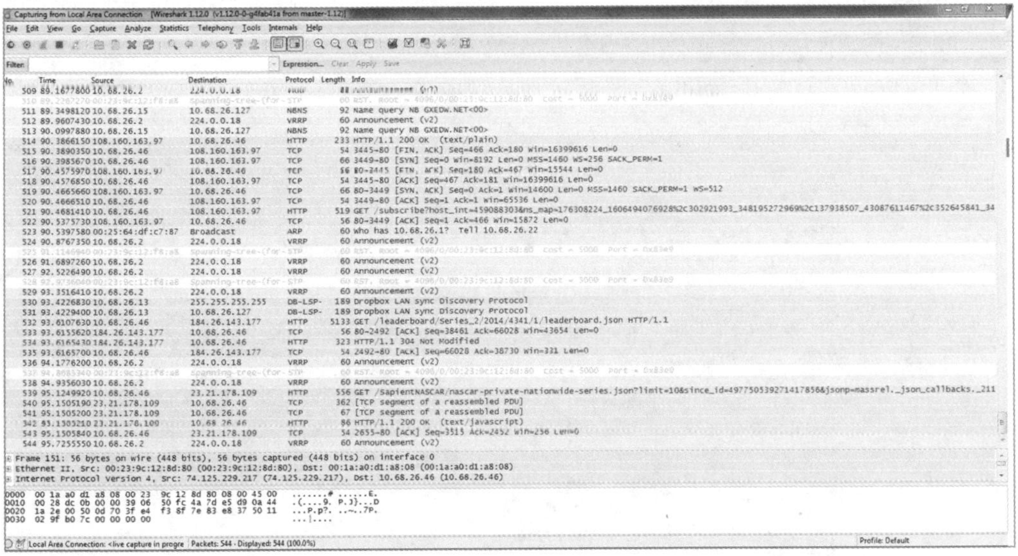

In the output shown in Figure 11.14, each line represents a packet captured on the network. You can see the source IP address, the destination IP address, the protocol in use, and the information in the packet. For example, line 511 shows a packet from 10.68.26.15 to 10.68.16.127, which is a NetBIOS name resolution query. Line 521 shows an HTTP packet from 10.68.26.46 to a server at 108.160.163.97. Just after that, you can see that the server is sending an acknowledgment back. To try to read the packet, you would click on the single packet. If the data were cleartext, you would be able to read and analyze it. So you can see how an attacker could acquire credentials and other sensitive information.

Protocol analyzers can be of help whenever you need to see what is really happening on your network. For example, say you have a security policy that says certain types of traffic should be encrypted. But you are not sure that everyone is complying with this policy. By capturing and viewing the raw packets on the network, you would be able to determine whether they are.

Telnet Clients

Although a Telnet client comes on every Windows machine, the client is not installed by default. It is a handy tool to have because it allows you to connect to a device at the command line and work at the command line. You should know, however, that Telnet transmits in cleartext so you would not want to use it to perform any sensitive operations (like changing a password). In Exercise 11.3 you will install the Telnet client in a Windows 10 computer.

EXERCISE 11.3

Installing the Telnet Client

1. Right-click the Start menu and select Programs And Features.

2. In the Programs And Features window, select Turn Windows Features On Or Off, as shown here:

3. In the Turn Windows Features On Or Off page, scroll down until you see the Telnet client, as shown here:

| Windows Features | — □ ✕ |

Turn Windows features on or off   ❓

To turn a feature on, select its check box. To turn a feature off, clear its check box. A filled box means that only part of the feature is turned on.

- ☐ RIP Listener
- ⊞ ☐ Simple Network Management Protocol (SNMP)
- ☐ Simple TCPIP services (i.e. echo, daytime etc)
- ☑ SMB 1.0/CIFS File Sharing Support
- ☐ Telnet Client
- ☐ TFTP Client
- ☐ Windows Identity Foundation 3.5
- ⊞ ☑ Windows PowerShell 2.0
- ⊞ ☐ Windows Process Activation Service
- ☐ Windows TIFF IFilter
- ☑ Work Folders Client
- ☑ XPS Services

  OK   Cancel

4. Check the box next to Telnet Client and then click OK. The client will be installed and you will be notified when the installation is complete. You can now use it at the command line to connect to a remote machine by its IP address.

Anti-malware/Antivirus

The primary method of preventing the propagation of malicious code involves the use of *anti-malware software*. This category includes antivirus, antispyware, and antispam software.

Antivirus software is an application that is installed on a system to protect it and to scan for viruses as well as worms and Trojan horses. Most viruses have characteristics that are common to families of virus. Antivirus software looks for these characteristics, or fingerprints, to identify and neutralize viruses before they affect you.

2021 saw the highest average cost of a data breach in 17 years, with the cost rising from US$3.86 million to US$4.24 million on an annual basis. New types of malware are added all the time. Your antivirus software manufacturer will usually work hard to keep the definition database files current. The definition database file contains all the known viruses and countermeasures for a particular antivirus software product. You probably won't receive a virus that hasn't been seen by one of these companies. If you keep the virus definition database files in your software up-to-date, you probably won't be overly vulnerable to attacks.

The best method of protection is to use a layered approach. Antivirus software should be installed at the gateways, at the servers, and at the desktop. If you want to go one step further, you can use software at each location from different vendors to make sure you're covered from all angles.

File Integrity

When a file has integrity, it means that the file has not been altered in an unauthorized manner. It is important to know that files you receive have not been altered en route because they could have been converted to malware with the same filename! In this section we'll talk about ensuring file integrity.

Checksums

Checksums are values that can be calculated based on the contents of a file that can be used later to verify that the file has not changed. There are a number of tools that can do this, such as the Microsoft File Checksum Integrity Verifier. Many third-party tools can be used to create checksums that can be verified at a later time.

Monitoring

One of the ways to monitor integrity issues with system files is to use a file-checking utility. In Chapter 10, "Troubleshooting Hardware and Software Issues," you learned about System File Checker (SFC), which is designed for this purpose. Please review that section.

Detection

Another tool that can be used for detecting integrity issues is Tripwire. You can use this in either Linux or Windows. While this requires you to take a hash of all of critical files (and update it each time you update the system) it checks the hash of the files to ensure they have not changed since you generated the hash value.

Enforcement

Some systems such as databases have the ability to enforce integrity by establishing rules about the changing of data in the database. Here's an example: numeric columns/cells in a table should be restricted to accept alphabetic data. Also only a single user can access an object at a time. Moreover, if a failure occurs during a transaction and it is not committed, it is rolled back. These rules can't address all integrity issues, but they help prevent some types of integrity issues.

User Access Controls

Controlling user access to resources has always been a tough job, but there are new tools that make this job easier. In this section we'll look at two tools that can prevent privilege escalations and other issues.

SELinux

Security-Enhanced Linux (SELinux) is a Linux kernel security module that, when added to the Linux kernel, separates enforcement of security decisions from the security policy itself and streamlines the amount of software involved with security policy enforcement.

SELinux also enforces mandatory access control policies that confine user programs and system servers, and it limits access to files and network resources. It has no concept of a "root" superuser and does not share the well-known shortcomings of the traditional Linux security mechanisms. In high-security scenarios, where the sandboxing of the root account is beneficial, the SELinux system should be chosen over regular versions of Linux.

User Account Control (UAC)

Administrator and root accounts are the most highly privileged accounts in an operating system. When a server is left logged on with a privileged account, it creates a huge security issue. Most of the server operating systems you will encounter today incorporate the ability of an administrator or a root account holder to use a nonprivileged account as standard operating procedure and elevate their privileges as needed without logging off and logging back in as root.

The User Account Control feature in Windows and the use of the sudo command in Linux make this possible. Using either system an administrator can elevate their privileges for a specific task and that security context ends when they are finished with that task.

In Windows this can be done in the GUI by right-clicking the icon representing the task and selecting Run As Administrator, as shown in Figure 11.15.

FIGURE 11.15   Run As Administrator

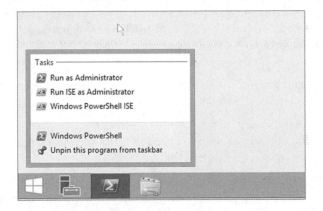

At the command line in Windows, you can accomplish the same thing by prefacing the command with the runas command, as shown here, opening the command prompt as administrator:

```
runas /user:troym@mcmillan.com\administrator cmd
```

Summary

In this chapter you learned about some of the common issues that prevent network connectivity, among them email failures, Internet failures, and DNS failures. You also learned many of the causes of these issues, such as misconfigured VLANs, improper subnetting, and

DHCP failures. You were also exposed to some of the tools that you can use to troubleshoot these issues.

Security misconfigurations can also cause connectivity issues. You learned that this can lead to an inability to open files, applications that will not load, and privilege escalations. We also discussed the causes of these issues, such as misconfigured policies and permission, firewall rules, and rogue processes. Finally, we covered the tools you can use to troubleshoot security-related issues, such as port scanners, sniffers, and checksum tools.

Exam Essentials

Identify common connectivity issues.   This includes Internet connectivity failures, email failures, a misconfigured DHCP server, destination host unreachable messages, unknown host messages, a misconfigured default gateway, failure of the service provider, and inability to reach a host by name/FQDN.

Identify common causes of connectivity issues.   Describe common causes such as improper IP configuration, VLAN configuration, port security, improper subnetting, component failure, incorrect OS route tables, bad cables, firewall misconfiguration hardware failure, software failure, misconfigured NICs, routing/switch issues, DNS and/or DHCP failure, misconfigured Hosts file, and IPv4 vs. IPv6 misconfigurations.

List common command-line tools.   Tools include ping, tracert/traceroute, ipconfig/ifconfig, nslookup, net use/mount, route, nbtstat, and netstat.

Identify common security issues.   These include file integrity issues, privilege escalation, applications that will not load, inability to access network file/shares, inability to open files, excessive access, and excessive memory utilization.

Identify common causes of security issues.   Causes include open ports, active services, inactive services, intrusion detection configurations, anti-malware configurations, local/Group Policies, firewall rules, misconfigured permissions, virus infections, and rogue processes/services.

List common tools.   Among these are port scanners, sniffers, cipher, checksums, Telnet clients, and anti-malware.

Review Questions

You can find the answers in the Appendix.

1. Which of the following addresses is used to test the functionality of the NIC?
   A. 0.0.0.0
   B. 127.0.0.1
   C. 255.255.255.255
   D. 0.0.0.1

2. Which of the following is *not* the proper application of a crossover cable?
   A. From one computer to another
   B. From a computer to a switch
   C. From a switch to a router
   D. From a switch to a switch

3. Which of the following attempts to avoid detection by masking itself from applications?
   A. Multipartite virus
   B. Stealth virus
   C. Armored virus
   D. Zero-day threat

4. Which of the following commands clears the local DNS cache?
   A. `ipconfig/flushdns`
   B. `flushdns`
   C. `cache/flushdns`
   D. `ipconfig/flush`

5. Which of the following should be the same on all devices in the same subnet?
   A. IP address
   B. Subnet mask
   C. Hostname
   D. FQDN

6. Which of the following are programs that enter a system or network under the guise of another program?
   A. Middleware
   B. Worms
   C. Trojans
   D. Viruses

7. To monitor traffic on the network segment, the network interface card (NIC) must be operating in what mode?

   A. Promiscuous

   B. Active

   C. Passive

   D. Autosense

8. Which of the following are APs that you do not control and manage?

   A. Fat AP

   B. Thin AP

   C. Rogue AP

   D. NIDAP

9. Which of the following would not be a cause of an inability to connect to the Internet?

   A. The IP address of the computer

   B. The MAC address of the computer

   C. The default gateway address of the computer

   D. The DNS server address of the computer

10. Which of the following commands could be used to see if HTTP is working on a server?

   A. `telnet 192.168.5.5`

   B. `ping 192.168.5.5 :80`

   C. `telnet 192.168.5.65 80`

   D. `pathping 192.168.5.5`

11. What is the code number of a destination unreachable message when it indicates the destination host is unreachable?

   A. 0

   B. 1

   C. 2

   D. 3

12. You receive a destination unreachable message with no source IP address. Where is it coming from?

   A. A remote router

   B. A remote DNS server

   C. A local DNS server

   D. The local router

13. When the default gateway address is incorrect on the router, which connections will succeed?

    A. From a local device to a remote device

    B. From a remote device to a local device

    C. From a local device to the Internet

    D. From a local device to a local device

14. Which server could be the source of an inability to connect to a local host by name?

    A. NAT server

    B. SQL server

    C. DNS server

    D. Web server

15. At what layer of the OSI model are devices in different VLANs separated?

    A. Layer 1

    B. Layer 2

    C. Layer 4

    D. Layer 7

16. Which of the following features can be used to prevent unauthorized devices from connecting to a switch?

    A. NAT

    B. Port security

    C. Portfast

    D. Cipher

17. Which of the following processes completes its work but is mistakenly marked as a dead process, preventing it from ending?

    A. Inactive process

    B. Orphan process

    C. Zombie process

    D. Active process

18. Which of the following features can administrators use to create smaller networks called subnets by manipulating the subnet mask of a larger classless or major network?

    A. NAT

    B. CIDR

    C. DHCP

    D. DNS

19. What command is used on a router to identify the routes of which the router is aware?

A. `show ip route`

B. `show route`

C. `route print`

D. `show ip route`

20. Which commands are used on a router to identify the path taken to a destination network? (Choose two.)

A. `traceroute`

B. `tracert`

C. `ipconfig/trace`

D. `trace`

Chapter 12

Troubleshooting Storage Issues

COMPTIA SERVER+ EXAM OBJECTIVES COVERED IN THIS CHAPTER:

✓ **4.3 Given a scenario, troubleshoot storage problems.**

- Common problems
    - Boot errors
    - Sector block errors
    - Cache battery failure
    - Read/write errors
    - Failed drives
    - Page/swap/scratch file or partition
    - Partition errors
    - Slow file access
    - OS not found
    - Unsuccessful backup
    - Unable to mount the device
    - Drive not available
    - Cannot access logical drive
    - Data corruption
    - Slow I/O performance
    - Restore failure
    - Cache failure
    - Multiple drive failure
- Causes of common problems
    - Disk space utilization
        - Insufficient disk space

- Misconfigured RAID
- Media failure
- Drive failure
- Controller failure
- Hot bus adapter (HBA) failure
- Loose connectors
- Cable problems
- Misconfiguration
- Corrupt boot sector
- Corrupt filesystem table
- Array rebuild
- Improper disk partition
- Bad sectors
- Cache battery failure
- Cache turned off
- Insufficient space
- Improper RAID configuration
- Mismatched drives
- Backplane failure
- Tools and techniques
  - Partitioning tools
  - Disk management
  - RAID and array management
  - System logs
  - Disk mounting commands
    - net use
    - mount
  - Monitoring tools
  - Visual inspections
    - Auditory inspections

Since long-term storage is where all the data resides, issues that prevent access to storage can prevent business processes from moving forward. Therefore, you should pay close attention to troubleshooting storage problems. As storage can be presented to the servers in various ways, some issues are technology-specific whereas others apply to any type of storage. In this chapter, common storage problems will be discussed along with possible causes. We'll also survey various tools that can be used to deploy, manage, and troubleshoot storage systems.

Given a Scenario, Troubleshoot Storage Problems

Although experience will expose you to most of the storage issues covered in this chapter, your value to the server support team and the organization in general will be greatly enhanced by your study of and preparation to address these issues. This section will describe signs of storage issues and the potential underlying causes of these issues.

Common Problems

You may never experience some of the following issues, but there are some that will return time and again. As you gain experience addressing these more common issues, you will begin to make consistent connections between the causes and the issues. Until that time, you must rely on the application of the troubleshooting method covered in Chapter 10, "Troubleshooting Hardware and Software Issues," and a clear understanding of the common problems discussed in this section.

Boot Errors

When multiple volumes or partitions exist on the computer or there are multiple hard drives and maybe CD/DVD and floppy drives as well, there are multiple potential sources for the boot files. If the system delivers an "operating system not found" message, it could be that the system is looking in the wrong location for the boot files.

The boot order is set in the BIOS. Check the boot order and ensure that it is set to boot to the partition, volume, and hard drive where the boot files are located. When the system is running down the list of potential sources of boot files, in all other cases if it looks in a location and finds no boot files, it will move on to the next location in the list. However, if a floppy is in the floppy drive and it checks the floppy drive and no boot files are present, it does not proceed but stops and issues the nonsystem disk message.

Failure to Boot

A failure of the system to boot can be caused by a number of issues:

- Failure of the system to locate the boot files.

- If you are presented with an "IDE drive not ready" message at startup, the drive may not be spinning fast enough to be read during startup. Enable or increase the hard disk pre-delay time. This setting is found in the BIOS settings where you can set a boot order.

- If you receive the message "Immediately back up all your data and replace your hard drive. A fault may be imminent," take it seriously. This means the drive is using Self-Monitoring, Analysis, and Reporting Technology (SMART) to predict a failure.

- The hard drive data or power cable may have become unseated. Sometimes even if the cable appears to be seated fine, reseating it can have a positive effect. Also ensure that the data cable has not been reversed.

Sector Block Errors

Many filesystems like NTFS are designed to identify bad sectors and to discontinue using those sectors to store information. In some cases, you may need to manually mark sectors as bad. To run a scan, use the following procedure:

1. Open This PC, right-click on System Drive, and choose Properties.

2. Go to Tools, and then click Check. Click Check under Error-Checking.

3. Review the scan result, then click Scan And Repair Drive.

4. Choose when to repair the filesystem. Wait for Windows 10 to scan and repair the hard drive bad sectors. If there are no issues, you will see the message box in Figure 12.1.

Cache Battery Failure

RAID arrays often use caching to improve performance. A battery-backed cache is one that can maintain the data in the cache during a power outage, preventing the loss of data still residing in the cache at the moment of the power failure. When this battery fails, it can cause the loss of data.

To change the battery, you must first put the battery in an error state. You can do so after powering on the device and using the tools provided with the operating system to force the battery into the error state. Even if you think that process went well, do *not* remove the battery if the Cache Present LED is flashing because that indicates data is still present in the cache. When the light is out, you can remove the cover and replace the battery. Use the tools to start the write cache again.

FIGURE 12.1 Scanning for errors

Cache Turned Off

Several methods are available that a server can use to cache information that it is preparing to send to long-term storage. The most beneficial to performance is a method called write-back cache. In this method, write I/O is directed to cache and completion is immediately confirmed to the host. This results in low latency and high throughput for write-intensive applications, but there is data availability exposure risk because the only copy of the written data is in cache.

When the cache is turned off, you lose all of those performance benefits. Cache can be enabled in both the operating system and in the storage software. While it must be done in both places, typically when you set it in the storage software it will be reflected in the settings in Windows as well, but it's always worth checking. In Windows Server 2022 this is done in the properties of the storage device in Device Manager, as shown in Figure 12.2.

FIGURE 12.2   Enabling write-back cache in Windows

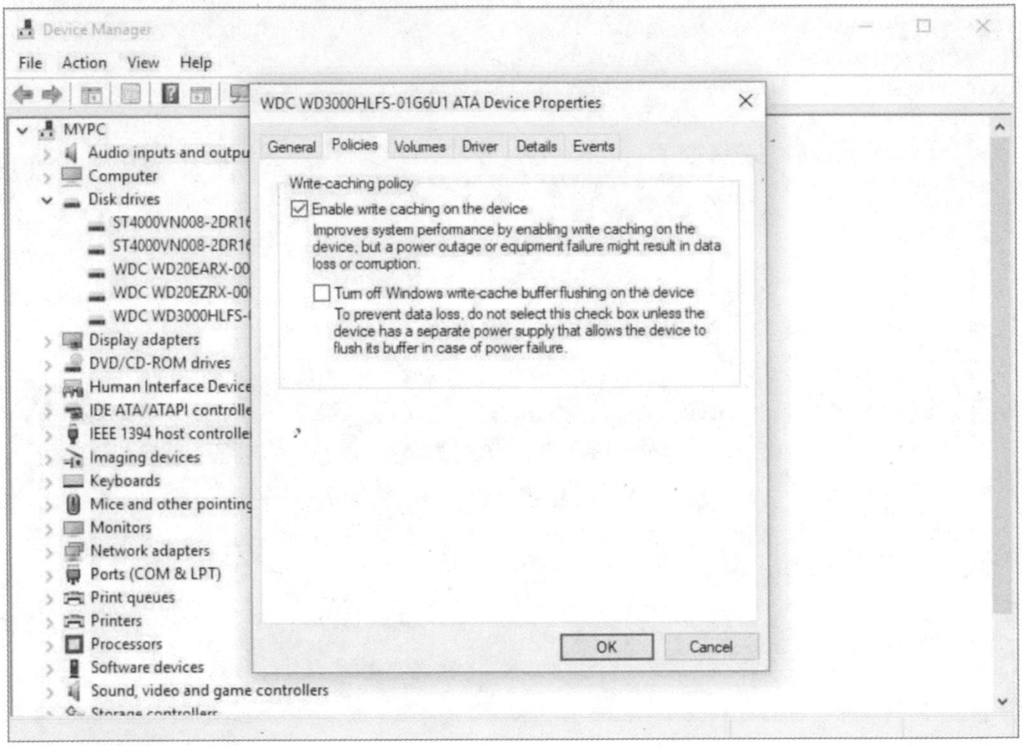

Read/Write Errors

Read/write failures occur when areas of the hard drive require repeated attempts before successful reads or writes occur. This is because these areas are at least partially damaged, although perhaps not enough for these areas to be marked as bad sectors.

Failed Drives

It has been said that it is not a matter of whether a hard drive will fail but rather when it will fail. Hard drives typically exhibit symptoms before they fail. Learning to read these clues is critical to troubleshooting. Review all the symptoms and solutions found in this chapter. Keep in mind that once a drive fails you may never be able to recover data that was on the failed drive. Make regular backups.

Page/Swap/Scratch File or Partition

In Chapter 2, "Installing and Configuring Servers," you learned that today's operating systems support the use of swap files. Let's review. Swap are files located on the hard drive that are utilized temporarily to hold items moved from memory when there is a shortage of memory required for a particular function. The running programs believe that their information is still in RAM, but the OS has moved the data to the hard drive. When the application needs the information again, it is swapped back into RAM so that the processor can use it. Providing adequate space for this file is a key disk management issue. Every operating system seems to have its own recommendations as to the optimum size of this file, but in all cases the swap file should be on a different drive than the operating system if possible.

Issues with the page or swap file or partition can sometimes be avoided by monitoring certain memory and disk metrics. Among them are:

Memory\Free System Page Table Entries   The number of entries in the page table not currently in use by the system. If the number is less than 5,000, there may be a memory leak. (Memory leaks occur when an application is issued memory that is not returned to the system. Over time this drains the server of memory.)

Memory\Pool Nonpaged Bytes   The size, in bytes, of the nonpaged pool, which contains objects that cannot be paged to the disk. If the value is greater than 175 MB, you may have a memory leak (an application is not releasing its allocated memory when it is done).

Memory\Pool Paged Bytes   The size, in bytes, of the paged pool, which contains objects that can be paged to disk. (If this value is greater than 250 MB, there may be a memory leak.)

Memory\Pages per Second   The rate at which pages are written to and read from the disk during paging. If the value is greater than 1,000 as a result of excessive paging, there may be a memory leak.

Page_Fault_in_nonpaged_area   This is another message that can be the result of adding faulty hardware or of hardware (usually memory of some type) going bad. Use the hardware diagnostics provided with the system to gain more information about the error. And as always, if you just added something, remove it and test the results.

Partition Errors

Partition errors can be dealt with in the same manner as sector block errors. You can use the Graphical User Interface (GUI)-based Check Disk option in the properties of the drive, but you can also do this from the command line using chkdsk. One of the advantages of the command-line version is that you can schedule a batch file to perform chkdsk on a regular basis.

1. Press the Windows key and type **cmd**.

2. Right-click Command Prompt and choose Run As Administrator.

3. Enter the following command:

   `chkdsk E: /f /r /x`

   (*E* represents the drive letter of the partition you want to repair.)
   This command will run chkdsk to check and repair disk errors in Windows 10.

While Check Disk and its command-line version chkdsk can be used to identify and repair partition errors, many find that some third-party partition tools offer functions not available with the default tools. Some examples are:

- MiniTool Partition Wizard
- AOMEI Partition Assistant Standard Edition
- Tenorshare Partition Manager

Slow File Access

Another symptom of hard drive issues is slow access to the drive. Oddly, one of the potential causes of this is insufficient memory. When this is the case, it causes excessive paging. Another cause can be a drive that needs to be defragmented. A fragmented drive results in it taking much longer for all the parts of a file to be located before the file will open. Other issues that cause slow performance are controller cards that need updating, improper data cables, and slower devices sharing the same cable with the hard drive.

OS Not Found

When you receive the "operating system not found" message, it's usually a software error rather than a hardware error. It could be that the master boot record or the active partition cannot be located. These issues can be corrected in Windows by rebooting the computer into Recovery mode and executing one of several commands at the command line of the Recovery environment. See the "Boot Errors" section earlier in this chapter.

In Linux and Unix, this issue can be caused by a missing or misconfigured GRUB. You will learn more about GRUB later in this chapter.

Boot problems can also occur with corruption of the boot files or missing components. Luckily, during the installation of the OS, log files are created in the %SystemRoot% or %SystemRoot%\Debug folder (C:\WINNT and C:\WINNT\DEBUG or C:\Windows and C:\Windows\Debug, depending on the operating system). If you have a puzzling problem, look at these logs to see whether you can find error entries there. They are primarily helpful during installation. For routine troubleshooting, you can activate boot logging by selecting Enable Boot Logging from the Windows Advanced Options menu (access the menu by turning on your computer and pressing the F8 key before Windows starts) to create an ntbtlog.txt log file in the %systemroot% folder.

Unsuccessful Backup

Most backup processes occur with no issues, but occasionally a backup will fail. This is a serious issue especially if it isn't discovered until you need to restore the data. There are many reasons for unsuccessful backups. In some cases, it is because some files could not be backed up because they were moved from the original location to some other location. In Windows, when using an automatic backup if you choose to remove unused library or folder locations this will sometimes solve this issue. Failures can also occur in these cases:

- If your computer is off, sleeping, or hibernating.
- If the backup destination isn't available.

- If the backup destination is a network location and it's not available or your network credentials have expired.

- If the backup destination is encrypted by BitLocker, it needs to be unlocked when it's time for your scheduled backup.

Unable to Mount the Device

If a device cannot be mounted, it cannot be accessed by the system. This can result from having no formatted partition or volume on the device or from filesystem corruption on the device. In Windows, you can try running Check Disk to attempt to repair any errors on the drive. Another possibility is to back up the data on the external device from a different system, format the drive again, and restore the data. This issue seems to happen most frequently when devices with NTFS partitions are introduced to Unix and Linux systems. Keep in mind that these systems only have native support for NTFS with versions 5.15 and above. An example is installing fuserfs-ntfs in Free BSD.

Drive Not Available

The "drive not available" message indicates the local or remote drive to which you are attempting to connect cannot be reached. Although it can always be a network issue in the case of a remote drive, there can be other reasons as well.

If the drive is local, one of the following can be the issue:

- The hard drive data or power cable may have become unseated. Sometimes even if the cable appears to be seated fine, reseating it can have a positive effect. Also ensure that the data cable has not been reversed.

- If you just added a drive, ensure that both drives have not been set to primary or secondary and that the boot drive is set as primary on the first channel.

- If the system uses serial ATA and you just added a drive, ensure that all of the onboard SATA ports are enabled.

- If you just added a drive, ensure that there is no conflict between the new drive and another device.

- If you receive the "No boot device available, strike F1 to retry boot, F2 for setup utility" message, it could be incorrect drive geometry (which is probably not the case if this drive has been functioning properly before), a bad CMOS battery, or an inability to locate the active partition or master boot record.

In the case of remote drives, any changes in the permissions associated with the drive may cause the problem as well.

Cannot Access Logical Drive

When a logical drive cannot be accessed, the error message could come in several forms since the issue can be from several sources. The two main issues that cause an inability to access a logical drive are corruption of the drive (bad sectors, for example) and encryption of the drive.

In Windows, if the error message says "Data error (cyclical redundancy check)," it could be either of these issues. First try turning off BitLocker on the drive. Then follow these steps:

1. Press Windows key+X, and select Control Panel.

2. Click the View By option at the top right and set it to Large Icons.

3. Click BitLocker Drive Encryption and then expand the options for the system drive (usually the C drive).

4. Click Turn Off BitLocker and check if you are able to access the drive.

If the drive is not encrypted or you still get an error message after turning off BitLocker, use Check Disk to attempt to locate and repair any bad sectors.

In cases where the operating system of a device must be reinstalled, there will sometimes be issues accessing the existing logical drives after the reinstallation of the operating system to its previous partition. If this occurs and the problem partition appears in Disk Management with a name rather than a drive letter, assign it a drive letter and that usually solves the issue. Of course, this issue can be avoided entirely by always backing up data.

In some cases, none of these methods will allow access to the drive. There are recovery tools such as Wondershare Recoverit Data Recovery that may allow you to at least recover the data off the drive. In that case, you will need to delete it and re-create it, and then restore the data afterward.

Data Corruption

Data corruption is also a possibility when data is being written to and read from a drive and when data is being transferred within a system and between systems. If even a single bit in a file is altered at any time, the data will no longer pass the CRC check and will be considered by the system to be corrupted.

So how does corruption occur? There are a number of ways:

-   Failure to eject external hard drives and related storage devices before disconnecting them or powering them off

-   Power outages or other power-related problems

-   Hardware problems or failures, including hard drive failures, bad sectors, bad RAM, and the like

-   Bad programming, particularly if it results in either hard restarts or data that is saved incorrectly

-   Improper shutdowns, like those caused by power outages or by performing a hard restart, pressing and holding the power button, or on Macs so equipped, the restart button

If the corrupted files are system files, the system may not even boot. If this is the case, try performing one of the system repair processes, which will check the integrity of all system files and replace any bad ones.

In Linux, you can use the `fsck` command to make a repair attempt. For example, the following command will check the sda1 partition:

```
fsck /dev/sda1
```

It is important to note that this command should *not* be used on a mounted drive. If you do so, you run the risk of damaging the filesystem and making the issue worse. If you want `fsck` to attempt to repair any errors it finds, add the -a or -y parameter after the command, as shown here for the same partition:

```
fsck -a /dev/sda1
```

Of course, if these recovery procedures are not useful, you can restore the data from backup.

Slow I/O Performance

Slow disk access can have a number or sources, some that may surprise you. While the actual disk itself may be the problem, it can also be low memory and CPU issues that manifest themselves as slow I/O.

The root of the problem can be found by using the Linux command `top`. While this command doesn't work in Windows, you can create a PowerShell script that will yield the same information. First let's look at the command output in Linux shown in Figure 12.3.

FIGURE 12.3 top output

```
top - 00:23:58 up 8 min,  2 users,  load average: 0.36, 0.55, 0.28
Tasks: 118 total,   3 running, 115 sleeping,   0 stopped,   0 zombie
Cpu(s):  6.0%us,  2.0%sy,  0.0%ni, 92.0%id,  0.0%wa,  0.0%hi,  0.0%si,  0.0%
Mem:   1026436k total,   478668k used,   547768k free,    15692k buffers
Swap:  1646620k total,        0k used,  1646620k free,   216820k cached
```

In this output, you are interested in six values:

- CPU% time
- Idle time
- I/O wait time
- Swap usage
- Memory usage
- Memory cached

In this example, the values are as follows:

- CPU% time: 6%
- Idle time: 92% (a high value is good)
- I/O wait time: 0% (anything above 10% is an issue)
- Swap usage: 1646620k
- Memory usage: 478668k
- Memory cached: 218620k

Other issues are indicated by the following combinations of values:

- I/O wait and idle time are low: A single process (probably the application in use) is causing the issue and should be killed.

- I/O wait time is low and idle time is high: This is caused by an application or an external process the server is waiting on.

- I/O wait time is high: Check the swap usage; if high, this is probably a memory issue.

- I/O wait time is high: Check the swap usage; if low, this is probably not a memory issue. Some process is hogging the I/O.

- High memory usage: Subtract the cached memory from the used memory to get this value. If this is an anomaly, it is an offending process that must be killed. If it is constantly high, you need more memory.

So in summary, a real I/O issue is only indicated when I/O is high, use of swap is low, and use of memory is high. If you need to create a PowerShell script for this process, run this command:

```
while (1) { ps | sort -desc cpu | select -first 30; sleep -seconds 2; cls }
```

The output will be different but the same information is displayed.

I/O Failure

I/O errors are typically related to the system reading or writing to its storage. An I/O error can occur with different types of hardware devices or media:

- External hard drives
- SD cards
- USB flash drives or pen drives
- CD-ROM or DVD drives
- CD or DVD discs

One of the most common error messages related to this says this:

```
The request could not be performed because of an I/O device error
```

When this message or other messages referencing I/O issues are generated, some possible causes are as follows:

- The hardware drivers are damaged or incompatible.
- The optical disk that you are trying to access is dirty or damaged.
- The operating system is trying to use a transfer mode that the hardware device cannot use.
- The device that you are trying to access is damaged or defective.
- There is a connection problem, such as a bad cable.

Here is a general approach to these issues:

- Restart the server, and then try to access the drive or disk again.
- Use a commercial disc cleaner to clean the disk.
- Move the disk or drive to another server and attempt to access the data to confirm that the drive or disk is not damaged.
- If no alternate and compatible server is available, try a different disk or drive on the original server to make sure that the problem is with the computer and not with the original disk.

If this doesn't solve the issue, check all cable connections and perform a clean boot of the server.

Clean Boot

When you start the server in a clean boot, it starts by using a preselected minimal set of drivers and startup programs, and because the computer starts with a minimal set of drivers, some programs may not work as you expected.

Restore Failure

When data restoration fails, it is never a good thing because the only reason you ever perform this activity is to replace deleted or damaged data that you need. Though most data recovery failures are due to human error in the data backup process (such as running multiple jobs simultaneously, failure to change tapes, or forgetting to remove a cleaning tape), some issues are beyond your control, including these:

- Software errors, such as scripts used to run backup operations, mount media, or perform other operations
- Resource contention during the process
- SAN or other connectivity problems
- Tape drive or media error
- Hardware errors

Although script errors are somewhat under your control, most of these issues are not. Your best defense against data recovery errors is to develop and maintain a backup procedure that includes frequent verifications of backups.

Cache Failure

During the boot process, the BIOS or UEFI of many systems will check the cache. If there is an issue with the cache, the boot process may stop or it may continue and simply disable the cache. This will impact the performance of the server if you consider the way in which the CPU uses this cache.

When this occurs, it can be either cache memory itself or it can be the motherboard to which the cache is attached. You will need to troubleshoot both—specifically:

- Check to see if the cache is securely inserted into the motherboard, if that is where it is located.

- If you have added or changed any cache, investigate whether any changes should have been made to any jumpers on the board as well.

- Check to see if the cache chips get hot after the system has been on a bit. This indicates the chip may be bad, but if you replace it and the same thing occurs, it's the motherboard.

Multiple Drive Failure

When drives fail and are replaced with new drives that subsequently fail, it is always possible that you were just unlucky and got two bad drives in a row, but odds are that is not the case. Typically, something else is causing the drives to fail. In some cases, design flaws in the positioning of the drive may be causing stress that is killing the drives. For example, many laptop owners experienced this, and some theories were that the drives were positioned in such a way that pressure from the user resting their palm on the laptop was causing pressure on the read-write heads, thus damaging the drives over time.

While we are dealing with servers and not laptops, design flaws can occur. Here are some of the issues to consider when multiple drives have failed:

- Are all of the fans functioning?

- Is the airflow from the fans impeded in any way?

- Have you made any firmware changes that may be causing the issue?

- Is the server room or datacenter sufficiently cooled and is airflow ensured?

- Have you protected the server from electrical outages, surges, and sags?

Multiple drive failures in RAID arrays are even more vexing. If two drives fail before you attempt to rebuild the array, you will not be able to do so. This illustrates the value of using hardware RAID with hot spares so that this possibility is reduced.

Causes of Common Problems

While incompatible programs and drivers are a possible cause of issues such as I/O problems, they are not the only causes of some of the issues raised in this section. We'll look at some other issues that can plague any computer and some that are specific to servers in the datacenter.

Disk Space Utilization

As you learned in Chapter 4, "Storage Technologies and Asset Management," capacity planning can prevent many disk space issues. Another tactic you can use to better utilize the space you have is to compress files that are used infrequently. This can be done in Windows at both the file and the folder levels. Review Chapter 2, which covered the use of compression files.

Insufficient Disk Space

When it comes down to it, this is the issue you are trying to prevent with proper capacity management. In some cases, you receive an error message from the storage system that there is insufficient space in the cache. For example:

```
WARNING: Failure to reserve space on any cache data file storage location.
 Failure has occurred '@1%d'times since last warning.
```

   or:

```
1006006 Failed to bring block into the memory. Data cache is too small. Please
increase the data cache size.
```

You can use the storage software to increase the cache available to the system. This may require adding more memory as well. The procedures for doing that are in the documentation that came with the software.

Misconfigured RAID

You learned about RAID and RAID controllers in Chapter 1, "Server Hardware." You also learned about software and hardware versions of RAID in Chapter 4. When RAID is misconfigured you may not experience the benefits you expect. For example, the choice of RAID type is very important to achieving the goals you have set for your RAID implementation. Examples of an improper choice include:

- Choosing RAID 0 when you need fault tolerance (there is no fault tolerance with RAID 0)
- Choosing software RAID when you need to protect the OS (that can only be done with hardware RAID)

You will learn much more about RAID and array management later in this chapter.

Media Failure

We usually think of media as CDs, DVDs, flash drives, and the like, but sometimes an error message will refer to a "media test failure." In this case, it may be referring to this type of media, but it can also be referring to the hard drive or to an ability to boot to a network. In most cases, the message is indicating an ability to locate boot files, and you'll see this message early in the boot process.

Ensure that the boot order is set correctly in the BIOS. If that is not the issue, attempt to run any hardware diagnostics that may be available to you from the server vendor. Reseating the drive cables may also solve the issue. In some devices this will occur if the boot order is set with Network Boot at the top of the list and there are no boot files on the network.

Drive Failure

Every drive is going to fail—it's just a matter of when. Frequent backups are the first line of defense, but sometimes even when your backup plan is sound, a drive fails that contains critical data that has not yet been committed to backup. If you locate this type of data in a fault-tolerant RAID array, your recovery options increase. You still have the data on the other drive in RAID 1, or in the case of RAID 5, you have the parity information required to re-create the data.

When all else fails, data recovery specialists may be able to get the data off the failed drive. They do this by opening the drive in a clean room and reading the data from the exposed platters with special equipment. In cases where the issue is electronics, they may replace the circuit board and attempt to start the drive. Whatever method they use will be costly.

Earlier in this chapter you learned about the impact of drive failures. A loud clicking noise, sometimes referred to as the click of death, is caused by the read/write heads making contact with the platters. After that happens, both the heads and the platters become damaged, and the system becomes unable to establish a successful starting point to read the drive. (Keep in mind that a bad fan can also make a clicking noise). This is serious damage and cannot be repaired. Be aware that solid-state drives have no moving parts and thus will never make this clicking noise. Back up all the data if that's still possible. If the drive is beyond readable, the only option to recover the data is with the help of a professional data recovery service. At that point, you must balance the cost of the recovery with the value of the data. This is a case where performing regular backups saves the day!

Controller Failure

In hardware RAID implementations, the RAID process is managed by a controller. If the RAID server has only one controller, this is a serious single point of failure. If it fails, you may not be able to recover the data on any of the drives. Many technicians put too much faith in RAID and become lax in preforming backups, which exacerbates the situation when it occurs. Some systems allow for a backup of the RAID configuration, which can mitigate this single point of failure.

Hot Bus Adapter (HBA) Failure

Host bus adapters (HBAs) are installed into expansion slots in a server and are used to allow the server to communicate on internal or external networks using technologies such as SCSI, Fibre Channel, and SATA. These networks are typically populated with storage devices.

When an HBA fails, it prevents the server from being able to communicate with the storage network and thus the storage devices. An HBA failure can cause a number of the scenarios we have discussed in which a storage device is unreachable and should always be considered as a possibility in a server that uses HBAs.

Whenever you suspect an HBA failure, you should first check the cables and reseat the adapter in its slot. One of the best mitigations for HBA failure is to implement redundant HBAs providing multiple paths to the storage network. Keep in mind that while a dual-port

HBA may provide another path to the network, if the HBA fails it's still a single point of failure.

Loose Connectors

In any of the situations we have covered where connections are involved, the connectors should always be checked. Even if the connection appears to be solid, disconnect it and reconnect it to be sure. Every technician can tell a story about a connection that appeared secure as could be but failed to work until this was done. So always check connections to HBAs, controllers, NICs, and other physical interfaces.

Cable Problems

The same approach you take with connectors should be taken with cables. Remember, just because a cable works doesn't mean it is working well. Issues such as cuts in the outer cover and stressed connectors can cause the cable to allow noise into the cable (RFI, EMI) that causes packets to be damaged or corrupted. This leads to retransmissions and lower throughout. Also keep in mind that you should always check the Physical layer first before attempting to troubleshoot issues higher in the OSI model.

Bend Radius

When working with cables, especially fiber cables, you must recognize that every cable has a maximum bend radius, which you cannot exceed without damaging the cable. The smaller the allowable bend radius, the greater the material flexibility. If you exceed the recommended bend radius, you will damage the cable. For twisted pair cabling, this is much less of an issue, but the bend radius should not exceed four times the cable diameter for horizontal UTP cables and 10 times the cable diameter for multipair backbone UTP cables.

For fiber-optic cables, if no specific recommendations are available from the cable manufacturer, the cable should not be pulled over a bend radius smaller than 20 times the cable diameter.

Misconfiguration

There are so many opportunities for misconfigurations with respect to storage, many of which we have discussed, such as improper RAID type. One final consideration is fragmentation. Over time as data is written and erased from a drive, the data becomes fragmented, which mean that pieces of the same file are scattered in various locations on the drive. This makes it more difficult for the system to find all the pieces when reading the drive so performance slows. This can be addressed by using a defragmentation tool, such as the one included in versions of Windows Server.

Corrupt Boot Sector

Booting problems can occur with corruption of the boot files or missing components. Common error messages include an invalid boot disk, inaccessible boot drive, a missing NTLDR file, or the BOOTMGR is missing.

When the boot sector is corrupted, the system is unable to locate the operating system. In Windows you have several options to remedy this situation. In Exercise 12.1 you will perform a system repair.

EXERCISE 12.1

Repairing the System in Windows Server 2012 R2

1. Insert the installation DVD or USB and boot Windows Server 2012 R2 from it.

2. On the Windows Setup page, specify Language To Install, Time And Currency Format, and Keyboard Or Input Method, and click Next.

3. Click Repair Your Computer.

4. Click Troubleshoot and then click Advanced Options.

5. Click Command Prompt and type the following commands (press Enter after each command):

   ```
   Bootrec /fixmbr
   Bootrec /fixboot
   Bootrec /rebuildbcd
   ```

6. Restart the computer. Check if you're able to boot now.

OS Boot Failure in Windows

Common error messages include an invalid boot disk and inaccessible boot drive. On Windows servers, additional messages could be a missing NTLDR file and a missing BOOTMGR. In Windows Server 2012 R2, there are four main issues that cause this:

- Corrupted system file
- Corrupted boot configuration data (BCD)
- Corrupted boot sector
- Corrupted master boot record (MBR)

Each of these issues can be addressed by booting the system to the installation disk and, during the process, selecting to repair the system. In Exercise 12.2 you will execute the four commands that address these issues.

EXERCISE 12.2

Repairing Boot Files in Windows Server 2012 R2

1. Put the Windows Server 2012 R2 installation disc into the disc drive, and then restart the server.

2. When the message "Press any key to boot from CD or DVD . . ." appears, press a key.

3. Select a language, a time, a currency, and a keyboard or another input method, and then click Next.

4. Click Repair Your Computer.

5. Click the operating system that you want to repair, and then click Next.

6. In the System Recovery Options dialog box, click Command Prompt.

7. To ensure the system files are all intact, execute the following command at the command prompt:

   ```
   sfc /scannow
   ```

8. To rebuild the boot configuration data (BCD), execute the following command:

   ```
   Bootrec /RebuildBcd
   ```

9. To repair the boot sector, execute the following command:

   ```
   BOOTREC /FIXBOOT
   ```

10. To repair the master boot record, execute the following command:

    ```
    BOOTREC /FIXMBR
    ```

11. Finally, to apply the master boot code that is compatible with BOOTMGR, execute the following command, where *Drive* is the drive where the installation media resides:

    ```
    Drive:\boot\Bootsect.exe /NT60
    ```

Missing GRUB/LILO

The GRUB is the bootloader package in Linux and Unix systems. If it is not present, the system will not boot. In some cases when you install Windows, it will overwrite the GRUB. If this occurs, or in any case where you need to reinstall or recover the GRUB, follow these steps, which are based on Ubuntu:

1. Mount the partition your Ubuntu Installation is on.

2. Bind the directories to which GRUB needs access to detect other operating systems.

3. Using chroot install, check, and update GRUB.

4. Exit the chrooted system and unmount everything.

5. Shut down and turn your computer back on, and you will be met with the default GRUB screen.

For more detailed assistance with this process visit http://howtoubuntu.org/how-to-repair-restore-reinstall-grub-2-with-a-ubuntu-live-cd.

Corrupt Filesystem Table

The fstab file (File System Table) is used by Linux operating systems to mount partitions on boot. The following messages may be displayed at boot time if the /etc/fstab file is missing or corrupted:

```
WARNING: Couldn't open /etc/fstab: No such file or direcctory
WARNING: bad format on line # of /etc/fstab
```

This prevents some or all filesystems from being mounted successfully. If you have a backup of fstab you can restore it. To restore a missing or corrupted /etc/fstab file:

1. Log in under Maintenance Mode.

2. Remount the root filesystem in read-write mode (an ext3 type root filesystem is assumed in this example; modify as appropriate):

   ```
   # mount -t ext3 -o remount,rw /dev/vx/dsk/rootvol /
   ```

3. Restore the /etc/fstab file from a recent backup, or correct its contents by editing the file.

4. Reboot the system.

Array Rebuild

Sometimes, the term *array rebuild* refers to the process of the redundancy regeneration in RAID 5. In this case we're talking about a degraded RAID array, one that has failed to rebuild for one reason or another. In cases where the rebuild must be done manually (which means no hot spare), if drives are not connected back in the correct position it can cause a failed rebuild.

To prevent this from occurring, follow these procedures when performing a manual rebuild:

- Clearly label the disks as you remove them and note the corresponding port.

- Identify, remove, and similarly label the faulty drive. The drives should be placed back in the reversed order of failures (failures, not removals).

- If you are replacing a failed drive, ensure that it and the other drives are connected to the original port numbers.

Improper Disk Partition

Partitions can get corrupted or damaged due to a number of reasons, such as these:

- Virus attack

- Installation of defective software

- Instant shutdown or power failure

There are a number of commercial partition tools that you can use to repair damaged partitions. Before you use one of these commercial tools, you might want to use one of the system tools available to you. One of these is chkdsk (Check Disk). You learned about using chkdsk earlier in this chapter, and in Exercise 12.3 you will use it again to identify and repair disk issues that may be part of the partition issue.

EXERCISE 12.3

Checking the Disk in Windows Server 2012 R2

1. Insert the installation DVD or USB and boot Windows Server 2012 R2 from it.

2. On the Windows Setup page, specify Language To Install, Time And Currency Format, and Keyboard Or Input Method, and click Next.

3. Click Repair Your Computer.

4. Click Troubleshoot and then click Advanced Options.

5. Click Command Prompt and type the following command:

   chkdsk /p

   If after the test completes, the message "One or more errors detected on the volume" appears, then proceed to step 6. If no errors are reported, then your drive cannot be repaired using chkdsk.

6. Type **chkdsk /r**.

When the repair process completes and you are returned to the command prompt, check to see if the repair worked by typing **chkdsk /p**

If no errors are reported, the repair worked. Check to see if this solved the partition issue.

Bad Sectors

When sectors on a hard drive go bad, many filesystems can mark the sector as bad so that it is not used again. You can also identify bad sectors using tools such as Check Disk on Microsoft systems, or badblocks on Unix-like systems. Bad sectors are one of the issues that the procedure you performed in Exercise 12.3 is designed to locate and repair (repair in this case meaning moving the data to a good sector and marking the old sector as bad).

badblocks has several different modes that enable you to detect bad sectors in Linux. One of those is destructive to the data and should be used only on new drives and not ones where you have data. The nondestructive method creates a backup of the original content of a sector before testing with a single random pattern and then restores the content from the backup. The command you want to run and an example of the output are shown here:

```
# badblocks -nsv /dev/<device>
Checking for bad blocks in non-destructive read-write mode
From block 0 to 488386583
Checking for bad blocks (non-destructive read-write test)
Testing with random pattern: done
Pass completed, 0 bad blocks found. (0/0/0 errors)
```

Cache Battery Failure

You learned earlier in this chapter about issues related to cache and the cache battery. Please review that section.

Cache Turned Off

Cache issues were covered earlier in the first occurrence of the section named "Cache Turned Off."

Insufficient Space

Regardless of how much storage space a server has, at some point you may fill that space! While lack of space in and of itself can slow the system down, issues that accompany the filling hard drive make the situation worse.

For one, this is typically accompanied by disk fragmentation (covered earlier in this chapter). Also as more data is added to the system, it takes the anti-malware program longer and longer to scan the system, and while it is doing this, in the background the performance dips.

There is one area that can be affected by lack of space if the situation gets critical. If the system has insufficient memory and frequently makes use of page or swap files on the hard drive, the lack of space will impact performance. The simplest solution to this issue is to add more space or archive some data and remove it from the drive.

In some cases, you receive an error message from the storage system that there is insufficient space in the cache. For example:

```
WARNING: Failure to reserve space on any cache data file storage location.
 Failure has occurred '@1%d'times since last warning.
```

or:

```
1006006 Failed to bring block into the memory. Data cache is too small. Please
increase the data cache size.
```

You can use the storage software to increase the cache available to the system. This may require adding more memory as well. The procedures for doing that are in the documentation that came with the software.

Improper RAID Configuration

As you have learned, most RAID misconfigurations involve a misunderstanding of the requirements and benefits of each type. Each has a minimum number of drives required, and each provides advantages and disadvantages that must be clearly understood or expectations will not be met. The common types of RAID and the requirements and benefits of each were covered in Chapter 4. Please review that chapter.

Mismatched Drives

When choosing drives for a RAID array, the best choice is to buy the same models from the same manufacturer with the same speed, size, and other characteristics. However, if you search for "mismatched drives," you will find many forums where experienced technicians are saying, "I know all the drives should be the same but they just aren't." Budgets and the real world sometimes interfere with best practices.

Although it is possible to use mismatched drives, you should have a clear understanding of the implications of each type of mismatch. The only requirement set in stone is that they be of the same architecture.

A speed mismatch will simply mean that the fastest drive will have to wait for the slower drives to finish writing in cases where data is being written to multiple drives. This is why it is sometimes said that it "dumbs down" the faster drives. A size mismatch will simply mean that the largest volume on any drive can be no larger than the smallest drive in the array. That results in some wasted drive space.

Backplane Failure

In Chapter 10, you learned about backplanes. You learned that the backplane provides a connection point for the blade servers in the blade enclosure. Some backplanes are constructed with slots on both sides, and in that case they are located in the middle of the enclosure and are called midplanes. They can host drives as well as servers in storage devices.

When a backplane fails, it affects all the drives that connect to it. Luckily backplane failures are much less likely than drive failures, so you should always suspect a drive failure first. Blade systems and rack servers typically come with several management tools you can use to identify the failing part.

If you confirm that the backplane is bad and must be replaced, ensure that you follow the directions in the documentation to the letter. Each system will have its own unique quirks and "gotchas" to avoid. Read through the entire operation before you start—otherwise you could make your situation much worse.

Tools and Techniques

You can use a number of common tools to monitor, configure, and troubleshoot storage and storage issues. We will survey some of these tools in this section. Keep in mind that there will probably be vendor-specific tools that come with the server or with the storage hardware that may provide more functionality because the tools were written specifically for the server or storage device.

Partitioning Tools

Partitioning tools are used to divide the storage media into sections called partitions or volumes. Some of these have GUIs and others operate from the command line. While there are many, many commercial and free software products that can do this, you can also use tools built into the operating system.

In Windows Server 2012 R2 the diskpart command lets you manage storage from the command line. Although there are GUI tools you can use, the command-line tool almost always provides more functionality. diskpart enables you to manage objects (disks, partitions, or volumes) by using scripts or direct input at a command prompt. It can perform all the functions that can be done with the Disk Management utility and quite a few that cannot be done with Disk Management. In many ways, it is an updated version of fdisk. It can be used to create and manage volumes on the drive.

An example of one of the things you can do with diskpart is initializing a disk. Initializing a disk makes it available to the disk management system, and in most cases, the drive will not show up until you do this. Once the drive has been connected or installed, you should initialize it. You can do so at the command using diskpart or by using the Disk Management tool. Keep in mind that initialization will wipe out the drive! To use diskpart to perform the initialization on 2 TB drives and smaller, follow these steps:

1. Open the Start menu, type **diskpart**, and press Enter.
2. Type **list disk**, and press Enter.
3. Type **select disk X** (where **X** is the number your drive shows up as), and press Enter.
4. Type **clean**, and press Enter.
5. Type **create partition primary**, and press Enter.
6. Type **format quick fs=ntfs**, and press Enter.
7. Type **assign**, and press Enter.
8. Type **exit**, and press Enter.

To use diskpart to perform the initialization on drives that are 2 TB drives and larger:

1. Open the Start menu, type **diskpart**, and press Enter.
2. Type **list disk**, and press Enter.
3. Type **select disk X** (where **X** is the number your drive shows up as), and press Enter.
4. Type **clean**, and press Enter.
5. Type **convert gpt**, and press Enter.
6. Type **create partition primary**, and press Enter.
7. Type **format quick fs=ntfs**, and press Enter.
8. Type **assign**, and press Enter.
9. Type **exit**, and press Enter.

fdisk

Although the fdisk command is no longer used in Windows Server 2012 R2, it is still the tool used on Linux to manage partitions. The sudo fdisk -l command lists the partitions on the system. To make any changes to a disk's partitioning, you must enter command mode for that device. That means you need to know how the system refers to that device, which can be found in the output of the fdisk -l command.

For example, in the output in Figure 12.4, the name of the first listed device is dev/sda.

FIGURE 12.4   fdisk

```
Disk /dev/sda: 21.5 GB, 21474836480 bytes
255 heads, 63 sectors/track, 2610 cylinders, total 41943040 sectors
Units = sectors of 1 * 512 = 512 bytes
Sector size (logical/physical): 512 bytes / 512 bytes
I/O size (minimum/optimal): 512 bytes / 512 bytes
Disk identifier: 0x0006c031

   Device Boot      Start         End      Blocks   Id  System
/dev/sda1   *        2048    39845887    19921920   83  Linux
/dev/sda2        39847934    41940991     1046529    5  Extended
/dev/sda5        39847936    41940991     1046528   82  Linux swap
/ Solaris
howtogeek@ubuntu:~$ sudo fdisk /dev/sda

Command (m for help): █
```

Therefore, to enter the mode required to manage it, type:

sudo fdisk /dev/sda

In command mode, you use single-letter commands to specify actions. At the following prompt, you can type **m** to list the actions and their letters.

Command (type m for help)

If you do so, you will get the output shown in Figure 12.5.

FIGURE 12.5   Actions menu

```
Command (m for help): m
Command action
   a   toggle a bootable flag
   b   edit bsd disklabel
   c   toggle the dos compatibility flag
   d   delete a partition
   l   list known partition types
   m   print this menu
   n   add a new partition
   o   create a new empty DOS partition table
   p   print the partition table
   q   quit without saving changes
   s   create a new empty Sun disklabel
   t   change a partition's system id
   u   change display/entry units
   v   verify the partition table
   w   write table to disk and exit
```

As you can see, you can create and delete partitions from this menu using **n** and **d**, respectively.

Defragmentation Tools

Defragmentation tools are used to reorganize the physical location of the data on the hard drive so that all pieces of a file are located together in the same place. When this is done, it improves the performance of the drive. All server operating systems come with built-in defragmentation tools, and their operation can be scheduled for a time convenient to the user. This also frees the user (and the technician) from having to think about running the tool on a regular basis. Figure 12.6 shows the Drive Optimization tool in Windows Server 2012 R2. This tool is available from the Tools menu in Server Manager.

FIGURE 12.6   Drive Optimization tool

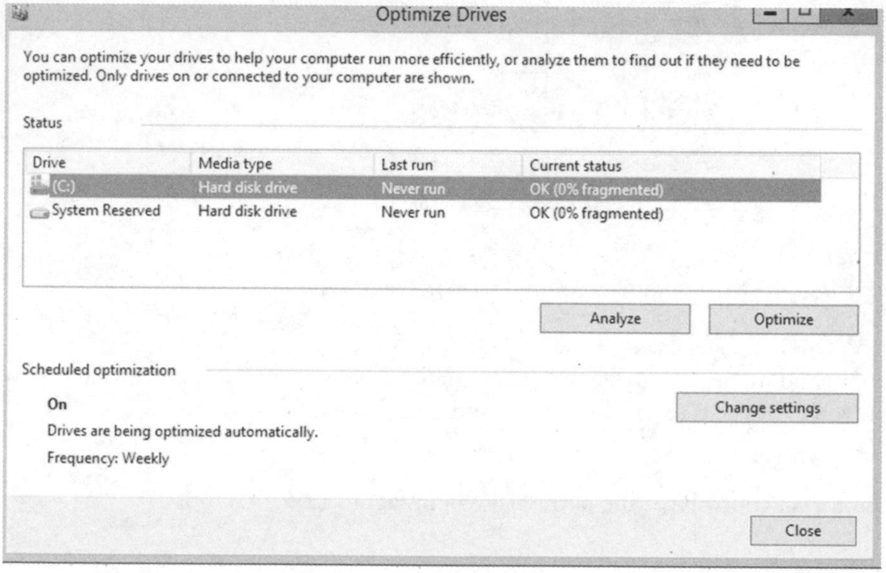

You can analyze the drive and the degree of fragmentation will be determined, or you can select Optimize and start the defragmentation process without analyzing. You can also make schedules so that this occurs automatically. The server in the figure is set for weekly defragmentation.

Disk Management

In Windows, you can manage your hard drives through the Disk Management component. To access Disk Management, access Computer Management from the Tools menu in Server Manager. Disk Management is one of the tools in Computer Management. The Disk Management screen lets you view a host of information about all the drives installed in your system, including CD-ROM and DVD drives, as shown in Figure 12.7.

The list of devices in the top portion of the screen shows you additional information for each partition on each drive, such as the filesystem used, status, free space, and so on. If you right-click a partition in either area, you can perform a variety of functions, such as formatting the partition and changing the name and drive letter assignment. For additional options and information, you can also access the properties of a partition by right-clicking it and selecting Properties.

FIGURE 12.7 Disk Management

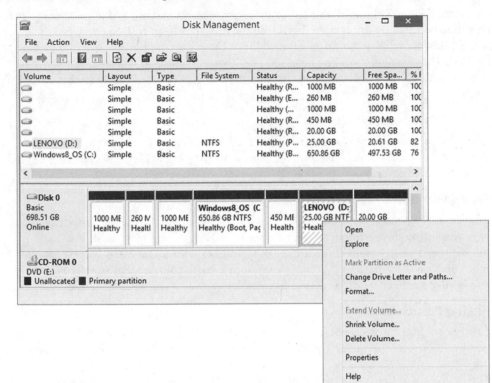

Drive Status

The status of a drive can have a number of variables associated with it (System, Boot, and so on), but what really matters is whether it falls into the category of *healthy* or *unhealthy*. As the title implies, if it is healthy, it is properly working and if it is unhealthy, you need to attend to it and correct problems. In Figure 12.7, in the Status column of Disk Management, we can see that all drives are Healthy.

Mounting

Drives must be mounted before they can be used. Within Windows, most removable media (flash drives, CDs, and so forth) are recognized when attached and mounted. Volumes on basic disks, however, are not automatically mounted and assigned drive letters by default. To mount them, you must manually assign them drive letters or create mount points in Disk Management.

 You can also mount from the command line using either the Diskpart or the Mountvol utilities.

Initializing

Initializing a disk makes it available to the disk management system, and in most cases, the drive will not show up until you do this. Once the drive has been connected or installed, you should do this. Initializing the drive can be done at the command line using diskpart or in the Disk Management tool. You need to know that initialization will wipe out the drive's contents! Using diskpart to perform the initialization was covered earlier in this chapter in the section "Partitioning Tools."

Extending Partitions

It is possible to add more space to partitions (and logical drives) by extending them into unallocated space. This is done in Disk Management by right-clicking and choosing Extend or by using the Diskpart utility.

Splitting Partitions

Just as you can extend a partition, you can also reduce the size of it. While generically known as splitting the partition, the menu option in Disk Management is Shrink. By shrinking an existing partition, you are creating another with unallocated space that can then be used for other purposes. You can only shrink basic volumes that use the NTFS file-system (and space exists) or that do not have a filesystem.

Shrinking Partitions

It is also possible to shrink a volume from its size at creation. To do so in Disk Management, access the volume in question, right-click the volume, and select Shrink Volume, as shown in Figure 12.8.

   This will open a dialog box that allows you to control how much you want to shrink the volume, as shown in Figure 12.9.

Assigning/Changing Drive Letters

Mounting drives and assigning drive letters are two tasks that go hand in hand. When you mount a drive, you typically assign it a drive letter in order to be able to access it. Right-click a volume in Disk Management to access the option Change Drive Letter And Paths, as shown in Figure 12.10.

Adding Drives

When removable drives are added, the Windows operating system is configured, by default, to identify them and assign a drive letter. When nonremovable drives are added, you must mount them and assign a drive letter, as mentioned earlier.

Adding Arrays

Arrays are added to increase fault tolerance (using RAID) or performance (striping). Disk Management allows you to create and modify arrays as needed.

FIGURE 12.8   Shrink Volume

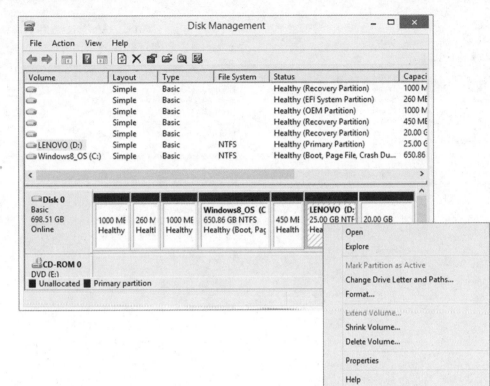

FIGURE 12.9   Set volume size

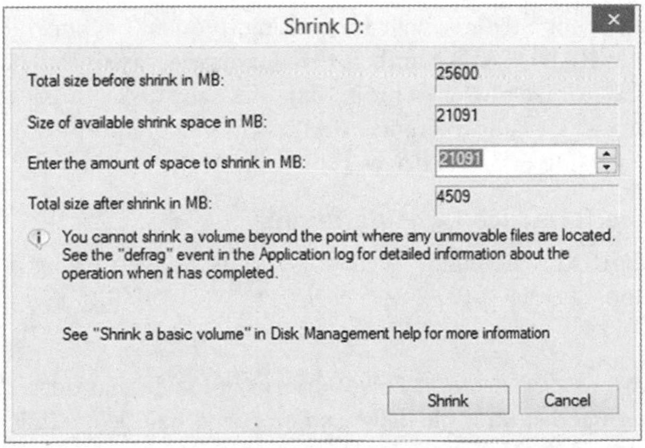

FIGURE 12.10 Change Drive Letter And Paths

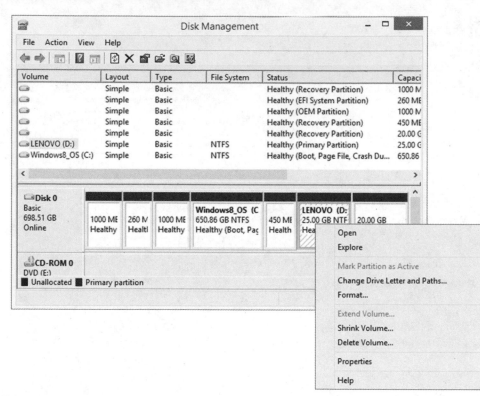

RAID and Array Management

In some cases you may want to maintain access to data even when there is a single drive failure (although this is not a replacement for making frequent backups). You can do so by deploying a version of RAID. RAID stands for Redundant Array of Independent Disks. It's a way of combining the storage power of more than one hard disk for a special purpose such as increased performance or fault tolerance. RAID is more commonly done with SAS drives, but it can be done with IDE or SATA drives.

RAID Levels and Performance Considerations

Not all versions of RAID provide fault tolerance, and they have varying impacts on performance. Let's look at each type.

RAID 0

RAID 0 is also known as *disk striping*. This is a form of RAID that doesn't provide fault tolerance. Data is written across multiple drives, so one drive can be reading or writing while the next drive's read/write head is moving. This makes for faster data access. However, if any one of the drives fails, all content is lost. In RAID 0, since there is no fault tolerance, the usable space in the drive is equal to the total space on all the drives. So if the two drives in an array have 250 GB each of space, 500 GB will be the available drive space. RAID 0 is illustrated in Figure 12.11.

FIGURE 12.11 RAID 0

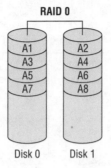

RAID 1

RAID 1 is also known as *disk mirroring*. This is a method of producing fault tolerance by writing all data simultaneously to two separate drives. If one drive fails, the other drive contains all the data and may also be used as a source of that data. However, disk mirroring doesn't help access speed, and the cost is double that of a single drive. Since RAID 1 repeats the data on two drives, only one half of the total drive space is available for data. So if two 250 GB drives are used in the array, 250 GB will be the available drive space. RAID 1 is illustrated in Figure 12.12.

FIGURE 12.12 RAID 1

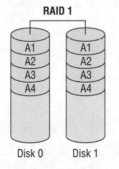

RAID 5

RAID 5 combines the benefits of both RAID 0 and RAID 1 and is also known as *striping with parity*. It uses a parity block distributed across all the drives in the array, in addition to striping the data across them. That way, if one drive fails, the parity information can be used to recover what was on the failed drive. A minimum of three drives is required. RAID 5 uses $1/n$ (n is the number of drives in the array) for parity information (for example, one third of the space in a three-drive array), and only $1 - (1/n)$ is available for data. So if three 250 GB drives are used in the array (for a total of 750 GB), 500 GB will be the available drive space. RAID 5 is illustrated in Figure 12.13.

FIGURE 12.13 RAID 5

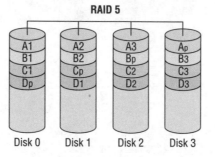

RAID 6

RAID 6 writes parity information across the drives as is done in RAID 5, but it writes two stripes, which allows the system to recover from two drive failures whereas RAID 5 cannot. As each set of parities must be calculated separately, performance is slowed during writing to the drive. The cost is higher due to the two drives dedicated to parity information.

RAID 6 uses $2/n$ (n = the number of drives in the array) for parity information (for example, two thirds of the space in a three-drive array), and only $1 - (2/n)$ is available for data. So if three 250 GB drives are used in the array (for a total of 750 GB), 250 GB will be the available drive space. In Figure 12.14 (which shows RAID 6), you can see the parity blocks are indicated with a small letter next to each and that they are in pairs.

FIGURE 12.14 RAID 6

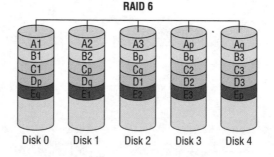

RAID 10

RAID 10 is also known as RAID 1+0. Striped sets are mirrored (a minimum of four drives, and the number of drives must be even). It provides fault tolerance and improved performance but increases complexity. Since this is effectively a mirrored stripe set and a stripe set gets 100 percent use of the drive without mirroring, this array will provide half of the total drive space in the array as available drive space. For example, if there are four 250 GB drives in a RAID 10 array (for a total of 1,000 GB), the available drive space will be 500 GB. RAID 10 is illustrated in Figure 12.15.

FIGURE 12.15   RAID 10

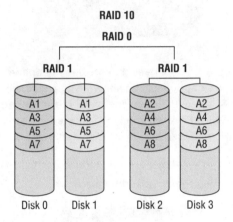

RAID Setup

The management of hardware RAID is usually done through a utility that you select to access during the boot process, as you would if you were selecting to enter setup. An example of this is the PowerEdge Expandable RAID Controller BIOS Configuration Utility. When you boot the server, you press Ctrl+M to launch this utility. From a high level you will use the utility and the arrow keys to perform Exercise 12.4.

EXERCISE 12.4

Managing Hardware RAID

This example uses a Dell PowerEdge. Your server may be different. Consult the documentation.

1. Select Configure ➢ View/Add Configuration on the initial screen, as shown in Figure 12.16

EXERCISE 12.4 *(continued)*

FIGURE 12.16   View/Add configuration

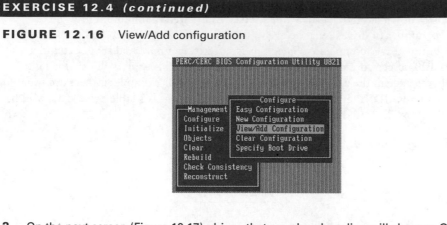

2. On the next screen (Figure 12.17), drives that are already online will show as ONLINE and any that have just been added will be shown with a status of READY. For any drives that still show as READY, select the drive and press the spacebar, which will change the status from READY to ONLINE. When you have selected the drives that will be in the array, they will be blinking. Press Enter to confirm that these drives will be members of this array.

FIGURE 12.17   Confirming the drive additions

3. Press F10 to display the Array configuration screen (Figure 12.18).

FIGURE 12.18   Array Configuration screen

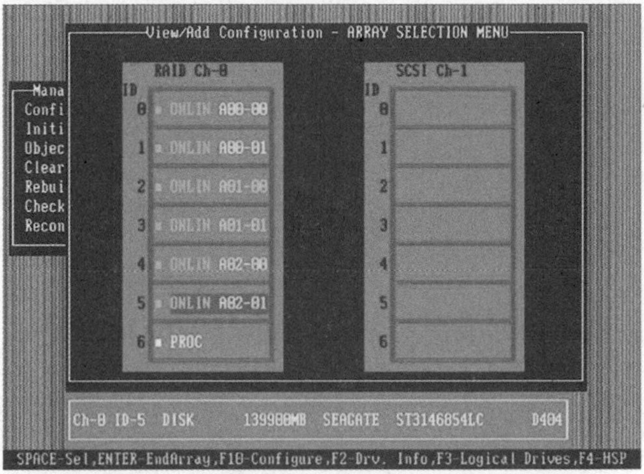

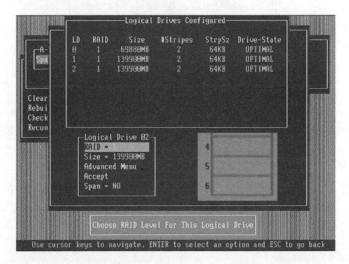

4. The array number that was assigned for the new disk drives from the previous step is displayed here. Press the spacebar to display the Span-1 message just below where the array number appears. Press F10 and you are now ready to select the RAID level, as shown in Figure 12.19.

FIGURE 12.19   Selecting the RAID level

5. Select the RAID level, keeping in mind the number of drives required for each type. Finally, select the size of the array.

6. Save the configuration and reboot the system.

Array Controller

The heart of a hardware array is the array controller. When choosing the controller you should be concerned with three issues. Let's talk about these three issues.

MEMORY

RAID cards will come with memory right on the card. This memory is used to cache information, and the more you buy, the faster the performance of the array. For example, a card with 512 MB onboard would be a better choice than one with 256 MB onboard. This memory can be configured into two caches: a read cache and a write cache. A common ratio used for the two is 75:25 write:read.

BATTERY-BACKED CACHE

Another interesting aspect of the cache that comes on a RAID controller is that it is typically supported by a battery so that if there is a loss of power, there is no loss of the information that may be residing in the cache. This can include changes to data that have not yet been written to the disk as well. A RAID card is shown in Figure 12.20. The battery pack is shown connected to the back of the card.

FIGURE 12.20   Battery-backed cache

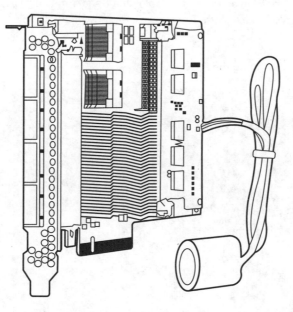

REDUNDANT CONTROLLER

To take the redundancy provided by RAID a step further, you can implement multiple RAID controllers so that you have fault tolerance not only at the disk level but at the controller level as well. An example of a single-piece RAID controller that provides redundancy is shown in Figure 12.21.

FIGURE 12.21   Redundant RAID controller

RAID ARRAY MANAGEMENT

The tool used to manage a RAID array depends on whether it is software or hardware RAID. If it is software RAID (which is highly unlikely on a server), you will manage it with the tools in the operating system. If it is hardware RAID, you will use the tools available with the system, which you can sometimes access by rebooting and selecting the RAID tool from the initial menu. In other cases, GUI tools may be provided that allow you to create and manage the array.

ARRAY MANAGEMENT

Some servers and storage solutions include array management software, but you can also buy it from commercial vendors. This software is specifically designed to make creating, troubleshooting, and managing storage arrays of various types easier.

The following are some of the features that may be available with this type of software:

- A single interface to use across many arrays
- Interactive service and maintenance reminders and information
- Proactive remote monitoring with alerts
- Management from anywhere
- Automated best practices

An example of the interface of an array manager is shown in Figure 12.22, which is the welcome page of the HP Array Configuration Utility.

FIGURE 12.22   HP Array Configuration Utility

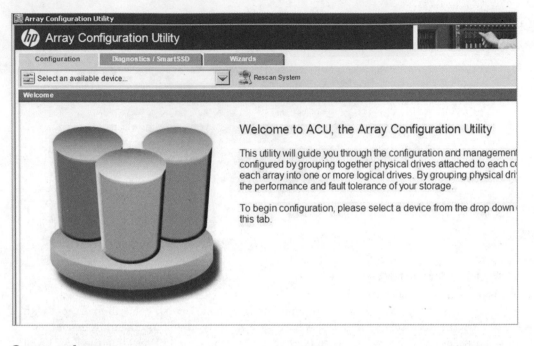

System Logs

All operating systems collect information about events that have occurred that are stored in log files. There are typically log files for different components, such as a security log, an application log, or a system log. These files can be used to troubleshoot operating system issues, and events related to this are usually in the System log.

If the enterprise is large, you may want to have all the devices send their logs to a central server, where they can be stored and analyzed. In Windows these logs can be viewed, filtered, and saved using a tool called Event Viewer. We'll look more closely at that tool later in this section.

In Linux the following are some of the major log files and their locations:

- /var/log/messages: General and system-related.

- /var/log/auth.log: Authentication logs.

- /var/log/kern.log: Kernel logs.

- /var/log/cron.log: Cron logs (cron job).

- /var/log/maillog: Mail server logs.

- /var/log/qmail/: Qmail log directory (more files inside this directory); qmail is a mail transfer agent (MTA) that runs on Unix.

- /var/log/httpd/: Apache access and error logs directory. Apache is a web server.

- `/var/log/lighttpd/`: Lighttpd access and error logs directory. Lighttpd is an open source web server.

- `/var/log/boot.log`: System boot log.

- `/var/log/mysqld.log`: MySQL database server log file.

- `/var/log/secure` or `/var/log/auth.log`: Authentication log.

- `/var/log/utmp` or `/var/log/wtmp`: Login records file.

- `/var/log/yum.log`: Yum command log file. Yellowdog Updater, Modified (yum) is an open source command-line package-management utility for Linux operating systems using the RPM Package Manager.

Windows employs comprehensive error and informational logging routines. Every program and process theoretically could have its own logging utility, but Event Viewer, through log files, tracks all events on a particular Windows computer. Normally, though, you must be an administrator or a member of the Administrators group to have access to Event Viewer.

With Windows Server 2012 R2, you can access Event Viewer from the Tools menu in Server Manager, as shown in Figure 12.23.

FIGURE 12.23 Tools menu

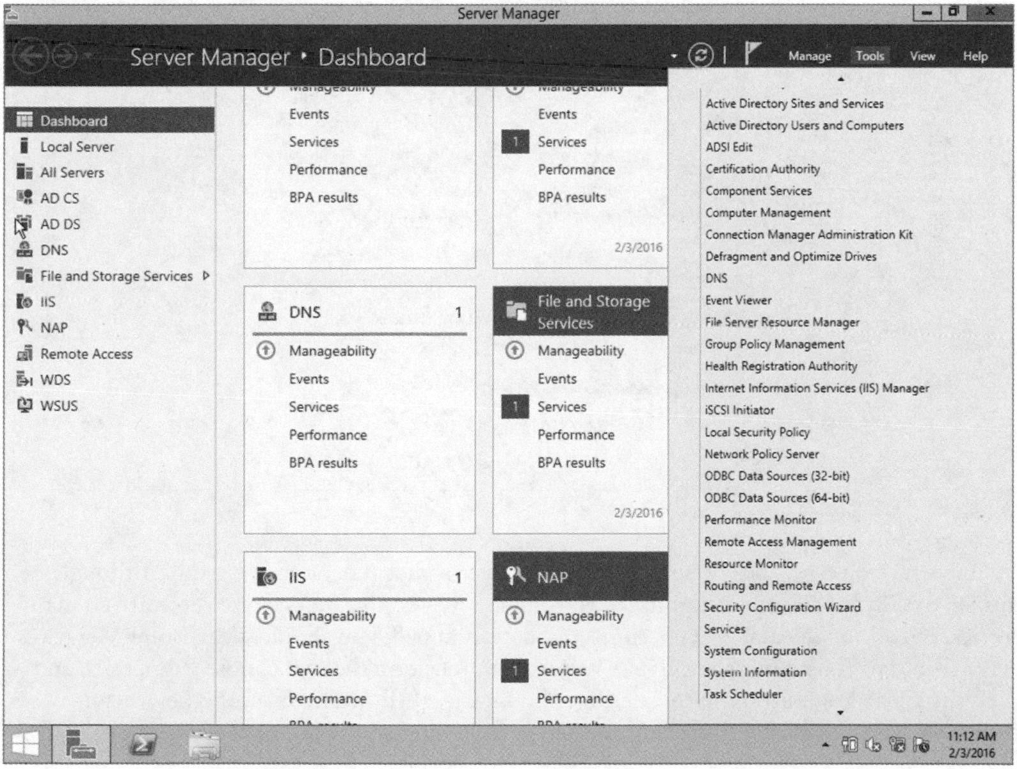

Once Event Viewer is selected, you see the opening page shown in Figure 12.24:

- The System log file displays alerts that pertain to the general operation of Windows.

- The Application log file logs application errors.

- The Security log file logs security events such as login successes and failures.

- The Setup log will appear on domain controllers and will contain events specific to them.

- The Forwarded Events log contains events that have been forwarded to this log by other computers.

These log files can give a general indication of a Windows computer's health.

FIGURE 12.24   The opening interface of Event Viewer

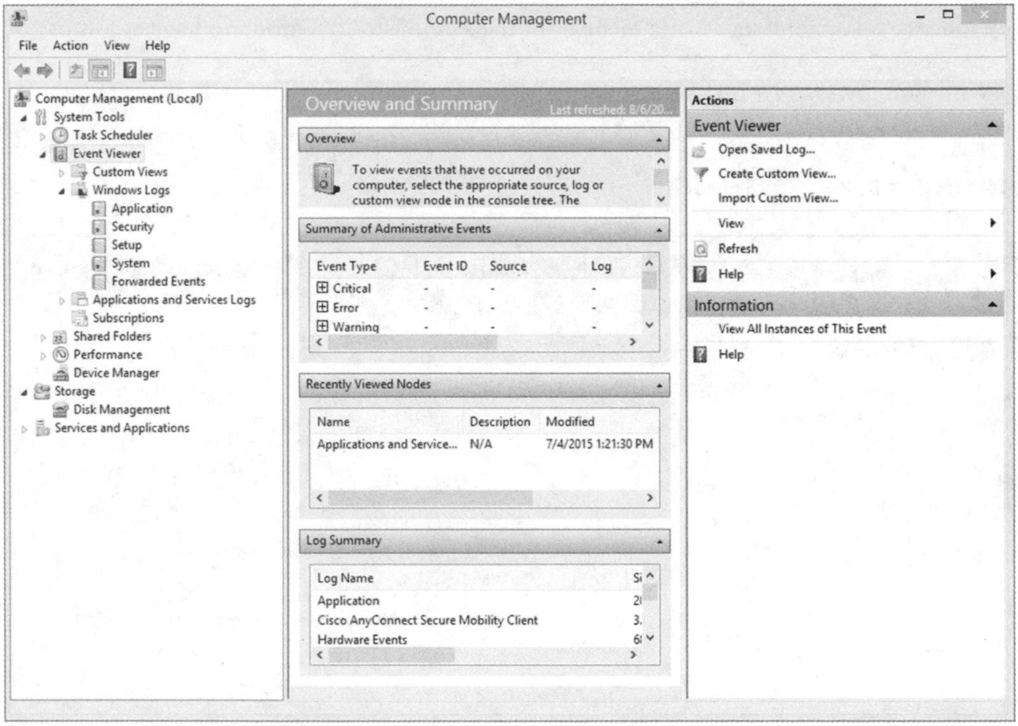

One situation that does occur with Event Viewer is that the log files get full. Although this isn't really a problem, it can make viewing log files confusing because there are so many entries. Even though each event is time- and date-stamped, you should clear Event Viewer every so often. To do this, open Event Viewer, right-click on the log, choose Properties, and click the Clear Log button; in earlier OSs, choose Clear All Events from the Log menu. Doing so erases all events in the current log file, allowing you to see new events more easily when they occur. You can set maximum log size by right-clicking on the log and choosing Properties. By default, when a log fills to its maximum size, old entries are deleted in first in, first out (FIFO) order. Clearing the log, setting maximum log size, and setting how the log is handled when full are done in the Log Properties, as shown in Figure 12.25.

FIGURE 12.25   Event log Properties

Log Properties - Security (Type: Administrative)		

General

Full Name:	Security
Log path:	%SystemRoot%\System32\Winevt\Logs\Security.evtx
Log size:	13.07 MB(13,701,120 bytes)
Created:	Friday, March 28, 2014 12:13:22 PM
Modified:	Thursday, February 4, 2016 10:12:16 AM
Accessed:	Friday, March 28, 2014 12:13:22 PM

☑ Enable logging

Maximum log size (KB):   131072

When maximum event log size is reached:

◉ Overwrite events as needed (oldest events first)

○ Archive the log when full, do not overwrite events

○ Do not overwrite events (Clear logs manually)

Clear Log

OK   Cancel   Apply

You can save the log files before erasing them. The saved files can be burned to a CD or DVD for future reference. Often, you are required to save the files to CD or DVD if you are working in a company that adheres to strict regulatory standards.

In addition to just erasing logs, you can configure three different settings for what you want to occur when the file does reach its maximum size. The first option is "Overwrite events as needed (oldest events first)," and this replaces the older events with the new entries. The second option is "Archive the log when full, do not overwrite events," and this will create another log file as soon as the current one runs out of space. The third option, "Do not overwrite events (Clear logs manually)," will not record any additional events once the file is full.

Disk Mounting Commands

Earlier in this chapter you learned there can be issues with mounting a drive. In this section you'll learn about commands related to disk or drive mounting.

Net use

The net command is one of the most powerful on the Windows-based network, as illustrated by net use. The options that can be used with the command differ slightly based on the Windows operating system you are using; you can view a full list by typing **net /?**.

The net use command is used on Windows-based clients to connect or disconnect from shared resources. You can see what is currently shared by typing **net use** without any other parameters, as shown in Figure 12.26.

FIGURE 12.26   Typing net use lets you see what is currently shared.

```
C:\Users\tmcmillan>net use
New connections will be remembered.


Status       Local     Remote                      Network
--------------------------------------------------------------------------
OK           G:        \\srat1060\groups             Microsoft Windows Network
OK           M:        \\srat1060\pstpickup\tmcmillan
                                                     Microsoft Windows Network
OK           P:        \\srat1060\personal\tmcmillan
                                                     Microsoft Windows Network
OK           Z:        \\10.88.2.132\fun             Microsoft Windows Network
The command completed successfully.
```

Mount

The mount command serves to attach the filesystem found on some device to the filesystem in Linux and Unix. The standard form of the mount command is as follows:

```
mount -t type device destination_dir
```

where type represents the type of device, device represents the device, and destination_dir represents the directory you want to mount. In the following example, a CD-ROM is mounted and the -o ro parameter indicates it should be mounted with read-only access. The iso9660 identifies the device as a CD-ROM.

```
# mount -t iso9660 -o ro /dev/cdrom /mnt
```

Monitoring Tools

There are a number of tools available in Windows Server 2012 R2 to monitor the use of resources. The two tools we'll discuss are Resource Monitor and Performance Monitor.

Resource Monitor

Resource Monitor, available from the same Tools menu in Server Manager where we accessed Event Viewer, can track the use of the CPU, memory, disk system, and network card in real time. It has a tab for each and an Overview tab, as shown in Figure 12.27.

FIGURE 12.27 Resource Monitor

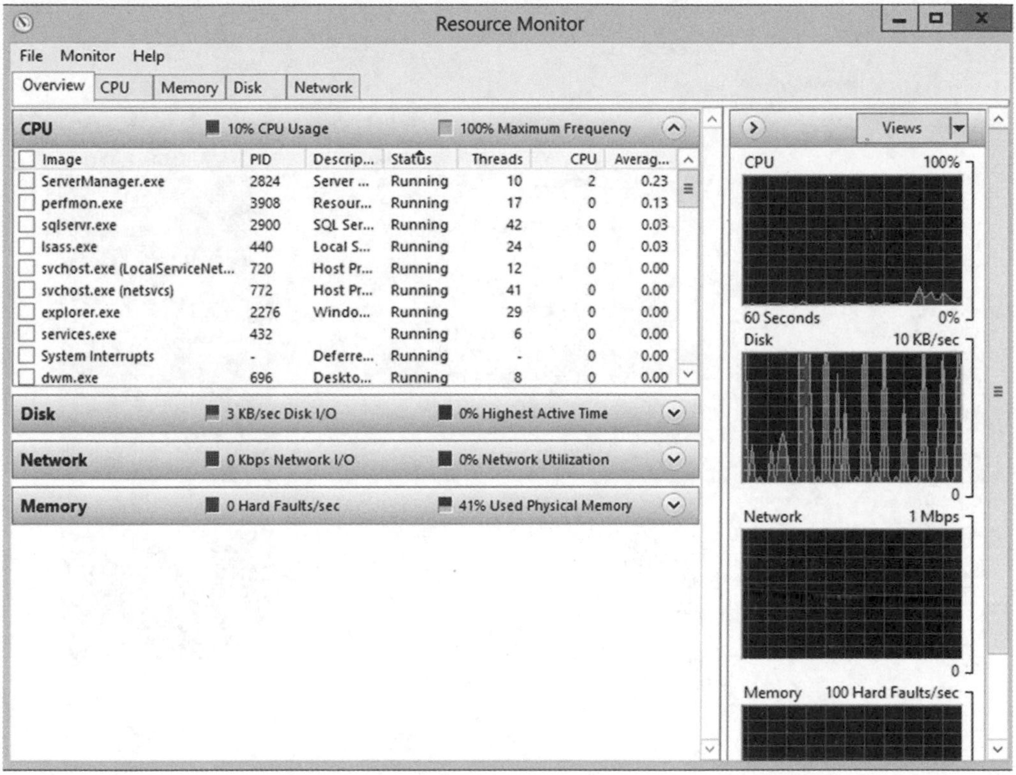

On each tab there are real-time details on the use of each resource. For example, in Figure 12.28 the Memory tab shows a graph of the memory usage (scrolling across in real time) and at the bottom, a bar chart shows how much memory is used, how much is available, and so on.

Storage Tools

Many servers and storage devices come with monitoring tools, and others can be used from within a storage array manager. For example, in Figure 12.29, you can see that the Solarwinds Storage Resource Manager has several monitors (or logs) available in the menus tree on the left side of the console.

Servers will also have performance monitoring tools you can use. In Windows you can use Performance Monitor, which differs a bit between versions but has the same purpose throughout: to display performance counters. While lumped under one heading, two tools are available—System Monitor and Performance Logs And Alerts. System Monitor will show the performance counters in graphical format. The Performance Logs And Alerts utility will collect the counter information and then send it to a console (such as the one in front of admins so they can be aware of the problem) or event log.

FIGURE 12.28   Memory tab

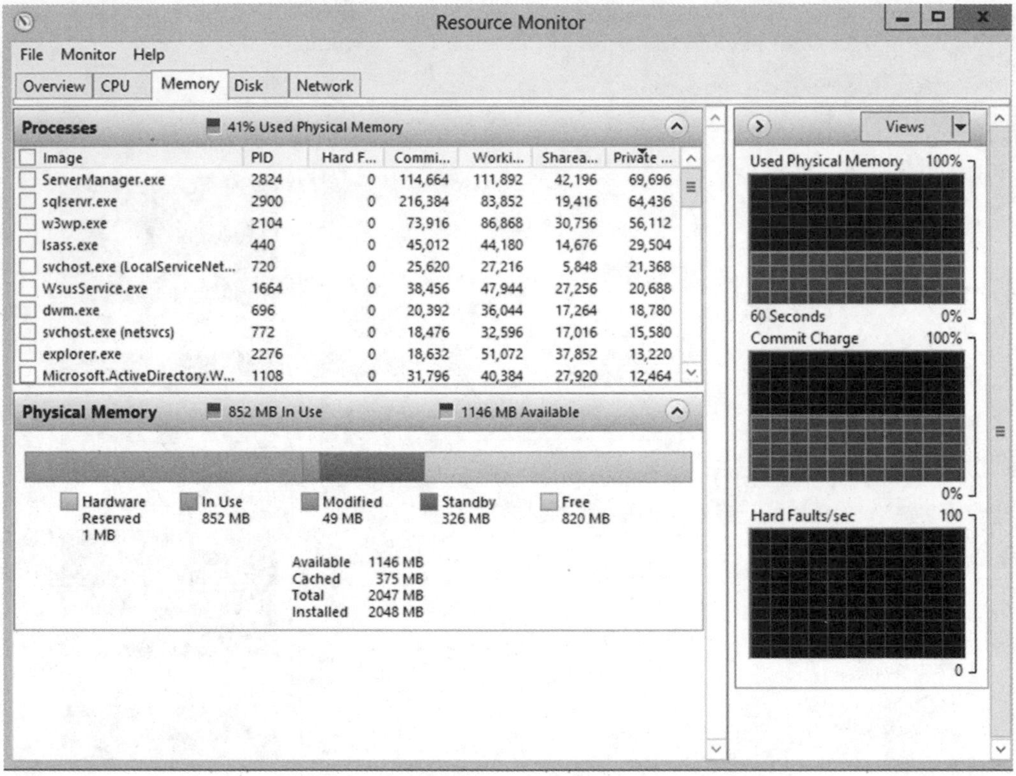

FIGURE 12.29   Solarwinds Storage Resource Manager

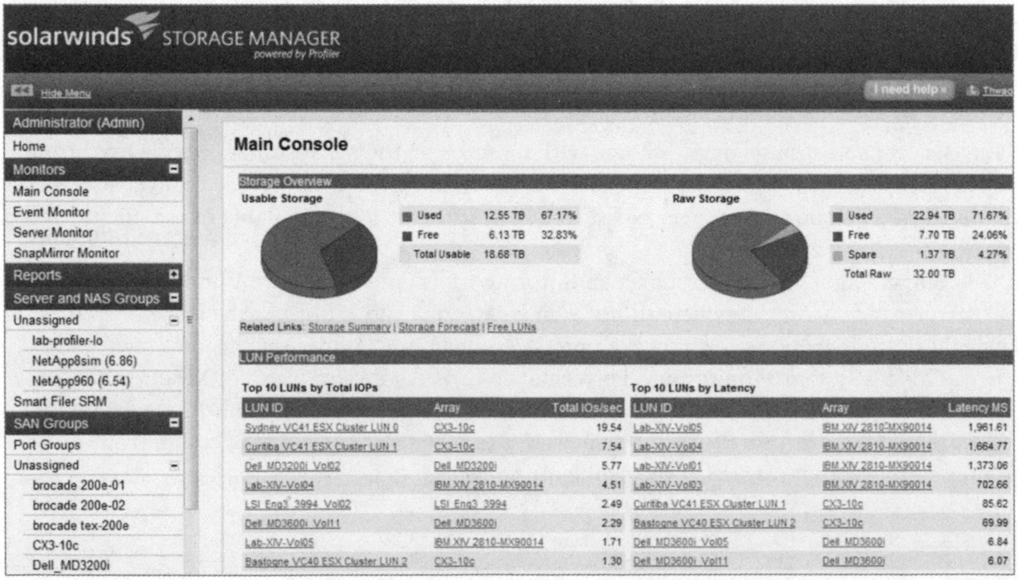

Visual/Auditory Inspections

From time to time, you need to physically visit the server and make some observations. While many issues can be detected remotely, nothing beats looking at the server for signs of issues such as:

- Smoke
- Odd odors, especially burning smells
- Clicking or whining sounds
- Stressed or damaged cabling
- Status lights indicating issues

Summary

In this chapter you learned about common issues that can plague storage system—issues such as slow file access, data corruption, slow I/O performance, and drive failures. This included a discussion of error lights, restoration failures, and cache issues.

You also learned the cause of many of these issues, including but not limited to hardware issues such as media failures, drive failures, controller failures, and HBA failures. We also looked at misconfiguration issues such as improper termination, having the cache turned off, improper RAID configuration, and mismatched drives.

Finally, you learned about the tools that can be used to manage and diagnose storage systems, such as partitioning tools, RAID array management, array management software, system logs, and monitoring tools.

Exam Essentials

Identify common storage issues.   These issues include slow file access, OS not found, data not available, unsuccessful backups, error lights, inability to mount the device, drive not available, cannot access logical drive, data corruption, slow I/O performance, restore failure, cache failure, and multiple drive failure.

Describe common causes of storage issues.   Describe common causes of storage problems, such as media failures, drive failures, controller failures, HBA failures, loose connectors, cable problems, misconfiguration, improper termination, corrupted boot sector, corrupted filesystem table, array rebuild, improper disk partition, bad sectors, cache battery failure, cache turned off, insufficient space, improper RAID configuration, mismatched drives, and backplane failure.

List common tools.   Understand the use of tools such as partitioning tools, disk management, RAID array management software, array management software, system logs, net use/mount commands, and monitoring tools.

Review Questions

You can find the answers in the Appendix.

1. In Linux, which of the following can cause an inability to locate the operating system?
   A. Missing NTLDR
   B. Missing GRUB
   C. Missing Bootmgr
   D. Missing boot.ini

2. Which of the following Windows commands lets you manage storage from the command line?
   A. `nslookup`
   B. `diskpart`
   C. `net use`
   D. `format/s`

3. What command can be used to attempt a repair of the dda drive in Linux?
   A. `fsck -a /dev/dda`
   B. `fdisk -s /dev/dda`
   C. `fsck /dev/dda`
   D. `fdisk /dev/dda`

4. Which of the following commands in Linux can be used to diagnose a memory issue?
   A. `fsck`
   B. `top`
   C. `grub`
   D. `grep`

5. Which of the following operations makes the drive available to the disk management system, and in most cases, the drive will not show up until you do this?
   A. Mounting
   B. Formatting
   C. Initializing
   D. Extending

6. Which of the following is the most common cause of backup failures?
   A. Tape drive failure
   B. Human error
   C. Software errors
   D. SAN issues

7. For fiber-optic cables, if no specific recommendations are available from the cable manufacturer, the cable should not be pulled over a bend radius smaller than how many times the cable diameter?

   A. 5

   B. 10

   C. 15

   D. 20

8. Which of the following symptoms is caused by the read/write heads making contact with the platters?

   A. Whining sound

   B. Clicking sound

   C. Burning smell

   D. Poor performance

9. Which of the following Windows commands is used to identify and repair disk issues?

   A. `nslookup`

   B. `diskpart`

   C. `chkdsk`

   D. `format/s`

10. Which of the following writes parity information across the drives and writes two stripes, which allows the system to recover from two drive failures?

    A. RAID 0

    B. RAID 1

    C. RAID 5

    D. RAID 6

11. What file is used by Linux to mount partitions on boot?

    A. `fstab`

    B. `grub`

    C. `lilo`

    D. `remount`

12. Which of the following is *not* a best practice when manually rebuilding RAID arrays?

    A. Clearly label the disks as you remove them and note the corresponding port.

    B. Identify, remove, and similarly label the faulty drive.

    C. The drives should be placed back in the reversed order of removals.

    D. If you are replacing a failed drive, ensure that it and the other drives are connected to the original port numbers.

13. What command can be used in Linux to detect bad sectors?

    A. fschk

    B. badblocks

    C. fstab

    D. grub

14. Which of the following *must* match when adding drives to a set of existing drives?

    A. Speed

    B. Capacity

    C. Architecture

    D. Vendor

15. What command is used to connect users to shared drives?

    A. net share

    B. net use

    C. mount

    D. dmap

16. Which of the following is used to manage storage in Windows Server 2012 R2 at the command line?

    A. fdisk

    B. format

    C. diskpart

    D. fstab

17. Which of the following commands lists the partitions in a Linux system?

    A. sudo fdisk -l

    B. sudo fdisk /dev

    C. fstab -a

    D. sudo fstab -a

18. Which of the following tools cannot be used to mount a volume on a basic disk in Windows Server 2012 R2?

    A. mountvol

    B. diskpart

    C. Disk Management

    D. fdisk

19. Which of the following can track the use of the CPU, memory, disk system, and network card in real time?

    A. Event Viewer

    B. Resource Monitor

    C. System

    D. Control Panel

20. In Linux the log file that contains general and system-related messages like any you would be interested in for storage issues is located where?

    A. `/var/messages`

    B. `/var/log`

    C. `/log/messages`

    D. `/var/log/messages`

Appendix

Answers to Review Questions

Chapter 1: Server Hardware

1. A. When we use the term *form factor* when discussing any computing device or component, we are talking about its size, appearance, or dimensions. It is typically used to differentiate one physical implementation of the same device or component from another. In the case of servers, we are talking about the size and dimensions of the enclosure in which the server exists.

2. B. Rail kits, when implemented, allow you to slide the server out of the rack for maintenance.

3. C. Each U is 1.75 inches (4.445 cm) high.

4. D. This technology consists of a server chassis housing multiple thin, modular circuit boards, known as server blades. Each blade (or card) contains processors, memory, integrated network controllers, and other input/output (I/O) ports.

5. C. The Level 1 cache, also known as the L1 or front-side cache, holds data that is waiting to enter the CPU. On modern systems, the L1 cache is built into the CPU.

6. B. The internal speed may be the same as the motherboard's speed (the external or bus speed), but it's more likely to be a multiple of it. For example, a CPU may have an internal speed of 1.3 GHz but an external speed of 133 MHz. That means for every tick of the system crystal's clock, the CPU has 10 internal ticks of its own clock.

7. C. When monitoring CPU performance, the following are common metrics and their meanings:
   - **User time**—The time the CPU was busy executing code in user space
   - **System time**—The time the CPU was busy executing code in kernel space
   - **Idle time**—The time the CPU was not busy; measures unused CPU capacity
   - **Steal time (virtualized hardware)**—The time the operating system wanted to execute but was not allowed to by the hypervisor, because it was not the CPU's turn for a time

8. D. When CPUs undergo revisions, the revisions are called stepping levels. When a manufacturer invests money to do a stepping, that means they have found bugs in the logic or have made improvements to the design that allow for faster processing.

9. A. ARM requires fewer resources than either x86 or the x64. In that regard they are suitable for tablets, smartphones, and other smaller devices.

10. B. The primary benefit of DDR3 over DDR2 is that it transfers data at twice the rate of DDR2 (eight times the speed of its internal memory arrays), enabling higher bandwidth or peak data rates.

11. A. True.

12. A. When installing the memory, install the same size modules in the same bank. If you do not, the modules will not operate in dual-channel mode. This will impair the performance of the bank.

13. A. Memory timing measures the performance of RAM and is composed of four components:

- **CAS Latency**—The time to access an address column if the correct row is already open

- **Row Address to Column Address Delay**—The time to read the first bit of memory without an active row

- **Row Precharge Time**—The time to access an address column if the wrong row is open

- **Row Active Time**—The time needed to internally refresh a row

14. A, D. You can mix speeds and manufacturers but not form factors or types.

15. B. PCI-extended (PCI-X) is a double-wide version of the 32-bit PCI local bus. It runs at up to four times the clock speed, achieving higher bandwidth, but otherwise uses the same protocol and a similar electrical implementation.

16. A. An auto-MDIX card is capable of detecting what type of device is on the other end and changing the use of the wire pairs accordingly. For example, normally a PC connected to another PC requires a crossover cable, but if both ends can perform this sensing, that is not required.

17. C. Many servers attach to storage networks and may run converged network adapters (CNAs), which act both as a host bus adapter (HBA) for the SAN and as the network card for the server.

18. C. The midplane or backplane also supplies power connections to various components. When a midplane is in use, connections are provided on the back side for power modules.

19. B. 1U and 2U systems are 1.75″ and 3.5″, respectively.

20. B. There are several types of RAID that provide varying degrees of increased performance and/or fault tolerance. All of these techniques involve two or more hard drives operating together in some fashion.

Chapter 2: Installing and Configuring Servers

1. C. Some of the enhancements this new interface provides are better security by helping to protect the preboot process against bootkit attacks; faster startup and resuming from hibernation times; support for drives larger than 2.2 TB; support for modern, 64-bit firmware device drivers that the system can use to address more than 17.2 billion GB of memory during startup; and capability to use BIOS with UEFI hardware.

2. C. Windows Server 2022 requires the following:

Processor: 1.4 GHz 64-bit processor compatible with x64 instruction set

Memory/RAM: 512 MB

Disk space: Minimum 32 GB (Windows Server 2022 using the Server Core installation option)

3. B. Introduced by Microsoft along with Windows NT (and available on all Windows Server operating systems), NTFS is a much more advanced filesystem in almost every way than all versions of the FAT filesystem.

4. B. The Zettabyte File System (ZFS) was developed by Sun Microsystems. It is part of Sun's Solaris operating system and is thus available on both SPARC and x86-based systems, but it's also an open source project.

5. C. Today's operating systems support the use of swap files. These are files located on the hard drive that are used to temporarily hold items moved from memory when there is a shortage of memory required for a particular function.

6. B. During an attended installation, you walk through the installation and answer the questions as prompted. Questions typically ask for the product key, the directory in which you want to install the OS, and relevant network settings.

7. A. You can use third-party monitoring tools or you can rely on some that are built into the system, such as the Performance Monitor tool in Windows Server 2012 R2. This tool can be used to take snapshots over a period of time as well so that you get a feel for the rise and fall of the workload on the server.

8. B. The swap file is often called the pagefile.

9. C. With Windows servers, set the pagefile to 1.5 times the RAM.

10. A. In a Windows classic unattended installation, this file is called an answer file and the file provides the answers to the question posed during the installation.

11. B. The Preboot Execution Environment (PXE) is an industry-standard client-server interface that allows networked computers that are not yet loaded with an operating system to be configured and booted remotely by an administrator.

12. D. Processor\% Processor Time represents the percentage of time the CPU spends executing a non-idle thread. This should not be over 85 percent on a sustained basis.

13. B. Mail servers run email server software and use SMTP to send email on behalf of users who possess mailboxes on the server and to transfer emails between email servers. Those users will use a client email protocol to retrieve their email from the server. Two of the most common are POP3, which is a retrieve-only protocol, and IMAP4, which has more functionality and can be used to manage the email on the server.

14. B. Developed by Microsoft, Remote Desktop Protocol (RDP) allows you to connect to remote computers and run programs on them. When you use RDP, you see the desktop of the computer you've signed into on your screen.

15. C. If you don't need access to the graphical interface and you just want to connect to a server to operate at the command line, you have two options: Telnet and SSH. Telnet works just fine, but it transmits all of the data in cleartext, which obviously would be a security issue. Therefore, the connection tool of choice has become Secure Shell (SSH). It's not as easy to set up because it encrypts all of the transmissions and that's not possible without an encryption key.

16. A. ext2, ext3, and ext4 are Linux filesystems. As you would expect, each version is more capable than the previous one.

17. B. If you don't need access to the graphical interface and you just want to connect to a server to operate at the command line, you have two options: Telnet and SSH. While Telnet works just fine, it transmits all of the data in cleartext, which obviously would be a security issue. Therefore, the connection tool of choice has become Secure Shell (SSH).

18. C. Type I hypervisor (or native, bare-metal) runs directly on the host's hardware. A Type II hypervisor runs within a conventional operating system. VMware Workstation and Virtual-Box exemplify Type II hypervisors.

19. C. Values such as Low, Normal, High, and Custom (using VMware as an example) are compared to the sum of all shares of all VMs on the server. Therefore, they define the relative percentage each VM can use.

20. A. The VMs reside on the host servers and the host servers are attached to the shared storage devices.

Chapter 3: Server Maintenance

1. A. Out-of-band management refers to any method of managing the server that does not use the network. This provides some advantages, among them:

    - It offers a solution when the network is down or the device is inaccessible.

    - It manages devices with no power and remotely reboots devices that have been crashed, turned off, or hibernating, or that are in sleep mode.

2. B. A forward-compatible license is one that, though purchased for an older version of software (for example, Windows Server 2012), can be used to demonstrate license compliance for a newer version (such as Windows Server 2012 R2).

3. C. Integrated lights-out (iLO) is technology embedded into HP servers that allows for out-of-band management of the server. Out-of-band management refers to any method of managing the server that does not use the network.

4. D. Some software is what we call a *combined work*, meaning it consists of multiple differently licensed parts. This can present an issue when the various parts have very different and incompatible licensing terms. Sometimes projects wind up with incompatible licenses, and the only feasible way to solve it is the relicensing of the incompatible parts. Relicensing is achieved by contacting all involved developers and other parties and getting their agreement for the changed license.

5. A. A Dell Remote Access Controller (DRAC) card provides out-of-band management for Dell servers. The iDRAC refers to a version of these interface cards that is integrated on the motherboard of the server.

6. B. A true-up occurs when a company compares the number of actual software license users to the good-faith estimate of the initial contract and corrects any issues.

7. B. Some network cards offer a feature called Wake on LAN (WOL). This allows the device to be started up from the network by sending a special packet to the NIC (which is not ever actually off).

8. C. Volume licensing is the process of purchasing a number of installation instances and then using a single volume license key to demonstrate that you have paid for the installations.

9. C. A crash cart is a mobile server room cart equipped with a secured laptop that is used to provide a direct connection to malfunctioning servers and computers for restoration of crashes.

10. D. Maintenance plans may include a service level agreement (SLA). These agreements specify the type of support to be provided and the acceptable amount of time allowed to respond to support calls. Typically, these time windows are different for different types of events.

11. A. A server may offer the option to connect to it using a special cable called a console cable. These cables are used to connect to and manage routers and switches as well. The port looks like an RJ-45 port, and the cable looks like an Ethernet cable except that it's flat and wired differently. Sometimes these cables are called rollover cables.

12. D. The license demonstrates that you have paid for the right to use the software and does not imply either a warranty or a promise of help and support.

13. A. This is a configuration that can be done in the BIOS settings in a fashion similar to the way you disable the USB ports.

14. B. This model evolved from the SaaS cloud model where the software is not installed but instead is run from the cloud.

15. C. Firmware includes any type of instruction for the server that is stored in nonvolatile memory devices such as ROM, EPROM, or flash memory. BIOS and UEFI code is the most common example for firmware.

16. D. Regardless of the exact procedure, the process is referred to as flashing the BIOS. It means the old instructions are erased from the EEPROM chip and the new instructions are written to the chip.

17. A. There are two main types of open source licenses, copyleft and permissive. Copyleft is a method for making a software program free while requiring that all modified and extended versions of the program also be free and released under the same terms and conditions.

18. B. While the update is completing, ensure that you maintain power to the device.

19. C. These keys work together to perform both encryption and digital signatures. To provide encryption, the data is encrypted with the receiver's public key, which results in ciphertext that only the receiver's private key can decrypt.

20. A. The rotational speed of the disk or platter has a direct influence on how quickly the drive can locate any specific disk sector on the drive. This locational delay is called latency and is measured in milliseconds (ms). The faster the rotation, the smaller the delay will be.

Chapter 4: Storage Technologies and Asset Management

1. A. RAID 0 is also known as disk striping. This is RAID that doesn't provide fault tolerance. Data is written across multiple drives, so one drive can be reading or writing while the next drive's read/write head is moving. This makes for faster data access. However, if any one of the drives fails, all content is lost.

2. B. RAID 1 is also known as disk mirroring. This is a method of producing fault tolerance by writing all data simultaneously to two separate drives.

3. C. When the hard disk manufacturer advertises a 120 GB hard drive, they are selling you 120,000,000,000 bytes. Windows divides this number by what it considers a GB (1073741824) and reports the hard disk size as:

120000000000 (bytes) / 1073741824 (bytes per GB) = 111.8 GB

4. B. One of the things that you can do in Windows to mitigate the amount of space used by constant updates is to manage a folder called the component store. This folder, called `windows\winsxs`, contains all the files that are required for a Windows installation.

5. B. Manually performing a disk cleanup will allow you to get rid of these files (and many other useless files as well), but if you would like to create a batch file, you can automate the process.

6. D. A minimum of three drives is required. RAID 5 uses $1/n$ (n = the number of drives in the array) for parity information (for example, one third of the space in a three-drive array), and only $1 - (1/n)$ is available for data. So if three 250 GB drives are used in the array (for a total of 750 GB), 500 GB will be the available drive space.

7. B. A minimum of three drives is required.

8. C. Volume licensing is the process of purchasing a number of installation instances and then using a single volume license key to demonstrate you have paid for the installations.

9. C. One disadvantage in using RAID 6 is that each set of parities must be calculated separately, which slows write performance.

10. D. The advantages of using software RAID are lower cost and the ability to implement disk duplexing.

11. B. The ability to implement disk duplexing is an advantage of software RAID, not hardware RAID.

12. C. Since this is effectively a mirrored stripe set and a stripe set gets 100 percent use of the drive without mirroring, this array will provide half of the total drive space in the array as available drive space.

13. C. Disk duplexing is the use of separate controller cards for each disk when implementing disk mirroring (RAID 1), thus providing fault tolerance at both the disk level and the disk controller level, protecting against both a single disk failure and a single controller card failure.

14. A. SATA is the slowest and least expensive of the options, with a maximum cable length of 1 meter (3 feet).

15. C. While Fibre Channel is the fastest and provides the longest allowable cable length, it is the costliest.

16. D. The faster the RPM, the faster the disk access will be.

17. A. Mixing any of the following drive specifications in the same array will result in the entire array using the least capable specification (also called "dumbing down" the array):
- Slowest speed (performance)
- Smallest size
- Smallest buffer

18. B. If you are using SATA disks, hot swapping is inherently supported due to the pin layout.

19. C. A cold spare is one that is attached to the system and available but cannot replace the bad disk without administrator intervention and in some cases a reboot.

20. C. One of the metrics that is used in planning both SLAs and IT operations in general is mean time to repair (MTTR). This value describes the average length of time it takes a vendor to repair a device or component.

Chapter 5: Identifying Fault Tolerance Requirements

1. A. In load balancing, a frontend device or service receives work requests and allocates the requests to a number of backend servers. This type of fault tolerance is recommended for applications that do not have a long-running in-memory state or frequently updated data.

2. A. Combining physical links can be done using proprietary methods, and there is also an IEEE standard for the process called 802.3ad, later replaced by 802.1ax-2008.

3. C. To configure Ethernet 6 to be used as a slave by a NIC team, open the `ifcfg-eth5` file and edit it as follows. In this case, the NIC team will be created and identified as bond0.

```
# vi /etc/sysconfig/network-scripts/ifcfg-eth5
DEVICE="eth1"
TYPE=Ethernet
ONBOOT="yes"
BOOTPROTO="none"
USERCTL=no
MASTER=bond0
SLAVE=yes
```

4. B. Failover is when a failed components workload is switched over to a backup component. In the case of a NIC team used for fault tolerance, this means that the backup NIC takes over for the failing NIC.

5. A. A heartbeat connection is a connection between servers in a load balancing scenario across which the servers send a signal (called a heartbeat) used to determine when the other server is down. If one server goes down, the other will service the entire workload.

6. C. An IEEE standard for the process called 802.3ad, later replaced by 802.1ax-2008, uses a protocol called Link Aggregation Control Protocol (LACP) to control the establishment of the aggregated link based on the proper combination of settings of the ends of the multiple links and on the agreement of certain settings on all physical links in the "bundle" (speed and duplex among them).

7. B. For links that run between switches, using an aggregated link is better than using two links that are not aggregated, because in switch networks that include redundant links (which they should, according to best practices) a switching loop prevention protocol called Spanning Tree Protocol (STP) will disable one of the links. When the links are aggregated, STP considers them to be a single link and does not shut any of the ports in the aggregation.

8. C. In an active–active cluster, both or all servers are actively servicing the workload.

9. A. The Most Recently Used (MRU) algorithm attempts to send clients into running servers, preferably the most recently used server, before starting new servers. The goal of this algorithm is to reduce the overhead of starting new servers by using servers that are already running.

10. B. Redundancy can be provided at the network interface level. NIC teaming is the process of combining multiple physical network connections into a single logical interface.

11. B. A server cluster is generally recommended for servers running applications that have long-running in-memory state or frequently updated data. Typical uses for server clusters include file servers, print servers, database servers, and messaging servers.

12. C. In a round robin allocation system, the load balancer allocates work requests to each server sequentially, resulting in each getting an equal number of requests.

13. B. Clustering is the process of combining multiple physical or virtual servers together in an arrangement called a cluster, in which the servers work together to service the same workload or application.

14. B. A form of fault tolerance that focuses more on providing high availability of a resource is load balancing. In load balancing a frontend device or service receives work requests and allocates the requests to a number of backend servers. This type of fault tolerance is recommended for applications that do not have long-running in-memory state or frequently updated data.

15. B. Failback is a term that describes when the original system goes back online and the workload is moved back to the original system.

16. A. Load balancing can be done using load balancing software or it can be done with a physical appliance called a load balancer.

17. A. NIC teaming is the process of combining multiple physical network connections into a single logical interface. This process goes by other names as well, including link aggregation and link bonding.

18. D. Combining physical links can be done using proprietary methods, and there is also an IEEE standard for the process called 802.3ad, later replaced by 802.1ax-2008.

19. C. In a round robin allocation system, the load balancer allocates work requests to each server sequentially, resulting in each getting an equal number of requests. This could mean that a user may make two requests that actually go to two different servers.

20. A. Load balancing can be done using load balancing software or it can be done with a physical appliance called a load balancer.

Chapter 6: Securing the Server

1. C. While passwords and usernames are examples of something you know and a retina scan is an example of something you are, possessing a smart card is an example of something you have.

2. A. A mantrap is a series of two doors with a small room between them. The user is authenticated at the first door and then allowed into the room. At that point additional verification will occur (such as a guard visually identifying the person) and then the user is allowed through the second door.

3. B. The drawbacks of this technology are that the tag signal can be read by any reader in range, multiple readers in an area can interfere with one another, and multiple devices can interfere with one another when responding. Active tags are more expensive but can transmit up to a hundred meters.

4. A. Biometric devices use physical characteristics to identify the user. Such devices are becoming more common in the business environment. Biometric systems include hand scanners, retinal scanners, and soon, possibly, DNA scanners.

5. B. Security guards offer the most flexibility in reacting to whatever occurs. Guards can use discriminating judgment based on the situation, which automated systems cannot do. This makes guards an excellent addition to the layers of security you should be trying to create.

6. A. With respect to fire, first understand that no safe is fireproof. Many are fire-resistant and will protect a document from being destroyed, which occurs at a much higher temperature than many of the other items (such as backup tapes and CDs) can tolerate without damage. For these reasons, items such as backup tapes should be stored off-site.

7. D. Assigning a BIOS password is considered a physical hardening technique.

8. B. When discussing network security, an endpoint or host is any point of entry into the network. A typical example of an endpoint is a laptop connected to the network with a remote access connection. Therefore, the process of providing endpoint security is the process of ensuring that every endpoint (including servers) has been secured in the same way in which you would secure the network gateway.

9. D. A host-based system is installed on the device (for purposes of our discussion, a server) and the system focuses solely on identifying attacks on that device only. This is in contrast to a network-based system, which monitors all traffic that goes through it looking for signs of attack on any machine in the network.

10. A. You might think it a bit off topic to discuss environmental controls in a security chapter. However, it makes perfect sense to do so if you consider what the A in the security triad CIA stands for. CIA is an acronym for the three goals of security: to provide confidentiality (data can be read only by those for which it is intended), integrity (the data has not been altered in any way), and availability (the data is available to those who need it when they need it).

11. B. While important, implementing strong authentication is a form of digital security.

12. B. Security information and event management (SIEM) utilities receive information from log files of critical systems and centralize the collection and analysis of this data. SIEM technology is an intersection of two closely related technologies: security information management (SIM) and security event management (SEM).

13. C. Signature-based recognition analyzes traffic and compares patterns, called signatures, that reside within the IDS database. This means it requires constant updating of the signature database.

14. D. Wet pipe systems use water contained in pipes to extinguish the fire. In some areas, the water may freeze and burst the pipes, causing damage. These systems are not recommended for rooms where equipment will be damaged by the water.

15. A. Dumpster diving is a common physical access method. Companies normally generate a huge amount of paper, most of which eventually winds up in dumpsters or recycle bins. Dumpsters may contain information that is highly sensitive in nature (such as passwords after a change and before the user has the new one memorized). In high-security and government environments, sensitive papers should be either shredded or burned.

16. C. Closing unneeded ports is a logical hardening method.

17. B. Barriers called bollards have become quite common around the perimeter of new office and government buildings. These are short vertical posts placed at the building's entrance-way and lining sidewalks that help to provide protection from vehicles that might either intentionally or unintentionally crash into or enter the building or injure pedestrians.

18. C. Crime Prevention Through Environmental Design (CPTED) refers to designing the facility from the ground up to support security. It is actually a broad concept that can be applied to any project (housing developments, office buildings, and retail establishments). It addresses the building entrance, landscaping, and interior design.

19. C. There are emissions coming from the servers themselves that can sometimes disclose sensitive information. This can be addressed by placing the server inside enclosures that can block signals. One example is called a Faraday cage, which implements an outer barrier or coating called a Faraday shield.

20. A. At one time, fire suppression systems used Halon gas, which works well by suppressing combustion through a chemical reaction. However, these systems are no longer used because they have been found to damage the ozone layer.

Chapter 7: Securing Server Data and Network Access

1. C. Whereas passwords and usernames are examples of something you know and a retina scan is an example of something you are, possessing a smart card is an example of something you have.

2. C. There is an interesting relationship between security groups and distribution groups. While a security group can also be used as a distribution group, a distribution group cannot be used as a security group.

3. A. Group memberships can be monitored using a Group Policy setting, Restricted Groups. When this policy is applied to a container in Active Directory, it checks the membership of each group each time the policy is refreshed (at login and startup), removes any members that are not approved, and readds any members that have somehow been deleted.

4. A. Biometric devices use physical characteristics to identify the user. Such devices are becoming more common in the business environment. Biometric systems include hand scanners, retinal scanners, and soon, possibly, DNA scanners.

5. B. List Folder Contents is an NTFS folder permission, not a file permission.

6. A. For the most part, members of Guests have the same rights as users except that they can't access log files. The best reason to make users members of the Guests group is if they are accessing the system only for a limited time.

7. C. When using encryption to protect data that resides on storage devices, the data is called data at rest.

8. C. Encryption at the file level is performed on each file or on a folder that contains files. In Windows this is done using the Encrypting File System (EFS). EFS is an encryption tool built into all Enterprise versions of Windows.

9. B. Disk-level encryption may use a Trusted Platform Module (TPM) chip. This chip is located on the motherboard of the system and provides password protection, digital rights management (DRM), and full-disk encryption.

10. B. A bootloader is a file that locates the operating system files and loads them into memory so that they can be executed to start the OS. For example, GRUB is the bootloader package in Linux and Unix systems.

11. B. Determining the relative priority of each dataset cannot be done until all data is classified. There should be a system of data classification that extends to cover sensitive documents such as contracts, leases, design plans, and product details.

12. D. We@kP@$$w0rd contains all four character types, making it the strongest password.

13. B. The term *superuser* applies to any user account that has total control and access to a system. This user will possess the Full Control permission to every resource and object on the device for which the user possesses this account type. Various operating systems attach different names to this account. Windows systems call this the Administrator account.

14. A. Every program and process theoretically could have its own logging utility, but Microsoft provides the Event Viewer, which, through log files, tracks all events on a Windows computer.

15. B. A password is an example of something you know.

16. C. The purpose of single sign-on (SSO) is to give users access to all the applications and systems they need when they log on. This has become a reality in many environments, including Kerberos, Microsoft Active Directory, Novell eDirectory, and some certificate model implementations.

17. D. A soft wipe describes any method that deletes data in such a way that the data can be recovered later using special data forensics software. The best example of this is the simple file deletion process.

18. B. A hard wipe is a term used to describe any deletion process that cannot be reversed using data recovery or forensics software. Most disk management software will provide this type of deletion and may refer to it in various terms, such as "scrubbing" the drive.

19. D. Physical destruction is always the best method.

20. D. Scope-based access control allows you to create a custom set of resources (called a scope) and assign access to them to a user.

Chapter 8: Networking and Scripting

1. C. In IPv6 the loopback address is all zeroes in every hextet except the last. Closing up the first seven hextets with a double colon results in ::, and the one in the last hextet results in ::1 after omitting the leading zeroes in the last hextet.

2. B. When autoconfiguration is used, the first hextet will always be FE80::. The rest of the address will be derived from the MAC address of the device.

3. B. Using CIDR, administrators can create smaller networks called subnets by manipulating the subnet mask of a larger classless or major network ID. This allows you to create a subnet that is much closer in size to what you need, thus wasting fewer IP addresses and increasing performance in each subnet.

4. D. The Class B range of private IP addresses is from 172.16.0.0 to 172.31.255.255.

5. D. Automatic Private IP Addressing (APIPA) is a TCP/IP feature Microsoft added to their operating systems. If a DHCP server cannot be found and the clients are configured to obtain IP addresses automatically, the clients automatically assign themselves an IP address, some-what randomly, in the 169.254.x.x range with a subnet mask of 255.255.0.0.

6. A. In IPv6, there is a type of address called a link local address that in many ways is like an APIPA address in that the device will generate one of these addresses for each interface with no intervention from a human, as is done with APIPA. The devices always generate the address using the same IPv6 prefix (the equivalent of a network ID in IPv4), which is FE80::/64. The reminder of the address is created by spreading the 48-bit MAC address across the last 64 bits.

7. A. Fully qualified domain names (FQDN) identify the host and the location of the hostname in the DNS namespace of the organization. They consist of at least two parts and perhaps more. All FQDNs will have a hostname and a domain name.

8. B. In many instances, users make references to unqualified hostnames when accessing resources. When this occurs, DNS needs to know how to handle these unqualified domain names. It is possible to configure a list of domain names called suffixes for the DNS to append to unqualified hostnames and the order in which they should be tried.

9. B. Batch files, or files with a .bat extension, are used to automate a command or set of commands each time you execute the batch file.

10. B. Firewalls are becoming available as appliances, meaning they're installed as the primary device separating two networks. Appliances are freestanding devices that operate in a largely self-contained manner, requiring less maintenance and support than a server-based product.

11. B. When EUI-64 is used, it doesn't actually change the format of the physical 48-bit MAC address. It is a method of spreading the 48-bit MAC address across 64 bits so that it can be used as the last 64 bits of the 128-bit IPv6 address.

12. C. Each part of this address communicates information. The left half of the address is called the organizationally unique identifier (OUI). The right half is called the universally administered address (UAA). Together they make a globally unique MAC address.

13. B. A VLAN security issue you should be aware of is called VLAN hopping. By default, a switch port is an access port, which means it can only be a member of a single VLAN. Ports that are configured to carry the traffic of multiple VLANs, called trunk ports, are used to carry traffic between switches and to routers. A VLAN hopping attack's aim is to receive traffic from a VLAN of which the hacker's port is not a member.

14. B. In TCP/IP, a gateway is the address of the machine to send data to that is not intended for a host on this network (in other words, a default gateway). It is the router that allows traffic to be sent beyond the internal network.

15. D. Memory is the most important resource because the entire DNS zone file will be loaded into memory. As you add zones, or as a zone gets larger, you should add memory.

16. C. Simple Mail Transfer Protocol (SMTP) is a protocol for sending email. SMTP uses port 25 by default.

17. A. Secure File Transfer Protocol over SSH, or SFTP, is a version of FTP that is encrypted by SSH. Since it operates over an SSH session and SSH uses port 22, SFTP uses port 22.

18. B. Telnet is a protocol that functions at the Application layer of the OSI model, providing terminal-emulation capabilities. Telnet runs on port 23 but has lost favor to SSH because Telnet sends data—including passwords—in plain-text format.

19. B. The default masks are:

Class	Default subnet mask
A	255.0.0.0
B	255.255.0.0
C	255.255.255.0

20. B. Although it requires a bit more setup than Telnet, SSH provides an encrypted command-line session for managing devices remotely.

Chapter 9: Disaster Recovery

1. C. A cold site is a leased facility that contains only electrical and communications wiring, air conditioning, plumbing, and raised flooring. No communications equipment, networking hardware, or computers are installed at a cold site until it is necessary to bring the site to full operation.

2. C. When constant replication is in use, each time a change is made (data addition, deletion, change, etc.) at the primary site, the same change is written to the secondary site. This results in the secondary site being constantly up-to-date and is generally an expensive option.

3. A. With asynchronous replication, the write operation to the primary system is acknowledged by the primary system before the write is sent to the secondary, whereas with synchronous replication, the write is sent to the secondary system without waiting for acknowledgment from the primary.

4. D. Background replication means that the replication process is performed as a background operation. A background operation is processing that occurs "in the background" while a user is performing other tasks in the system.

5. D. One interesting feature with respect to the various versions of LTO is the use of colors to indicate a specific cartridge type. For example, though not a standard, LTO-6 cartridges are typically black whereas LTO-5 cartridges are red (unless they are from HP, which has its own color scheme).

6. D. This type of snapshot is created every time a change is made and is a snapshot of everything rather than just the changes. However, it takes significant storage space and the restore process is slower.

7. B. The archive bit is used to communicate to the backup system whether a particular file has changed since the last backup. When the archive bit is cleared (0), it communicates that the file has been backed up already and has not changed since. When the bit is on (1), it communicates that the file has changed since the last backup and should be backed up again.

8. B, D. Neither the differential nor the copy backup clears the archive bit.

9. B. While a full backup requires only one backup tape for restoration and the number of tapes required when using incremental and copy methods depends on when the failure occurs, when the differential method is used you always only need the last full backup and the last differential backup tapes to restore.

10. D. You will need the last full tape from Saturday and the incremental tapes from Sunday, Monday, Tuesday, Wednesday, and Thursday.

11. B. This type of snapshot is taken every time a user enters data or changes data, and it only includes the changed data. Although it allows for rapid recovery from a loss of data, it requires you to have access to all previous snapshots during recovery.

12. A. Backup programs that use the Windows Volume Shadow Copy Service (VSS) can back up open files. However, you should know that when you back up open files in this manner, changes that may have been made to the file while it was open and the backup job was proceeding will not be present in the backup of the open file and will not be recorded until the next backup.

13. A. A live failover test is one in which the primary site is taken down and operations are completely switched over to the secondary site. While this is the riskiest test to perform, it will also generate the best data about the sufficiency of your disaster recovery plan.

14. B. While younger technicians may be unfamiliar with the task of rewinding or fast-forwarding a music tape or cassette to access a particular song, it illustrates the way linear access works. A song cannot be played until the tape head (reader) is positioned over the location where that song resides. Accessing data on a tape must be done the same way.

15. A. Checksums are used to verify that the data has not been corrupted during the backup.

16. A. While replication is considered to be from database to database, mirroring is from machine to machine or server to server. In server-to-server replication, also called host-based replication, software on the servers handle the replication process.

17. A. In this scheme, three sets of backups are defined. Most often these three definitions are daily, weekly, and monthly.

18. C. In this scheme, the newest backup is saved to the oldest media. Although this is the simplest rotation scheme, it does not protect against data errors. If an error in data occurs, this system may result over time in all copies containing the error.

19. B. A tape library contains a number of slots to hold tape cartridges and a barcode reader that is used to identify the cartridges.

20. C. Conducting a tabletop exercise is the most cost-effective and efficient way to identify areas of vulnerability before moving on to more involved testing. A tabletop exercise is an informal brainstorming session that encourages participation from business leaders and other key employees.

Chapter 10: Troubleshooting Hardware and Software Issues

1. B. The steps in order are:

    1. Identify the problem and determine the scope.

    2. Establish a theory of probable cause.

    3. Test the theory to determine cause.

    4. Establish a plan of action to resolve the problem and notify affected users.

    5. Implement the solution or escalate as appropriate.

    6. Verify full system functionality and, if applicable, implement preventive measures.

    7. Perform a root cause analysis.

    8. Document findings, actions, and outcomes throughout the process.

2. B. You may find yourself making significant changes on a server in an attempt to locate and/or solve the issue. Be sure that you do a backup before you make any changes so that all your actions can be undone, if necessary.

3. A. When you make multiple changes at a time, those changes might interact with one another and make the picture even muddier.

4. B. Chip creep—the unseating of components—is one of the more common byproducts of a cycle of overheating and cooling off the inside of the system.

5. B. Replacing slot covers is vital. Servers are designed to circulate air with slot covers in place or cards plugged into the ports. Leaving slots on the back of the computer open alters the air circulation and causes more dust to be pulled into the system.

6. B. In Linux you can use the `kill` command to stop the process. To do so, you must identify the guilty process using the `ps` command.

7. C. A serious issue is a STOP message or Blue Screen of Death (BSOD) message. Once a regular occurrence when working with Windows, blue screens have become less common.

8. A. Some firewalls offer the ability to filter based on zones. A zone is a group of different interfaces that share the same security attributes or the same level of trust. You define which interfaces are in the same zone and then you create rules controlling traffic between zones.

9. B. Safe mode starts Windows in a basic state, using a limited set of files and drivers. If a problem doesn't happen in safe mode, this means that default settings and basic device drivers aren't causing the issue.

10. B. Network Time Protocol (NTP) servers are used as a time source by the devices in the network. When the devices are configured with the address of an NTP server, they will periodically check in with the server to ensure their time is correct.

11. C. SQL servers have no impact on users logging into to servers. When users have difficulty logging on to a server, it can be one of several things:
- User error typing the password
- Incorrect password
- Account disabled
- Account expired
- Inability to contact the domain controller
- DNS server failure
- Incorrect DNS server IP address on the server
- Unauthorized user

12. A. Backplanes are advantageous in that they provide data and control signal connectors for the hard drives. They also provide the interconnect for the front I/O board, power and locator buttons, and system/component status LEDs. Unfortunately, this creates a serious single point of failure because if the backplane fails, we lose communication with the servers to which it is connected.

13. B. You can remove dust and debris from inside servers with compressed air blown in short bursts. The short bursts are useful in preventing the dust from flying too far out and entering another machine, as well as in preventing the can from releasing the air in liquid form.

14. C. Maintain the relative humidity at around 50 percent.

15. B. It is a balancing act keeping humidity at the right level since low humidity causes ESD and high humidity causes moisture condensation.

16. B. This tab shows the system resources in use (I/O, IRQ, and so on) and whether there are conflicts.

17. B. When the system makes noises, you should listen. A grinding or clicking noise can be a failing drive. A whining sound could be a fan on its way to failing.

18. D. Spyware would compromise the privacy of the users browsing but would not prevent them from logging on.

19. C. Memory leaks occur when an application is issued some memory to use and does not return the memory nor any temporary file to the operating system after the program no longer needs it.

20. B. Buffers are portions of system memory that are used to store information. A buffer overflow is an attack that occurs when the amount of data that is submitted to is larger than the buffer can handle.

Chapter 11: Troubleshooting Network Connectivity and Security Issues

1. B. Ensure that the NIC is functional and the TCP/IP protocol is installed and functional by pinging the loopback address 127.0.0.1.

2. C. Crossover cables are used when:
- Connecting a computer to a computer
- Connecting a router to a router
- Connecting a switch to a switch
- Connecting a hub to a hub
- Connecting a router to a PC because both devices have the same components

3. B. A stealth virus attempts to avoid detection by masking itself from applications. It may attach itself to the boot sector of the hard drive. When a system utility or program runs, the stealth virus redirects commands around itself to avoid detection.

4. A. If recent changes have occurred in the DNS mappings or if your connection to the destination device has recently failed because of a temporary network issue that has been solved, you may need to clear the local DNS cache using the `ipconfig/flushdns` command.

5. B. Sometimes an incorrect mask will prevent all communication, but in some cases it results in successful connections locally but not remotely (outside the local subnet). The subnet mask value should be the same mask used on the router interface connecting to the local network.

6. C. A Trojan horse may be included as an attachment or as part of an installation program. The Trojan horse can create a backdoor or replace a valid program during installation.

7. A. The most common IDS, a network-based IDS (NIDS), monitors network traffic on a local network segment. To monitor traffic on the network segment, the NIC must be operating in promiscuous mode.

8. C. There are two types: those that are connected to your wired infrastructure and those that are not. The ones that are connected to your wired network present a danger to your wired and wireless networks.

9. B. This issue can have a number of sources, including:

- The IP configuration of the user's computer
- The IP configuration of the user's default gateway or router
- The IP configuration of any routers that stand between the gateway and the Internet
- The DNS server
- The ISP
- The DHCP server

10. C. You can determine this by attempting a Telnet connection to the IP address of the device and adding the port number.

11. B. It will appear as a destination unreachable message (this is a group of message types that all have code numbers) with a code number of 1.

12. D. If the message comes with no source IP address, the message is coming from the local router (the default gateway of the sender). If it has the source IP address of the sender, then it is another router in the path.

13. D. If the computers cannot connect to the default gateway (which will be the case if the gateway is incorrect), it will be confined to communicating with devices on the local network.

14. C. It is a name resolution or a DNS issue.

15. B. Even if you assign devices in different VLANs with IP addresses in the same subnet, they will not be able to communicate because they are separated at Layer 2.

16. B. Some of the things you can specify using the port security feature are the only MAC address or addresses allowed to send traffic in the port, the total number of MAC addresses that can transmit on the port, and an action to be taken when a violation occurs (either shut the port down or prevent transmissions by the guilty MAC address).

17. C. A zombie process (work performed on behalf of services is done using processes) is one that is a child of another process. It becomes a zombie when it completes its work but is mistakenly marked as a dead process, preventing it from ending.

18. B. To allow for the creation of smaller networks that operate better, the concept of classless routing, or Classless Interdomain Routing (CIDR), was born.

19. A. The `show ip route` command can be used to identify the routes of which the router is aware.

20. A, B. The `tracert` command (called `traceroute` in Linux and Unix) is used to trace the path of a packet through the network on routers.

Chapter 12: Troubleshooting Storage Issues

1. B. In Linux and Unix, this issue can be caused by a missing GRUB/LILO.

2. B. `diskpart` enables you to manage objects (disks, partitions, or volumes) by using scripts or direct input at a command prompt. It can perform all the functions that can be done with the Disk Management utility and quite a few that cannot be done with Disk Management.

3. A. If you want `fsck` to attempt to repair any errors it finds, add the `-a` or `-y` parameter after the command.

4. B. Among the issues that can be diagnosed with the `top` command are memory issues.

5. C. Initializing the drive can be done at the command line using `diskpart` or with the Disk Management tool. You need to know that initialization will wipe out the drive's contents!

6. B. While most data recovery failures are due to human error in the data backup process (running multiple jobs simultaneously, failure to change tapes, forgetting to remove a cleaning tape), there are some issues that are beyond your control.

7. D. When working with cables, especially fiber cables, you must recognize that every cable has a maximum bend radius, which you cannot exceed without damaging the cable. For fiber-optic cables, if no specific recommendations are available from the cable manufacturer, the cable should not be pulled over a bend radius smaller than 20 times the cable diameter.

8. B. A loud clicking noise, sometimes referred to as the click of death, is caused by the read/write heads making contact with the platters. After that happens, both the heads and the platters become damaged, and the system becomes unable to establish a successful starting point to read the drive.

9. C. There are a number of commercial partition tools that you can use to repair damaged partitions. Before you use one of these commercial tools, you might want to use one of the system tools available to you. One of these is chkdsk (Check Disk).

10. D. RAID 6 writes parity information across the drives as is done in RAID 5, but it writes two stripes, which allows the system to recover from two drive failures whereas RAID 5 cannot. As each set of parities must be calculated separately, performance is slowed during writing to the drive. The cost is higher due to the two drives dedicated to parity information.

11. A. fstab (File System Table) is a file used by Linux operating systems to mount partitions on boot.

12. C. The drives should be placed back in the reversed order of failures (failures, not removals).

13. B. badblocks has several different modes that allow you to detect bad sectors in Linux.

14. C. While it is possible to use mismatched drives, you should have a clear understanding of the implications of each type of mismatch. The only requirement set in stone is that they must be of the same architecture.

15. B. The net use command is used to connect users to shared drives.

16. C. In Windows Server 2012 R2, the diskpart command is used to manage storage from the command line.

17. A. The sudo fdisk -l command lists the partitions on the system.

18. D. fdisk is not available in Windows Server 2012 R2.

19. B. Resource Monitor, available from the same Tools menu in Server Manager where you access Event Viewer, can track the use of the CPU, memory, disk system, and network card in real time. It has a tab for each and an Overview tab.

20. D. In Linux this log file is located at /var/log/messages.

Index

O

S

Online Test Bank

To help you study for your CompTIA Server+ certification exam, register to gain one year of FREE access after activation to the online interactive test bank—included with your purchase of this book! All of the practice questions in this book are included in the online test bank so you can study in a timed and graded setting.

Register and Access the Online Test Bank

To register your book and get access to the online test bank, follow these steps:

1. Go to www.wiley.com/go/sybextestprep. You'll see the "How to Register Your Book for Online Access" instructions.
2. Click "here to register" and then select your book from the list.
3. Complete the required registration information, including answering the security verification to prove book ownership. You will be emailed a pin code.
4. Follow the directions in the email or go to www.wiley.com/go/sybextestprep.
5. Find your book on that page and click the "Register or Login" link with it. Then enter the pin code you received and click the "Activate PIN" button.
6. On the Create an Account or Login page, enter your username and password, and click Login or, if you don't have an account already, create a new account.
7. At this point, you should be in the test bank site with your new test bank listed at the top of the page. If you do not see it there, please refresh the page or log out and log back in.